FROM VILLAGE BOY
TO GLOBAL CITIZEN

With Compliments
to the Morgan
family

Shelton Gunaratne
June 2014

FROM VILLAGE BOY TO GLOBAL CITIZEN
(VOLUME 2)

THE TRAVELS OF A JOURNALIST

SHELTON GUNARATNE

To order additional copies of this book, contact:
Xlibris Corporation
1-888-795-4274
www.Xlibris.com
Orders@Xlibris.com
117397

CONTENTS

Part 3: The Travels of a Journalist

PART 3

THE TRAVELS
OF A JOURNALIST

Note

This is the second volume (Part 3) of the book *From Village Boy to Global Citizen*. The first volume contained Part 1 (*The life journey of a journalist*) and Part 2 (*About Bowers, boats and buddies*) of the book.

The essays appearing in all three parts are interconnected, interrelated and interdependent on one another.

This volume opens with chapter 36 because the first volume carried the initial 35 chapters. The *Foreword* and *Preface* appearing in the first volume are relevant to all three parts of the book.

Whereas the first volume emphasizes the autobiographical aspects of the author's life as a journalist, this volume emphasizes his inveterate commitment to become a global traveler. The drama of travel in the company of his nuclear family provides fascinating reading for people of all ages.

The author has published another related book *Village Life in the 'Forties: Memories of a Lankan Expatriate* (published in 2012 by iUniverse), in which he tries to give a dramatic picture of his birth village with no holds barred.

CHAPTER 36

England: Jogging along London's Canals, Glimpses of Dickens

WHEN I WAS a child (in Sri Lanka), my father and I had a lot of fun conversing with each other in lyrical "free" verse (in Sinhalese) to bemuse ourselves during walks to the Mullewatte well for bathing or on other occasions when our minds turned to leisurely pursuits. Although my father had never visited England, his "colonial" education at Mahinda College had fostered in his mind a picture of London as the "greatest" city in the world. So he would often tease me with the following question:

> *Loken itha uttama nagaran-vitaya*
> (The greatest city in the world—)
> *Kima dai kiya pawasanu mage run-putaya*
> (what's it, my dear son?)

He had taught me to respond with the following couplet:

> *Dannay nedda piyatuma London-vitaya*
> (Dad, don't you know that London—)
> *Loken itha uttama nagaran-vitaya*
> (—is the greatest city in the world)

I was determined to explore London, the city my father held in high esteem, for another reason. I had developed "nostalgia" for experiencing the ethos of London described in the classical literary works of Charles Dickens, all of which I had read avidly in my undergraduate days at Peradeniya.

Although I first visited London in 1966, the circumstances for exploring the Dickensian ethos of London did not come about until the summer of 1990, when I accepted an internship at the then headquarters of the World Association for Christian Communication on Kennington Lane, Vauxhall. The late Michael Traber, the research director of WACC, was aware of my Buddhist credentials. He and I saw no conflict of interest because my internship involved no religious propaganda.

In 1966, a representative of the British Information Service took me to see the sixteenth-century Tudor building that bears the name of Dickens's 1840 novel *The Old Curiosity Shop*. This creaking, half-timbered building (at 13 Portsmouth Street, Westminster) is believed to have inspired Dickens to construct the details of the place where the principal characters of the novel, Nell Trent and her grandfather, lived. But my stopover in London was too short to absorb and analyze the smells, tastes, sights, feelings, and perceptions related to England that I had stored in my stream of consciousness as a scholar of Dickensian literature.

In 1990, I was able to enjoy the late twentieth-century remains of the English ethos portrayed in Dickens's novels and mull over his social criticism while exploring the backyards of London and its surroundings along the Regent's Canal, which links the Paddington Arm of the 137-mile (220 km) Grand Union Canal (from Birmingham) at Little Venice (just to the northwest of central London) and flows east into the Thames at Limehouse in Docklands.

Over its 8.5-mile (13.5 km) length, the Regent's Canal drops 86 feet (26 meters) through twelve locks followed by a ship lock. Those who like walking can use the canal paths to access a variety of London attractions, such as Regent's Park, London Zoo (both south of Camden Town), and Charles Dickens Museum (48 Doughty Street, a block behind Gray's Inn Road). The only guide needed is a good map of London.

In my view, a visit to London without walking, jogging, or cycling along the pathways on the canal is to deprive oneself of the idyllic and the Arcadian dimensions of London, as well as the Dickensian ethos still lingering in the "greatest" city of the world. The one who takes the tube or the bus to Limehouse and engage in self-propulsion all the way to Little Venice will enjoy the scenes (landscapes, architecture, and buildings), smells (peculiar to English countryside), sounds (of wildlife), and feelings (roused by Dickensian fiction) that others miss through their supreme ignorance.

If one wants to enjoy the nature's bounty in the English countryside, one could continue further along the Paddington Arm of Grand Union Canal. The terminus of GUC—a canal with 166 locks—is the River Thames at Brentford wherefrom the mainline canal climbs over fifty locks up into the Chiltern Hills. It descends, and then climbs again to a new summit in Birmingham. What is called Brentford Arm of GUC runs southeastwards along River Brent, a tributary of Thames, from Bulls Ridge Junction to Brentford.

In August 1990, I jogged on the walking trail along the Regent's Canal and the Paddington Arm of the Grand Union Canal covering the area from Limehouse Basin in the east to Southall in the west.

I spent the summer of 1990 with my youngest sister, Nayana, who lived in Shepherd's Bush, just outside Hammersmith Park. After work, I would return home, don my jogging gear, and take public transportation to a spot where I could jog for an hour or more. I also took public transportation to return home from the spot I finished jogging. Thus, it took me several days to explore and enjoy the canals from Limehouse to Southall.

My diary entries show that I covered segments of the canal in no particular order. My canal exploration commenced on August 2, 1990, when I entered the Paddington Arm of GUC from Scrubs Lane (north of Wormwood Scrubs) and headed west all the way to Victoria Road in North Acton.

August 10, 1990: I again entered the Paddington Arm from Scrubs Lane. This time, I headed east all the way to Little Venice, where the Regent's Canal begins. Along the way, I passed the huge Kensal Green cemetery with its monuments. I jogged parallel to Harrow Road up to Westbourne Green. The barge dwellers of Little Venice reminded me of Dickensian characters like Uriah Heep (a devious hypocrite), Bill Sikes (a thief), Krook (an alcoholic landlord), and Fagin (leader of a team of pickpockets) The picturesque narrow boats with all of their flowers provided a contrast to the open basin at Little Venice, where I tarried to enjoy the Rembrandt Gardens—a little island.

August 14, 1990: I turned my attention to exploring Regent's Canal. Starting from Little Venice, I headed east all the way to York Way. Along the way, I stopped to see Camden Lock (in Camden Town) and observed how the scenery changed from residential apartments to commercial developments. The stretch parallel to Prince Albert Road appeared to me as the most scenic area of the canal. I got off the towpath at Maiden Lane Bridge (two bridges ahead of Islington Tunnel), close to King's Cross.

August 15, 1990: I completed my exploration of Regent's Canal. In spite of a slight downpour, I started from Limehouse Basin, where I had a good look at the canal flowing into River Thames. I jogged northwards along the towpath until I reached Copperfield Road at King George's Fields. Then past Mile End and Globe Town, I deviated northeast to jog along Bow Canal on the eastern boundary of Victoria Park. I got into the park at Three Colt Bridge to admire its lakes and flower gardens. Back on Regent's Canal, I jogged westward past Cat and Mutton Bridge to Kingsland Basin, where I stopped at a pub for beer. I used the energy input so gained to propel myself all the way to the Islington canal tunnel, which is at least half a mile long. Two hours of exercise exhausted me so much that I paid scant attention to the townhouses and barge homes along the canal in East London.

I resumed my passion for canal exploration when I returned to London two years later. I was determined to complete some unfinished business, viz., exploring the western end of Paddington Arm of GUC.

July 17, 1992: I resumed my exploration of the western section of Paddington Arm from the Victoria Road access to the canal in North Acton (where I stopped two years ago). I jogged westward past Lower Place and Alperton, all the way to Horsenden Lane North, savoring the Arcadian charm of the area. Then I left the canal and walked south to Perivale station to return home.

July 30, 1992: I entered the canal at Horsenden Farm and jogged from Perivale (northwest of North Acton) to Southall (for a taste and smell of

"Little India"), a distance of about six miles. On my way, I headed south from Greenford Green, crossed Western Avenue, and left the Paddington Arm at Uxbridge Road. (Brentford, the southern terminus of the mainline Grand Union Canal, lies to the southeast of Southall. Paddington Arm stretches 12 miles from Bull's Bridge Junction, northwest of Brentford, to its terminus at Little Venice.) This is a picturesque area abounding with birds and rustic greenery that makes the explorer feel he or she was in the Midlands. However, the towpaths could confuse the explorer without a map between the GUC and River Brent to the south. My diary entry says, "I really enjoyed the bucolic aspect of the environment along the canal."

In 1992, I retraced segments of my 1990 canal explorations but paid special attention to enjoying the recreational potential of the Brentford Arm (or the stretch of River Brent from the Hanwell locks to Brentford) and the lower reaches of River Thames.

Walking and jogging allows you to fall in love with the "greatest" city in the world. The next chapter will describe my exploits on Brentford Arm and the lower Thames, as well as one of the strangest things that happened to me on my travels.

CHAPTER 37

England: London Escapades, Color-Bar Mishap Mars Joy of Jogging

THE "STRANGEST THING" that could happen to a traveler struck me at about 4:45 p.m. on Friday, July 20, 1990. It shattered the image of London that my father had impressed on me as the "greatest" city in the world.

I purchased a few groceries from Marks & Spencer in Hammersmith and was about to leave the store to walk toward the tube station along King Street when a security guard (later identified as George Cox of Storewatch Ltd.) pounced on me to search my waist for "shoplifted goods."

It had never occurred to me that anyone could ever suspect me of being a shoplifter. But a suspicious Cox had been watching me moving to a quiet nook of the store to open up my waist. The prejudiced mind of the white security guard instantly made him cocksure that I, a colored Asian, was stuffing my waist with goods to avoid payment.

True, I was meddling with my waist away from the crowds. But I was merely counting the bills in the moneybag wrapped around my waist—a safety measure suggested by travel experts to elude the wily thieves and pickpockets of Dickensian fame.

By a strange coincidence, a passerby took offence at the manner the security guard was searching me on a public street. Using his high-decibel vocal chords, he demanded an explanation from the store personnel, who seemed relentlessly unapologetic about their foul procedure despite my explanation that I was merely searching my moneybag. It turned out that the passerby who came to my defense was a gentleman by the name of Bryan LaBroy, a Dutch Burgher who had left Ceylon in the late 1950s. To show my gratitude, I bought him a drink at the nearest pub, and we talked about our mother country. LaBroy volunteered to be a witness in case I decided to file a suit against the store.

When I told Martin Axon, my English brother-in-law, about the lack of remorse that Marks & Spencer personnel showed through their self-righteous behavior, he decided "to make a fuss over this matter." Three days later, he lodged a complaint with the company protesting its callous treatment of a customer of color.

On August 2, I received a set of gift certificates valued at £100 from Marks & Spencer as a "material gesture" of regret for the indignity to which a security guard subjected me on July 20. F. J. Kieran, solicitor for the company, in a letter dated July 25, said, "We wish to offer you our unreserved apologies . . . our staff who were involved in the incident have specifically asked that they be permitted to associate themselves with the apology."

We decided not to pursue the hassle of legal recourse for higher compensation.

I used the gift certificates to purchase a St Michael jacket (£ 49.50) and a pair of shoes of the same brand (£ 17) at Marks & Spencer in Marble Arch. On another shopping spree at Marks & Spencer on Kensington High Street, I exhausted the gift certificates to buy more St Michael products, including another pair of leather shoes (£ 20) and a pair of trousers (£ 19).

I never went back to Marks & Spencer in Hammersmith, which was the closest to Shepherd's Bush where I stayed during my London visits.

Shepherd's Bush was a good location for me to explore the delights of exploring the Brentford Arm of the Grand Union Canal and the lower reaches of River Thames. The mishap at Marks & Spencer robbed my confidence as a globetrotter of Asian origin for a while, but my adventures as a jogger helped my rejuvenation.

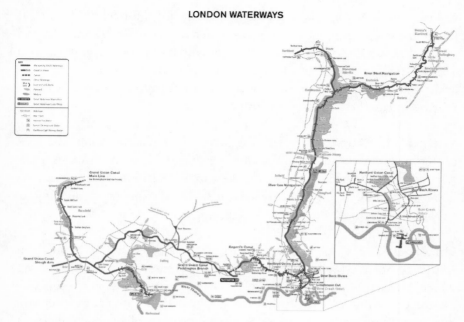

Map 37.1: Map of London Waterways. ©H. Henniker-Major.
The lower portion details the Grand Union Canal and its Paddington
Arm (with the linking Regent's Canal) and Brentford Arm (linked
with River Brent).

Brentford Arm

First, I shall recount my encounter with the Brantford Arm of GUC,
which follows the engineered course of River Brent from the Hanwell
Locks to Brentford, the terminus of the GUC.

August 4, 1992: After getting off the bus in Acton Town late afternoon,
I crossed Gunnersbury Park from the north and walked southwestward
to Brentford to see the confluence of River Brent with mother River
Thames. Then I crossed the Brent at Dock Road to watch Thames Lock
101 and explore the scenic Marina area. Thereafter, I walked along
Augustus Close and recrossed the Brent to find the public footpath
alongside the stretch of river-cum-canal (a.k.a. Brentford Arm) that
heads northwestward from Brentford to Hanwell Flight of six locks.
Brentford Gauging Lock 100 lies just to the north of High Street. I left
the canal at the crossing point of Motorway 4 on the eastern edge of

Osterley Park. Then I proceeded to Boston Manor station to take the tube home.

August 6, 1992: I continued my exploration of River Brent this evening. I got off the tube at Northfields station and walked southward to Boston Manor Park, where I joined the Brentford Arm footpath again to resume my walking and jogging from where I stopped at the M4 crossing on August 4. I passed through Clitherow's Lock and Osterley Lock to reach Hanwell, where the River Brent departs the GUC and heads northeastward and crosses the Paddington Arm at Alperton.

The Hanwell Flight of six locks raises the GUC by just over 53 feet (16.2 m). These locks have turned into a safe haven for birds, insects, small mammals such as water voles and wild flowers. Almost every lock has a lock-keeper's cottage. At the top of the flight of locks toward Norwood Green is the Three Bridges designed by engineer Isambard Kingdom Brunel. From this point, the Grand Union Canal Walk takes you southwestward to North Hyde and northwestward to Bull's Bridge, where the Paddington Arm branches off to Little Venice. I left the canal at Uxbridge Road thereby completing my exploration of the Brentford Arm.

River Thames

Next, I shall focus on the delightful spots I enjoyed along the lower reaches of River Thames, which runs from west to east demarcating the south side of London. It runs parallel to the Paddington Arm of GUC, which demarcates the north side of London. My jogging excursions included long patches of pathways along the Thames from the Limehouse-Greenwich end in east to the Bushy Park-Hampton Court end in west.

> *My No. 1 choice is jogging on any of the twenty-four bridges that span River Thames from Kew Bridge to Tower Bridge and exploring the pathways in the vicinity to absorb the unique beauty and splendor of each.*

I fell in love with the charm of Hammersmith Bridge, not very far from Shepherd's Bush. Many a time, I would sit on a bench along this 310-meter suspension bridge to enjoy the river scenery at sunset or simply walk or jog from Hammersmith on the north side to Barnes on the south side. The bridge, when lit up at nightfall, provides scenic solace to the pub crowd along the newly repaved River Walk, a joggers' paradise. Once I jogged all the way from the bridge to Chiswick House, a medium-sized Jacobean mansion built in 1774 as a summer residence for the Earl of Burlington.

The 262-meter London Bridge, often shown as a hallmark of the "greatest" city, has a history going back to the Roman period. Its sad history is captured in the following nursery rhyme:

London Bridge is falling down,
Falling down, falling down.
London Bridge is falling down,
My fair lady.

The neighboring sixty-meter-long Tower Bridge (built in 1894) is the only Thames bridge that can be raised to allow large vessels to pass through. The two bridges closest to the Palace of Westminster—Westminster Bridge (green) and Lambeth Bridge (red)—bear the respective colors of the House of Commons and the House of Lords. Those who visit the British Parliament and listen to political debates might find a few minutes of self-propulsion on these two bridges and the adjoining Vauxhall Bridge enough payback to clear their minds.

Further to the west are a number of bridges that could add immeasurably to a jogger's joy. A few of my favorites are the charming Putney Bridge (1729-1826), the only bridge in Britain to have a church at both ends; Kew Bridge (1759-1903), close to the Royal Botanic Gardens; Battersea Bridge (1773-1890), a cast iron and granite five-span cantilever bridge; and Richmond Bridge (1777), a stone-arch bridge close to Richmond Palace.

I also pick one of the seventeen underwater tunnels in Greater London
built beneath the river Thames as a high-priority choice for exploration
by foot: the Greenwich Tunnel in East London.

The Greenwich Foot Tunnel, classed as a public pedestrian highway, connects Island Gardens at the tip of the Isle of Dogs with Greenwich on the south side. Part of the fun is getting to Island Gardens by Docklands Light Railway. The entrance shafts at both ends of the tunnel lie beneath glazed domes. Lifts, as well as spiral staircases, take the walkers to the sloping tile-lined tunnel.

August, 11, 1990: My ten-year-old son Junius and I found the walk through the tunnel awe-inspiring and adventurous. We stopped at the tea clipper *Cutty Sark* exhibit near the glazed dome and visited Greenwich Park, the home of the Old Royal Conservatory. After walking around to admire the flower gardens, we took a train from Maze Hill to Charing Cross.

August 22, 1990: Junius and I returned to Greenwich to visit the Royal Naval College. The temptation to walk through the tunnel again was irresistible.

Although I have focused on canals and the Thames River bridges as a bonanza for joggers, I must in passing mention the London parks as an added bonanza. For example, an excellent jogging path is available in Green Park—one of London's royal parks in the vicinity of Buckingham Palace. The forty-seven-acre park is located between Hyde Park and St. James Park, which is another excellent place for a run. The three-hundred-acre Royal Botanic Gardens at Kew—featuring more than sixty thousand species of plants as well as dozens of decorative structures, museums, galleries, glasshouses, and wildlife areas—can be another paradise for joggers. The Broad Walk and its network of pathways are all too tempting.

June 9, 1990: Junius and I spent the day at Kew Gardens. We visited the Kew Palace, a favorite of George III and Queen Charlotte's Cottage. We walked around the entire garden and ate lunch at Kew Bakery. We enjoyed the exhibits of the six glasshouses—palms, temperate, Alpine and Australian plants, as well as the bamboo, heather, rhododendron, and rock gardens.

CHAPTER 38

England: Pommy's Tour of London by Night Shows Sites in Different Light

ON THE NIGHT (Tuesday, July 27, 2010) before my wife and I left England and went back to Minnesota, a bright idea sparked in the mind of my "Pommy" brother-in-law, a longtime resident of Shepherd's Bush. In postprandial conviviality, he offered to take us to central London to see "London by night." The thought intrigued me, particularly because he was associated with the London club circles in his youth.

"Pommy" clarified that what he had in mind was a two-mile (or so) walking tour of central London to see the nocturnal charm of shades, shadows, and reflections of streetlights and security lights imposed upon Her Majesty's majestic buildings that housed the legendary bureaucracy and the political elite who ruled Great Britain. In short, "Pommy" invited us to join him for a power walk through the portals of power sans the jostling crowds and parking hassles of a daytime tour.

However, there was one hitch: the continual drizzle outside. That was not a problem for "Pommy," the consummate Londoner. "Warm jackets and umbrellas are all we need," he said. Three of us—"Pommy's" first daughter, Camilla, my wife Yoke-Sim, and I—agreed to join the "London by night" tour, the brainchild of my *machan* (Sinhala slang for brother-in-law). So he drove us seven miles from Frithville Gardens (Shepherd's Bush) to St. James's Park (Westminster), where he parked his Volvo in Queen Anne's Gates.

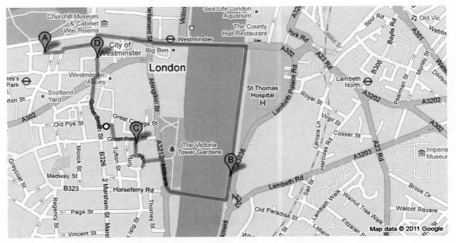

Map 38.1 Pommy's Walking Tour of "London by Night" offers charming views of London's historical institutions illuminated by bright lights. *A*, St. James Park (area between Queen Anne's Gates and Birdcage Walk allows inexpensive or free parking at night); *B*, Promenade along the right bank of River Thames, *C*, Lord N Street; *D*, Termination of tour. Distance is two miles. Walking time is forty minutes.

"Pommy's" Walking Tour

We put on our rain gear, stretched out the umbrellas, and began our walk from the vicinity of St. Stephen's Club (34 Queen Anne's Gates), originally the club of the Conservatives founded in 1870. Prime Minister Harold MacMillan opened the club in the current premises in 1963. The club has been apolitical since 2003.

We crossed the Cockpit Steps to go east on Birdcage Walk on the south side of the twenty-three-hectare St James's Park, the oldest royal park in London. Buckingham Palace stood at the western edge of the park.

Cockpit Steps is associated with the urban legend of a headless woman dressed in red that two soldiers encountered in 1802. The *Times* reported that the soldiers had seen the headless figure (believed to be the wife of an officer who killed her and tried to bury her mutilated body in the park) drifting from Cockpit Steps toward St. James's Park. Again, in

1972, a motorist claimed that he hit a lamppost on the road as he tried to avoid a ghostly figure dressed in red. The court cleared the motorist of the charge of dangerous driving. I am glad that nothing spooky appeared as we crossed the Cockpit Steps.

Past the Horse Guards Road at the east end of the park, we continued walking east on Great George Street. Horse Guards Road runs north to join The Mall. Downing Street, which demarcates the center of political power in Britain, was just two blocks north of us straddling the Horse Guards Road and Whitehall.

On Downing Street, 10 is the official residence of the first lord of the treasury (the prime minister); 11, the official residence of the second lord of the treasury (chancellor of the exchequer); and 12, the official residence of the chief whip of the ruling party. The Foreign and Commonwealth office is also on Downing Street, which currently allows only restricted public access. The stone-faced and dark brick structures on Downing Street could not possibly add any nocturnal charm except perhaps for the headless lady in red whom we missed at Cockpit Steps.

We walked past the Churchill Museum and Cabinet War Rooms (at Clive Steps, King Charles St.; Admission is £15) and Her Majesty's treasury (at 1 Horse Guards Road), where "Pommy's" daughter worked. The multistory treasury building, originally designed by architect John Brydon and later modified by Sir Henry Tanner, was built with Portland stone. Bright lights highlighted the building as we walked past.

Turning south on Little George Street, we were fascinated by the brightly lighted Parliament Square (first laid out in 1868), a large open patch of green in the middle with a cluster of trees to its west, surrounded by the imposing structures of the Big Ben (1858), the largest four-faced chiming clock and the third-tallest free-standing clock tower in the world; the Houses of Parliament, also called the Westminster Palace, a perpendicular Gothic structure with origins in the eleventh century; the Westminster Abbey, a mainly Gothic church with origins in the tenth century; and the Middlesex Guildhall (UK Supreme Court), which took over the judicial functions of the House of Lords in 2009. Sir Peter Blake was the designer of the guildhall.

Strategically placed statues of famous statesmen—e.g., Winston Churchill, Benjamin Disraeli, Abraham Lincoln, Nelson Mandela, Lord Palmerston, Robert Peel, and Jan Christian Smuts—adorned the Parliament Square. This is the place where daytime tourists gathered to relax and compare notes. It was equally fascinating to watch the square after nightfall, even on a rainy, spooky night.

Picture 38.1 The "London Eye" at night. It's a 135-meter high Ferris wheel, the tallest in Europe (2005). (Photo by Benutzer Swgreed. *Source:* Wikimedia Commons)

As we walked around the Parliament Square to turn eastward to Bridge Street, we tarried at St. Stephen's Tavern, an ever-popular waterhole of the hoi polloi standing side-by-side with the Big Ben, the most familiar symbol identifying London. A closer look at Big Ben is necessary to understand why the people called it big. Augustus Pugin designed the clock and the dials more than a century and half ago. "The clock dials are set in an iron frame seven meters (23 feet) in diameter, supporting 312 pieces of opal glass, rather like a stained-glass window," explains the Wikipedia. Big Ben is the name of the biggest bell in the tower, although popular parlance has bestowed the name on the whole tower.

Picture 38.2 A panoramic view of the Parliament Square (2010)
(Photo by Wjh31. *Source:* Wikimedia Commons.)

Now, in the drizzle, we were crossing the Thames on the renowned Westminster Bridge, thoroughly enjoying the illuminated night scenery over the Thames. On the north side, we saw the scintillating "London Eye," the massive Ferris wheel. Resisting the temptation of the "carnival," we got off the east end of the bridge to proceed southward. (The Westminster Bridge has a history going back to 1739-1750. The current bridge, designed by Thomas Page, was opened in 1862. The green paint of the bridge honors the House of Commons' preferred color.)

Our saunter on the bridge turned into a jog as we raced down the ill-lit promenade along the east bank of the Thames on the back of St. Thomas's Hospital right up to Lambeth Bridge. We surmised that the northern end of the east bank promenade provided the best night view of the Big Ben and the Westminster complex.

Even at 10:00 p.m., romantic couples occupied the public benches along the promenade to enjoy the magnificent well-lit scenery of Westminster on the opposite bank. The uneven cobblestone almost tripped me as I jogged.

We crossed the Lambeth Bridge, painted red to honor the preferred color of the House of Lords and turned north on Millbank at the foot of the Victoria Tower Gardens. (The original Lambeth suspension bridge opened in 1862. The current five-span steel arch structure replaced the suspension bridge in 1932. Dorman Long built the Lambeth Bridge designed by Sir George Humphreys and Sir Reginald Blomfield.)

Then, we walked northwest (via Dean Stanley St., Smith Square, Lord N St., Great Peter St., Tufton St., Little Smith St., and Great Smith St.) to reach Westminster Abbey. Finally, we turned east on Lewisham Street that merged into Queen Anne's Gates where "Pommy" had parked his Volvo.

This wasn't the first nocturnal sightseeing tour that I had joined on "Pommy's" initiative. I recalled the midnight car tour of Cardiff, Wales, which he gave me in the early 1990s after we visited his sister's family in Churchill (Bristol)—a story I will narrate in another chapter. It was almost midnight when we returned to Shepherd's Bush.

CHAPTER 39

England: On Tour with a Ten-Year-Old—Fire and Joy

PATRICK BENNET, AN Englishman, was our tour director. David Price, a Welshman, was our coach driver. Trafalgar Tours had assigned them to take good care of us and show us the best of England and Scotland over eleven days beginning June 12, 1990.

If we add up the motorway distances between the cities where we were scheduled to stay overnight, Price had the enviable task of driving us through a distance of at least 2,520 km. My hunch was that he did more driving than that because a sightseeing tour cannot always stick to the shortest or fastest distance between two points.

My son Junius, then ten years old, and I submitted ourselves to the mercy and care of Bennet and Price at the Victoria Station in London that morning. With Yankee Doodles making up the majority of the tour group, our coach headed southwestward to Devon.

Bennet was a proud raconteur of English history. As we approached Runnymede, about 35 km from where we started, he gave us a vivid description of the water-meadow on River Thames where King John in 1215 most likely sealed the Magna Carta, not too far from Windsor Castle.

More than 100 km further, we stopped at Stonehenge, the center of England's most dense complex of Neolithic and Bronze Age monuments, including several hundred burial mounds. But these stone monuments are not as old as those found in Newgrange in the Boyne Valley of Ireland.

The Stonehenge monuments are believed to be 2,500-3,000 years old. Pagans and Druids have made Stonehenge a site of pilgrimage.

Our stop for lunch was Salisbury, about 15 km to the south, the location of the Anglican cathedral with the tallest (123 m) church spire in England. Built by Bishop Richard Poore in the thirteenth century, the cathedral also has one of the four surviving original copies of the Magna Carta. Junius still remembers the "church mouse" lunch of grilled cheese and tomato soup we ate at the cathedral. Because my brother-in-law Martin's mother lived in Great Wishford, near Salisbury, until her death, we subsequently got to know the area quite well. Junius was literally bitten by a white boy during a visit to see the old lady!

Price patiently drove the coach for another 180 km southwest to reach our resting place for the night, the Valley of the Rocks Hotel, in the cliffy coastal village of Lynton, adjoining Lynmouth. We got there via Taunton and the northern boundary of Devon's Exmoor National Park along the Bristol Channel. Coincidentally, we passed by Minehead, the birthplace of the late Arthur C. Clarke, the science-fiction writer who made Sri Lanka his country of residence, on the northeast corner of the park.

After dinner, Junius and I walked to Hollerday Hill to enjoy the breathtaking views of the Valley of the Rocks. Content with our adventures, we fell asleep.

I took Junius with me on this tour because I thought his was the right age to start hobnobbing with inveterate cosmopolitans so that he too would aspire to be a global citizen. He left Queensland, where he was born, at the age of six, and came to Minnesota with the rest of the family in 1986. Now, in 1990, I brought him to England to stay with his youngest aunt (my youngest sister) and her two daughters, Camilla and Georgina, for the entire summer.

Junius and I had already visited many of the London landmarks prior to joining the tour of the rest of England we were now on. Although I had studied European and British history both at Ananda College and Peradeniya University, most of the historical tidbits that Junius learnt from Bennet and the sites we visited gave him a sort of education-on-the-go.

Junius had already expanded his knowledge of British history and culture after our visits to the British Museum and Library, the Tower of London, the Hampton Court Palace, and many other sites in and around London. As well, the coach tour enabled us to enjoy the countryside and get to know the British hoi polloi at close range, thanks to our good driver Price.

Fear of a fire

Hearing cries of arson, we got up from our cozy sleep about 2:30 in the morning. We saw the building adjoining our hotel on fire. Deadly smoke buffeted against the window of our hotel room forcing Junius and me to eject ourselves from the room into the lobby.

Luckily for us, the fire brigade was able to control the rogue fire. But the shock that engulfed us failed to put us back into sleep.

Bennet and Price, our *gardiens temporaires*, were highly apologetic about what transpired. They joined us for breakfast at the hotel and got us ready to leave Lynton about 9:00 a.m. promising to relieve us from our fire scare with a scenic tour of the coast of Devon and Cornwall. (When Junius and I interviewed Sir Arthur Clarke at his home in Colombo in August 1993, we told him about this incident that scared us only a few miles away from his birthplace.)

Leaving Exmoor National Park, Price drove along the enchanting A39 route southward from Bideford all the way to Tintagel, a distance of 116 km from Lynton.

Bennet told us the story of the legendary King Arthur, who was born in Tintagel. Legend has it that this noble king was born to the beautiful Queen Igerna and protected from evil by the magician Merlin, who lived in a cave below the mighty fortress. The 'Arthnou' stone, a 1400-year-old inscribed slate discovered at the site, supports the contention that Tintagel was a royal palace for the Dark Age rulers of Cornwall.

We stopped for lunch at the picturesque town of Looe, 58 km southeast of Tintagel, on Whitesand Bay. We walked on the beach while eating genuine Cornish pastry from Kelly's.

Our place of rest for the night was the hotel Novotel in Plymouth, about 35 km east of Looe. A city of 582,000 people, Plymouth is known for its Royal Navy Dockyard, Plymouth Hoe and Mayflower Steps, among other landmarks. To forget our memories of the fire early this morning, we took a boat ride in the harbor at the mouth of River Tamar. After a hearty dinner, Junius and I walked to the nearby Alpine Lodge to see the steep artificial ski slope.

Arthur and Shakespeare

The following day, Bennet proudly introduced us to more of Arthurian mystery, the glamour of Roman baths, the life and times of Shakespeare, and the titillating legend of Lady Godiva and Peeping Tom.

We left Plymouth in the morning for the 373 km northeastward trip to Coventry in the West Midlands. Price drove on route 38, which runs parallel to the southeastern limits of Dartmoor National Park, and joined Motorway 5 at Exeter. North of Bridgwater, we turned east on route 361 to Glastonbury (in Somerset)—161 km from Plymouth.

- We stopped to see the ruins of Glastonbury Abbey, believed to be the burial place of the legendary King Arthur and Queen Genevieve—yes, the same Arthur brought up in the castle at Tintagel. On display here was a leaden cross with the inscription *Hic jacet sepultus inclitus rex Arthurus in insula Avalonia* ("Here lies interred the famous King Arthur on the Isle of Avalon") found in 1191.

Our next stop was Bath, about 44 km north of Glastonbury (and about 21 km southeast of Bristol). Bath is a city of 84,000 people. The Romans made this city a spa resort in AD 43. It became a popular spa resort during the Georgian era.

- We visited the Great Roman Bath, which has four main features: the Sacred Spring, the Roman Temple, the Roman bath house, and finds from Roman Bath. The Georgian Pump Room is on the ground level. The sacred spring lies at the very heart of the ancient monument. Water rises here at the rate of more than a million liters a day and at a temperature of 460 C. The spring rises within the courtyard of the Temple of Sulis Minerva, and water from it feeds the Roman baths.

Junius found the Roman Bath to be one of the most interesting spots we saw on our tour. We purchased a cup of mineral water for 30 pennies, sipped some of it, and washed our hands in the main pool. Later, we had a quick lunch of fruits.

Price then guided us further 136 km northeast to Stratford-upon-Avon, the birth and burial place of William Shakespeare (1564-1616), the famous English bard, through the Cotswold Hills scenic route via villages like Tetbury, Cirencester, and Burford in the county of Gloucestershire.

Stratford-upon-Avon (on the banks of River Avon) in the rural county of Warwickshire has a current population of 23,700. The Royal Shakespeare Company provides a full set of programs throughout the year for Shakespeare buffs. Shakespeare wrote thirty-eight plays of varying type: historical romances (*Romeo and Juliet*, *Henry VIII*); light, fantastic comedies (*As You Like It*, *The Merchant of Venice*, *The Taming of the Shrew*), and several tragedies (*Hamlet*, *Othello*, *King Lear*).

Although we did not have the time to "Shakespearience" the town, Junius declared his satisfaction with this unforgettable stopover: the thrill of seeing the Bard's birthplace (on Henley St.), the school the Bard is believed to have attended (on Church St.), and the childhood home of Anne Hathaway, the Bard's wife (in Shottery).

Two days after his death, Shakespeare was buried in the chancel of the Holy Trinity Church. A curse against moving his bones appears on the stone slab covering his grave:

> *Good frend for Iesvs sake forbeare,*
> *To digg the dvst enclosed heare.*
> *Blest be ye man yt spares thes stones,*
> *And cvrst be he yt moves my bones.*

We also learned another tidbit about Stratford-upon-Avon that might interest the fans of Sir Arthur C. Clarke, who served the RAF in the town during the 1940s. The plot in Clarke's short story "The Curse" takes place in a post-apocalyptic Stratford-upon-Avon.

Lady Godiva

Our final destination for the day was Coventry (pop 309,800), another 31 km to the northeast, where we visited the Saint Michael's Cathedral, the city's best-known landmark. German bombing during World War II destroyed the original fourteenth-century cathedral. The new edifice was opened in 1962 next to the ruins of the old. Coventry, which is also associated with the legend of Lady Godiva (fl. 1040-1080), wife of Leofric, the Earl of Mercia. Wikipedia relates the legend thus:

> Lady Godiva took pity on the people of Coventry, who were suffering grievously under her husband's oppressive taxation. Lady Godiva appealed again and again to her husband, who obstinately refused to remit the tolls. At last, weary of her entreaties, he said he would grant her request if she would strip naked and ride through the streets of the town. Lady Godiva took him at his word and, after issuing a proclamation that all persons should stay indoors and shut their windows, she rode through the town, clothed only in her long hair. Only one person in the town, a tailor ever afterwards known as Peeping Tom, disobeyed her proclamation in one of the most famous instances of voyeurism. In the story, Tom bores a hole in his shutters so that he might see Godiva pass and is struck blind. In the end, Godiva's husband keeps his word and abolishes the onerous taxes.

We stayed overnight at Leofric Hotel (named after Godiva's husband), where we saw the Lady Godiva and Peeping Tom recreation under the clock tower.

CHAPTER 40

Scotland: On Tour with a Ten-Year-Old—Learning about Battles, Massacres, Firths, Lochs, and Monsters

THE MOST MEMORABLE of our five-day tour of Scotland (16-20 June 1990), from the point of view of a ten-year-old, was our breathtaking scenic tour through the rugged highlands and lochs west and southwest of Aviemore (a small town of fewer than seventy thousand people in 1990, but more than 108,000 now). From Aviemore, we fanned out southwest to see the site of the Massacre of Glencoe (1692) and northwest to see the site of the Battle of Culloden Moor (1746) at Inverness and to get a glimpse of the legendary Loch (lake) Ness monster at Drumnadrochit.

I, as a student of British history during my Peradeniya years in the late 1950s, had yearned to visit Glencoe and Inverness. My son, Junius, was at the time more interested in a chance meeting with "Nessie," the monster inhabiting Loch Ness.

Massacre of Glencoe

The chorus of "The Battle of Glencoe," the ballad that Jim McLean wrote in 1963, captures the essence of the Glencoe tragedy:

> O, cruel was the snow that sweeps Glencoe
> And covers the grave o' Donald
> O, cruel was the foe that raped Glencoe
> And murdered the house of MacDonald

Poet T. S. Eliot also makes implicit references to this sad incident in his poem "Rannoch, by Glencoe," which describes the scenic splendor of the glen lying along Loch Linnhe, and its tributary Loch Leven, with Loch Rannoch further to the east.

While observing this famous site, I imagined how this quiet glen would have turned into a killing field the early morning of Friday, February 13, 1692.

It is now known that the massacre of clan McDonald was a royal plot hatched by William of Orange and his cohorts to prevent the Stuart pretenders from capturing the English crown. Scotland was divided between the supporters of William and the Jacobites—the backers of the Stuarts.

In August 1691, William III issued a proclamation requiring the chiefs of all Scottish clans to take an oath of allegiance by year's end. His intention was to crush the deposed Stuart pretenders. Alasdair MacIan, chief of Clan MacDonald of Glencoe, swore his fealty to William only a week into the new year of 1692 because officials had deliberately delayed his efforts to meet the deadline. This trifling delay allowed Lord Advocate John Dalrymple, who was one of the plotters, to make an example of clan MacDonald by ordering that all "under seventy" die by the sword, and "these miscreants be cutt off root and branch."

Some 120 men, under the command of Captain Robert Campbell of Glenlyon, had made their way to Glencoe on February 1, under the pretence of collecting tax in arrears. They persuaded clan MacDonald to give them shelter, producing military documents as proof. Campbell's niece was also married to Alexander MacDonald, the youngest son of MacIan. This kinship gave further vindication to the nature of their visit.

Campbell's conduct was a mere ruse to gain the "trust" of clan McDonald while awaiting orders from his superior officer, Major Duncanson. Campbell and Duncanson spent the evening of February 12, dining and playing cards with their unsuspecting hosts, even making plans for a festive meal the following evening. But at 5:00 a.m. on February 13, the killing began.

The hospitable MacIan was stabbed to death before he could arise from his bed and alert his family to Campbell's treachery. In all, thirty-eight members of clan MacDonald were slain as they tried to escape from their former guests. Another forty family members, mostly women and children, died from exposure to the cold as they fled the dwellings they had generously shared with those who now set them ablaze. An additional forty women and children died of exposure after their homes were burned.

Map 40.1: Routes We Traveled in Scotland
First Leg: Etna Green (G) to Edinburgh (H)
Second Leg: Edinburgh (H) to Aviemore (A)
Third Leg: Aviemore (A) to Luib (M) (roundtrip)
Fourth Leg: Aviemore (A) to Glasgow (F)
Final Leg: Glasgow F) to Etna Green (G)
Estimated distance traveled=1,200km+)

Imagine how contemporary human rights activists would have reacted if the ruling elite used the strategy and tactics that the perpetrators of the 1692 Massacre of Glencoe used to consolidate the power of the ruler.

Battle of Culloden Moor

Poet Robert Burns (1759-1796) opened his *Lament for Culloden* thus:

> *The* lovely lass o' Inverness,
> Nae joy nor pleasure can she see;
> For e'en and morn she cries, "Alas!"
> And aye the saut tear blin's her e'e:
> "Drumossie moor, Drumossie day,
> A waefu' day it was to me!
> For there I lost my father dear,
> My father dear and brethren three.

We visited the site of the Battle of Culloden Moor (a.k.a Drumossie) five kilometers east of Inverness and 46 km to the northwest of Aviemore, where we lodged at the elegant Highlands Hotel for two nights. Inverness is located on Moray Firth (fjord).

The Battle of Culloden, which took place on April 16, 1746, marked the decisive victory of the British Army commanded by William Augustus, Duke of Cumberland, against the Jacobite and the French forces under the command of Charles Edward Stuart, better known as "Bonnie Prince Charlie" or the "Young Pretender."

The Jacobites were mainly Scottish Highlanders (comprising clans of Catholic and Episcopalian faiths) who sided with James Stuart, the "Old Pretender" to the British Throne. The 1688 Revolution had ousted James, a Roman Catholic, from the British Throne, and installed William of Orange (William III), the Protestant nephew of James, as the successor.

The first Jacobite uprising to restore James to the throne resulted in the 1690 Battle of the Boyne (the site of which also I visited in Drogheda on my Ireland tour). James lost that battle, which took place two years before the Massacre of Glencoe, against William III. The second and final Jacobite uprising culminated in the Battle of Culloden Moor, which pitted the Army of George II of the House of Hanover against the ill-prepared Jacobites under the command of Charlie, the grandson of James.

In the battle, some 1,500-2,000 Jacobites were killed or wounded. Another 154 Jacobites and 222 "French" were taken prisoner. In striking contrast, the Government forces suffered fifty dead and 259 wounded, although a high proportion of those recorded as wounded are likely to have died of their wounds.

Loch Ness Monster

Loch Ness is the second largest inland lake in Scotland next to Loch Lomond. Drumnadrochit, where the visitor center is located, is just about 23 km south of Inverness. Gordon Nicol takes poetic license to relate the story of "Nessie," the Loch Ness monster, in a manner appealing to children:

The very first person to see "Nessie," says Nicol, was Saint Columba who reported seeing a serpent in the loch in AD 565—"a monster with humps rising up and down." Columba described the monster as a shy creature who preferred to stay beneath the loch "only coming up every so often, when she needed to have a break."

Trouble started when people got scared of a monster suddenly appearing in their loch.

One day, Wee Angus McDonald was walking with his mother on the shores of the loch looking for the monster, who was nowhere to be seen. But just when they were about to leave, Angus saw "a big splash and a churning of water with foam." He hugged on to his mother unable to believe what he saw—a huge, ugly, bigger-than-a-whale monster with a long bumpy tail standing just next to them.

> Nicol ends his poem, thus:
> Nessie's eyes looked and saw them. She knew they were afraid.
> So she gave out a mighty roar and mother and son . . . they prayed.
> But then the great big monster had a great big change of heart.
> She decided to leave them alone and with a friendly roar, she did depart.

Junius, my ten-year-old son, was fairly confident just like Angus MacDonald in the preceding story that he could get a glimpse of the ugly monster if he kept both of his eyes open while at Drumnadrochit, where visitors can examine the controversy on the putative monster through the natural history of Loch Ness. Some believe that the monster comes from a line of long-surviving plesiosaurs. However, although we searched for him on a boat, the wily monster failed to respond to Junius's exhortations to show up and prove his existence.

Overall Scotland Tour

Our tour of Scotland comprised five major excursions involving more than 1,300 km of travel.

The first was our 180 km trip from Gretna Green, the southern entry point to Scotland, to Edinburgh, the capital, which lies 75 km east of Glasgow, the largest city. We stayed two nights in Musselburgh in east Edinburgh to explore the vicinity. Among other things, we visited the Holyroodhouse Palace and Edinburgh Palace on the Royal Mile and attended a fascinating "Scottish Night" out at Prestonfield House (I skipped the details for space reasons.)

The second was our 282 km excursion from Edinburgh to Aviemore in the Highlands via St. Andrews, Dundee, and Perth. In St. Andrews, we saw the home of the Royal and Ancient Golf Club, which exercises legislative authority on golf worldwide (except United States and Mexico). On this trip, a bunch of Aussies, who relished their newly acquired fame as "Crocodile Dundees" (following the success of the 1986 Paul Hogan movie) insisted on stopovers in Dundee on the Firth of Tay, Perth, and Dunkeld.

Crossing the Pass of Drumochter on the Grampians to reach Aviemore was an awesome experience. A close-up satellite map of the area between the Pass of Drumochter and Dalwhinnie at the head of Loch Enoht could instill fear in feeble travelers.

The third was our 409 km roundtrip excursion from Aviemore to Luib in the Isle of Skye via Inverness, Achnasheen, Kyle of Lochalsh, and Kyleakin. This trip took us to Culloden and Loch Ness, which we reached from its southern end.

The fourth was our 317 km journey from Aviemore to Glasgow via Fort William, Glencoe, and Loch Lomond. On this trip, we saw Ben Nevis at close range, lamented the Massacre of Glencoe on the spot, and took a boat ride on Loch Lomond in rainy weather.

The fifth was our 160 km exit journey from Glasgow to Etna Green, the exit point to Hadrian's Wall. I explored Glasgow when I returned to the city to attend a conference in 1998 because this trip virtually skipped it except for an overnight stay at a hotel near the airport in Paisley.

Our Scotland tour was an educational treat and an outdoor delight for ten-year-old Junius. He was no longer puzzled by the difference between firths (fjords) and lochs (lakes). He could proudly claim that he ate haggis with Scottish Highlanders and that he had a close view of Ben Nevis, the highest mountain in the British Isles, and that he got as close as possible to look for the infamous Loch Ness monster. He also learnt some British history.

CHAPTER 41

Northern England: Learning about Lake District and Yorkshire

ALTHOUGH OUR 1990 tour of Northern England, which covered more than 1,000 km, was not a literary tour for the egghead types, it so happened that our tour director Patrick Bennet took us through the scenic Lake District National Park, which is also closely associated with the Romantic poetry of William Wordsworth (1770-1850), who was England's poet laureate from 1843 until his death, and his circle of fellow poets.

"Wordsworth Country"

Wordsworth was one of the three Lake Poets identified as the Lake School. The other two were Samuel Taylor Coleridge (1772-1834) and Robert Southey (1774-1843). These Lake Poets initiated the Romantic Age in English literature.

As our tour coach entered England's largest national park in Cumbria on a Saturday morning (June 16, 1990), I recalled reading extracts of the works of the Lake Poets in an anthology that I, as a high school student, was required to study. I can still recall four lines from Coleridge's lengthy poem "Rime of the Ancient Mariner," which my old schoolmaster Mr. Karunaratne at Carey College relished to read aloud:

> Water, water, everywhere,
> And all the boards did shrink;
> Water, water, everywhere
> Nor any drop to drink.

Of the three main Lake Poets, the "true" native of the Lake District was Wordsworth, who was born in a Georgian townhouse in Cockermouth, Cumbria. We visited the site where he and his wife lie buried at the Church of St Oswald in Grasmere (pop 800).

Our coach driver David Price took us on a scenic tour of the national park along the eastern bank of Lake Windermere—past Bowness, Ambleside, and Rydal—to Grasmere. The 18-km long Windermere is the largest natural lake in England. As we drove north, we saw the 978-meter Scafell Pike, England's highest peak on to our left. (Ben Nevis in Scotland is the highest in Britain. Snowdon in Wales is the second highest.) This stretch of the park, which comprises ribbon-shaped lakes and steep hills, is called "Wordsworth Country."

We left the park through Keswick. Southey, who was a resident of Keswick for forty years, lies buried in Crosthwaite churchyard. Coleridge lived for some time in Keswick and also at Grasmere.

Wedgwood Pottery

We started the northward journey on June 14 after an early breakfast at the Leofric in Coventry still thinking about Lady Godiva's magnificent gesture. Price, our tireless driver, took us via Birmingham, 36 km northwest of Coventry, to Liverpool, our destination for the day, another 188 km north.

On the way, Bennet, our tour guide, exercised his authority to get us off the motorway to visit the Wedgwood Pottery in the village of Barlaston, eight km south of Stoke-on-Trent.

Founded in 1759 by Josiah Wedgwood, the company employs 1,800 people to produce luxury brands of tableware—Kutani Crane, for example. I am still not sure whether the stopover here was a commercial subterfuge.

My son Junius, then ten, and I would have preferred to walk a few kilometers on the 429-km long Pennine Way national trail (opened in 1965), which starts at Edale in the Peak District National Park, crosses the Yorkshire Dales National Park, and ends at Kirk Yetholm at the Scotland border with the Northumberland National Park. Edale was only 54 km northeast of Stoke-on-Trent. (I compensated for the disappointment of not making it to Edale by getting on to the Pennine Way on a subsequent visit [August 23, 1992] to Yorkshire Dales and jogging more than two kilometers along the trail from Thwaite to Muker.) This national trail was the brainchild of journalist Tom Stephenson, who was inspired by his experience of the Appalachian Trail in the United States.

Chester and Liverpool

Our second stop for the day was Chester (pop 77,000), where we willy-nilly spent four hours trying to make sense of its city walls, the Rows, and its black-and-white architecture. Junius and I walked the three-km long footpath atop the walls (encompassing the medieval city limits) crossing roads by bridges over Eastgate, Northgate, St Martin's Gate, Watergate, Bridgegate, Newgate, and Wolf Gate.

We also explored the Rows, the aboveground network of shopping walkways unique to Chester. We learned that the peculiar architecture of the Victorian buildings was a result of "the black-and-white revival."

We ate a "pilgrim's lunch" at the refectory of the cathedral. As well, we visited the Chester Castle, the remains of the Roman fortress, the Roman Garden, the Roman amphitheater, and the remains of St John's Church. The Romans had named this city (on the River Dee) Deva Victrix in AD 79.

Price picked us up at 5:00 p.m. and drove us to Liverpool (pop 435,500) in Merseyside, 34 km to the northeast, to spend the night. After eating dinner at Jenny's, we walked to the Metropolitan Cathedral of Christ the King (Roman Catholic) and the Liverpool Cathedral (Anglican), the largest cathedral in Britain.

The next morning, we left Liverpool driving through the city's famous waterfront and the docks. Our tour did not allow for much exploration of this city associated with the Beatles.

We were on our way to Grasmere in the heart of the Lake District—167 km from Liverpool. We passed through Lancashire and drove parallel to the western bounds of Yorkshire Dales to reach Cumbria. This travelogue had already outlined our Lake District experience. The Scotland border was another 74 km to the north.

England-Scotland border

Hadrian's Wall marks the border between England and Scotland. Roman Emperor Hadrian initiated its construction in AD 122. It was largely completed within six years. We had a close look at the wall when Price drove us some 100 km eastward from the Gretna-Carlisle (western) end of the wall to Newcastle-Upon-Tyne (pop 273,600). We observed the tranquil beauty of the Northumberland National Park to the north as the eastern end of the wall faded away into our horizon. Kirk Yetholm, the northern terminus of the Pennine Way, lay hidden from our view.

At Newcastle upon Tyne, we crossed the river to Gateshead on the south side. Our lunch stop was Durham (pop 43,000), another 18 km to the south in the county bearing the same name. Junius and I ate our lunch on a bench along the River Wear. Then we walked to the Durham (Norman) Castle and Durham Cathedral in the premises of Durham University.

Yorkshire Experience

We were now ready for the putative Yorkshire experience. Yorkshire is supposedly different from the rest of England because the Yorkshire folks use a dialect called Broad Yorkshire or Tyke—a mixture of Old English and Old Norse. Those who have watched the TV drama "All Creatures Great and Small" (written by a veterinary surgeon under the penname James Herriot and mostly filmed on location in the Yorkshire Dales by the BBC) would be familiar with this dialect. Therefore, some claim, that Yorkshire has its own culture.

Yorkshire County, the largest in England, has been divided into four parts—North, South, East, and West—for administrative convenience. But our activities on this tour were confined to North Yorkshire, where we spent two hours in the afternoon in the city of York (pop 195,400) and spent the night in the city of Middlesbrough (pop 142,300).

York is a walled city on the River Ouse founded by the Romans, just like Chester in Cheshire (177 km to the southwest diagonally across the Peak District NP). The Romans called it Eboracum when they founded the city in AD 71. Angles took over the city when the Romans departed in AD 415. When the Vikings captured the city in AD 866, they renamed it Jórvík (York in Scandinavian). (Another walled city that I later in May 1994 visited was Xi'an, China's ancient capital. But it had nothing to do with the Romans.)

The walls encircling the city center also serve as popular walkways. In the city center stands the York Munster, the second largest Gothic cathedral in northern Europe. Its three towers dominate the city. In contrast to the Rows in Chester, York has The Shambles, a narrow medieval street lined with shops, boutiques and tearooms. Such narrow pedestrian streets, called "snickelways," are a feature of York. A number of museums also adorn the city.

I was unhappy that our Yorkshire experience failed to give us a sense of the literary genius of Yorkshire—for instance, the memorabilia associated with the Bronte sisters (Anne, Charlotte, and Emily) or with other literary giants like poets W. H. Auden and William Empson, novelists like J. B. Priestly and Barbara Taylor Bradford or best-selling authors like James Herriot (Alf Wight). We also had no time to listen to authentic Tyke.

The next day, we completed our tour of Britain. We left Middlesbrough in the morning for London—covering a distance of 435 km. On the way, we stopped at Cambridge to replenish our tired intellects. Back in London, we thanked Bennet and Price for being our *gardiens temporaires* and said good-bye with a handsome tip. They smiled.

CHAPTER 42

North Wales: Snowdon Range Lays Unwelcome Mat

OUR (JULY 25) 2010 trip to North Wales was unplanned and unexpected. After attending the annual conference of the International Association for Media and Communication Research (IAMCR) in Braga, Portugal, Yoke-Sim, and I returned to London to visit with my youngest sister Nayana Axon's family in Shepherd's Bush. On the day after our arrival, we met with a couple from Westlake, Queensland—Geoffrey and Kathy Hagan—at Cutty Sark in Greenwich. The Hagans have been our mates since we originally settled down in Central Queensland in the mid-1970s.

While eating our lunch at the Taste of India in Greenwich, after visiting the National Observatory, the Hagans told us that they planned to rent a car and explore the area surrounding the 3,560-ft (1,085 m) Snowdon or *Yr Wyddfa* ("the tumulus"), the second highest peak in Britain after Ben Nevis in Scotland. Because we had no important engagements for the next couple of days, we decided to join the Hagans to explore the Snowdon National Park (*Parc Cenedlaethol Eryri*) in Gwynedd, a largely Welsh-speaking county in Northwest Wales.

My son Junius and I whizzed past the 4,409-ft. (1,344-m) Ben Nevis in 1990, when we participated in a Trafalgar tour of Britain (see the three preceding chapters). Although I wanted to get close to Snowdon as well, the occasion never arose until now—twenty years later! I grabbed the opportunity although it was Yoke-Sim who was vocal in expressing enthusiasm to explore the peculiarities of Welsh-speaking Britain. I was more interested in seeing the rustic splendor of the scenic A5 route from Shrewsbury (pop 70,700), the county town of Shropshire in the West Midlands, to Bangor (pop 13,725) in Wales.

Day 1

The next morning, we rejoined the Hagans at terminal 1 of Heathrow Airport, where the Hagans rented a stick shift Avis car for the journey. Geoffrey, a retired math teacher of Irish ancestry born in Sydney, chose to be the driver. We bundled ourselves into the little Chevrolet with Yoke-Sim and me in the back seats. Kathy, an Aussie retired teacher of South Indian origin, volunteered to be the navigator. Hers was quite an easy task. She fed the Global Positioning System (GPS) to give directions to the driver to go to specific destinations.

Geoffrey did not reveal the specific destinations of the journey. He followed the driving directions of the GPS robot seemingly hiding his own understanding of directions and routes. Usually, I spend hours looking at the geographical layout of a trip well before the journey. On this occasion, I did not know that we were going to spend overnight at Dinas Dinlle, a fishing village along the east coast of the Irish Sea seven miles southwest of Caernarfon (pop 9,611), the most Welsh-speaking community in all of Wales.

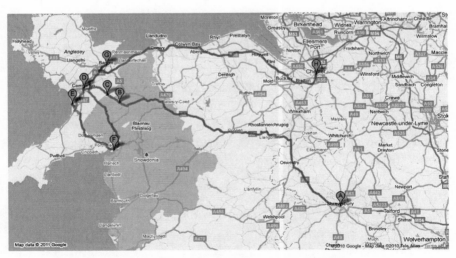

Map 42.1: The A5 Route to Snowdon National Park.
A=Shrewsbury; B=Snowdon; C=Llanberis; D=Caernarfon; E=Dinas Dinlle; F=Portmeirion; G=Bangor; H=Chester.

Leaving Heathrow about 10:00 a.m. on a Sunday (July 25), Geoffrey followed the automated directions of the GPS right up to Shrewsbury, some 160 miles to the northwest on M40. We stopped on a wayside service area for brunch. Thereafter, Geoffrey drove along the narrow but extremely scenic and idyllic route A5 right up to Capel (Chapel) Curig in the heart of Snowdon National Park. A5 crosses into Wales near the village of St. Martin's in Shropshire. Afon (River) Ceiriog and Afon Dee demarcate the England-Wales border.

The distance from Shrewsbury to Snowdon is about 74 miles. After crossing over to Wales, the Celtic flavor of the territory becomes all too obvious not only in people's shrill accents but also in signs giving pride of place to Welsh with tongue-twisting place names like Llangolen (Denbighshire), Druid, Cerrig-y-drudion (Conwy), Rhydlydan, Pentrfoelas, and Merddwr (where A5 enters the Snowdon National Park).

Within the national park, we passed through picture-postcard villages such as BroGarmon; Betws-y-Coed ("Prayer house in the wood") known for its Pont-y-Pant Falls and Swallow Falls, as well as the converging point of Afon (River) Conwy and its two tributaries Llugwy and Lledr; Pont (Bridge) Cyfyng; and Capel (Chapel) Crunig on the Llugwy (where we turned west on A4086 to reach Caernarfon via Snowdon and Llanberis. This road runs southwest and then curves northwest to suit the contours of the mountains. We arrived in Dinas Dinlle about 3:30 p.m. and went straight into Bryn Mor Beach Hotel on the seafront.

Ram and Sandhya Ananthraman, the couple who ran the hotel, greeted us and checked us into our respective rooms. They were friends of the Hagans. The lust for travel and adventure had landed them in Wales after stints in Botswana and Papua New Guinea. They established the hotel in 2003. After a brief rest, Yoke-Sim and I walked more than a mile along the sand and pebble beach admiring the canine creatures their owners were promenading. Back at the hotel, we joined Ram and the Hagans for tea and wine with Indian delicacies.

Because we saw hundreds of rams (uncastrated male sheep) and other sheep, including black sheep, grazing in the pastures, I introduced some humor into our conversation when I asked Ram whether the Welsh had any difficulty distinguishing him from the other rams in the area. He responded that the people maintained the distinction by pronouncing his Sanskrit name with the "are" sound.

Picture 42.1 The sand and pebble beach at Dinas Dinlle in North Wales. The author climbed the cliff Boncan Dinas, where he rehearsed Aussie-style coo-eeing. (Picture by L. J. Anderson. *Source:* Wikimedia Commons)

After the refreshments, the Hagans and we went to climb Boncan Dinas, the majestic cliff by the beach, just south of the hotel. We followed the winding pathway that enabled us to reach the top without mishap. However, I reached the top first through a steep shortcut. I fell down flat on my face as I negotiated a slippery descent, but I was unhurt. I celebrated the event by coo-eeing from the peak as I used to do at Cooee Bay in Yeppoon, Queensland, Australia.

Back in the hotel, it was time for dinner. Another surprise: Seated next to us was an Indian Malaysian family—a female law student; her accountant brother; her mother, a retired teacher; and her uncle, a telecommunication businessman. We instantly established rapport because Yoke-Sim was a Malaysian by birth and I was a lecturer in Penang in the midseventies. We exchanged preliminaries in Bahasa Malaysia and then veered into Malaysian politics, Tamil conundrum in Sri Lanka, etc., until close to midnight.

Day 2

Yoke-Sim and I planned to return to London in the evening so that we have a day of rest before flying back to the United States Wednesday. The Hagans had planned to stay a few more days to explore all of Wales. Before we joined the Hagans for the day's tour, we offered to settle our account for the night's stay. But the Ananthramans refused to issue us an invoice asserting the Eastern tradition of offering hospitality to friends with no financial gain in mind. We diffused the situation by placing on the reception desk an envelope with £50 enclosed.

Ram told us that the light rain and mixed weather conditions in the morning would prevent us from seeing the summit of Snowdon even if we succeed in getting a ride from Llanberis to the Summit (*Yr Wyddfa*)—a 4.7-mile stretch on Snowdon Mountain Railway. Ram was right. When we went to the Llanberis station, the counter clerk bluntly told us that although the narrow gauge rack and pinion mountain railway was running, he saw no point in purchasing tickets at £25 per person to see nothing of the mountains. We regretted the hefty £4 we had to pay to park the car just to turn back.

Alternatively, we could have gone on the sixty-minute return train trip along the north coast of Llyn (Lake) Padarn from Gilfach Ddu (where we ate lunch at the café and visited the slate museum) to Penllyn on the Llanberis Lake Railway for £7.20 a person. However, this option did not appeal to us.

We spent the morning driving through the northern mountain range of Snowdonia (*Eryri*), which is roughly synonymous with the 827-square-mile (2,140-sq.-km) Snowdon National Park. (The UK goverrnment established it as the third national park of Britain in 1951.) The Wikipedia explains the following:

The northernmost area is the most popular with tourists and includes (from west to east) Moel Hebog, Mynydd Mawr, and the Nantlle Ridge; the Snowdon Massif; the Glyderau; and the Carneddau. These last three groups are the highest mountains in Wales, and include all Wales' 3000-foot mountains.

Northern Snowdonia is the only place in Britain where the Snowdon Lily, an arctic-alpine plant, and the rainbow-colored Snowdon beetle (*Chrysolina cerealis*) are found, and the only place in the world where the Snowdonia hawkweed *Hieracium snowdoniense* grows.

Although the intermittent drizzle and the ensuing mist prevented us from seeing the Snowdon summit at close range, we saw enough of it from a distance over two days. Ram told us that the area was one of the wettest in Britain and that the visibility of the summit was unpredictable from day to day.

We spent most of the morning in the Italian-style tourist village of Portmeirion, which Sir Bertram Clough Williams-Ellis (1883-1978), an architect, established between 1925 and 1975. We drove 17 miles southeast from Dinas Dinlle to visit it at Penrhyndeudraeth, on the estuary of Afton (River) Dwyryd, two miles southeast of Porthmadog. A charitable trust owns and operates Portmeirion, which is one of the top tourist attractions in north Wales. The establishment has always been run as a hotel, which uses the majority of the buildings as hotel rooms or self-catering cottages, together with shops, a café, tearoom, and restaurant. Portmeirion's grounds contain an important collection of rhododendrons and other exotic plants in a wild-garden setting. Incidentally, we saw even a large Buddha statue ensconced in a dome. Admission to the village is £8 per adult. Spending a night at the luxury hotel costs a minimum of £200.

The Hagans dropped us at the Bangor Railway Station to catch the 4:00 p.m. Arriva train to Chester, where we changed over to the London-bound semiexpress Virgin train. The Bangor-London one-way ticket cost us £75.70 each, a hefty rip-off by the privately run British railway system.

Picture 42.2 A panoramic view of the Snowdon Mountain Range from Mynydd Mawr, 10 miles east of Dinas Dinlle. Snowdon is on center right. The Glyderau are in the background. (*Source:* Wikimedia Commons)

Picture 42.3 Panoramic view of the central piazza at Portmeirion (*Source:* Wikimedia Commons)

CHAPTER 43

Ireland: An Irish Escapade in Glencolumbkille

I CREATED ADVENTURE out of my global peregrinations even after I turned fifty. I was thinking as if I were a man of half that age when I got engrossed in jogging along the towpaths of the canals of London, the alleys of Tianjin, the footpaths of Happawana, or around the golf course in Moorhead, where I live.

My sense of adventure and my proclivity to explore in relative solitude put me in a situation of unexpected danger during a two-week tour of Ireland involving some 1,262 km of travel in July 1990.

After a 225-km coach-ride northwest from Dublin, we—a group of American egghead-types cobbled together by an American journalism professor from Chico State—arrived in Sligo on July 1 to experience and savor the environs where poet and dramatist William Butler Yeats (1865-1939) spent his childhood. Yeats won the Nobel Prize for literature in 1923 for his "inspired poetry, which in a highly artistic form gives expression to the spirit of a whole nation."

We spent three nights in Sligo, Ireland's smallest city with a current population of 17,900, at the Sligo Park Hotel. Although well known for its abundance of shellfish and Yeats, Sligo's population has remained stagnant, perhaps declined by a hundred or so, over the last twenty years.

On the first night, tour leader John Sutthof enticed our ragtag tour group to converge for postprandial coffee and conversation. We introduced ourselves to one another.

Yeats Mania

The next morning, we earnestly ventured into exploring Yeats's country further. We saw the Lake Isle of Innisfree that Yeats immortalized in the lines:

> I will arise and go now, and go to Innisfree,
> And a small cabin build . . . wattles made:
> Nine bean-rows . . . for the honeybee,
> And live alone in the bee-loud glade.

I experienced the crowning point of the day's exploration when I had the thrill of reading the epitaph on Yeats' grave at Drumcliff. Yeats "leaves the world of reason and embraces the spiritual world of eternity" in one of his last poems "Under Ben Bulben." The sixth verse of this poem ends with his famous epitaph.

> Under bare Ben Bulben's head
> In Drumcliff churchyard Yeats is laid.
> An ancestor was rector there
> Long years ago, a church stands near,
> By the road an ancient cross.
> No marble, no conventional phrase;
> On limestone quarried near the spot
> By his command these words are cut:
> > *Cast a cold eye*
> > *On life, on death.*
> > *Horseman, pass by!*

Risky Escapade

I had reason to mull over Yeats's epitaph—"cast a cold eye on life, on death"—the very next day (July 3) when our tour group took a day trip to Donegal town, 53 km northeast of Sligo, to see what remained of the Donegal Castle, the stronghold of the powerful O'Donnell clan, built on a bend of the River Eske. (The castle was fully restored in the late 1990s.). We also saw the friary where the Four Masters of the Franciscan Order completed their epic annals in the seventeenth century.

Just before noon, Sutthof offered those of us who wanted to explore more of the Gaeltacht—the Irish-speaking region of Ireland—a bonus tour to Glencolumbkille, 55 km west of Donegal town along a frog-shaped peninsula. I jumped at the offer together with a few others. We took off to this remote village of 734 people passing through places bearing amusing names like Rossylongan, Dunkineely, Killybegs, and Carrick.

In Glencolumbkille (the valley of Saint Columba), our instant inclination was to walk to the scenic beach before repairing to the cafeteria in Father McDyer's Folk Village Museum for lunch. Sutthof decided that we could do our own thing until 2:15 p.m., when the coach would leave back to Donegal to pick up the rest of the group at Abby Hotel and return to Sligo for the night.

Tucked against a rocky hillside, the folk museum is a composite of cottages grouped to form a traditional, tiny, village (clachan). The thick, thatched roofs of the cottages—each a replica of the living quarters of locals over three successive centuries—are tied down with heavy rope and anchored with stones, securing them from the harsh Atlantic winds. Period furniture and utensils adorn each little home.

It turned out that while I was exploring the hills behind the museum meticulously keeping track of time, Sutthof and the group had departed the village. So when I returned to the coach stop at the stipulated time, there was no sign of the coach.

With no cell phones at our disposal those days, the only recourse I had was to leave a landline message for Sutthof with Abby Hotel in Donegal. Then my spirit of adventure egged me on to try hitchhiking all the way back to Donegal town.

In retrospect, this 54 km hitchhiking ride turned out to be a very risky adventure. I made it to Donegal early evening in five stages. First, I received a ride from a local woman, who deposited me at the village junction. Second, a local man dropped me in Carrick (Gaelic for "rock") on R263.

Carrick was and still is a small but busy village, to the southwest of the village lies the fishing village of Teelin, once the main fishing port in Ireland, a place where beauty erupts from the clash of land and sea. (Quote from a native)

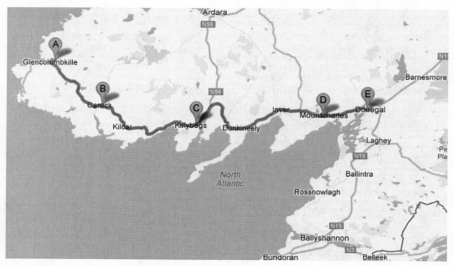

Map 43.1: From Glencolumbkille to Donegal: The Hitchhiked Trail
A=Glencolumbkille. B=Carrick. C=Killybegs. D=Mountcharles. E=Donegal Town]

Third, a touring German couple took me up to Killybegs (pop 1.280), Ireland's premier fishing port, where one can see the country's largest fleet of trawlers.

Fourth, a couple of Gaelic-speaking youngsters took me on a "wild" ride and dropped me off at Mountcharles. It was this ride that engendered me to mull over Yeats's epitaph and think of my rebecoming. The youngsters, who couldn't communicate with me in English, seemed to enjoy driving on byways at breakneck speeds to infuse fear in me either intentionally or unintentionally. All I know is that they confused my map reading by not sticking to R256 all the way and not explaining to me their actions. I was immensely relieved when they dropped me off without harming me to get my money.

Fifth, a local man picked me up at Moun tcharles, a place named after Charles Conyngham, an ancestor of Lord Mountcharles, and took me to Donegal, where a message from Sutthof was awaiting me at Abby Hotel.

Sutthof was apologetic about the agony he had put me through and took me for dinner at the Atlantic Café. Jim Wilson, our bus driver, returned to Donegal with Sutthof's wife Barbara to pick up the two of us. It was almost 10:00 p.m. when we got back to Sligo Park Hotel.

The next day, on our way to Galway, driver Wilson handed me the coach's public address system to recount my Glencolumbkille adventure. I put the following rhetorical question to the members of our tour group: How could you not notice the absence of the only colored Asian in the group when the coach left Glencolumbkille a few minutes before the stipulated departure time? No one volunteered a reply.

The rest of the tour of Ireland included stopovers in Galway (two nights), Limerick (one night), Killarney (three nights), Cork (one night), Kilkenny (one night), and Wexford (one night) before the group went their separate ways in Dublin.

CHAPTER 44

Ireland: Visiting Thoor Ballylee, Coole Park, Etc.

TWO DAYS AFTER the July 1990 Glencolumbkille episode (recounted in the preceding chapter), I, Weligama Podda (the brat from Weligama) of yore, was eating dinner at the Dunguaire Castle in the seaport village of Kinvara (pop 945) on the southeastern shore of Galway Bay. The castle's seventy-five-foot tower and its encompassing defensive wall stood majestically against the backdrop of the enchanting bay.

Not that I was trying to hobnob with the siblings of surgeon and poet Oliver St John Gogarty, who purchased the castle, originally built in 1520 by the Hynes clan, in the early twentieth century and turned it into the meeting place for the leading figures of the Celtic Revival—literary giants like dramatist and folklorist Isabella Augusta, Lady Gregory (1852-1932); playwright George Bernard Shaw (1856-1950); poet and playwright John Millington Synge (1871-1907); and Nobel Prize winner W. B. Yeats (1865-1939).

I was a mere participant in a ragtag group of literature buffs seeking to sense the flavor of the places and memories associated with the cream of the Irish literati.

July 5, 1990: I joined our "gang" of putative literary connoisseurs for a very pleasant medieval banquet. The entertainment included dramatizations of literary pieces of those connected to south County Galway—Lady Gregory, (James) Joyce, Shaw, Synge, Yeats and others.

(Since 1963, Shannon Heritage has owned and operated Dunguaire Castle, together with Bunratty and Knappogue castles. The castle is open to visitors from April to October. Its "medieval banquets" continue to be popular.)

Map 44.1: Google Map of my Ireland tour from Sligo to Dublin
A=Sligo.   B=Galway.   C=Limerick.   D=Killarney.   E=Cork.
F=Kilkenny. G=Wexford. H=Dublin

We arrived in Galway traveling 139 km southwards from Sligo along a scenic route via Ballina, County Mayo's largest town, to see some lovely lake country; Pontoon, an anglers' haven between lakes Conn and Cullin; Castlebar, the administrative seat of Mayo; Ballintubber Abbey, where St Patrick baptized local peasants; and Ballinrobe, the oldest town in South Mayo.

When we left Galway 100 km southeastwards for Limerick the next day, we learnt more about Yeats and Lady Gregory.

Some six km northeast of the town of Gort, named after King Guaire, we visited Thoor Ballylee, the sixteenth-century tower house that Yeats used as his summer home from 1918 to 1929. It inspired him to write *The Tower* (1928) and *The Winding Stair and Other Poems* (1929). Yeats deemed it appropriate to acknowledge his sojourn at the tower house in a tablet on the wall:

> I, the poet William Yeats,
> With old mill boards and sea-green slates,
> And smithy work from the Gort forge,
> Restored this tower for my wife George;
> And may these characters remain
> When all is ruin once again.

(Yeats, fifty-two, married George Hyde Lees, twenty-five, in 1917. Although Yeats was infatuated with Maud Gomme, eighteen months younger than he, she refused his proposal to marry him thrice.)

Some 3 km northwest of Gort, we also visited Coole Park, the home of Lady Gregory until 1927, when she sold it to the state. The home was demolished soon after. Yeats and (Edward) Martyn, who cofounded the Abbey Theater with Lady Gregory, often converged here with others of their ilk to enjoy its awesome beauty. Yeats's 1919 poem, "Wild Swans at Coole," immortalized it in the lines:

> THE TREES are in their autumn beauty,
> The woodland paths are dry,
> Under the October twilight the water
> Mirrors a still sky;
> Upon the brimming water among the stones
> Are nine-and-fifty swans.

The park's 4.5-km "Seven Woods Trail" connects the different woods celebrated in the poetry of Yeats. The "Autograph Tree," an old beech whereon the literary celebrities carved their initials, still remains.

(The Abbey Theater (now located at 26 Lower Abbey St., Dublin)—the brainchild of Lady Gregory, Yeats, Martyn and others associated with the Irish Literary Revival—celebrated its centenary in 2004. The recipient of an annual state subsidy, it is also known as the National Theater of Ireland.)

Other Attractions

Before we reached Limerick, we viewed the Cliffs of Mohr and visited the Bunratty Castle and Folk Park.

The awesome cliffs, near the village of Doolin in County Clare, rise 120 meters (394 ft) above the Atlantic Ocean at Hag's Head, and reach their maximum height of 214 meters (702 ft) just north of O'Brien's Tower, eight km away. The "Cliffs of Mohr Visitor Experience" facility opened in 2007—some seventeen years after our visit.

Bunratty (Castle at the Mouth of the Ratty) is another castle operated by Shannon Heritage. The castle, associated with the O'Brien Clan and the earls of Thomond, had its beginnings as a Viking trading camp in 970. Popular with the visitors are the castle's Great Hall, the four towers with spiral stairwells, and the dungeons. It also entices visitors with "medieval banquets" just like Dunguaire and Knappogue.

July 7-9, 1990: We left Limerick for the 110-km trip southwestwards for Killarney, which became our base for exploring the vicinity for three days. Our activities included the following:

- Visiting the model village of Adare (pop 2,592) located 15 km southwest of Limerick, with broad streets, half-timbered houses, thatched roofs, and rose-covered cottages.
- Doing the 170-km *Ring of Kerry* tour around the Iveragh peninsula. Popular points included Muckross House (near Killarney), Staigue Stone Fort, and Derrynane House, home of Daniel O'Connell. Other major attractions were Ross Castle, Lough Leane, and Ladies View.
- Touring the *Dingle Peninsula*. At Inch, we saw the beach where the movie "Ryan's Daughter" was shot on location. We passed through the Gaeltacht villages of Dunquin and Ballyferriter.

The two peninsula excursions took us to the furthest nooks and corners of southwestern Ireland.

July 10, 1990: We left Killarney for the 88-km trip eastward to Cork. This route marked the southern end of our tour of Ireland. The several sights we stopped to see included:

- Eccles Hotel in the small town of Glengariff, where Bernard Shaw wrote his masterpiece "Saint Joan" in 1914, more than a decade before he received the Nobel Prize for literature. Nestled between the harbor and the wooded hillsides, this scenic town still hangs on to its Victorian aura.
- Bantry House and Gardens constructed in the mid-eighteenth century by the Earl of Bantry on the scenic Bantry Bay.
- Blarney Castle, where I climbed up to the top of the tower to kiss the legendary Blarney Stone of Eloquence. For I was forewarned, "Kiss it and you'll never again be lost for words."

July 11, 1990: We left Cork, the second largest city in Ireland, for Kilkenny, 156 km to the northeast. With only two more days to end our long tour of Ireland, the clutter of place names mattered little to distinguish between Killarney and Kilkenny. But my journalistic commitment to fact checking ensured the accurate identification of the highlight of this day's tour:

- A visit to the Kilkenny Castle built in 1195 by William Marshal, the Earl of Pembroke. It was the home of the Butler family for five centuries from 1391. In 1967, the ownership of the castle and the grounds passed on to the people of Kilkenny with the Office of Public Works as their trustee. I walked the Royal Mile up to the Cathedral Church of St Canice, where I climbed up to the top of the Round Tower to see the environs.

July 12, 1990: We left Kilkenny and headed 79 km southeastwards for Wexford. A day for explorers of churches and cathedrals in Waterford and Wexford, the spot that impressed me was Wexford's twelfth century Selskar Abbey, where Henry II reputedly spent Lent 1172 doing penance for the murder of Thomas Beckett.

On the final day of our Ireland tour (July 13), on our way 130-km northwards from Wexford to Dublin, our ragtag group of literature buffs stopped by to savor the scenic Meeting of the Waters (of the rivers

Avonbeg and Avonmore) in the Valley of Avoca, which the Irish poet and lyricist Thomas Moore (1779-1852) immortalized in his famous lyric:

> *There is not in the wide world a valley so sweet,*
> *As the vale in whose bosom the bright waters meet.*
> *Oh, the last rays of feeling and life must depart,*
> *Ere the bloom of that valley shall fade from my heart.*

CHAPTER 45

Ireland: Dublin Is Rich with History and Culture

WHEN I FIRST visited Dublin in June 1990, it impressed me as a city that takes great pride in its history and culture. While every city has a history and a culture, not many cities can produce solid evidence to support their greatness.

Dublin is the place to visit the haunts of such literary giants as essayist Jonathan Swift (1667-1745), playwright William Congreve (1670-1729), dramatist Oliver Goldsmith (1730-1774), playwright R. B. Sheridan (1751-1816), lyricist Thomas Moore (1779-1852), folklorist Lady Gregory (1852-1932), playwright Oscar Wilde (1854-1900), playwright Bernard Shaw (1856-1970), poet W. B. Yeats (1865-1939), novelist James Joyce (1882-1941), and dramatist Sean O'Casey (1880-1964).

Moreover, Dublin is the home of some of Ireland's greatest museums, castles, markets, and parks.

Dublin is a global city with a metropolitan population of 1.6 million. Thus, about 38 percent of the republic's population lives in the Greater Dublin Area that includes Fingal, South Dublin, and Dun Laoghaire-Rathdown.

I arrived in Dublin on a Sunday (June 24, 1990). At the Dublin Airport, I took the express bus south to Busaras (in Dublin city), and then crossed over to Connolly Station to board the Dublin Area Rapid Transit (DART) train for a 20-km trip southeast to Bray, a seaside town of thirty-two thousand people (although the 1990 figure was only 22,700).

The Experiment for International Living had arranged for me to stay with the Hanafin family (Leo and Marie of 16 Raheen Park) for a week while I was attending the annual conference of the International Communication Association at Trinity College. Austin Babrow, a conference participant from Purdue University, was also staying with the Hanafins.

In the afternoon, the two Hanafin boys—Daragh, then twelve; and Mark, then twenty-two—took Babrow and me on a walking tour to the top of Bray Head, which has a large concrete cross, visible from the famous Victorian promenade overlooking the Irish Sea. Carlos, a Spanish boy staying with the Hanafins, also joined us.

After dinner, the Hanafins took Babrow and me for a drive through the Dublin Hills and the Wicklow Mountains. We stopped at Glencree to see the World War II German cemetery and also stopped on the wayside to absorb the scenery of the lakes below.

Such was my introduction to Dublin, which I explored over a week while attending the conference. Since the beginning of the Anglo-Norman rule in the twelfth century, Dublin served as the administrative seat of the Kingdom of Ireland (1541-1800) and of the Irish arm of the United Kingdom of Great Britain and Ireland (1801-1922). Dublin became the capital of the Irish Free State in 1922 and then the capital of the Republic of Ireland in 1949.

The absorption of Ireland into the United Kingdom for well over a century explains part of the resentment of the Irish against the British. The Irish claim that the English treated them disdainfully from the time that Ireland became the property of the English crown in 1171—the year when Strongbow (Richard Gilbert de Clare) and his fellow Normans resentfully acknowledged themselves to be the subjects of Henry II.

After the conference, I joined a ragtag group of Yankee eggheads cobbled together by professor John Sutthof to explore the famous Boyne Valley with Irish commentator John Killeen as our guide. We stopped at Drogheda, about 50 km to the north of Dublin, to see the site of the Battle of the Boyne (on July 12, 1690 in which William of Orange defeated James Stuart to win the crown of England. History buffs can tour the well-marked battlefield. Oliver Cromwell burned Drogheda in the 1640s.

But of greater interest to me were the nearby megalithic passage tombs of Newgrange, Knowth and Dowth, which are older than the pyramids of Egypt and predate Stonehenge by one thousand years. Some forty passage tombs built by the prehistoric inhabitants of the area are believed to exit. The four-feet-high tomb covers an acre of ground, with twelve large pillars surrounding it.

We ate lunch in Slane and proceeded to see the ruins of the twelfth century Mellifont Abbey, the first Cistercian abbey in Ireland. Then we stopped to see Monasterboice, an ancient monastic settlement noted for its intricately carved tenth century Cross of Muireadach and two other crosses varying in height from sixteen to twenty-one feet.

We also visited the archaeological complex named Hill of Tara, a sacral site associated with kingship rituals, between Navan and Dunshaughlin. This was the legendary seat of *Árd Rí na hÉireann*, or the High King of Ireland. There is an abundance of mythical stories associated with this place of mystery.

Dublin's Best

The preceding background allows me to make the claim that a fascinating aspect of touring Ireland is exploring the country's rich history, literary and otherwise. In Dublin, those interested in literature can visit the following:

- St Patrick's Cathedral, where Swift, the author of Gulliver's Travels and dean of the cathedral from 1713 to 1745, lies buried. Swift's own epitaph—"He lies where furious indignation can no longer rend his heart"—appears on a slab near the entrance.
- Trinity College, the oldest university in Ireland founded by Queen Elizabeth I in 1591. Among its famous alumni are Swift, Congreve, Goldsmith, Moore and Wilde. (Incidentally, the Long Room of the Trinity College Library attracts many visitors to see its chief treasure, the Book of Kells, an eighth-century

manuscript transcript of the four gospels described as "the most beautiful book in the world.")

- The new Abbey Theater, designed by architect Michael Scott, on the site of the original building that the Coole Park pals headed by Yeats and Lady Gregory founded in 1904. The original building succumbed to a fire in 1951 at the close of a performance of O'Casey's play *Plough and the Stars* that end with Dublin blazing in the aftermath of the 1916 Easter rebellion.
- Merrion Square where Wilde lived at No. 1 and Yeats at No. 82. This Georgian square housed several other celebrities as well. It is absorbing to read the historical signs outside the doorways.
- Dublin Writers' Museum opened since 1991 that features the lives and works of Dublin's literary celebrities over the past three hundred years—Swift and Sheridan, Shaw and Wilde, Yeats, Joyce, and Beckett.
- James Joyce Center that houses the Guinness Reference Library, Its "Ulysses Experience" contains a mural based on Joyce's most famous novel and incorporates the door of No. 7 Eccles Street—the fictional home of Leopold and Molly Bloom.

Dublin's share of Ireland's greatest museums, castles, markets and parks that a visitor should visit include the following:

- Christ Church Cathedral, which Viking King Sitric Silkenbeard founded in 1038. This is the Protestant cathedral for the diocese of Dublin. Rebuilt after its destruction in the twelfth century, it has one of Ireland's largest vaulted crypts.
- Leinster House, the meeting place of the Dail (House) and Seanad (Senate) since 1821. Built by Lord Kildare, Earl of Leinster, in 1745, it was used as a model for the White House by architect James Hoban of Carlow, who studied in Dublin. (I spent an afternoon in the visitors' gallery to watch then Prime Minister James Haughey fending questions from the opposition. The frequent shift to Gaelic both amused and confused me.)
- Mansion House, the residence of the lord mayors of Dublin since 1715. The 1919 Irish Declaration of Independence and the 1921 Anglo-Irish Treaty were signed in its Round Room. Nearby are the National Museum, the National Gallery and the Museum of Natural History.

- Dublin Castle, where the inauguration of the president of Ireland and related ceremonies take place in St. Patrick's Hall.
- General Post Office (1818), the headquarters of the Irish Volunteers during the 1916 Easter Rising. Two blocks to the west is the Moore Street Market, which no visitor to Dublin should miss. The voluble fruit and flower sellers supposedly represent the true voice of Dublin. They speak a sort of English that is straight Sean O'Casey.
- The 1,760-acre Phoenix Park, within which are the People's Gardens, the Zoological Gardens, the municipal race course, the Magazine Fort and the residences of the president of Ireland and the US ambassador.

Much of the joy and some of the agony of my tour of Ireland were the result of the company of my tour mates comprising John Sutthof' and his ragtag group of Yankee egghead-types. During the tour, we celebrated the forty-sixth wedding anniversary of two of them—Lou and Jean Chrysler. John Killeen, the Stewarts, Bill Todd-Mancillas and Charles Soderstrom were good dinnertime conversationalists. The group celebrated its dissolution on Friday (July 13, 1990) with their "last supper" at the Court Hotel in Dalkey facing the beautiful Killiney Bay.

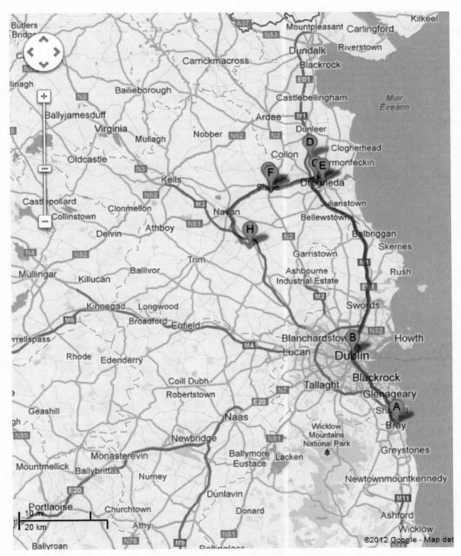

Map 45.1: A Google Map of Greater Dublin and the **Boyne** Valley A=Bray. B=Dublin. C=Site of the Battle of Boyne. D=Monasterboice. E=Old Mellifont Abbey. F=Newgrange. G=Slane. H=Hill of Tara

CHAPTER 46

Germany: A Drive on *Weinstrasse* (Wine Route)

S A HABIT, I invariably combined my professional (journalistic) and scholarly interests in planning my travels. My winter 1992 tour of the Rhine Valley wine route (*Weinstrasse*) and the Black Forest (*Schwarzwald*) was no exception.

I had made arrangements to visit the editorial office of the Frankfurter Allgemeine Zeitung (FAZ) one of the superb elite newspapers of the world and to enjoy the luxury of a grand hotel before I set off to the Black Forest to write a freelance travel piece for The (Fargo, North Dakota) Forum.

My flight landed in Frankfurt-am-Main Airport just before 9:30 a.m. on a Friday (February 28, 1992). I rented a stick shift Ford Fiat from Hertz at the airport. After getting lost several times, I finally got to the *FAZ* office at Hellerhofstrasse about noon. Because I was both a journalist and a professor of international communication, I received a warm welcome from managing editor Werner D'Inka whom I interviewed for about one hour. We discussed the possibilities for American students to work as *FAZ* interns and as foreign correspondents. (D'Inka became coeditor of *FAZ* in 2005, and he still continues in that position).

Then I drove 40 km west straight to Wiesbaden (pop 275,000), the capital of the federal state of Hessen, on A66 and checked in at Hotel Nassauer Hof on Kaiser Friedrich Platz, one of Europe's remaining grand hotels. Julia Reichert, the guest relations officer of the hotel, showed me all the facilities of the establishment, including the luxury suites graced by eminent celebrities. Later in the evening, I was the dinner guest of Heidi Gokeler, the hotel's executive secretary. Finishing the full-course dinner European style at the restaurant Die Ente von Lehel took us about three hours. After dinner, I visited the Kurhaus Bath Quarter (Kurviertel) located around the Wilhelmstrase promenade, the Brunnenkolonnade, and the Spa Park (Kurpark).

Map 46.1 The 805-kilometer route of my winter 1992 tour of Germany's Wine Route (*Weinstrasse*) and Black Forest (*Schwarzwald*). *A-N*, Frankfurt; *B*, Wiesbaden; *C*, Mainz; *D*, Worms; *E*, Bad Durkheim; *F*, Edenkoben; *G*, Dahn; *H*, Karlsruhe; *I*, Baden Baden; *J*, Freiburg; *K*, Donaueschingen; *L*, Stuttgart; *M*, Heilbronn; and *N-A*, Frankfurt. (A screen shot of a customized Google map.)

I learned that the Nassauer Hof had blended wellness, physical fitness, and beauty on its fifth floor facility to create an oasis of well being with an ambience of subtle design. The next morning, a hotel employee of Sri Lankan Tamil origin directed me to the hotel's thermal pool. Guests walked on light brown bamboo floors in a winter garden-like atmosphere and relaxed on teak loungers in front of arched windows.

I visited the Russian Orthodox Church of Saint Elizabeth and made it to the summit of the Neroberg Hill to get a panoramic view of Wiesbaden late morning. Then, I headed southward for Mainz (pop 200,300), the capital of the federal state of Rhineland-Palatinate, across the River Rhine. Although these two capitals are only 15 km apart, I lost my way a few times before I reached Mainz around midafternoon.

Lying at the confluence of the Rhine and the Main, the city is noted for its fine university named after Johannes Gutenberg (1398-1468), the supposed inventor of movable type and the printing press. Gutenberg was born in Mainz, where he also died. (Now, it is widely accepted that Bi Sheng, a Chinese alchemist, experimented with movable type for eight years from 1041 to four centuries before Gutenberg.). The Gutenberg Museum in the city proudly exhibits the original Bible that Gutenberg printed in the mid-fifteenth century.

Mainz also serves as a center of Germany's wine industry with the *Weinstrasse,* where I was heading, located within 100 km of its reach. Mainz is the home of the *Haus des Deutschen Weines* (House of the German Wine).

After stopping at Stadtpark to visit the Favorite Parkhotel, I drove north on Rheinestrasse to see the city's Cathedral Quarter. I entered the one-thousand-year-old Mainz Cathedral of St Martin (the Mainzer Dom) through a doorway on the Market Square. To my surprise, what I saw was a carnival going on inside. Carnivals are a regular feature in Mainz.

Luther and Worms

My plan was to stay overnight in Worms (pop 86,000), another 50 km to the south. I got there on the scenic highway along the Rhine. Having got there about 6.30 p.m., I inquired about a place to stay when a kind-hearted old couple directed me all the way to the Youth Hostel or Jugendgästehaus Worms, Dechaneigasse 1.

Worms is Germany's oldest city (or one of the three claimants to be the oldest with Trier and Cologne). Established by the Celts, who named it Borbetomagus, Worms became well known during the Protestant Reformation. My thoughts went back to the days when Mr. Dissanayake taught us European History at Ananda College in the midfifties. The connection between the Diet of Worms and the Protestant Reformation came to my mind.

Let me dramatize the proceedings of the Diet of Worms (with the help of Wikipedia), which took up matters relating to dissident Martin Luther from 16 to April 18, 1521.

- April 16: Luther arrives in Worms. Ulrich von Pappenheim, the reichmarschall, tells Luther to appear the following day at 4:00 p.m. before the diet. Jeromee Schurff, Wittenberg professor in Canon Law, acts as Luther's lawyer before the diet.
- April 17: The Imperial Herald Sturm and Pappenheim come for Luther. Pappenheim reminds Luther that he should speak only in answer to direct questions from the presiding officer, Johann von Eck. Eck asks if a collection of books is Luther's and if Luther is ready to revoke his heresies. Schurff says, "Please have the titles read." There are twenty-five of them, including *The 95 Theses, Resolutions Concerning the 95 Theses, On the Papacy at Rome, Address to the Christian Nobility, The Babylonian Captivity of the Church*, and *On the Freedom of a Christian*. Luther requests more time for a proper answer, and gets time until 4:00 p.m. the next day.
- April 18: Luther prays for long hours, consults with friends and mediators, and presents himself before the diet. A large crowd gathers. Luther is no longer in awe or feeling timid. When the counselor puts the same questions to him, Luther begins, "The Most Serene Lord Emperor, illustrious princes, most clement Lords, etc." He concedes that he lacks the etiquette of the court and admits, "They are all mine, but as for the second question, they are not all of one sort." Luther goes on to place his writings into three categories: (1) Works pertaining to the Protestant

Reformation that no one disputed. (2) Works attacking the abuses, lies, and desolation of the Christian world and the papacy. "If I now recant these, then, I would be doing nothing but strengthening tyranny," Luther declares. (3) Works that attacked individuals. He apologizes for the harsh tone of these writings but insists that he cannot reject them until he could be shown from the scriptures that he is in error. Luther concludes, "Here I stand. I can do no other. God help me. Amen."

The Edict of Worms, issued on May 15, 1521, declared Luther an obstinate heretic and banned the possession or reading of his books.

On the *Weinstrasse*

The next morning, after eating breakfast at the youth hostel, I went for a walk in Worms mulling over the historical events while visiting the Romanesque Cathedral and the Church of St Martin (both built in the thirteenth century). I also went to pay my respects to the Luther Monument (*Lutherdenkmal)* and the Jewish Cemetery.

Then I set out to explore the *Weinstrasse* (officially opened in October 1935), which runs approximately 85 km from the Alsace-Palatinate (French-German) border to north of the Palatinate Forest along B 38 and B 271 terminating at the House of German Wine in Bockenheim, which is just 15 km west of Worms.

Although the geography was clear in mind, I still lost my way when I found myself in Horchheim, where a young man asked me to follow him until I was on the correct road to the *Weinstrasse*. He left me at Dirmstein in the vicinity of the wine route. I looked around me to see vast stretches of plains with vineyards prospering under the watchful eyes of the Hardt Mountains. Being the warmest region in Germany, this area is most conducive to the cultivation of figs, lemons, grapes, and the like. The almond blossoms, which painted the area pink and white, pleased me.

I stopped at Frensheim because the ramparts encircling it and its twelfth-century church intrigued me.

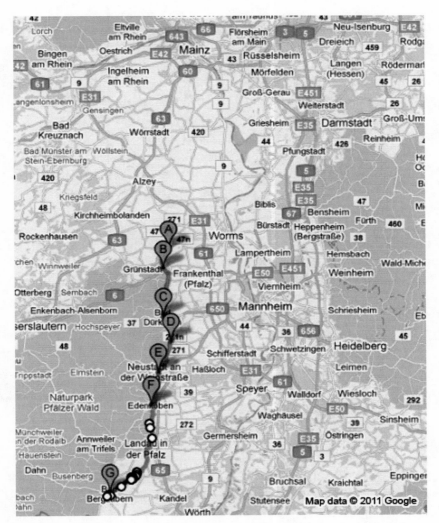

Map 46.2 The 85-km long *Weinstrasse* lies on the eastern bounds of the Palatinate Forest straight south of the Frankfurt-Wiesbaden-Mainz tri-city metropolitan area.

Then I crossed more vineyards to get to Weisenheim am Berg, where I joined the official wine route and proceeded driving southward tasting wine at places that caught my fancy. (Although I was not a habitual wine drinker, I was not averse to wine tasting, which I first did during a visit to Napa Valley in California during my travels as a WPI journalist.)

The spa park in Bad Durkheim caught my special attention. I stopped there for a leisurely walk. Bad Durkheim hosts the world's largest wine festival every September at the Wurstmarkt in front of the world's largest wine barrel. I drove past the wine towns of Wachenheim and Deidisheim and stopped at Neustadt an der Weinstrasse to fill up my rented car.

Just to the south of Neustadt, I stopped to see the Hambach Castle, considered to be the symbol of the German democracy movement because of the Hambacher Fest that took place in its premises in 1832. Although parking was free, a young lady at the parking lot was seeking donations.

I turned west at Maikammer to go to the Kalmit (673 m) lookout, the second highest point in the Palatinate. A short walk uphill to a *Pfaelzerwaldhuette* rewards the visitor with great views of the upper Rhine Valley in the east. On the way back, I also stopped at the tiny town of St. Martin, the location of Kropsburg, once the residence of the highest barons of the Reich, the knights of Dahlberg.

Fascinated by the enchanting beauty of the area, I decided to stay overnight at the nearby town of Edenkoben (pop 6,800), where I checked in at Pfaltzer Hof. A German couple, Walter and Margaret Ecker from Karlsruhe, joined me for dinner and conversation.

After a hearty breakfast at the hotel next morning, I paid a visit to the nearby Villa Ludwigshohe, the Italian-style summer residence of Ludwig I of Bavaria. Ludwig bought the grounds from the municipalities of Edenkoben and Rhodt in 1845 and built the castle in 1852. The abdication of Ludwig I in 1848 delayed its construction. The villa now houses the Max Slevogt gallery.

My "discovery" of the charm of Pfaltzer Wald committed me to spend an additional day to go deeper into the forest. Thus, after leaving Edenkoben, I headed 50 km west to Dahn (pop 4,800) via Rhodt under Rietburg (known for its 350-year-old Traminer vineyard, the oldest in Germany), Frankweiler and Annweiler am Trifels, where I stopped to see the ruins of the castle of Trifels on the Sonnenberg (493 m).

Rain spoilt my enjoyment of the steep climb to the castle, where Richard the Lionhearted of England was imprisoned in April 1193 after his return from the crusades. Trifels (three-fold rock) occupies one of the three peaks arising from the split of a red sandstone mountain. Anebos Castle is on one peak and Munz Castle is on the other.

Dahn, a rock-encircled country resort lying on the headwaters of the Lauter creek just 15 km from the Alsace-Palatinate border, was the ideal place for me to spend my last night in Rhineland-Palatinate. The place is a magnet for rock-climbers. Its landmark is the 70-meter high *Jungfernsprung* rock. Spending the night at Jugendherberge Dahn Am Wachtfelsen 1 was a pleasure because it gave me much needed rest and time to prepare for my adventures in the Black Forest.

CHAPTER 47

Germany: A Drive in *Schwarzwald* (Black Forest)

M Y ENCOUNTER WITH Germany's Schwarzwald (Black Forest) began on Tuesday (March 3, 1992) morning, when I arrived in Karlsruhe (pop 289,000) in the federal state of Baden Württemberg. Karlsruhe is the country's judicial capital or home of justice because it is the location of the *Bundesverfassungsgericht* (Federal Constitutional Court) and the *Bundesgerichtshof* (Federal Court of Justice).

I left Dahn soon after breakfast and drove east on the mountainous B427 to see the ruins of Burg Berwartstein at Erlenbach bei Dahn. The old castle had turned into a restaurant. I tarried at a park with a beautiful lake. Then I turned north on L493 to reach Voderweidenthal to view the looming Rodelstein rocks. Back on B427, I left the Palatinate Forest at Bad Bergzaben on the Weinstrasse, about 22 km from Dahn. After a rest stop at the spa park, I continued east on B427 to Kandel, near the boundary of Rhineland-Palatinate and Baden-Württemberg, and headed a few kilometers southeast on autobahn 65 to Karlsruhe.

I whiled away some time in Karlsruhe walking in the *Schlossgarten* (although the eighteenth-century castle that Margrave Karl Wilhelm built, now the Baden Regional Museum, was closed for the carnival) and the *Botanischer Garten* with its palm, cactus, and orchid house.

Karlsruhe is on the northwestern bounds of the Black Forest, renowned for its picturesque farms, sporting opportunities, and folklore. The forest runs for more than 200 km from Bad Sackingen (on the Swiss border) to Durlach (east of Karlsruhe) parallel to the Rhine, which separates Baden-Württemberg from Alsace-Lorraine in France. With an estimated width of 60 km, the Black Forest covers a rectangular mountainous region of approximately 12,000 square km. The forest area offers a network of some 23,000 km of tracks for walking, biking, and cross-country skiing. E1, the European long-distance trail, crosses the Black Forest.

Leaving Karlsruhe about 1:30 p.m., I drove south on B36 to visit the massive Schloss (castle) Rastatt built in the first decade of eighteenth century by the orders of Markgrafen Ludwig Wilhelm von Baden. The building now accommodates the military and national museums, as well as various administrative offices.

Curiosity enticed me to visit the Baroque-style Schloss Favorite in nearby Forch. Built by Margravine Franziska Sibylla Augusta of Sachsen-Lauenburg (1675-1733), it served as a pleasure and hunting palace.

Baden-Baden

I decided to spend my first night in the *Schwarzwald* at Baden-Baden (pop 55,000), the main northwestern gateway to the forest, where I arrived about 3:30 p.m. after driving some 100 km from Dahn. Baden-Baden, which literally means "bathing-bathing," is renowned for its thermal springs.

In the late afternoon, I had a pleasant walk on the Lichtentaler Allee, which runs besides the (artificial) Oos River. One of the most beautiful promenades in Europe; it attracts some of the world's most fashionable people as they emerge from the luxury hotels on the east side of the river. Some three hundred different trees and shrubs, including azaleas, ginkgos, oaks, magnolias, maples, silver poplars, rhododendrons, and tulips, adorn the park.

I ate dinner—farmhouse-style roast chicken with wine—at the Wienerwald restaurant, and checked in at Jugendherberge Baden-Baden Hardbergstraße 34, located on a hill, for the night.

I spent the next morning exploring the foremost attractions in Baden-Baden. The northern end of Lichtentaler Allee converges into Goetheplatz around which are the two hundred-year-old Spielbank (casino), the Kurhaus (cure house), and the Trinkhalle (pump room). The Kurhaus, built in the early 1820s, contains stately rooms, restaurants, bars, and spa rooms. (Germans have a predilection for baths, spas, and casinos, as is evident in place names that includes *Bad* as a prefix, as in *Bad* Durkheim, or as a suffix, as in Wies*bad*en.)

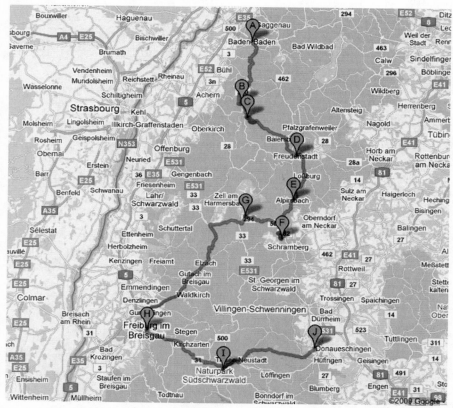

Map 47.1 The 65-km Black Forest Crest Road (Route B500) runs from Baden-Baden to Freudenstadt, where the 90-km "Kingdom of the Cuckoo Clock" Road (Route B294) takes over all the way to Freiburg. *A*, Baden-Baden; *B*, Mummelsee; *C*, Ruehestein; *D*, Freudenstadt; *E*, Alpirsbach; *F*, Schiltach; *G*, Wolfach; *H*, Freiburg im Breisgau; *I*, Titisee; *J*, Donaueschingen.

Spielbank is the oldest casino in Germany. Some believe that Fyodor Dostoyevsky wrote his short novel *The Gambler* (published in 1867) after losing his money at the Spielbank. As Europe's summer capital in the nineteenth century, the town became known for its opera house, concert halls, sports facilities, theaters, and the convention center.

SHELTON A. GUNARATNE

I also visited the Neues Schloss, which houses the Zahringen Museum. Completed in 1847, it was the residence of the margraves of Baden. Its terraces offer magnificent views of the town. I walked down steep stairs to see the *Stiftskirche* (a church that has the tombs of fourteen margraves of Baden) and the *Romanische Badruinen* (the ruins of Roman baths).

I left Baden-Baden about 11:30 a.m. heading southward to Freiburg im Breisgau, the main southwestern gateway to the Black Forest, through the Black Forest Crest Road and the Central Black Forest—a distance of about 155 km.

Black Forest Crest Road

In all my travels, the closest "route to heaven" that I ever encountered was the Black Forest Crest Road (*Schwarzwald Hochstrasse*) and its circular extension to the "Kingdom of the Cuckoo Clock."

A drive along this road reveals some of Germany's most beautiful scenery. As I passed the vineyard and orchard fringe south of Baden-Baden, the dark crests of the forest's conifers came into view. Mass logging had damaged patches of the forest's pines and firs at the time of my tour. Storm Lothar also damaged the ecology of the forest in 1999.

A couple of kilometers away, I was intrigued by the walking tracks that ran through the dense forest. As I backtracked and drove a kilometer or so off the Crest Road, I found myself at the portal of the luxurious Schlosshotel Buhlerhohe, a castle turned into a hotel, which provides 45 acres of private park grounds for its guests to indulge in jogging, golfing or just playing in the woods. Not too far away is the Badener Hohe, a popular destination for hikers.

I stopped at Mummelsee to see the small dark lake at the Hornisgrinde (1,164 m), the highest peak of the Northern Black Forest. Between Mummelsee and Ruehestein, the Crest Road circles the upper reaches of the Seebach Valley, and then finds its way through a plateau region and the Forbach Valley to Freudenstadt.

I stopped in Freudenstadt, which is strategically located on a high plateau at the confluence of all the main roads in the Northern Black Forest. I visited the town's *marktplatz*, its showpiece, and the seventeenth century church with identically domed belfries.

My research failed to yield a definitive answer to the question why this natural treasure of Germany is called the Black Forest. However, a native of the region expatiates:

> The Black Forest is called black because of [its] special trees [identified as "Tannenbaum." You might know this from the Christmas song ["O Tannenbaum, O Tannenbaum"]. They are so dense that the light cannot really get through [. . .] the really dark green of the Tannenbaum [creating the illusion of the color] black.

Fairy-Tale scenery

Then I moved on to explore the "Kingdom of the Cuckoo Clock." Cuckoo clocks originated in this region of Germany. Triberg native Franz Anton Ketterer built the first cuckoo clock. Ketterer's clocks soon became popular and many other people in the Black Forest began making them. In the early 1800s, the region had more than six hundred cuckoo-clock makers. The only memento I brought home from this tour was a cuckoo clock, which I bought for DM25 at Titisee the next day.

Proceeding southeast, I tarried at Alpirsbach to see the abbey some have described as "the most important Romanesque building in the Black Forest."

At Schiltach, I admired the wooden gabled houses and old inns. I found fairy-tale scenery along the way to Wolfach, the town with an unusual vista because of its confinement between a mountain and a bend in the Kinzig. (Triberg is 23 km south of Wolfach.)

However, I was disappointed that on my tour I did not encounter any of the fauna unique to the Black Forest—the *Hinterwalderberg* cows, the *Lumbricus badensis* giant earthworms, or the breed of horses called Black Forest Foxes—although I faintly recall a few eagles and owls swooping overhead.

SHELTON A. GUNARATNE

Freiburg im Breisgau

Finally, I drove southeast along the Elz Valley to Freiburg im Breisgau (pop 217,600—an increase of more than forty thousand since 1992), my destination for the night. After arriving at 6:00 p.m., I had no time or energy to tour the city. I stayed overnight at Jugendherberge Freiburg Kartäuserstr. 151.

I spent the morning of my last day in the Black Forest exploring Freiburg, which literally means "free city." Set among vineyards, this old university city has a unique gutter system called the *Bachle*—narrow brooks of swift-flowing water that run along the streets and alleys. The Bachle was a city-planning idea in medieval times to carry away the sewage and ensure a supply of fresh water.

The city is also known for the Freiburg Munster, a medieval Gothic cathedral adorning the largest square in the old city. This square resembles an Oriental bazaar with stalls protected by cotton umbrellas or makeshift awnings, on which are piled newly picked vegetables, fresh fruit, fish, tripe, poultry, honey, and flowers.

Some historical buildings grace the south side of the cathedral across the square: the Archiepiscopal Palace (1756), the Kaufhaus (1524) and the Wenzingerhaus (1761).

This flourishing city has many more attractions and features than what a passing journalist can see in half a day. I had to be in Stuttgart in the evening after completing my tour of the *Weinstrasse* and the *Schwarzwald*.

I left Freiburg about 11:30 a.m. and headed east on B31across the southern Black Forest to Titisee and Donaueschingen. As I reached the ski-jumping resort of Hinterzarten, the 1,493-meter Feldberg, the highest peak in Germany, was majestically staring at me at close range. The lovely lake at Titisee called for a stop and enticed me to buy a cuckoo clock. One of the goals of this tour was to see the source of the Danube—the Donauquelle. I achieved that goal in Donaueschingen, where I saw the confluence of the Brigach and the Breg to form the

Danube. A 19th century circular fountain officially marks the source of the Danube, Europe's second longest river (2,850 km), after the Volga. The Blue Danube (*An der schönen blauen Donau*) has become a romantic vision of the European life world. The waltz that Johann Strauss II composed in 1866 bearing that rubric "has been one of the most consistently popular pieces of music in the classical repertoire" (Wikipedia).

I left Donaueschingen about 3:30 p.m. headed for Stuttgart, 124 km north on Autobahn 81in the Neckar Valley. This road marks the eastern bounds of the Black Forest. Stuttgart, where I spent the night, lies parallel to the northern limits of Schwarzwald.

On this tour, I spent two more nights in Germany—in Heilbronn and Frankfurt. The highlight of these two days of leisurely travel was a visit to the Heidelberg Castle (Schloss Heidelberg), the earliest structure of which was built before AD 1214. Although it was expanded into two castles in the late thirteenth century, a lightning bolt destroyed the upper castle in 1537. A second lightning bolt destroyed the rebuilt structures of the castle in 1764. Wars and fires also affected the state of the castle. In short, it has been a very unlucky castle. Today, the hall of the castle is used for various festivities. During the Heidelberg Castle Festival in the summer, the courtyard becomes the venue for open-air musicals, operas, theatre performances, and classical concerts.

CHAPTER 48

Portugal: A Day in Porto

LUIS MIGUEL GONCALVES Pereira, a graduate student from the Communication and Society Research Center (CSRC), Universidade do Minho, was at the Francisco de Sá Carneiro Airport in Pedras Rubras to greet us—Yoke-Sim and me—when we landed in Portugal on Saturday (July 17, 2010) to attend the annual conference of the International Association for Media and Communication Research (IAMCR) in Braga.

Named after a Porto-born politician who died at the age of forty-six in an airplane crash just eleven months after he became Portugal's prime minister in 1980, the airport serves as the international gateway to both Porto (pop 221,800), 16 km to the southeast; and Braga (pop 175,063), 56 km to the northeast. The state-of-the-art airport underwent a massive program of refurbishment for the Euro 2004 football championships, partly hosted in Porto.

Portugal Visit 1972

I had visited Portugal in 1972 for an overnight stay in Lisbon on my way back from Sri Lanka to Minnesota to submit my doctoral dissertation. My diary documents that on Tuesday March 7 (1972) I spent $5 to get a visa at the Portugal consulate in Madrid, Spain, and flew to Lisbon on an Iberia flight the same day. I stayed overnight in Hotel Tivoli Jardim (at Rua Julio Cesar Machado from March 7 to 9) and explored the nearby Avenida da Liberdade and Praça (square) dos Restauradores early evening, later ending up at Cabaret Maxime, still a fixture at Praça da Alegria, 58.

I vividly remember a faux pas I committed on the evening I checked in at Hotel Tivoli Jardim. The bellhop who directed me to my room dillydallied obviously expecting a tip. I had no change in my possession except a US dime, which I passed over to him. He promptly returned the dime to me expressing the thought "You probably need it more than I do." I learned the lesson that giving no tip at all is better than a small tip.

On Wednesday March 8 (1972) morning, I explored the shopping area south of Restauradores; then, walked down Av 24 de Julho along the banks where Rio Tagus flows into the Atlantic Ocean; and returned on board a train to Praça (square) do Comercio. After stopping at Pan Am office to confirm my flight alterations, I took a taxi to the Lisbon Portela Airport for my flight to New York.

Background

Lisbon (pop 584,477) is the largest city and capital of Portugal, a "small" country in the Iberian Peninsula with 11.3 million people, about 30 percent of whom (3.4 million) live in the Lisbon Metropolitan Region. Portugal occupies an area of 35,645 square miles compared with Sri Lanka's 25,332 although in population size Sri Lanka is bigger (with 21.3 million people).

Porto (Port), also known as Oporto (The Port), is the second largest city. The name Portugal is derived from Portus Cale, the Latin name for Porto. It lies on the estuary of the Rio Douro. Porto comprises fifteen civil parishes. In 1996, UNESCO declared the historic center of Porto a World Heritage Site. The famous Port wine comes from the cellars of Vila Nova de Gaia, a city in the Porto Greater Metropolitan Area (GMA) just south of the Douro estuary.

Braga is the fifth largest, after Vila Nova de Gaia (pop 178,255) and Amadora (pop 176,239; in the Lisbon GMA). Two other cities—Almada (pop 102,357; in the Lisbon GMA) and Coimbra (pop 101,069; between Porto and Lisbon)—are big population size. (*Note:* area is smaller than region)

On this occasion (2010), I chose to land in the closest airport to Braga because I had already been to Lisbon although what I saw of it was very much restricted to the downtown and riverbank area. We—Yoke-Sim and I—reasoned that this arrangement would enable us to focus on north Portugal during the conference period.

So it happened that Louis Pereira and a coterie of communication students from Minho were at the airport to welcome the conference participants as they arrived. The CSRC coterie wore IAMCR T-shirts with the "Ask Me" sign to easily identify themselves.

Pereira took charge of the delegates who arrived on our flight from Gatwick late afternoon, seated them in a comfortable van, and got his doctoral thesis adviser and aunt Sara de Jesus Gomes Pereira to drive us all the way to Braga. On the way, he proved to be a good conversationalist as he used his command of English to pass on a few football tidbits to us—probably a bunch of cricket fans. He dropped Yoke-Sim and me at the Comfort Inn on the southwestern skirts of Braga.

It occurred to me that the numerous Pereiras and Pereras in Sri Lanka owed their names to the Portuguese who occupied parts of Sri Lanka from 1505 to1658. The Portuguese called the captured territory on the island Ceilao. Captains and captain majors ruled Ceilao until governors took over in 1594. One of the governors was Nuno Alvares Pereira (1616-1618). Thus, on the way to Braga, I had the privilege of meeting with two representatives of the Pereira Clan.

Yoke-Sim and I ate a lavish dinner at the hotel restaurant late that evening despite the communication problems we had with the young waitress, who had to summon front-desk to help understand what we wanted. Raquel Queirós, the very amiable woman who felicitously checked us into the hotel on our arrival, came to our rescue again. During a post-prandial conversation, Queirós persuaded us to go explore the sights and delights of Porto the next day (Sunday, March 18).

Sunday in Porto

Sunday morning we got on to a public bus and told the driver that we wanted to get off at the Braga Railway Station. Although the bus was not heading in that direction, he allowed us in. When the passengers disembarked at the terminal, he asked us to stay on and dropped us off right in front of the station. We thanked him profusely.

The Braga-Porto train service (2.20 euro one way) runs every hour. We were able to catch the 9:00 a.m. train, which took more or less one hour to reach our destination.

We got off at Porto's main central station, better known as Sao Benito, a tourist attraction itself. Located in the Almeida Garret Square, the station (opened since 1916) is known for its tile (*azulejo*) panels that depict scenes of the History of Portugal. Wikipedia elaborates that some 20,000 tiles constituting the panels show the work of Jorge Colaço, an important *azulejo* painter from 1905 to 1916.

After withdrawing some euro from the ATM at the Sao Benito Station, we walked downhill to the nearby Portugal Tours booth, where the man in charge suggested that we first get a feel of the city by hopping on and off the double-decker tourist buses that ran on two designated routes covering the attractions in both Porto and (Vila Nova de) Gaia. To do so, we bought two city-sightseeing tickets for 13 euro each valid for two consecutive days.

Picture 48.2 Sao Benito Train Station in the Almeida Garret Square to the east of which lies the city's red-light district. (Photo by Joseolgon at pt.wikipedia. Wikimedia Commons.).

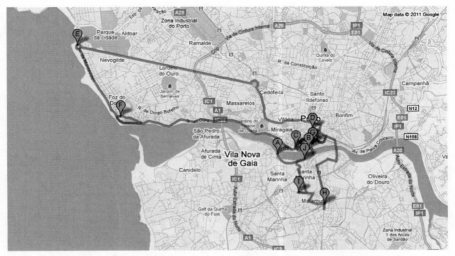

Map 48.1 Route of bus tour in Porto-Gaia. *A*, Gaia Wharf; *B* Ribeira Wharf; *C*, Bolsa Palace-Sao Francisco Church; *D*, Sao Benito Station; *E*, Fort San Francisco Xavier; *F*, Castelo Esplanade; *G,* Dom Luis Bridge; *H*, Joao de Deus; *I*, Cruz; *J*, Avenue Diogo Leite. Rio Douro separates Porto from Vila Nova de Gaia.

First, we tried the shorter Blue Line route with twenty-one stops. After lunch, we tried the Red Line route with thirty-three stops. The first nine stops are common to both lines, which enable visitors to explore the sights, mostly churches, closest to the Porto city center—such as Si Catedral (cathedral), Estacao (station) de Sao Bento, Igreja (church) de Santa Clara, Igreja de Santo Ildefonso, Mercado (market) do Bolhao, Igreja Trindade, Igreja Torre des Clerigos, Museu do Vinho (wine) do Porto, Museu dos Transportes, and Communicacoen, and Palacio (palace) da Bolsa—without having to walk excessively on the city's hilly terrain. Just to the east of Sao Benito Station is Hotel-Restaurante Mondariz, which shares the block (Rua Cimo de Vila 139) with several "remarkably staid" bordellos.

A popular tourist attraction is Porto's cable railway Funicular dos Guindais, which runs down a steep cliff from Batalha (on the higher ground of central Porto) to the quayside at Ribeira. The three-minute ride through the ninety-meter tunnel is claimed to provide the passengers with spectacular views of Ponte (bridge) de Dom Luis and the wharfs of both sides of Rio Douro. The funicular track is 281 meters long and descends 61 meters, giving an average gradient of around 20 percent.

Porto Metro, the company that operates the light railway network of electrified mass transportation in the Porto Metropolitan Region, also runs the funicular.

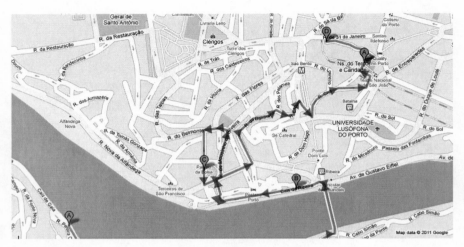

Map 48.2 Closeup of Central City, Porto. *Red A*, Hotel Mondariz.

The Blue Line crosses the Rio Douro to Gaia on Ponte (bridge) de Dom Luis I and stops at Largo Miguel Bombarda and Caves Croft to allow wine tasters to visit the cellars. Several other attractions are on its route: Cais (wharf) de Gaia, Corpus Christi, Casa-Museu (house museum) Teixeira Lopes, Camara (chamber) Municipal de Vila Nova de Gaia, Casa (house) Barbot and Mosteiro (monastery) da Serra do Pilar.

The Red Line takes the visitor all the way to the Atlantic beaches (*Praia*) on the western suburbs of Nevoglide, Foz do Douro, and Lordello do Ouro. The attractions on this route include Museu Nacional de Soares dos Reis, Casa de Musica, Estadio (stadium) do Bessa, Forte (fort) Sao Francisco Xavier, Castelo (castle) de Sao Joao de Foz, Farol (lighthouse) de Sao Miguel, Ponte (bridge) de Arrabida, and Alfandega Nova (new customs).

The two bus trips, which covered about 30 km, oriented us to much of Porto and part of Vila Nova de Gaia (see Map I) and gave us a notion of the many attractions that a visitor could explore, given more time and money. We had to catch the 4:00 p.m. train to get back to Braga to attend the opening ceremony of the IAMCR Conference.

World Heritage Site

We weren't able to see all the attractions we wished to see in Porto. We missed the Port wine tasting too. However, we saw the attraction we were determined to see—the Palacio da Bolsa (Stock Exchange Palace)—an edifice built in the nineteenth century by the city's Commercial Association (*Associação Comercial*) in Neoclassical style. It is now a World Heritage Site.

We bought admission tickets (5.50 euro each) for the early afternoon conducted tour. Our guide, a young woman fluent in several European languages, showed us the building's several rooms—Hall of Nations, General Assembly Room, Golden Room, Court Room, President's Room, Portraits Room, and the Arabic Room.

Picture 48.1 The Arabian Room of the Palacio de Bolsa. The structure of the palace was ready by 1850. Several artists magnificently decorated the interior of the palace, only finished in 1910. (Photo by Josep Renalias. Wikimedia Commons)

She particularly drew our attention to Portugal's coat of arms and the flags of its twenty friendly nations in the 119-meter high Hall of Nations ensconced in a metal and glass dome. The magnificent chandelier and the paintings in the General Assembly Room impressed us although the guide explained that the room's old oak and gold decorative appearance is a fake. A gold leaf implanted on the decorated plaster ceiling was the distinctive feature of the Golden Room. The Court Room evinced its affinity with French Renaissance. The President's Room is noted for its elegant pavement engraved in rare wood. The Portraits Room contains the portraits of the last six kings of Portugal in Louis XVI style.

However, the highlight of the palace is the Arabian Room, built between 1862 and 1880 by Gonçalves e Sousa. Built in Moorish style, this room engenders a feeling of luxury and grandeur.

Despite its fame, we fumbled locating the entrance to the palace. First, we by passed the building it is located. Second, we entered the wrong entrance and paid 3.50 euro each just to find out that we were in Igreja de Sao Francisco, the prominent Gothic monument adjoining the palacio. A thirteenth-century polychrome granite statue of Saint Francis of Assisi stands inside the church next to the entrance within a Baroque altarpiece. Out of curiosity, we also went to see the church's catacombs.

SHELTON A. GUNARATNE

CHAPTER 49

Portugal: Relishing Braga and Bom Jesus

ON ARRIVAL BACK at the Braga Railway Station Sunday (July 18) evening, Yoke-Sim and I bluffed our way by foot to Theatro Circo on Avenida da Liberdade, the venue of the official opening ceremony of the IAMCR conference. Because we did not have a detailed street map, we depended on amiable passers-by to give us directions. Our hunch was that the distance between the station and the theater was about 1.5 km.

Picture 49.3 Panoramic view of Braga, Portugal. (*Source:* Wikimedia Commons)

Exploration by Default

From the station, we hurried north on Largo da Estacao, where the bus driver dropped us off in the morning. At the Avenida Antonio Macedo roundabout, we turned east on Rua Andrade Corvo until we reached the Arco do Porta Nova ("arc of the new door" or New City Gate), which has decorated the western gate of the medieval wall in Sé parish since 1512.

The wall reminded us of the ancient origins of Braga, which was known as Bracara Augusta, the capital of Gallaecia province, under the Roman Empire. Today, the Braga Municipality (pop 177,183) is slightly larger than the city. It is now the center of the Greater Metropolitan Area of Minho with a population of 826,833.

From the Arc, we walked along a narrow pedestrian lane called Rua de Souto, which seemed to legitimize the claim that Braga is the oldest Portuguese city and, to boot, one of the oldest Christian cities in the world. We walked past the Museu Imagem (photography museum) opened in 1999; the Igreja (church) da Misericordia de Braga, an edifice of the Renaissance period built in 1562; the Sé Catedral, one of the most important historical buildings in Portugal; and the Casa Paivas ou da Roda [house of the wheel] until we reached Avenida da Liberdade. A female street musician and a young woman who was walking toward our destination were the last two to give us directions.

Ours was an unintended and unorthodox method of exploring the heart of a strange city—exploration by default.

At Theatro Circo

Although we missed the opening speeches of Braga Mayor Francisco Mequita Machado and IAMCR President Annabelle Sreberny, the "Ask Me" coterie of CSRC, helped us find seats in the 899-seat auditorium to listen to the remaining heavyweights. After the speeches, the Theatro took on its proper role as a place of entertainment when it presented a musical bonanza by the inimitable Portuguese singer Maria Joao with Mario Laginha on the piano. The international audience gave them a standing ovation for this magnificent welcome.

The organizers had apparently wanted the 1,300 or so conference participants from all over the world to spread the word about the historical Theatro Circo, "one of the largest and most beautiful theaters of Portugal." The theater, designed by architect Moura Coutinho, was inaugurated on April 21, 1915 with the Leoncavallo Operetta *La reginetta delle rose*. The building is one of the most important architectural works in Braga built in the early twentieth century.

Although the usual post-opening-ceremony reception was absent on this occasion, yet participants gathered in front of the theater to meet old friends and make new ones. Yoke-Sim and I got engrossed in conversation with an Indian couple, Abhijit Sen and his wife Sanchala, who were attending the IAMCR conference for the first time.

Picture 49.2 Abhijit Sen and his wife Sanchala whom the author met at the IAMCR Conference in Braga. (July 21, 2010)

The Sens joined us for dinner at a restaurant facing the city's elegant water fountain in Praca (square) da Republica, about 300 meters north of the Theatro. Sen, an associate professor of mass communication at Winston Salem State University in North Carolina, had read my academic work on de-westernizing the communication field. Both of us were specialists in international communication. After dinner, we returned to our respective hotels by taxi since we missed the free bus.

The conference went on from Monday through Thursday. The organizers had taken pains to arrange courtesy transportation for all participants on local bus routes. Thus, the municipal bus drivers, as well as the city dwellers, were well aware of our presence in Braga for the next four days. Clearly, the remote city of Braga considered it an honor to host an international conference!

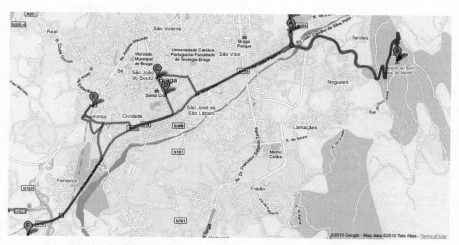

Map 49.1 Braga Map. The highway from *A* (Universidade do Minho [Gualtar Campus]) to *F* (Comfort Inn lies along Rio Este). *C* (Theatro Circo) and *D* (Praca da Republica are in the Braga City Center), *E* (Braga Train Station) and *B* (Bom Jesus do Monte).

On Gualtar Campus

Luis Pereira was back in action as our chief transportation organizer. Each day, he appeared at the Comfort Inn sharp at 8:00 a.m. to see that its share of participants got a ride on the courtesy bus to the Gualtar campus of Universidade do Minho, the conference venue, six kilometers

SHELTON A. GUNARATNE

northeast of Comfort Inn on the highway that runs parallel to the Rio (river) Este (see Map 49.1).

Monday morning, we found out that reaching the conference venue from the bus stop on hilly Gualtar campus was a mildly uphill task. Good exercise for indolent eggheads, though.

Our registration packets contained all the meal tickets we needed, the conference program souvenir, and other important tidbits. We became official participants of the conference when we attended the first plenary session.

We had to climb uphill another one-half kilometer or so to eat our lunch at the Gualtar Campus cafeteria. The Sens joined us for lunch. The walk back to the parallel sessions automatically took care of the digestive problems of the participants. After eating lunch Monday afternoon, I walked in to watch Sen's presentation of his paper "Media, Hinduism and Buddhism: Mainstream media coverage of Asia's two major religions."

A public university founded in 1973, Universidade do Minho has an enrollment of more than fifteen thousand students (including some two thousand in graduate studies), a faculty of 1.100 and a staff of about six hundred employees.

Braga and Bom Jesus

Courtesy of the IAMCR, we had the privilege of visiting a remarkable religious sanctuary in Braga—Bom Jesus do Monte (Good Jesus of the Mount), a notable example of a pilgrimage site with a monumental, Baroque stairway that climbs 116 meters (381 feet).

Located four kilometers east of the Gualtar campus, this was the venue of the conference dinner Wednesday.

Archbishop Rodrigo de Moura Telles of Braga initiated work on the sanctuary in 1772. Its design placed the temple of God, the church, at the top of the hill with an awesome set of stairways divided into three broad areas: The first stairway row has chapels dedicated to the *Via Crucis* (Way of the Cross). The next set of stairways, which takes a zigzag form, is dedicated to the five senses—sight, smell, touch, hearing, and taste—each represented by a different fountain. The third stairway, which also follows a zigzag pattern, is dedicated to the *three theological virtues*—faith, hope, and charity—each with its fountain. As the Wikipedia explains:

> As the pilgrims climbed the stairs, they encountered a theological program that contrasted the senses of the material world with the virtues of the spirit, at the same time as they experienced the scenes of the Passion of Christ. The culmination of the effort was the temple of God, the church on the top of the hill. The presence of several fountains along the stairways gives the idea of purification of the faithful.

Picture 49.1 The author and his wife Yoke-Sim on the top stairway below the Temple of God, Bom Jesus do Monte. (July 21, 2010)

SHELTON A. GUNARATNE

The Bom Jesus funicular, which the Swiss engineer Nicklaus Riggenbach built in 1882, has a 274-meter long track that descends the hill's 116-meter height at an average gradient of 42 percent. It is the oldest water-ballast funicular in the world. The journey on the two-car funicular (with a capacity of thirty-eight people per car) takes 2.4 to four minutes.

We ate dinner on the grounds of the Good Jesus Sanctuary—a place where we listened to the Burgundian Combo while eating and chatting with an international group of colleagues. On the terrace of Hotel du Parque, I had a nostalgic conversation with longtime friend John Lent who was instrumental in placing me on the faculty of Universiti Sains Malaysia in the early 1970s. He is still teaching full-time at Temple University.

Bits and Pieces

Yoke-Sim and I took the public bus to the Braga city center on Thursday afternoon for exploring the area around Praca da Republica again. We cut through the Santa Barbara shopping area to the Arco da Porta Nova for the second time. Then, we returned to the campus by another bus in time to attend the IAMCR General Assembly session. We went to the city center Monday evening as well to regale ourselves at the opening reception of IAMCR at Casa dos Coimbras (Largo Santa Cruz 506).

The Braga experience made me wary of using toilets in Portugal. To conserve energy, the good Portuguese have set the toilet lights to switch off automatically. If a toilet user failed to meet that time limit, he or she would have to toil in the pitch dark. I faced this situation both at the Theatro Circo and the Gualtar Campus.

We checked out of Comfort Inn on Friday after breakfast. Luis Pereira made all the arrangements for our transportation to the Francisco de Sá Carneiro Airport in Pedras Rubras for our return trip to Gatwick, London. We wished that Luis was there to say good-bye.

CHAPTER 50

Australia: Crossing the Nullarbor Back and Forth

FTER MY WIFE Yoke-Sim and I settled down in Central Queensland in 1976, we decided to get better acquainted with our adopted land by criss-crossing the big island (continent?).

Since I had considerable experience exploring the United States by Greyhound during my year (1966-1967) with the World Press Institute, I convinced Yoke-Sim that we should explore Australia by coach to get a better feel of our new country. Moreover, our transportation would be quite inexpensive because each could purchase a $225 Aussiepass or Eaglepass for unlimited travel for a month. Accommodation would also cost less because our travel would entail sleepovers aboard the bus several nights.

The ideal opportunity came when Howard Gaskin of the Western Australia Institute of Technology (which became Curtin University of Technology in 1986) invited both of us to visit Perth for the general meeting of the newly formed Australian Association for Tertiary Education in Journalism (December 14-15, 1978), where I was scheduled to present a paper titled "Public Affairs Reporting, Precision Journalism and Specialisms."

(In 2010, Greyhound Australia offered two types of passes:

- Aussie Explorer Pass on predetermined routes. The All Australian Pass, valid for twelve months, cost $2,998.
- Aussie Kilometer Pass starting at 2,000 km and increasing in blocks of 1,000 km to a maximum of 20,000 km. Price ranged

from $382 for 2,000 km to $2,239 for 20,000 km. Valid for twelve months.

The $225 Aussiepass we bought in 1978 is a thing of the past!)

Mixing business with pleasure, we set off on a month-long bus tour of Australia leaving our home in Rockhampton Saturday December 9, 1978. We traveled about 17,000 km on this trip, enjoyed meeting and hobnobbing with numerous "Crocodile Dundees" (a term that became synonymous with folks in the Aussie outback less than a decade later with Paul Hogan's 1986 movie), and suffered the sorrows of all bus travelers on bumpy outback roads like the Stuart Highway.

In retrospect, I look at this long trip as a well-planned travel adventure divisible into three parts:

- From Rockhampton, Queensland, to Perth, Western Australia—a distance of 5,600 km—through New South Wales (Armidale, Dubbo, Broken Hill) and South Australia (Adelaide, Ceduna).
- From Perth, Western Australia, to Darwin, Northern Territory—a distance of 6,300 km—through South Australia (Adelaide, Coober Pedy) and lower Northern Territory (Ayers Rock, Alice Springs).
- From Darwin, Northern Territory, to Rockhampton, Queensland—a distance of 4,000 km—through lower Northern Territory (Tennant Creek), northwestern, and northern Queensland (Mount Isa, Cairns, Townsville, Marlborough).

On the Way to Perth

The Ansett Pioneer Express picked us up at the Leichardt Hotel in Rockhampton (current population 60,000, about 8,000 more than in 1978) at 1:30 a.m. on Saturday (December 9), and we were on the way on our long journey West. I recalled the famous advice that New York Tribune editor Horace Greeley gave in an 1851 editorial: "Go West, young man." As a journalist, I was happy to follow Greeley's exhortation because Australia's pioneer country was also its West.

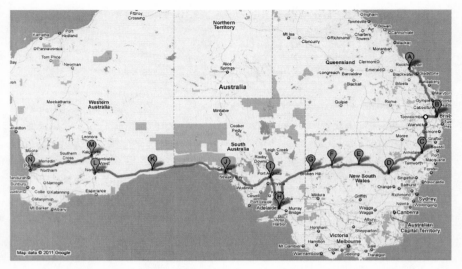

Map 50.1 Our 5,600 km bus tour from Rockhampton, Queensland, to Perth, Western Australia.

After a brief stop in Bundaberg, Queensland, the coach arrived in the Queensland capital of Brisbane (current metro population of 1.9 million) at 12:15 p.m. We figured out that since it took the bus almost eleven hours to cover the 616 km from Rockhampton, our road speed would be about 56 k.p.h.

Our plan was to stay overnight in Brisbane at the University of Queensland International House and to eat dinner with a few Thai students attending UQ.

The next day, after we ate a hearty breakfast at the International House, a friend brought us to the Ansett terminal, where we got on a Melbourne-bound coach to continue our journey. The coach captain drove 125 km west to Toowoomba and another 83 km south to Warwick, where he stopped for lunch before crossing the Queensland border to New South Wales.

Our dinner stop was Armidale (pop 19,500), the home of the University of New England, 308 km south of Warwick. The stop, north of the town, was close to a motel in peaceful surroundings. An elderly lady from Toowoomba who was going to Melbourne to see her grandchildren joined us for dinner.

From Armidale, our tour route took a southwestern direction. Our coach captain handed over his driving seat to a new one at Tamworth, 112 km further away. He explained that safety precautions did not permit any coach captain to drive more than 700 km a day. Although it was 9:00 p.m., the new driver put on some soothing music to lull us into sleep.

Our coach arrived in Dubbo, New South Wales (pop 30,200)—342 km southwest of Tamworth—at 1:30 a.m. the next day. Those heading west had to disembark here while those going southeast to Melbourne remained in the same coach.

We boarded the Adelaide-bound coach, which took us a further 296 km northwest to Cobar, NSW, where we stopped for breakfast at 6:00 a.m. Our driver had to knock on the door to get the café open. We ate poached eggs on toast at a cost of $4.50.

The 261 km stretch of the Barrier Highway from Cobar to Wilcannia, NSW, turned out to be to be "a cockatoo (galah) paradise" with birds crossing the road quite often. (Bird lovers, please note.) The refuelling stop in Wilcannia enabled me to take a quick shave.

Our driver covered another 196 km west on Silver City Highway to reach the isolated mining center of Broken Hill (pop 18,900), the last NSW town near the South Australia border. BHP Billiton, the world's largest mining company, had its roots here.

We ate lunch at the Barrier Social Democratic Club (218 Archer St.). I ate a porterhouse steak while Yoke-Sim preferred fish and chips.

A new driver took over the coach to take us all the way to the South Australian capital of Adelaide (metro population 1.3 million), another 511 km to the southwest. We checked in at the Plaza Hotel, east of the Rundle Mall, to rest and recuperate and prepare ourselves for crossing the Nullarbor the next day.

On Tuesday (December 12), as we finished eating breakfast at a snacker and walked to the Pioneer bus terminal in Adelaide, we mulled over the daunting prospect of having to drive through another stretch of more than 2,700 km to Perth soon after completing a massive stretch of more than 2,800 km from Rockhampton. Rather than repeating the same syntax to express the routine procedures the coach captain executed during the rest of the trip, let me just summarize them to convey a sense of the tyranny of distance

- December 12, lunch stop: Port Augusta, South Australia (306 km from Adelaide)
- December 12, dinner and driver-change stop: Ceduna, South Australia (466 km from Port Augusta)
- December 13, driver-change stop: Madura, Western Australia (676 km from Ceduna)
- December 13, breakfast stop: Norseman, Western Australia (532 km from Madura)
- December 13, driver-change stop: Kalgoorlie, Western Australia (187 km from Norseman)
- December 13, lunch stop: Merredin, Western Australia (334 km from Kalgoorlie)
- December 13, destination stop: Perth, Western Australia (264 km from Merredin)

At Ceduna (pop 2,300), where the local water supply was so salty as to be undrinkable, Yoke-Sim and I prepared our own sandwiches for dinner from groceries we purchased in Port Augusta (pop 13,300). After dinner, the new driver who took charge of the coach advised us to take a good look at our right and at our left "and then go to sleep because the next few hundred miles would look exactly the same." The Nullarbor is roughly the plain stretching 1,142 km from Ceduna to Norseman, immediately north of the Great Australian Bight.

But crossing the Nullarbor (treeless) Plain is a matter of great pride for the Crocodile Dundees. The Eyre Highway, opened in 1941, connecting Norseman, Western Australia, with Port Augusta, South Australia, enabled the crossing of the Nullarbor.

The next driver, who took over the coach in Madura, a roadhouse community, while most of us were fast asleep, stopped at Caiguna for those who wanted to get refreshments. At Norseman (pop 1,000), our breakfast stop, I had enough time to shave and refresh myself. Before he left us in Kalgoorlie, this driver gave us interesting accounts of Kambalda, Boulder and Kalgoorlie as we reached these towns.

Kambalda (pop 4,300), located on the western edge of Lake Lefroy, a large 510-square km salt lake, is a mining town divided into East and West within the Goldfields-Esperance region. Percy Larkin, a gold prospector, initiated the settlement at the base of Red Hill in 1897.

Kalgoorlie-Boulder (pop 28,300) was founded in 1893 during the Yilgarn-Goldfields gold rush after three prospectors—Paddy Hannan, Tom Flanagan, and Dan O'Shea—found signs of gold in the area when one of their horses cast a shoe. The town grew as a mining center ever since.

Picture 50.1 The author, with his wife Yoke-Sim, at the Hainault Tourist Mine ("The Super Pit" on the Golden Mile) between Kalgoorlie and Boulder in Western Australia (December 18, 1978).

The Super Pit is the main attraction in Kalgoorlie. Other places of interest include its Hay Street (named after Hay Street, Perth) brothels; its two-up (an Aussie gambling game involving coin throwing) school; the goldfields railway loop line; the Kalgoorlie Town Hall; the Paddy Hannan statue and drinking fountain; and the Mt Charlotte lookout. One of its infamous brothels also serves as a museum and is a major national attraction. We decided to explore Kalgoorlie on our return journey. The last driver took us all the way from Kalgoorlie to Perth. For me, the long water pipeline, designed by C. Y. O'Connor to bring in fresh water from Mundaring Weir near Perth, was an eyesore. Yoke-Sim took advantage of our lunch stop, Merredin, to buy some essential groceries. We reached the Western Australian capital of Perth (metro population 1.6 million) about 6:00 p.m.

Doug White of Mount Lawley CAE (subsequently renamed Edith Cowan University), an AATEJ representative, met us in Perth and took us to the Ocean Beach Hotel in Cottesloe (between Perth and Fremantle) for us to rest and recover from fatigue.

Yoke-Sim prepared our dinner. Later, we went for a leisurely stroll on the beach and joined the teenyboppers at the hotel for a drink.

As we discovered soon, Cottesloe (named after an Aussie prime minister) was the best deal we had in the West. Ocean Beach Hotel still exists.

CHAPTER 51

Australia: Backtracking the Nullarbor and Reaching the Top End

I PARTICIPATED IN the AATEJ (subsequently renamed Journalism Education Association) general meeting in Perth December 14-15, 1978. Doug White transported us from Cottesloe to the meeting venue on the WAIT (subsequently renamed Curtin University of Technology) campus. The first day's highlight was a discussion with high-school journalism teachers.

My paper elicited heated comments on the second day. Doug Golding and Charles Stokes, both of Queensland, opposed my advocacy of precision journalism (application of the scientific method to journalism) while Murray Masterton (South Australia) and Maurice Dunlevy (Canberra) gave it qualified support.

Friday evening, we joined a barbecue organized by Tony Hoffman of WAIT's School of Arts and Design at his hacienda-style home in Kalamunda in the eastern suburbs. Good food and lively company at this social gathering gave added value to our Perth visit. Although we left the party at 11:00 p.m., we couldn't get back to Cottesloe until 12:30 a.m. because Don Woolford, who agreed to give us a ride, lost his way.

Exploring Perth

My wife Yoke-Sim and I explored Perth's Hay Street Pedestrian Mall Saturday (December 16) morning. At Beaufort Street, we rented a Letz car to tour the city because it would ease our transportation problems until our departure Sunday.

Armed with guides and maps, first we visited the Mount Lawley CIA (now Edith Cowan University) campus; then the 110-hectare Lake Monger Reserve to see the flocks of black swans, cormorants, pelicans, and spoonbills. Other inhabitants of this wetland reserve include skunks, tortoises, and frogs.

Picture 51.1 The author at the Two Rocks Town Center in Yanchep Sun City (January 16, 1978). The background shows the Waugal Monoliths, an Aboriginal legend recreated in limestone dominated by a winged serpent, 19 m high, carved from two Garrah trees

Proceeding north to Wanneroo, we stopped to see the elegant suburbs of Quinn's Rocks, Yanchep and Two Rocks. We ate lunch at Loch McNess (perhaps so named to remind one of Loch Ness in Scotland) in the Yanchep National Park, where we also joined the conducted tour of the Crystal Cave. We couldn't resist drinking a beer at a tavern in the magnificent shopping center in Two Rocks.

Back in Perth late afternoon, we stopped to see the Old Mill (Shenton's Mill), a restored tower mill constructed in 1835, at Mill Point. The highlight of the evening was a visit to King's Park, where we enjoyed the landscaped botanic garden, which exhibited some two thousand of the twelve thousand plant species of Western Australia. We climbed the observation tower to view the city from all directions.

Sunday morning, Yoke-Sim and I checked out of the Ocean Beach Hotel (a complete hotel suite at $14 per night was an unexpected bonanza) to explore metropolitan Perth further in our rented car before we boarded the coach at 3:10 p.m. for backtracking the Nullarbor to reach Darwin via Adelaide.

Picture 51.2 The author at Fremantle's Old Gaol and Courthouse built with convict labor in 1855-56. It is one of the best examples of colonial architecture. The architect was R. R. Jewell.

We started with a visit to the port of Fremantle. From the lighthouse on Port Beach Road, we drove along the inner harbor to the lighthouse at Arthur Head and climbed on to the Round House from the ocean side. We also had a good look at the fish market, the slipway, the boat pen, and the pottery gallery. Then we went around the Fishing Boat Harbor on Mews Road to the city.

Next, we drove further south to Robb Jetty and the Coogee Beach Reserve. In the vicinity of Woodman Point, off Cockburn Road, our car got stuck in the sand. A passing motorist helped us tow the car to the sealed road. Our next "brilliant" idea was to visit Bibra Lake and the Murdoch University campus just north of it. Having thus become familiar with the vicinity, we returned to the city center and stopped briefly at the WACA oval to watch the England versus Australia cricket test.

As our departure time came closer, we returned the rented car and boarded the bus at the coach terminal. To reach Darwin, we had to backtrack all of the 2,700 km distance from Perth to Adelaide. In the late 1970s, coaches didn't travel the bad outback roads from Broome to Darwin although today coaches are available to proceed directly from Perth to Darwin (Route 680/860 via Kalbarri) on the sealed highway.

Kalgoorlie Stopover

At Kalgoorlie, where we arrived before midnight, we disembarked the bus and decided to check in at Glendevon Hotel on Egan Street. This hotel, currently run by a couple named Stew and Chrissy, was originally built circa 1930.

Monday morning, after a sumptuous breakfast at Glendevon, Yoke Sim and I took a taxi to Hainault Gold Mine on the Golden Mile to join the $3 tour conducted by an old miner. He took us 61 meters underground in a cage to explain how the mine operated. (Hainault was closed as a tourist attraction in 1993. But Hannan's North Tourist Mine, seven km north of Kalgoorlie, provides a tour for $22/adult.).

Rick and Yoonne Atkinson, a couple from Woomera, South Australia, gave us a ride from the mine to the scenic Hammond Park, which had a lake, rustic bridges, and a miniature castle made of local stones. We bought our lunch at Woolworth's and returned to the hotel to rest.

In the afternoon, we visited the other attractions in the city: the British Arms Hotel or the Golden Mile Museum, the Mineral Museum, and the art gallery in the Town Hall. I also had a leisurely walk on the infamous Hay Street.

Backtracking the Nullarbor

Tuesday (December 18) morning, just after midnight, we boarded the Adelaide-bound coach to continue with backtracking the Nullarbor. We fell asleep until we arrived at the Cocklebiddy (pop 80) roadhouse for breakfast. Sleeping was a better option than watching the "identical landscape" for hundreds of kilometers. The lunch stop was Eucla (pop 50), the last Western Australia roadhouse before crossing the border to

South Australia. In my view, Eucla had the best facilities (for example, a swimming pool with shady picnic tables) for passers-by than any other roadhouse on the Nullarbor Plain.

On the way to Ceduna, the scheduled dinner stop, our coach encountered a mechanical glitch. We prepared our own dinner with groceries purchased at a local shop since the coach captain confessed that he could not continue driving without "safety repairs." After a delay of four hours, we left Ceduna at 3:00 a.m. (Wednesday). We ate breakfast at Port Augusta and arrived back in Adelaide at 1:00 p.m. Again, we checked in at the Plaza Hotel for two nights.

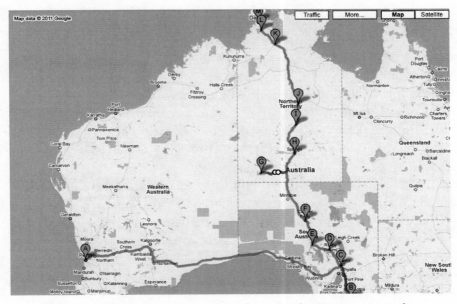

Map 51.1 The route that took us from Perth, Western Australia, to Darwin, Northern Territory, via Adelaide, South Australia. We backtracked the entire Eyre Highway spanning the Nullarbor and covered the entire length of Stuart Highway from Darwin to Port Augusta. *A*, Perth; *B*, Adelaide; *C*, Port Augusta; *D*, Pimba; *E*, Kingoonya; *F*, Coober Pedy; *G*, Ayers Rock or Uluru; *H*, Alice Springs; *I*, Barrow Creek; *J*, Tennant Creek; *K*, Katherine; *L*, Adelaide River; *M*, Darwin.

We spent the afternoon at the Rundle Mall purchasing clothes and shoes needed for outback travel and planning a trip to the Barossa Valley at the tourist bureau. In the evening, we ate an enjoyable Sri

Lankan-style dinner at the Ceylon Hut (27 Bank St.), including sparkling wine, for $12. (Three decades after our visit, this restaurant is still in operation.)

Barossa Valley

Although I am not a regular wine connoisseur, I have not been averse to tasting wine during vineyard excursions (such as Napa Valley in California and the *Weinstrasse* in Rhineland-Palatinate). Therefore, a tour of the Barossa Valley during our layover in Adelaide had an inherent appeal to me. The tour cost at $14 per person seemed quite reasonable to imbibe all the wine one needed.

We joined the Premier Roadlines' fine wine tour of the Barossa Valley, 56 km northeast of Adelaide, Thursday. Our first stop was the Seppeltfield winery, founded in 1851 by Joseph Ernst Seppelt. The winery is well known for its signature wine, the hundred-year-old Para Tawny Port. After taking us on a conducted tour, the winery offered us a variety of wines to taste. (Barossa is known for its red wines, like the Shiraz. An estimated fifty wineries are located in Barossa.)

Then we visited the Mengler's Hill lookout in the Barossa Ranges for a view of the valley. Lunch was awaiting us at Weintal Hotel-Motel in Tanunda. The tour then took us to the Gramp's Orlando winery at Rowland Flat. We returned to Adelaide about 4:00 p.m. via Williamstown and the spectacular Torrens Gorge.

Onward to Alice

We left Adelaide Friday (December 22, 1978) morning on the Alice Springs-bound coach heading northward to Port Augusta, the terminus of The Track (also identified as Stuart Highway). Three decades ago, Australia's West actually appeared to begin about a stone's throw to the area west of this partly bumpy, ill-kept main artery of traffic. I suspected that coach drivers who had to steer their vehicles on The Track, stretching 2,834 km from Darwin in the north to Port Augusta in the south, went through much *dukkha* (suffering). Our adventure was to conquer this track (designated N1, N87, or A87 at various points) over the ensuing few days. (*Note*: The road was completely sealed in the

1980s as a bicentennial project. What we experienced in late 1978 was a partly unsealed Stuart Highway.)

Life along The Track gave us a general sense of life in the Aussie outback (as lived by bushrangers, swagmen, and squatters "beyond the Black Stump"). Their language was distinct and raunchy. They loved liquor and "Waltzing Matilda." Thus the quirks we noticed on the tour got etched in our memory. Just after midnight, we reached Coober Pedy (pop 2,000), "the world's largest opal center" 540 km northwest of Port Augusta.

The unsealed parts of the Track between Pimba/Woomera and Coober Pedy (through Glendambo/Kingoonya, Mount Soward, Mount Sandy, and Mount Penrhyn) induced in us revulsion for bus travel. Ansett had assigned two coach captains to share the agony of driving on rough terrain in two-hour shifts. We had some relief from "back pain" when the coach stopped at Kingoonya, "the township with the widest main street in Australia," for dinner.

At the Kingoonya Hotel, a friendly old white man, who was drinking with a friendly old aborigine, approached us with mild interest to talk about our countries and exchange other information. It turned out that the townsfolk, living in relative isolation, converged on the hotel for the evening chitchat and enjoyed greeting travelers who stopped at their railway-support settlement, about 160 km northwest of Pimba.

We stopped at a "dugout" in Coober Pedy (boys' waterhole) for coffee and refueling. Part of this dugout was a church. We learned that the underground churches, the mines, and the graveyard distinguished the town. Many townspeople lived in *dugouts* (refurbished old mines) to avoid the scorching sun during the day. About 1,000 km from Port Augusta, we crossed the South Australia-Northern Territory border and stopped at the Kulgera (pop. 50) roadhouse in Northern Territory for Saturday (December 23) breakfast.

Climbing Ayers Rock

A few kilometers further to the north, we got off the Ansett coach at Erldunda Station, where we boarded another bus heading 270 km west to Ayers Rock. We established the acquaintance of two people—an

English lady, Jean Clough, who was traveling on a shoestring budget; and a French girl named Christine—during lunch at Curtin Springs.

After reaching Ayers Rock, we checked in at the Uluru Motel for our stay.

In the late afternoon, we joined a tour of the Olgas, the second major feature and attraction of what is currently named Uluru-Kata Tjuta National Park. The Olgas (Kata Tjuta), consisting of thirty-six steep sided monoliths, are located 32 km west of Ayers Rock (Uluru). As we trudged the track to see the gorge between Mount Walpa and Mount Olga, a seven-year-old precocious English kid, John Coulson, surprised me as a conversationalist.

Sunday (December 24) morning, both Yoke-Sim and I managed to climb the Uluru, the 3-km-long and 348-meter high world's largest sandstone rock. Yoke-Sim was the last in our group to reach the top. The climb up and the descent took us nearly two hours. A few chickened out even before reaching the "Chicken Rock." A Canadian in our group couldn't climb to the top because the rock had "no trees."

Tony, the manger of Uluru Motel, took us on an afternoon tour to show the Maggie Springs and the caves on one side of the rock. Then we took a dip in the swimming pool of the Inland Motel, where the Christmas spirit appeared to have taken over. Jack, a sort of "Crocodile Dundee" sporting a beard, let Yoke-Sim use his bicycle. I borrowed Jack's bicycle to go around the rock fighting against the wind. On the way, I saw three plaques in memory of people who died attempting to climb the rock.

We left Ayers Rock about 9:00 p.m. with hearty greetings from everyone. Our coach headed toward Alice Springs, some 470 km northeast. Early Christmas morning, about two o'clock, our coach captain stopped the bus at Palmer Valley on the Stuart Highway to "boil the billy" for tea to kick off Christmas. We enjoyed this stopover very much. He told us the story of the lady who ran the Erldunda Station, which we just passed.

We reached Alice Springs (current population 27,500) about 4:00 a.m. But the coach captain allowed us to sleep on the bus until dawn, when we walked across the dry Todd River to check in at Bindalong Guest

House (10 Start Terrace). Ruth Backney, our hostess, made us breakfast. We ate Christmas 1978 breakfast right in the geographical center of Australia half way between Adelaide and Darwin.

The Alice is the home of the Arremie Aborigines. The aborigines constituted 29 percent of the Northern Territory population (including 17 percent in Alice). The "Yankee Doodles" serving the United States-Australia satellite tracking station in Pine Gap (since the station opened in 1968) have also become part of the area scene in addition to a small population of Asians.

Soon afterwards, we joined a Trailway tour of the Finke River and West MacDonnell Ranges to visit the Heavitree Gap Lookout, Ellery Gorge, Ochre Pits, Ormiston Gorge, and Glen Helen Gorge. This tour westward started along the unsealed Namitjira Drive. A few people with whom we rubbed shoulders at the Uluru were on this tour as well. We topped the day with a grand Christmas meal at the Glen Helen Tourist Camp. Our table companions were a couple from Melbourne. We returned to Alice at 6:30 p.m.

The next morning, Yoke-Sim and I went on an exploratory tour of downtown Alice. We walked all the way north to the old Telegraph Station on Stuart Highway and returned to our guesthouse on the track from Charitja Hill to Spencer Hill along the River Todd. Then, we said good-bye to Ruth Backney, who gave us a cold lunch to take with us.

We resumed our journey north to Darwin, another 1,500 km north, at 3:00 p.m. Our dinner stop was the Wauchope Roadhouse, about 90 km north of Barrow Creek, where we already had an unofficial stop. We noted that the hotels at both stops had rather bawdy anecdotes pasted on to the walls. We whiled away more than one hour listening to a garrulous woman yarning her world travels.

Wednesday (December 27) morning, the coach stopped at the Dunmara Waterhole, where a new coach captain took over. He stopped at Katherine to allow us eat our breakfast. After another stop for refreshments at Adelaide River, we reached Darwin at 12:30 p.m.

CHAPTER 52

Australia: From Top End Back to Central Queensland

THE FORDAY FAMILY of Darwin—Harry Forday; his sister, Pauline; his daughter-in-law, Sylvia; and her daughters, Penney and Leanne—gave my wife Yoke-Sim and me a warm welcome at the Darwin coach terminal on Saturday (December 27, 1978) early afternoon. Apparently, the Forday family of Rockhampton, headed by Albert and Winnie, had advised their relatives in Darwin to accord us their "royal" treatment! Harry took us to his home in Rapid Creek (2 Roma Place) and made us his guests. He had already prepared us a hearty lunch of prawns.

On the Top End

Later in the afternoon, the Fordays took us on a tour of Darwin (pop 120,700), the capital city of Northern Territory, located on a low bluff overlooking the Timor Sea. Starting from Rapid Creek, we drove northeast to see the community college, the Royal Darwin Hospital, the free beach in Casuarina, and the fishing area at Lee Point. We stopped at Berrimah in the southeast for ice cream and drove through Winnellie in the south and Stuart Park, where I sighted the Ceylon Restaurant, in the southwest. The compact city surrounds the Darwin Airport. Then we toured the area covering the Darwin Botanical Gardens, in the vicinity of downtown Darwin. We returned via Mindil Beach and Fannie Bay. Palmerston, Darwin's satellite city, lies to the south on the Stuart Highway.

Earlier, we dropped by at the home of Pauline and John at Ludmilla. Later, they joined us for dinner, before which a heavy rainstorm blacked out our area.

We got up very early next morning to join the six o'clock Sunrise Wild Tour ($18 per adult) to see the flora and the fauna along the first 100 km of the Arnhem Highway on the western edge of the Nature Reserve linking Howard Springs, Humpty Doo, Fogg Dam and Marrakai Plains. We had the company of a Japanese and a couple from Western Australia on this tour. The giant termite mounds we saw were awesome compared to those I had seen in Sri Lanka. Although we did not make it to the Kakadu National Park, we at least had the satisfaction of experiencing the wildlife along the highway that would have taken us there.

Having returned to the city by noon, Yoke-Sim and I ate lunch at Woolworths and got acquainted with the layout of Darwin. We visited the public library, the chamber of the Legislative Council, and the Chinese Joss House. When Harry came to pick us up at 5:00 p.m., Yoke-Sim presented him with a hefty bag of groceries.

Harry had organized a dinner party in honor of us that evening. This gave us the opportunity to meet the other members of the Forday family and a number of other local Chinese.

Friday (December 29) morning, Harry dropped us off at the Casuarina Shopping Center, where Penney provided us guidance. In the afternoon, Vincent and Beverly Hee of Fannie Bay took us on a tour of Berry Springs in the Territory Wildlife Park, 56 km south of Darwin. Then they drove us another 13 km south to see the Darwin River Dam. On the return journey, they stopped briefly at Jack the Slasher and the Yarrowonga Zoo. Later, we had a dip in the Hees's swimming pool and joined them for dinner. Much later, after we came back to Rapid Creek, Yoke-Sim joined our hosts to visit the family of Tim Forday while I watched on television the first day's play of the third England-Australia cricket test in Melbourne.

The Fordays were remarkable hosts who took immense pains to make us feel at home in Darwin. Our company was their pleasure. They accompanied us to the coach terminal Saturday morning to say good-bye.

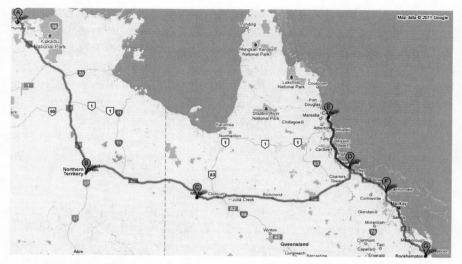

Map 52.1 The last leg of our tour route from Darwin, Northern Territory, to Rockhampton, Queensland. Floods forced us to return to Rockhampton on January 5 1979. We completed the Townsville-Cairns roundtrip (January 8-11) on the same Aussie Pass with no additional fees.

Backtracking the Track

The Stuart Highway begins in all its glory as a dual carriageway for 30 km from Darwin to Howard Springs. It continues as National 1 for another 190 km southeast to Katherine (pop 9,200), once a gold town now better known for its gorge and river bearing the same name. The Track continues from Katherine onwards as National 87 down to the SA border where it becomes A87.

Our destination on this coach ride was Mount Isa, Queensland, 1,650 km southeast from Darwin on the main highway. Of this distance, 990 km would be backtracking The Track down to Three Ways (north of Tennant Creek), where we would turn east on Barkly Highway to cross the Queensland border.

The coach captain on this trip was the same one who brought us to Darwin on Wednesday. His smile of recognition summed up more than thousand words of a greeting. Our lunch stop was Katherine. The next break was at Daly Waters, where we saw a Progress Hall with nothing in it. The dinner stop was Dunmarra (637 km from Darwin), where our coach captain completed his shift. Here we had the time to walk to the woods across the highway to observe some wildlife near the lake. The bag of cooked prawns that Harry Forday passed on to us before our departure served as our lunch, as well as the dinner.

Our new coach captain took us all the way to the Three Ways Roadhouse, 330 km further south at the Stuart-Barkly highway intersection, where we arrived at 10:20 p.m. Here we were delighted to run into a young South Australian couple—Hank and Anna Doolette—that we got acquainted with at the Uluru. They were on their way to Darwin. One hour later, our bus headed southeast on Barkly Highway with two new drivers.

Mount Isa Experience

The coach crossed over to the border town of Camooweal in Queensland while we were asleep. We reached Mount Isa (pop 22,600) about 7:00 a.m. Sunday (December 31). We were walking to our motel when a "Good Samaritan," Arthur Yamaguchi of the Kalkadoon Aboriginal Sobriety House, offered us a ride. He dropped us at Copper City Motel, where we checked in and ate breakfast.

In the afternoon, we set out on a walking tour of the city. We went to the City Lookout and stopped by at the infamous Boyd Hotel, where Neville Bonner, the aboriginal senator from Queensland, had been refused service. The barmaid asked Yoke-Sim what she wanted to drink without paying attention to me. We wondered whether this was a subtle expression of color resentment. We ate dinner at Kentucky Fried Chicken. On the way back to our motel, we visited the Salvation Army.

We relaxed on the New Year's Day morning. Because of unbearable heat, I decided to celebrate the New Year by jumping into the motel's swimming pool both morning and evening.

In the afternoon, we joined a free tour of the Mount Isa Holdings Ltd. mine on the western edge of the city. Ray Pagett, a public relations man from the company, picked us up at the Memorial Swimming Pool for the tour, which took almost two hours. Pagett, originally from Birmingham,

England, gave thorough details as he drove our party from point to point on the mine surface. I was impressed with the mine's new cement stack towering so high, although a tad smaller than the Empire State.

Next, we joined Horst Horkins' Tiki Hi tour of the Kalkadoon Park, the venue of the annual rodeo; and Lake Moondara, which provided Mount Isa's water supply. Horst took us on the dirt roads around the lake to show the abundance of wildlife.

On our third day in Mount Isa, we joined Horst's full-day Tiki Hi tour of the Selwyn Range area—a safari on a 4WD covering some 220 km. for $20 per person. Our group comprised the Ahrens, a couple from Brisbane; Davy, Horst's small son and helpmate; Yoke-Sim and me.

The highlights were visits to Mary Kathleen, a uranium-mining town; the abandoned Rosebud Dam; Balara, an abandoned copper-mining settlement; Lady Jenny Camp, where silica mining has replaced copper; Wee McGregor copper leeching mine; a field where visitors could pick Maltese Cross stones; and the Mount Frosty open-cut calcite mine. We thanked Horst for the "very interesting and unusual tour."

Davy played his role by giving us a demonstration of eating "blood apples," bugs, and all. I adamantly refused Davy's generous offer to eat them. We learned a lot about the outback and the bushrangers on this safari.

Grand Finale

On Wednesday (January 3, 1979) morning, we left Mount Isa (in northwestern Queensland) for Townsville (in north Queensland), 904 km away. We proceeded via Cloncurry, the birthplace of the Qantas Airlines. Our refreshment stop was Julia Creek and the lunch stop Hughenden, where we arrived at 2:00 p.m. Our route took almost a horizontal eastern direction up to this point; then it took a gradual northeasterly direction up to Charters Towers and a steeper diagonal direction from there. We reached Townsville about 7:30 p.m. We crossed paths with the young South Australian couple, the Doolettes, again on this trip.

Our original travel plans came to an abrupt end in Townsville because rains caused by Cyclone Peter had made the roads to Cairns impassable. So we checked in at Coral House in Hale Street for the night.

The next morning, we learned about the official cancellation of the bus service to Cairns. Therefore, Yoke-Sim and I spent the morning in downtown Townsville exploring the shops and the arcades.

At the bus terminal, we were told that the southbound coach had room for both of us if we wanted to make the 700-km journey back to Rockhampton. We accepted the offer.

About 6:00 p.m., we stopped for dinner at Proserpine, where I chanced into Jan Ward, a former journalism student of mine. She told me she was about to change her reporter's job from the Proserpine to the Townsville newspaper. We returned to Rockhampton at 1:30 a.m. on Friday (January 5, 1979).

We visited Cairns from January 8-11 using the same Aussie Pass with no extra fees because our originally planned trip was disrupted for no fault of ours. On Tuesday (January 9), we visited the Green Island. On Wednesday, we toured the Atherton Tablelands via the Cairns-Kuranda scenic route. We celebrated the successful completion of our long journey with a spicy Indian dinner at Thuggee Bill Restaurant on Aplin Street.

CHAPTER 53

New Zealand: Crossing the Alpines on South Island

MY SON JUNIUS was barely two years old when my wife Yoke-Sim and I took him on a three-week-long tour of New Zealand. We landed in Christchurch, the big city of the South Island, on a Saturday (December 12, 1981) at 4:30 p.m. although we left Brisbane, Queensland (Australia), at 10:30 a.m. and the Qantas flight itself took only three hours. But the New Zealand time zone was also ahead of Queensland by three hours.

Our intention was to introduce Junius to the joys and sorrows of foreign travel from a very early age. Therefore, I arranged the Tiki Tour of New Zealand to celebrate his second birthday on January 19. We left Auckland (New Zealand) back to Brisbane on January 1, 1982. I suspect that because of the eighteen-day time gap between the two events, Junius did not associate the tour with his birthday at all.

Tiki Tours, the company that organized the tour of our choice, had no objection to a two-year-old joining the long excursion. And we had confidence that Junius had the mettle to withstand the strains of a two-week coach tour.

At the Christchurch Airport, we reported to the Tiki Tours Center, where a Mr. McIlwraith took us in a coach to Shirley Lodge on Marshlands Road, Shirley, northeast of the city, where we checked in. Our room had excellent facilities, and we enjoyed a sumptuous dinner as well. Our first impression of New Zealand was very positive.

I laid back and read the *Star* newspaper. The quality and depth of its political analyses impressed and surprised me.

(The Shirley Lodge is still in operation and so are the Tiki Tours.)

Crossing Arthur's Pass

Mt. Cook Coachlines's "steerologist" (coach captain and driver) Merv Papakura commenced our Tiki Tour of the South Island Sunday morning.

First, Papakura gave us a short tour of Christchurch (current population 386,100), the second largest urban area of New Zealand, after Auckland. The estimated population of the entire country is 4.4 million (78 percent European and other; 15 percent Maori; 9 Percent Asian; and 7 percent Pacific Islander).

Among the points of interest in Christchurch are its Cathedral Square, which accommodates a speakers' corner (an obvious replication of London's Hyde Park Corner); the pedestrian-only urban mall along Cashel Street; and the Cultural Precinct that promotes arts, cultural, and heritage attractions.

After a stop at Cathedral Square, Papakura gave us a panoramic view of the city by driving south on Colombo Street (next to Madras St.) from Hagley Park through Sydenham and Cashmere to the Sign of the Takahe and beyond to the scenic northern Summit Road at the southwestern edge of Victoria Park overlooking the bay. My diary entry doesn't record how he got to Highway 73 for our 242-km ride northwest across the island's mountainous middle to Greymouth (pop 10,000) on the West Coast.

Our tea stop was at Springfield, the center of a farming and sheep-raising district, 64 km from Christchurch. The plains ended and the mountains took over from there. Less than 16 km ahead was Porters Pass (elevation 939 meters), close to Lake Lyndon, reaching which required a steep climb. The highway zigzagged uphill across the steep cliffs for almost 65 km when we reached Arthur's Pass (elevation 922 km), where we tarried to eat lunch at a quaint Alpine restaurant. (In addition to Arthur's Pass, two other passes—Haast and Lewis—enable motorists to cross the Alpine Mountains of the South Island). Rainy weather greeted us here. Papakura steered the coach uphill with meticulous skill for another 15 km to Otira, wherefrom he focused on the gradual descent to the West Coast's Kumara Junction, 63 km further to the west. Then he headed north (on Highway 6) some 15 km to Greymouth, located on the mouth of the River Grey. Ashley Motor Inn, where we checked in, was 2.5 km south of the town center. This motel is still in operation.

(Since our journey three decades ago, the New Zealand government has stabilized and improved the condition of Highway 73. For example, in 1999, the government completed the Otira Viaduct spanning 440 meters of unstable terrain at a cost of $45 million.)

Map 53.1 Crossing the Alpine Range on Highway 73 via Arthur's Pass. *G*, Christchurch; *F*, Springfield; *E*, Porters Pass; *D*, Arthur's Pass; *C*, Otira; *B*, Kumara Junction; *A*, Greymouth.

SHELTON A. GUNARATNE

After dinner, I walked north to explore the town. My walk got longer when I got lost north of Victoria Park. Back in the motel after the walking exercise, I relaxed reading the *Weekend Star* and the Saturday edition of the *Greymouth Evening Star*.

Franz Josef Glacier

We left Greymouth at 9:00 a.m. in rainy weather. Our first stop was the township of Hokitika (pop 3,000), 38 km southwest of Greymouth on Highway 6. Founded in 1864 as a gold-mining center, Hokitika became the capital of the short-lived Westland Province from 1874-1876. In the 1980s, the township was heavily dependent on dairying and sawmilling. We visited a glass-blowing factory and a greenstone-carving factory in the town.

Continuing our journey in the rain, we passed Lake Ianthe and stopped briefly at Hari Hari to see the La Fontaine Swamp where the Australian aviator Guy Menzies (1909-1940) crash-landed on January 7, 1931 when he flew the first solo trans-Tasman flight from Sydney to the West Coast of New Zealand.

The purpose of the day's trip was to experience the Franz Josef Glacier, a major tourist attraction that draws in some 2,700 visitors a day. Therefore, on arrival in Franz Josef (pop 330), 134 km from Hokitika, we checked in at the Westland Motor Inn.

The 12-km long glacier is located in the Westland National Park. To cite the Wikipedia:

> Together with the Fox Glacier 20 km to the south, it (Franz Josef Glacier) is unique in descending from the Southern Alps to less than three hundred meters above sea level, amidst the greenery and lushness of a temperate rainforest.

> The area surrounding the two glaciers is part of Te Wahipounamu, a World Heritage Site park. The river emerging from the glacier terminal of Franz Josef is known as the Waiho River.

Picture 53.1 The author, with his almost two-year-old son Junius strapped onto his back, landed on Franz Josef Glacier by helicopter on Monday, December 14, 1981.

Yoke-Sim and I decided that having traveled this far in the world, it was sheer folly for us not to experience the actual glacier. So we spent an extra $35 per head for a Heli-Hike tour of the glacier. We had to put on boots and Alpine stock before we got on the helicopter to land on Luncheon Rock, about 800 meters above sea level. A guide helped us to walk on the glacier ice. It was an awesome experience for all three of us.

After dinner, we visited the Westland National Park Visitor Center to learn more about glaciers.

SHELTON A. GUNARATNE

On the Way to Queenstown

Tuesday morning, Papakura transported us from Franz Josef to Queenstown for a two-night stay.

Although the distance between these two places was only 354 km on Highway 6, our detours along the way increased the day's traveled distance by an extra 60 km. After leaving the motor inn heading south on Highway 6, we stopped briefly at the foot of the Franz Josef Glacier to pay our respects and acknowledge its majesty. However, by failing to spare even a moment to acknowledge its collaborative role to enhance our understanding of the glacial life cycle, we silently but arrogantly miffed Fox Glacier.

We stopped for rest at Lake Paringa and Knights Point, where we saw the plaque marking the opening of the Haast Pass by Prime Minister Keith Holyoake in November 1965. Highway 6, which is the main drag from one end of the South Island (Invercargill) to the other (Nelson) on the western side of the Alpine Range, takes on different names at different points. The stretch between Fox Glacier and Makarora bears the name Haast in three variations. At Haast Pass, Highway 6 crosses the Alpines.

At Haast Beach on West Coast, Highway 6 takes a sharp turn east in the vicinity of the Haast township, where we stopped at the restaurant for tea. The restaurateur served us complimentary scones to celebrate our crossing the border from Westland to Otago through the Gates of Haast and the steep Haast Pass (562 meters above sea level), where the highway would turn southward to Makarora at the northern end of the enchanting Lake Wanaka.

Our lunch stop was Wanaka, further to the south. The scenery of this lake region was breathtaking. On the stretch from Wanaka to Queenstown, we stopped at Nevis Bluff and Kawarau Bridge. In Queenstown (pop 10,500), we checked in at the (now defunct) Mountaineer Establishment Hotel.

Queenstown is an international resort built around the Queenstown Bay, an inlet of Lake Wakatipu "that is shaped like a staggered lightning bolt"

(Wikipedia). It has earned a reputation for adventure tourism (bungy jumping, whitewater rafting, mountain biking) and snow sports (skiing, skateboarding). TSS Earnslaw, a century-old coal-fired steamship, provided tours of the lake.

On our first night in Queenstown, we (Junius, Yoke-Sim, and I) did a postprandial walk in the town to see the jetty, the marine parade, the mall, Camp Street, Isle Street, etc. On our second night, we walked to the Queenstown Gardens, a patch of greenery that juts into the lake, where Junius had a lot of fun chasing after the ducks and other birds. Both evenings, I relaxed reading the excellent local newspaper, the *Otago Daily Times*.

Although our second day in Queenstown turned out to be cloudy and drizzly, we took a boat ride (on "Moana") across Lake Wakatipu to the Walter Peak sheep and cattle station, where we had tea and short eats ($2 per person). On this three-hour excursion, we watched wool-spinning and sheepdog trials at the homestead. Costs have dramatically escalated since our 1981 trip as evident from the following cotemporary account of a visitor:

> You can just ride the ship across the lake and back for NZ$40 (adult), you can ride across and get off at the Walter Peak Farm (a working sheep farm) to get a tour and sheep-shearing show for NZ$60 (adult) or with lunch included for NZ$82 (adult), you can also get a more historical tour of the farm for NZ$70, or you can do what we did, which was to ride across the lake and get off at Walter Peak Farm for a horseback ride for NZ$99 (adult)

Back in town, we ate lunch on the mall, where a very amiable female barber gave me a $6 haircut. Later, we took a 445-meter Skyline Gondola ride ($3.50 per person) to the chalet overlooking the town. But the clouds marred our view of the vicinity. (Again, I have mentioned these 1981 prices only as a historical record.)

SHELTON A. GUNARATNE

CHAPTER 54

New Zealand: Exploring the East of South Island

I N NEW ZEALAND, the West (in the sense of Horace Greeley's "Go West, young man") refers to the West Coast of the South Island—the area to the west of the Alpine range that you can penetrate through the Haast Pass on Highway 6, Arthur's Pass on Highway 73, or Lewis Pass on Highway 7. The 600 km coastal strip between Kahurangi Point in the north and Awarua Point in the south encompassing an area of 23,336 square km is called the West Coast. With only 32,800 people, it is the most sparsely populated region of New Zealand.

Our West Coast tour of the Tiki Tour guided by our "steerologist" Merv Papakura terminated when we crossed the Haast Pass to the Otago region. Now, Papakura was guiding us through what I call the East of the South Island (meaning, all other regions except the West Coast).

Thursday (December 17, 1981) morning, with a pleasant sunshine greeting us, Papakura transported us to see a few more attractions in Queenstown's vicinity: the Cattledrome; the Coronet Peak Ski Grounds; and Arrowtown (20 km northeast), where Yoke-Sim purchased a sheepskin for $279. We returned to Queenstown for lunch. I ate pancakes on the mall while Yoke-Sim shared a soup with Junius.

Heading for Milford Sound

In the afternoon, Papakura took us off to our next destination, Te Anau (pop 2,000) in the Southland region, 171 km southwest of Queenstown. We drove south on Highway 5 along the eastern bank of Lake Wakatipu to its southern tip at Kingston, where we crossed from Otago to Southland region.

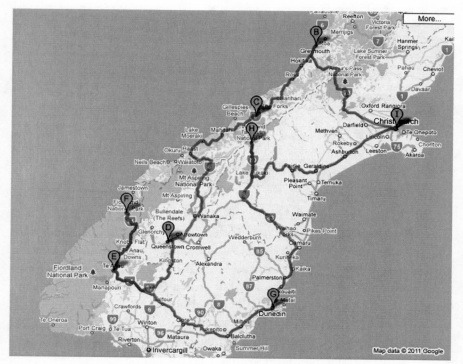

Map 54.1 The route of our South Island Tiki Tour of New Zealand:
A/I, Christchurch; *B*, Greymouth; *C*, Franz Josef; *D*, Queenstown;
E, Te Anau; *F*, Milford Sound; *G*, Dunedin; *H*, Mt. Cook National
Park. We covered more than 2,111 km.

We continued going south up to Five Rivers, where we turned into
Highway 97, a shortcut route going southwest to Mossburn. After
stopping there for refreshments, we proceeded northwest on Highway
94 all the way to Te Anau, located on the southeastern tip of the 65 km
long Lake Te Anau, the second largest lake in New Zealand after Lake
Taupo. Te Anau serves as the gateway to the Fjordland National Park,
the eastern boundary of which includes Lake Te Anau.

We checked in to the Vacation Hotel for two nights. After dinner,
Yoke-Sim and Junius joined me for a walking tour of the town. Back
in the hotel, I was thinking of the next day's visit to Milford Sound
when Junius interrupted my reverie by accidentally smashing my
eyeglasses.

In the morning, we drove 117 km northwest on Highway 94 to visit the Milford Sound, located almost on the northern boundary of Fjordland National Park. Here we were not too far (as the crow flies) from the northern tip of Lake Wakatipu, just across the Alpine barrier.

Milford Sound (fjord) is considered one of the world's topmost tourist attractions with about 1,500 people visiting it every day. (Wikipedia explains that *sound* or *seaway* is a large sea or ocean inlet larger than a bay, deeper than a bight, wider than a fjord, or it may identify a narrow sea or ocean channel between two bodies of land called a strait).

We rested for a while at the Milford Hotel before boarding the boat Mitre Peak 2 for the two-hour Milford Sound experience along the fjord's 15 km run inland from the Tasman Sea. I lay snugly on the boat relishing a chicken and Champaign lunch as I observed sheer rock faces that rose 1,200 meters (3,900 ft) or more surrounding the inlet on each side. I saw the peak The Elephant at 1,517 meters (4,980 ft), resembling an elephant's head; and the peak Lion Mountain, 1,302 meters (4,270 ft), resembling a crouching lion. I saw the lush rain forests clinging precariously to these cliffs, while seals, penguins and dolphins danced and pranced in the waters. An occasional whale too might have appeared.

(*Post-tour note*: On February 8, 2004, a spill of thirteen thousand liters of diesel fuel was discovered, resulting in a 2-km oil spill, which closed the sound for two days.)

We returned to our hotel in Te Anau late afternoon. After dinner, Junius, Yoke-Sim, and I took a boat ride to the Glow-Worm Caves, 14 km away on the western shore. Junius, whom I was carrying strapped on to my back, cuddled on to me, and closed his eyes as we explored the dark grotto. The chorus of the American popular song of the 1950s crossed my mind:

> Shine, little glow-worm, glimmer
> Shine little glow-worm, glimmer!
> Lead us lest too far we wander.
> Love's sweet voice is calling yonder!

Dinner in Dunedin

Saturday (December 19) morning, we left Te Anau on the 290 km trip to Dunedin (pop 115,700), the administrative center of the Otago region. Papakura's plan was to drive on a southeast direction on Highway 94 up to Gore and then drive northeast to Dunedin on Highway 1. We crossed back to Otago region from Southland at Arthurton on Highway 1.

Picture 54.1 At the Timbertop Sheep Farm in Lumsden, Otago, on Saturday, December 19, 1981: The writer helps himself to mid-morning tea while his son Junius and wife Yoke-Sim try to bottle-feed a baby sheep introduced by a farm girl.

On the way, we stopped at Lumsden to visit the seven-hundred-acre Timbertop Sheep Farm. The farmer-in-charge gave us a talk on sheep farming and also provided a demonstration of sheep sheering. Junius had the distinct privilege of bottle-feeding a baby sheep that a farm girl introduced while we all helped ourselves to refreshments (see picture)

Our lunch stop was Peggydale, three km south of Balclutha. We had a chat with Bill, Peg, Mervyn, and Alison Jones, who operated the Peggydale Tourist Center. Yoke-Sim bought a cardigan here. Peg gave Junius a souvenir and told me about a Sri Lankan living in the area. (Google maps have wiped out Peggydale although the place still exists.)

In Dunedin, we stopped to see the glory of Overton House, an old home built by an idealist from Bristol in the inner suburb of City Rise, which is notable for its grand townhouses dating back to late nineteenth century.

We checked in at the Southern Cross Hotel (118 High St.), where our tour group had their first formal dinner. Thereafter, I walked alone to Belleknowes Parkland (now converted to a golf course) via York Place and returned via Russell Street.

Night at Mount Cook

Sunday (December 20) morning, we moved from Otago back to Canterbury region, where we set forth on this long excursion nine days ago. Papakura's directions were to take his Tiki Tour group to enjoy their final night on the South Island at the Aoraki/Mount Cook National Park, situated near the town of Twizel some 220 km to the northwest of Dunedin. Accordingly, we left the Southern Cross after breakfast heading north on Highway 1 passing through some of the city's landmarks—like the Dunedin Hospital, the University of Otago campus, and the Botanic Gardens. We stopped for tea at Oamaru (pop 13,000), 113 km north of Dunedin. It is the largest town in north Otago, and is the eastern gateway to the Mackenzie Basin, via the Waitaki Valley. We went to a hilltop to get a good view of Oamaru and the Pacific coast below.

Then we headed northwest to the Waitaki Valley and crossed over to Canterbury region about 40 km away, near Duntroon. After Kurow, we went past a succession of lakes—Waitaki, Aviemore, and Benmore—until we reached Omarama, our lunch stop.

This is where Highways 8 and 83 merge to climb up to the foot of Lake Pukaki, where they separate again, one (Mt. Cook Road 80) going north to the Mount Cook Village (where we were heading), the other (Tekapo-Twizel Road 8) going east.

We continued our climb past Clearburn to the town of Twizel, where we stopped at the Information Center to watch a film on the hydro-electric scheme combining four lakes in the area. Thereafter, we climbed up the road going north alone the western shore of Lake Pukaki and crossed

Birch Hill to reach the Aoraki/Mount Cook National Park, of which the Mount Cook Village is a part. We checked in at the Glencoe Lodge, now a wing of The Hermitage.

The Aoraki/Mount Cook National Park comprises an area of more than 700 square km. Glaciers make up 40 percent of the park area, notably the Tasman Glacier on the slopes of Aoraki/Mount Cook. All of New Zealand's twenty peaks higher than three thousand meters, except Mount Aspiring, lie in this national park, which bears the name of New Zealand's highest mountain, Aoraki/Mount Cook (3,753 meters).

The Mount Cook Village lies 12 km south of Aoraki/Mount Cook's summit. The Hermitage is the village's easiest locator. In fact, we were now not too far from the glacier region of the West Coast. As a satellite map would show, the Haast Pass was incredibly close to where we were.

Unfortunately, rain spoilt our evening. Rain made everything surrounding us virtually invisible. With many activities canceled, the only thing I could do was to eat our dinner, and walk to the Visitors Center on Bowen Drive and The Hermitage on Terrace Road. But there was a happy event too: Yoke-Sim and I noticed that Junius could get out of the cot by himself!

On Monday (December 21) early morning, Yoke-Sim and I (with Junius strapped on my shoulders) climbed up to The Hermitage and took photos with New Zealand's highest peak in the background.

However, the drizzle, the rain, and the mist prevailed most of the day as Papakura took us on the 333 km journey from the Mount Cook Village back to Christchurch. At the foot of Lake Pukaki, we turned east on Highway 8 and stopped at the dog-shaped Lake Tekapo for refreshments. Our lunch stop was Geraldine, where I had the time to make a quick trip to the public library.

We arrived in Christchurch just after 3:00 p.m. We thanked our "steerologist" Merv Papakura for his tireless service over the last nine days. Having thus terminated the South Island Tiki Tour, Papakura took the tour group members continuing on the North Island leg of the tour to the Christchurch Airport to fly to Wellington.

CHAPTER 55

New Zealand:
From Capital City to Big City

ON ARRIVAL IN Wellington (current population 386,000), the capital and the third largest city in New Zealand, Monday (December 21, 1981) evening, we—my almost two-year-old son Junius, wife Yoke-Sim, and I—checked into the now defunct Waterloo Hotel. After dinner, I went for a stroll from Boulcott Street, down Willis Street, to Vivian Street.

Wellington is approximately 400 km northeast of Christchurch on the South Island, which we toured since December 12. Now the contrasts between the two islands were gradually becoming clear to us.

The South Island is dominated by the mighty Southern Alps from one end to the other with two hundred perpetually snow-capped mountains. This geographical phenomenon has created distinct climatic divisions within the island—a wet West Coast, a sunny north, a cold south, and a mild east. The warmer North Island contains all of New Zealand's volcanoes and thermal springs. It accommodates 76 percent of the country's 4.3 million population although South Island is 33 percent bigger in land area. Glaciers and the very high peaks are on South Island.

Ivan Brown, who took over as our coach captain on the Tiki Tour of North Island, guided us on a sightseeing excursion of Wellington the next morning. We skirted the Lambton Harbor, Oriental Bay and Evans Bay; then drove through the 623-meter-long Mount Victoria Tunnel opened in 1931 to connect the suburbs of Mount Victoria and Hataitai. Pedestrians and cyclists use an elevated ramp on the north side of the tunnel roadway, which became part of Highway 1 in 2001. Atop the tunnel is Alexandra Park.

Brown steered us to the lookout on Alexandra Road, just south of Roseneath, but the fog marred our view of much of the city, five kilometers to the west. On our return to the city, we saw the New Zealand Parliament Buildings on Molesworth Street before we stopped for tea at the Wellington Botanical Gardens by the bay.

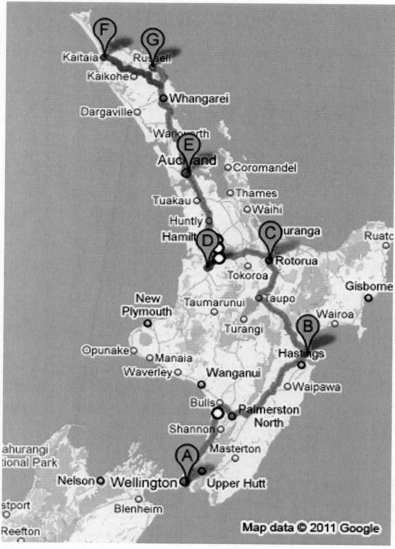

Map 55.1 Our tour route on North Island. *A*, Wellington; *B*, Hastings-Napier; *C*, Rotorua; *D*, Waitomo Caves; *E*, Auckland; *F*, Kaitaia; *G*, Russell.

SHELTON A. GUNARATNE

On the Way to Napier

Our Tiki Tour was not designed to give anyone an in-depth understanding of any of the major New Zealand cities. So that's all we saw of Wellington, when we commenced the day's 346-km trip to Napier at 11:30 a.m. We reached our destination at 6:00 p.m. via Carnarvon and Waipukurau. Our lunch turned out to be an enjoyable barbecue at the Duralyn Stud owned by the Gloyn family in Carnarvon. Yoke-Sim and Junius tried some horseback riding at the stud. At Sanson, a few kilometers to the north on Highway 1, we turned southeast on Highway 3 to Palmerston North and then northeast to Woodville, where we continued northeast on Highway 2. The next two short stops were at a lookout on a hill overlooking Waipukurau, and at Hastings (pop 65,100). The detours added an extra 30 km to the direct distance between the start and the finish.

In Napier (pop 58,100), a port city on Hawke's Bay in the east coast, we checked into the Masonic Establishment Hotel on Tennyson Street. The Twin Cities (also called the Bay Cities) of Napier and Hastings, less than 20 km apart, have a combined population of 123,200, a high concentration of urban people by New Zealand standards.

After dinner, we went for a family stroll on the Marine Parade (the "Golden Mile"), the location of the statue of Maori mythology's Pania of the Reef, a beautiful maiden who lived in the sea. Then I relaxed in my hotel room reading the (Napier) *Daily Telegraph* and the (Hastings) *Hawke's Bay Herald Tribune*. These two papers later merged to become the Hawke's Bay Today.

We spent Wednesday (December 23) morning enjoying the attractions of Napier. We took Junius to the Lilliput animated village and Model Railway ($2 per head) and the Hawke's Bay Aquarium ($2.50 per head). Napier's unique concentration of Art Deco architecture, a byproduct of reconstruction that followed the havoc caused by the 1931 earthquake, attracts many admirers, particularly in February.

Thermal Country and Maori Culture

Brown got us back on the coach at noon to start on the 222 km trip to Rotorua. He drove 62 km northwest along Highway 2 and Highway

5 before stopping briefly at Te Hanoto. Our lunch stop, Taupo, was a further 79 km to the northwest, located on the northeastern tip of the lake bearing the same name. When I went to purchase a copy of the Taupo Times, I noticed the presence of Indian and Chinese retail merchants in the town.

Then we visited the beautiful Huka Falls of the Waikato River, six kilometers to the northeast. The Wairakei thermal valley, which has the world's second geothermal power station, was only three kilometers away. The sight and smell of thermal activity in the valley gave us a much different experience than the glacier and fjord experience we had on South Island.

About 5:00 p.m., we reached Rotorua (permanent population 55,600) on the southern tip of the lake bearing the same name. With seventeen other lakes dotting the city's east and the south, Rotorua has developed into an aquatic paradise for fishing, waterskiing, and swimming. We checked in at the now defunct Grand Establishment Hotel on Hinemoa Street for two nights.

After dinner, our tour group attended the Tudor Towers Maori Entertainers Concert, which included three acts. I was thrilled by the Maori love song of all time, "Pōkarekare Ana."

Pōkarekare ana	(They are agitated)
ngā wai o Waiapu,	(the waters of Waiapu)
Whiti atu koe hine	(But when you cross over girl)
marino ana e.	(they will be calm.)

Rotorua represents the heart of Maori culture in New Zealand in addition to being a resort and a health spa. The next morning, we immersed ourselves in three of its famous attractions: the Maori Arts and Crafts Institute and Whakarewarewa Thermal Reserve, the Agrodome, and the Rainbow Springs.

At the thermal reserve, we saw the silica terraces, the boiling springs, and the geysers, notably the Pohutu (Big Splash) whose spurts sometimes reach 100 meters. At the Agrodome, we saw nineteen of New Zealand's top rams. At Rainbow Springs, we saw a kiwi, in the Nocturnal Kiwi

House, and thousands of rainbow and brown trout. Junius became friends with a ten-year-old girl while we ate lunch here. We also stopped at the Ohinemata Maori Church.

In the afternoon, Junius and Yoke-Sim joined for a stroll on the Government Gardens and walked up to Lake Rotorua behind the Tudor Towers. After dinner, the three of us walked to the Polynesian Pools to bathe in a private thermal pool ($2 per head). We liked the satin smooth (37-40 degree) mineral water fed by Priest, Rachael, and Radium springs. Back in my hotel room, I read the (Rotorua) *Daily Post* and the (Auckland) *New Zealand Herald*.

Christmas in the Big City

Christmas morning, Brown took us to explore the Waitomo Caves, 147 km west from Rotorua on Highway 5 and Otorohanga Road. Our first stop was at Arapuni, the location of the seventh and penultimate hydroelectric power station on the 425-km Waikato River, the longest river in New Zealand. It was late morning when we reached the caves, situated nine kilometers southwest of Hangatika.

A mishap delayed our cave tour when Merle Grubb, an elderly woman from San Diego, California, fell down while stepping off the coach and hurt her forehead. Brown took the Grubbs—Merle and John—to the Te Kuti Hospital. They quit their tour on our arrival in Auckland. (Two years later, on August 23, 1983, we had the privilege of being the guests of the Grubbs at their home in San Diego.)

The Waitomo Caves system includes four main caves: Waitomo Cave, Ruakuri Cave, Aranui Cave, and Gardner's Gut—all noted for their stalactite and stalagmite displays, and for the population of glowworms known as *Arachnocampa luminosa*. Therefore, they are similar to the caves we had already visited in Lake Te Anau on South Island.

The tour took us through three levels, starting with the Catacombs. The second level, called the Banquet Chamber, linked us back to the upper level to see the Pipe Organ, the cave's largest formation. The third level led us into the Cathedral, demonstration platform, and the jetty. The Cathedral, an eighteen-meter-high enclosed area with rough surfaces, provides for great acoustics. Dame Kiri Te Kanawa is among the artistes who reputedly performed here. A boat ride through the Glowworm Grotto took us onto the underground Waitomo River where the only light came from the tiny glowworms creating a sky of living lights.

We ate lunch at the Waitomo Hotel, perched on the brow of a hill. Brown picked up the Grubbs at the hospital and steered us 200 km north to the country's big city, Auckland (current urban population 1.3 million). On the way, our first stop was at the Te Awamutu Rose Garden, 45 km from the caves. We passed 61 km through Obaugo, Hamilton, and Ngaruwahia to reach Huntly, where we stopped next.

We reached Auckland about 4:00 p.m. and checked in at the Royal International to spend the Christmas night.

Junius, Yoke-Sim, and I spent the Christmas evening strolling on Auckland Domain, Albert Park, and Quay Street. As we returned to the hotel, we ran into three Sri Lankan sailors working for a Greek ship.

I wondered whether we could ever experience another Christmas of sulfur smells, glowworm sights, and big city phobia as this one was. However, as Buddhists we did not have to worry.

CHAPTER 56

New Zealand:
A Peep into the Far North

THE FINAL LEG of our Tiki Tour focused on the Northland Region, more commonly known as the Far North or less commonly as the Winterless North (because of its mild climate). Comprising a land area of 13,789 square km, it arrogates 80 percent of the 285-km-long North Auckland Peninsula. The region has three administrative districts: Far North, Kalpara and Whangarei.

Ivan Brown, our coach captain, welcomed fourteen new people to our tour group, as he departed Auckland in the morning after Christmas on the 325-km trip north to Kaitaia, a town of 5,200 people at the base of the Aupouri Peninsula, which is a tombolo—a deposition landform in which an island is attached to the mainland by a narrow piece of land such as a spit or bar.

On the Way to Far North

Our first stop on the way north was the Dome Valley Roadhouse, just south of Wellsford, about 75 km north of our starting point. Our lunch stop was at Whangarei (pop 51,400), located on the Hatea River, almost 160 km north of Auckland. It is the northernmost city in New Zealand and the regional capital of Northland Region. Here we visited the Bounty Museum (see photo) and ate lunch at the Grand Establishment Hotel.

At Kaikohe, 85 km further to the northwest, we visited the now defunct High Lake Dairy Farm, where the farmhands gave us a tour of the farm and a demonstration of milking.

We reached Kaitaia, the last major settlement on the main road north to the capes and bays on the peninsula, after driving 81 km further northwest. We checked in at Kaitaia Hotel.

After dinner, Yoke-Sim and I accompanied our son Junius to the children's playground in the park to the east of the hotel. He derived immense enjoyment climbing up and down the train engine and the tractor placed in the park.

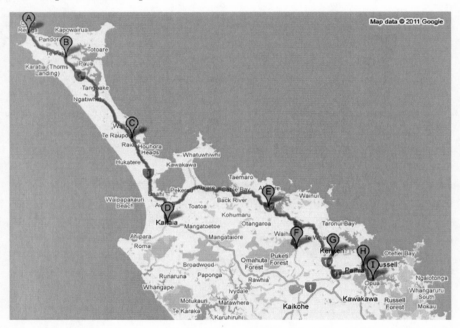

Map 56.1 Our exploration tour route of Aupouri Peninsula (Tombola) and the Bay of Islands in the far north of New Zealand. *A*, Cape Reinga; *B*, Waitiki Landing; *C*, Hauhora Harbor; *D*, Kaitaia; *E*, Kahoe; *F*, Manginangina Scenic Reserve; *G*, Kerikeri; *H*, Waitangi; *I*, Opua (from where we took a ferry ride to Okiato [old Russell] and drove nine km north to Russell [old Kororareka]).

Exploring the Tombolo

Sunday (December 27) morning, we had to get onto a new bus that could withstand the unsealed terrain and the sand dunes of the Aupouri Peninsula for our adventure trip to Cape Reinga ("Place of Leaping"), 111 km north of Kaitaia.

Five km west of the town lies Ahipara/Shipwreck Bay, from where the so-called Ninety Mile Beach (actually an 88-km long beach) stretches all the way northwest to Scott Point, five km south of Cape Maria van Diemen. In 1932, Ninety Mile Beach was used as the runway for some of the earliest airmail services between Australia and New Zealand. Our return trip from the cape took this long beach route so popular with surfers and water boarders.

However, our forward journey to the northernmost cape in New Zealand followed the old faithful Highway 1, which is sealed except for the last 20 km. It starts in Kaitaia as North Road and ends as Cape Reinga Road.

We took the North Road to Awanui, then turned northwest to cross over to the tombola through the narrow isthmus between Waipapakauri and Waiharara—a 10 km stretch.

Picture 56.2 The author, with Junius in his arms, stands in front of the Wagener Museum at Houhora Harbor in the Aupouri Peninsula (December 27, 1981).

Then, 44 km north of Kaitaia, we stopped at the Wagener Museum overlooking the Houhora Harbor and Mount Camel. The museum had an interesting collection of old musical instruments, clocks, washing machines, insects, shells, etc.

Back on the main drag, we had a look at Houhora Hotel, the northernmost hotel in New Zealand. About 25 km further northwest, we paused on a hilltop to look at the Parengarenga Harbor, the assembling place of thousands of bar-tailed godwits in late February to early March for their 12,000-km journey to Siberia.

We stopped for a smorgasbord lunch at the Waitiki Landing, the northernmost restaurant in New Zealand, about 20 km southeast of the cape. Then, past Te Paki station, we reached Cape Reinga (photo), where all of us took a walk down to the lighthouse.

On the return journey, we backtracked Highway 1 to Te Paki and drove south on the unpaved Te Paki Stream Road to the sand dunes of the Ninety Mile Beach, which serves as the alternative to Highway 1 during floods and landslides.

Many stop for boogie boarding or tobogganing down the huge sand dunes flanking the Te Paki Stream. Because none in our tour group was enticed by sand dunes, our special sand-resistant vehicle headed southeast for the return trip.

We stopped at The Bluff (see photo) briefly, then proceeded past Hukatere to Waipapakauri Beach, where we turned inland on West Coast Road to visit the Sweetwater Nursery of radiata pines, near Lake Ngatu.

We returned to Kaitaia about 4:30 p.m. The dinner was very good. Junius had a marvelous time dancing to music. But all was not well. I experienced a sore throat and other symptoms of a detested cold.

In the Bay of Islands

Monday (December 28) morning, we left Kaitaia for Russell on the Bay of Islands via scenic Highway 10. Past the Kaingaroa Valley, Lake Chia, Charles Bay, Coopers Beach and Mangonui Harbor, we crossed the Paewhenua Island to reach the Kahoe Township, our first stop of the day, 57 km east of Kaitaia.

Driving another 31 km southeast, we reached the Manginangina Scenic Reserve on the eastern edge of Puketi Forest. Here we tried to hobnob

SHELTON A. GUNARATNE

with the giant kauri trees, some of which are more than one thousand years old. But the giants didn't pay attention to our brief exercise of self-propulsion.

After backtracking to Highway 10, we stopped to eat lunch at the Tea Rooms in Kerikeri (pop 6,000), also called the Cradle of the Nation because it is the site of the first permanent mission station (1822) in New Zealand, and it has some of the most historic buildings in the country, including the old stone store (1823).

The purpose of our visit to the Bay of Islands was to get acquainted with the historic towns associated with the emergence of New Zealand as a colony of the British Crown. Therefore, we next visited the township of Waitangi (Weeping Waters) (photo), the place where the Crown rupees representatives and the Maori chiefs of the Far North signed the Treaty of Waitangi on February 6, 1840. The English and the Maori versions of the treaty were later found to be not the same. The treaty established a British governor in New Zealand, recognized the land and property rights of the Maori, and gave Maori the rights of British subjects. However, the treaty was ineffective until 1975, when the Waitangi Tribunal was set up as a permanent body to adjudicate on complaints.

Picture 56.1 Yoke-Sim, carrying Junius, stands at the entrance to the Waitangi Treaty House and Grounds (December 28, 1981).

Waitangi was also the place where the Declaration of Independence was signed on October 28, 1835, which was effectively nullified by the treaty that established New Zealand as a Crown colony. The government built the Maori Meeting House (Te Whare Runanga) next to the Treaty House (the house of the British representative James Busby) to celebrate New Zealand's centenary celebrations in 1940.

Located to the south of Waitangi, Paihia (pop 1,770) is the main town in the Bay of Islands. South of Paihia, we (bus included) took the ferry at Opua to cross over to Okiato (old Russell, New Zealand's first capital) on the eastern side of the Bay of Islands. Nine km north is new Russell (earlier called Kororareka), the first permanent European settlement in New Zealand, dating from the early 1800s. Old Russell was New Zealand's first capital before the capital shifted to Auckland and eventually to Wellington.

Our ferry trip saved us more than 100 km of driving around the Russell Forest to reach Russell (pop 816), where we checked in at the Duke of Marlborough Hotel on The Strand. Before dinner, I strolled the streets of the town with my family and purchased a copy of The (Whangarei) Northern Advocate for later reading.

The next morning, we got on board the boat Waikare II for a cruise on the Bay of Islands. This three-hour outing gave us a closer look at the islands lying to the northeast of Russell: Motorarokia (Robertson), Moturua (Mita's), Motukiete, Okahu, Waewaetoria, and Urupukapuka—not a bunch of easy-to-remember names. We also saw the two neighboring bays, Pakura and Waipiro, lying to the south of the chain of islands, which I decline to spell out again! Since, it took me several attempts to spell out each of these names with accuracy; I wondered why every bay, tombola, fjord, and loch in the world should bear a name.

Back in Russell, we ate lunch at the now defunct Traders Inn. In the afternoon, Junius, Yoke-Sim, and I had a very enjoyable bushwalk to the top of Flagstaff Hill (see photo), which the British used to fly the Union Jack following the Treaty of Waitangi. The Maori resented the flag as a sign of slavery. Shifting the capital to Auckland in 1841 angered the Maori so much that Hone Heke, a local Maori chief, had chopped the flagstaff on three occasions.

As my sore throat and other symptoms of a cold disappeared from my system, I fell more at ease to end our long Tiki Tour, which began in Christchurch on December 12, 1981.

Au Revoir Auckland

Wednesday (December 30, 1981): Ivan Brown, who had been our inestimable guide and "steerologist" in North Island, took us back to Auckland leaving Russell about 8:30 a.m. This time we took the ferry from Okiato (old Russell) to Opua, from where Auckland lies 224 km to the south. Heading southwest on Highway 11, we merged into Highway 1 at Kawakawa.

Our first stop was at Whangarei Falls, 62 km from Opua. Then we drove to the top of the Parahaki Nature Reserve to get a good look at Whangarei, where we stopped in the forward journey as well. Our lunch stop was Dome Valley Roadhouse. We reached Auckland about 3:00 p.m.

Before our Tiki Tour grouped dispersed, Brown took us on a small-scale sightseeing excursion of the Big City, something he failed to do on our first stop on Christmas Day. Perhaps he intended it as his act of farewell. He drove us along Tamaki Drive to Bastion Point to see the memorial to M. J. Savage (1872-1940), who was the first Labor prime minister of New Zealand during the last five years of his life. Bastion Point, which overlooks the Waitemata Harbor, is a coastal stretch of land in Orakei associated with Maori protests of 1977. Then, he took us to see the magnificent homes on Paritai Drive in the same eastern suburb. The property values in the vicinity ranged from $3 million to $12 million. Finally, he took us through the Auckland Domain to the top of Mount Eden Reserve (196 meters), almost 10 km to the southwest, from where "one could see the city all round."

Our plan was to stay two more nights at the Royal International in Auckland before returning to Australia Friday (January 1, 1982) evening.

We spent Thursday morning shopping in downtown Auckland. In the afternoon, we watched Junius chasing pigeons at the Aotea Square created in 1979 to accommodate public events, including fairs, protest rallies, music festivals, rock concerts, and the annual seeing-in of the New Year. We spent the rest of the afternoon at the Zoological Park in Western Springs ($3 per head).

This evening, Yoke-Sim and I decided to celebrate the end of our Tiki Tour as well as the old year, with a grand Indian dinner at the Maharajah Restaurant at the top of Khyber Pass. Junius appeared to relish Indian cuisine. The cost of the meal ($25) was insignificant compared to the enjoyment we derived.

We celebrated the New Year with a trip to the Rangitoto Island the next morning. There, we joined a two-hour adventure tour of the island—an active volcano only two hundred years ago—on board the Magic Bus. We were back at the Waitemata Harbor on the mainland at 2:30 p.m. Later, a limousine took us from the hotel to the Auckland Airport well in time for our Qantas flight to Brisbane at 7:30 p.m.

CHAPTER 57

California:
Mingling with Giant Sequoias

[*B*ACKGROUND: I WAS an exchange instructor at Fullerton College in 1983, occupying the residence of my exchange partner, Larry Taylor, at 2903 Wellesley Court, Fullerton, a suburb of Los Angeles. I arrived with my family in California on February 2, 1983, and we decided to make use of our weekends and the summer break to explore the West Coast to the fullest.]

Exploring the outstanding geographical features of the Sierra Nevada (Snowy Mountain Range), which stretches 400 miles (650 km) from Fredonyer Pass in the north to Tehachapi Pass in the south, became our primary recreational concern in the summer of 1983, though our tours extended to as far north as Corvallis, Oregon.

My son Junius, who had become a seasoned traveler after the long coach tour of New Zealand, where we experienced the delights of crossing the Alpine passes in December 1981, had grown 1.5 years older when he faced the next challenge of crossing (at least a sample of the twelve) mountain passes of the Sierra Nevada, which is bounded on the west by California's Central Valley and on the east by the Great Basin. The Sierras determine the boundary between California and Nevada. The mountain passes of the Sierra were higher than those crossing the Southern Alpines.

Those days, we were very much dependent on the maps and tour books of the American Automobile Association and the tour routes prepared by the AAA specialists for road travel. The Internet and the World Wide Web were the preserves of the elite. Our desktops were not equipped to spew out customized maps, direction finders, distance calculators, and satellite photographs of streets and places all over the world. (Larry Page and Sergey Brin, who founded Google in 1998, were just ten-year-olds in 1983!)

Thus, we planned our camping tour for the Sierra Nevada experience the old-fashioned way. We planned the trip based on three considerations. First, it should be a self-conducted camping tour. Second, it should be confined to the summer vacation, not during the school year. Third, it should include the following distinctive geographical features of the Sierra:

- Groves of giant sequoias (*Sequoiadendron giganteum*), the most massive trees in the world, populated along the narrow band of altitude on the western side of the Sierra Nevada.
- Lake Tahoe, the large, clear freshwater lake in the northern Sierra, with an elevation of 6,225 feet (1,897 m) and an area of 191 square miles (489 square km). Lake Tahoe lies between the main Sierra and the Carson Range, a spur of the Sierra. Water from Lake Tahoe eventually reaches Pyramid Lake, where it evaporates.
- Mount Whitney, the highest point in the "Lower 48," with an elevation of 14,505 feet (4,421 m), located on the eastern border of Sequoia National Park. Mount Whitney ranks eleventh in the United States, after Mount McKinley with an elevation of 20,320 feet (6,194 m) and nine other peaks in Alaska.
- Yosemite National Park, which is filled with stunning features, such as waterfalls and granite domes.
- The beautiful, glacially scoured canyons such as Hetch Hetchy Valley, Yosemite Valley, Kings Canyon, Kern Canyon, and Tehipite Valley on the western side of the Sierra.

However, we soon discovered that reservation of camping sites in popular national parks during the crowded summer required very advanced planning or some luck. Because we could not find back-to-back accommodation at Sequoia and Yosemite national parks at the same time, we had to make two separate trips to accomplish our travel goals.

As it turned out, the first trip was a ten-day excursion (July 15-25) of the Sequoia National Park, the King's Canyon National Park, Lake Tahoe and western Nevada. It involved a driving distance of more than 1,500 miles roundtrip from Fullerton.

The second trip was a twenty-two-day excursion (July 30-August 21) of a larger area of the West Coast, including five days (August 12-17) of camping in Yosemite and four days (August 17-21) exploring the Great Basin in the immediate vicinity of Mt. Whitney.

The Sequoia Experience

On Friday, July 15, 1983, we—Junius, Yoke-Sim, and I—drove 286 miles northeast of Fullerton to reach the Ash Mountain entrance to Sequoia National Park. We reached our destination via Bakersfield, which lies parallel to the Tehachapi Pass at the southern end of the Sierra; Tulare, where we ate lunch at Zumwalt Park; Visalia, where we visited the 155-acre Mooney Grove Park, Lake Kaweah, and Three Rivers.

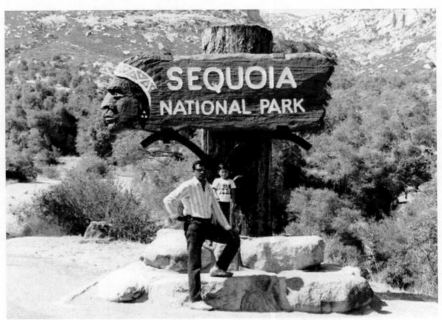

Picture 57.1 The author and his son at the Ash Mountain entrance (via Tulare-Visalia) to Sequoia National Park on July 15, 1983.

When we paid our $2 park fee at the Ash Mountain ranger station, we received a packet of literature, which included a copy of The Sequoia

Bark that gave all the news about the park's daily activities. After entering the park, we zigzagged along the Generals Highway (SR 198), with brief stops at Hospital Rock and Amphitheater Point and passed through the Four Guardsmen (giant sequoias) to make our way to the Lodgepole Campground on Lodgepole Road.

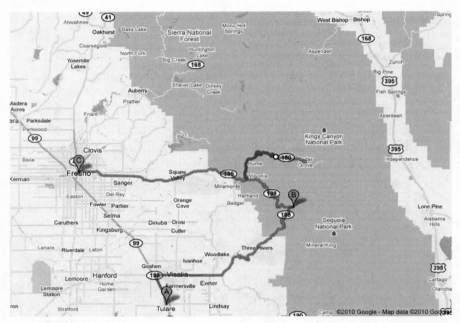

Map 57.1 Sequoia and Kings Canyon National Park has two entry and exit points: *A* (Tulare-Visalia) to the south or *C* (Fresno to the north). *B* = Lodgepole Campgrounds within the national park.

It being 5:00 p.m., we set up our tent, not too far from the South Fork of Kaweah River. After dinner, we went to the Lodgepole Amphitheater to listen to ranger Jack Stitt's talk on "Rock glaciers and running water." The night was freezing cold.

Established in 1890, the Sequoia National Park covers 404,051 acres (1,635 square km).

Saturday (July 16) morning, we joined a small group of people led by ranger Gail Cording for a hike to Tokopah Falls. The trail followed the Marble Falls of the Kaweah River, a typical U-shape of a glaciated gorge. The falls is a series of cascades totaling nearly 1,000 feet in vertical

SHELTON A. GUNARATNE

drop. On the way up, Cording gave a simple account of the geological formation of the area, as well as of the flora and the fauna. She taught us to eat "fiddle nets."

In the afternoon, we drove south and west past Wuksachi Village to see the Crystal Cave, nine miles from the Giant Sequoia Forest, along a narrow paved road. The temperature inside the cave was a constant fifty degrees. The cave had a remarkable gate built like a giant spider. The uphill return hike was quite arduous.

Picture 57. 2 Lilliputians (author's wife and son) at the feet of a Brobdingnagian (General Sherman) on July 16, 1983.

On the way back, we stopped at the General Sherman, a giant sequoia with a height of 275 feet (83.8 meters). (As recently as 2002, the volume of its trunk measured about 1,487 cubic meters, making it the largest non-clonal tree by volume. General Sherman lost its largest branch in early 2006, but that didn't affect its status as the largest tree.) Thereafter, we walked on the two-mile long Cypress Trail that took us to the middle of the Giant Forest with numerous giant sequoias. We were very much the Lilliputians.

Back at the Lodgepole, I took Junius to a children's campfire at the amphitheater. He and I also ambled along the riverbank. At 8:30 p.m., Yoke-Sim joined us for the Lodgepole campfire program. The highlight was ranger Vaughn Folkman's slide presentation on "Tooth, Fang, and Claw," a look at the Sierra animals.

Clarification from Wikipedia

Lest there be confusion, I should explain that the Kings Canyon National Park, which lies to the north, is territorially contiguous with the Sequoia National Park. Wikipedia clarifies that Kings Canyon National Park consists of two sections:

One is the readily accessible General Grant Grove section, which preserves several groves of giant sequoia, including the General Grant Grove, with the famous General Grant Tree, and the Redwood Mountain Grove—the largest remaining natural giant sequoia grove in the world (covering 3,100 acres, with 15,800 sequoia trees measuring more than 1 foot in diameter at base). Both Sequoia and Kings Canyon national parks share the Giant Sequoia forests.

Other is the remaining 90 percent of Kings Canyon National Park, lying to the east of General Grant Grove. This section forms the headwaters of the South and Middle forks of the Kings River and the South Fork of the San Joaquin River. Both the South and Middle forks of the Kings River have extensive glacial canyons. The park derives its name from the portion of the South Fork canyon called the Kings Canyon, one of the deepest canyons glaciers have carved out of granite. The Kings Canyon, as well as its developed area called Cedar Grove, is the only portion of the main part of the park that is accessible by motor vehicle. Both the

Kings Canyon and its Middle Fork twin, the Tehipite Valley, are glacial "Yosemites"—deeply incised glacial gorges with relatively flat floors and towering granite cliffs thousands of feet high. The canyon also contains a cave formation called Boyden Cave.

More of Sequoia Experience

Sunday (July 17) at 7:30 a.m., we left Lodgepole to explore Cedar Grove and Grant Grove sections of the Kings Canyon National Park.

Back on the main drag (Generals Highway), we tarried at Lost Grove and stopped at Stony Creek Village for gasoline. A friendly old attendant served us. At Quail Flat, we took the scenic route northeast to nearby Lake Hume, which deserved a brief stop. Then we joined highway 180 heading east for the breathtaking descent to Kings Canyon. East of Boyden Cave, SR 180 snaked parallel to the South Fork of Kings River—a geographical formation similar to that of Yosemite Valley. (We could not spot the Tehipite Valley on the Middle Fork of Kings River, further to the north. Kern Canyon was further to the south on Sequoia National Park.)

SR 180 provides the only peek into the "Other 90 percent" of the KCNP for motor vehicle exploration. We stopped at Roaring River Falls, a drop of eighty feet through a granite gorge. Next, we walked around the famous Zumwalt Meadow (which offers "magnificent views of high granite walls, a lush meadow, and the meandering Kings River") after turning back at Road's End. The meadow featured a moraine deposited by a glacier. It overlooked the granite monoliths North Dome and Great Sentinel. We ate lunch on the riverbank. Then we headed west again on the Motor Nature Trail and stopped at the Cedar Grove Village.

Finally, we backtracked SR 180 to visit the General Grant Grove, which has the second largest living thing in the world, the General Grant tree, also called "The Nation's Christmas Tree." There we ran into the family of an expatriate Sri Lankan, Francis Perera. After visiting the Grant Grove Visitor Center, Junius and I explored the Big Stump Trail. It was 7:30 p.m. when we returned to the Lodgepole. I had a headache.

Monday (July 18) was our last day at the Sequoia National Park. In the morning, we headed south on the main drag, and then turned east on

Crescent Meadow Road, close to the Giant Forest Village. We exercised ourselves on the pretext of following the trails to Crescent Meadow and Huckleberry Meadow. Names such as Tharp's Log, Chimney Tree, Squatters Cabin, and Dead Giant aroused our curiosity that induced us to touch, smell or sit on them.

We were disappointed that we were unable to get a view of Mt. Whitney from the western flank of SPN/KCNP because many of the snowcapped peaks in the Great Western Divide reached altitudes of twelve thousand feet (3,657 meters) or higher. It was, therefore, impossible to see over them to view Mt. Whitney from the 6,725 feet (2,050 m) Moro Rock, a granite monolith overlooking the deep canyon of the Middle Fork of Kaweah River. Yet it was most remarkable that we walked to the top of this rock (trudging each of the four hundred steps of the stairway) to see the Castle Rocks and the divide.

The Sierra has no mountain pass in an eastwest direction for 200 miles from Tioga Pass to Tehachapi Pass. Although no motor vehicle can access the eastern side of S/KCNP on this horizontal band, hikers and horseback riders can cross the forest through the Kaweah Gap on the 49-mile High Sierra Trail from the plateau of the Great Forest at Crescent Meadow to Bearpaw Meadow. Via this trail, the distance between Crescent Meadow and Mt. Whitney Portal is 72 miles.

We ate lunch on a log along Round Meadow, adjacent to the Lodge. On the return journey to Lodgepole, we stopped at the Visitor Center to watch a slide presentation of "Fungi in Sequoia" by John Taylor, a mycologist from UC Berkeley.

One of the delights of camping in US national parks is attending a choice of ranger-led programs and activities. Therefore, even on the eve of our departure from Sequoia, we did not want to miss the evening's postprandial activity: a very interesting presentation on "Awareness in pictures" by ranger John Satnet and Kodak specialist John Greene.

CHAPTER 58

California-Nevada: Crossing the Sierra Passes to Lake Tahoe and Reno

WE LEFT THE Lodgepole Campground of Sequoia and Kings Canyon National Park Tuesday (July 19, 1983) morning at 6.30 through the northern gate heading west to Fresno. Our destination was D. L. Bliss State Park in Emerald Bay, Lake Tahoe, on the Great Basin east of the Sierra—some 342 miles from Lodgepole.

This trip enabled us to get acquainted with the eastern bounds of California's Central Valley, which roughly stretches some 500 miles from Bakersfield in the south to Redding in the north. The lower half is better known as the St. Joaquin Valley and the upper half the Sacramento Valley. The two halves meet at the shared Sacramento-San Joaquin River Delta, a large expanse of interconnected canals, marshes, peat islands, sloughs, and streambeds.

From Fresno, we drove north on SR41 to Oakhurst, close to the South Entrance to Yosemite; then northwest on SR49 (Golden Highway) to Mariposa, the middle (Arch Rock) entrance to Yosemite; and further on SR49 to Moccasin, the northwest (Big Oak Flat) entrance to Yosemite. (We entered Yosemite National Park on August 12, through the northwest entrance on our second tour.)

At Mariposa, we visited California's oldest courthouse. Between Bear Valley and Coulterville is "Hells Hollow," the Merced River canyon, near Ragby. It gave me a thrill to drive on this stretch of the highway, which twisted its way from the ridge to the bottom by many loops and sharp, frightful turns.

Our next two stops were Chinese Camp and Jamestown, which lie parallel to Stockton in the Central Valley. Our leisurely driving delayed us from reaching Placerville, the terminus of SR49 northeast of Sacramento, until dinnertime.

From Placerville, we drove northeast on US50 (Lincoln Highway) to cross the Eldorado National Forest of the Sierra through the 7,382 ft (2,250 m) Echo Summit mountain pass between Twin Bridges and Meyers, south of Lake Tahoe. Echo Summit is the seventh highest of the twelve main mountain passes in the Sierra.

We reached D. L. Bliss State Park Campground, located north of Emerald Bay on the southwestern edge of Lake Tahoe, at 8:30 p.m. We set up our tent in the Lester Beach Road camp area for a two-night stay. It was pleasing to find hot water for a bath after the cold-water spell at Sequoia.

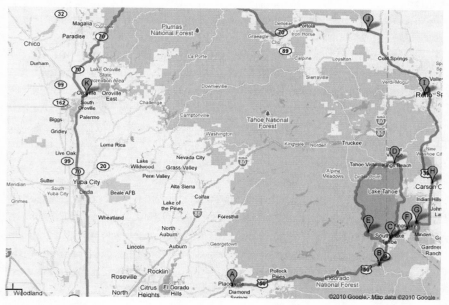

Map 58.1 Crossing the Sierra from California's Central Valley to Lake Tahoe or Reno via *B* (Echo Summit Pass) and recrossing the Sierra via *J* (Beckwourth Pass). Other letter signs: *A*, Placerville, California; *C*, South Lake Tahoe, California; *D*, Crystal Bay, Nevada; *E*, Emerald Bay, California; *F*, Kingsbury Grade, Nevada; *G*, Genoa, Nevada; *H*, Carson City, Nevada; *I*, Reno, Nevada; *K*, Oroville, California; *L*, Sacramento, California.

SHELTON A. GUNARATNE

Lake Tahoe Experience

California and Nevada share Lake Tahoe, a large freshwater lake (in the Great Basin) with a length of 22 miles (35 km), a surface area of 191 square miles (490 square km), and a shoreline of 72 miles (116 km). It is the second deepest lake in the United States, after Crater Lake in Oregon. California has the lion's share of the lake arrogating the west and the south.

The lake's largest city is South Lake Tahoe, Calif. (pop 23,600), adjoining Stateline, Nevada (pop 1,215). Tahoe City, California (pop 1,800) is located in the lake's northwest.

We spent Wednesday (July 20) exploring the perimeter of Lake Tahoe. In the morning, we—son Junius, wife Yoke-Sim, and I—walked from our campsite to Lester Beach. Then, we walked on the Rubicon Trail to Rubicon Point and the lighthouse.

To get things rolling, we drove seven miles north on the west beach to a laundromat in Tahoma to clean up the clothes we soiled over a week of camping. Eleven miles further north, we stopped for lunch at Tahoe City, where we also visited the Gatekeepers Cabin and Watson Cabin—the oldest house built on-site in this area. We also looked at the population of trout under Fanny Bridge.

Reaching the northern part of the lake, we drove another thirteen miles northeast along the beach highway past Carnelian Bay, Tahoe Vista, Kings Beach, and Brockway to cross the state border to Crystal Bay in Nevada. There, Yoke-Sim and Junius got excited about playing the "one-armed bandits" at the nearest casino in Incline/Tyrolian Village. I went through a brief shock when the casino folks warned us that Junius shouldn't be even close to a slot machine. We agreed.

We left the north shore of the lake and drove twenty-two miles south on the east shore, past Glenbrook and Oakridge, to Zephyr Cove-Round Hill Village, lying almost parallel to our campsite on the western shore. We tarried here to observe the boat ramp. Next, we drove another seven miles to Stateline, a hive of activity with famous casinos on the Nevada side.

Back in California, we stopped in South Lake Tahoe to eat dinner and visit the boat harbor. Later, we visited the Tallac Historic Site—the grounds of the Baldwin-McGonagle, Pope, and Valhalla summer homes, near Kiva Beach. The trail leading to the site rambles under aspen past the remains of Lucky Baldwin's Tallac House, gambling casino, and Tallac Hotel. At the Valhalla home, we attended a slide presentation by two rangers of the US Forest Service.

Our campground was only fourteen miles away. Thus, we took the entire day to immerse ourselves in Lake Tahoe over a driving distance of seventy-five miles, which should have taken no more than two hours had we not dillydallied to satisfy our touristic instincts.

On the Way to Reno

Nevada became our focus for the next two days. I first visited Las Vegas, Nevada, early January 1967 during my West Coast tour as a World Press Institute fellow. Again, in late August 1969, I crossed Nevada (Wells, Elko, Reno) with three fellow graduate students of the University of Minnesota (Jim Bowers, Dennis Davis, and Kurt Kent) on the way to attend the Association for Education in Journalism Convention in Berkeley. I remembered eating breakfast in Reno on that Sunday morning and visiting several casinos. But for both Yoke-Sim and Junius, Nevada was new and utterly exciting.

On Thursday (July 21), we travelled only eighty-four miles, but the quality of what we absorbed was exemplary. After leaving our campground in the morning, we drove three miles south to visit Vikingsholm, a thirty-eight-room mansion on the shore of Emerald Bay built by Lora Josephine Knight in 1929 to create a replica of an eleventh-century Viking castle. Behind the castle, we walked further to see Eagle Falls. The castle provided a good view of Fannette Island in the Emerald Bay.

Our second stop was South Lake Tahoe, where we saw the Stream Profile Chamber, the primary attraction at the Forest Service Visitor Center complex at Taylor Creek since it was constructed in 1968. The chamber provides a view of the stream environment allowing visitors to study a diverted section of Taylor Creek through a panel of aquarium-like windows. These windows enabled us to watch the Kokanee silver trout in their natural habitat.

Picture 58.1 The author (with cap on) and his son Junius in front of Vikingsholm on Emerald Bay, Lake Tahoe (July 21, 1983).

Crossing back to Nevada at Stateline, we drove east on the hilly Kingsbury Grade, and then north on Foothill Road to Genoa, the first permanent settlement in Nevada. We ate lunch at the Mormon Station Historic State Monument, and then visited the Genoa Court Museum opposite.

Sixteen miles north of Geneva, we reached Carson City (pop 53,000), the capital of Nevada. We improved our knowledge about how the state governs by visiting the state Legislative Building and the state Capitol (built c. 1871).

For more than fifty years, the Capitol housed all three branches of the state government. The Supreme Court met here until 1937, when it moved into an adjacent building; and the Nevada Legislature met here until 1971, when it moved to its new quarters just south of the Capitol. However, every Nevada governor except the first has had his office in the Capitol. Today, the Capitol continues to serve the governor and contains historical exhibits on the second floor (Wikipedia).

Although Nevada is the seventh largest US state in area (with Mojave Desert to the south and Great Basin to the north), it has a (current) population of only 2.6 million. About 86 percent of its land area belongs to the federal government. Also, about 85 percent of the population of Nevada lives in the metropolitan areas surrounding the Las Vegas-Paradise-Henderson area and the Reno-Sparks area. It's called the "Silver State" because of its numerous silver deposits.

We also visited the city's diamond attraction—the Nevada State Museum in the Old Mint Building. The basement had been converted into a silver mine at the time of our visit. Before we left for Reno, Nevada's fourth largest city, we drove around to see the governor's mansion and other Victorian buildings.

We arrived in Reno (pop 218,000), thirty-three miles north of Carson City, in the evening. After stopping at Liberty Bell to see the antique slot machines, we checked in at Motel 6 (South) for the night.

Reno, the birthplace of the gaming corporation Harrah's Entertainment, is best known for its casinos and as the western portal to legalized debauchery at the Mustang Ranch in Sparks and various other communities. Visiting such places was not an objective of our family camping adventure, which focused on enjoying the remarkable geological features of the Sierra: its mountain passes, glacier-cut canyons, freshwater lakes, endless trails, and forests.

The next morning (July 22), we toured the University of Nevada-Reno campus, including the mining museum, the planetarium, the library, and, of course, the journalism department. Thereafter, we treated ourselves to a 36-mile scenic tour of Reno starting at North Sierra Street, at the southern end of the campus; stopping at Idlewild Park by the Truckee River, where Junius exercised in the playground; moving on to Virginia Lake Park, where we ate lunch with countless ducks roaming around us; driving past the southwestern residential district along the posh Skyline Boulevard to Windy Mill; and ending up at Virginia City in the southeast.

Virginia City was a mining metropolis in the 1870s. At the time of our visit, the city had been restored to its original boomtown appearance with several small museums on C Street. We enjoyed ambling on the boardwalks, looking at quaint things and readily accepted the offer of two free beers. We enjoyed watching a documentary on the city at the visitors' center. Then, we drove to Dayton State Park via Gold Hill and Silver City to set up tent for our second overnight stay in the Reno area.

Picture 58.2 The author in front of the reconstructed gold-rush town of Virginia City, southeast of Reno, Nevada (July 22, 1983).

Crossing Beckwourth Pass

Saturday (July 23) morning, we left the Dayton campground back to Reno after a short stop at Washoe Lake, just to the northeast of Lake Tahoe. In the city, we visited several casinos, including Circus Circus and Harrah's and bought a Lake Tahoe T-shirt for Junius.

We left Reno at 11:00 a.m. on our return trip to California's Central Valley across the Sierra on SR70 through the Beckwourth Pass, lying at an elevation of 5,221 feet (1,591 m). It is the second northernmost pass in the Sierra, after Fredonyer Pass. However, it ranks as the second lowest pass in terms of elevation, next to Tehachapi. Our destination was the Loafer Creek Campground of the Oroville State Recreation Area, about 160 miles west. We reached the pass, immediately to the west of Hallelujah Junction, just thirty miles northwest of Reno.

I cannot recall the reason for choosing the Beckwourth Pass over the more pragmatic 7,085 ft (2,160 m) Donner Pass on Interstate 80 for recrossing the Sierra to the Central Valley. On I-80, the distance between Reno and Sacramento is 132 miles. Perhaps the booking of Oroville for camping overnight determined the route. Oroville is almost seventy miles north of Sacramento.

Following the overnight stay in Oroville, we headed south on the Central Valley to Sacramento, the state capital, where we embarked on a rushed tour of the Capitol, Sutter's Fort (1839) and Old Sacramento. We were the overnight guests of a friend of ours in Stockton (Jan Mullen of 1250 Elmwood Ave.) that evening. On Sunday (July 25), we returned to Fullerton, 363 miles further to the south.

CHAPTER 59

California: Getting Jitters at Hetch Hetchy in Yosemite

LATE AFTERNOON ON Friday August 12, 1983 we—my wife Yoke-Sim, three-year-old son Junius, and I—entered the Yosemite National Park in the Sierra through the northwest "Big Oak Flat" gateway designated SR120. From Moccasin, California (which we passed by on July 19 on our way north from Sequoia along the eastern edge of the Central Valley), we drove fifty-four miles east to reach the Upper Pines Campground of the Yosemite Valley, where we set up our tent.

(Now, we were on the last leg of our second long trip of the West Coast that we began on July 30. I shall write about what we did in between in a separate article.)

A Climb like "Empire State"

Our objectives for visiting Yosemite National Park, which covers an area of 761,266 acres (308,073 ha), included the following:

- Observing the stunning features of the park, such as waterfalls and granite domes.
- Exploring the beautiful, glacially scoured canyons such as Hetch Hetchy Valley and Yosemite Valley. (We had already seen Kings Canyon, Kern Canyon, and Tehipite Valley in the Kings Canyon/ Sequoia national parks to the south.)

Saturday (August 13) morning, we took the shuttle bus to the visitors' center to see the orientation slide show and other exhibits. Just behind the center, we visited the Indian Village and the Indian Cultural Museum, which depict Miwok and Paiute history.

The day's adventure was defying the challenge of a steep climb along the Upper Yosemite Falls Trail, a 3.8-mile (6 km) stretch from the Lower Yosemite Falls trailhead to the top of Yosemite Falls. The slow-and-tiring trudge involved climbing 2,600 feet (790 m)—the equivalent of climbing the Empire State Building in New York. Junius and Yoke-Sim managed to walk about 1.5 miles to get a closer look at the falls while we ate our lunch on the trail. They turned back, while I continued to walk the entire trek and reached the top of the falls about 4:00 p.m.—a four-hour climb! I puddled on the Yosemite Creek after crossing a footbridge. On this spot, I felt as if I were the king of all I surveyed—the entire Yosemite Valley, including the renowned Half Dome.

I resisted the temptation of climbing another 410 feet (125 m) to reach Yosemite Point (elevation 6,936 ft or 2,114 m) because time was against me. Having thoroughly enjoyed the fantastic view from the top of Upper Yosemite Falls, I started on my return trip at 4:45 p.m. and reached the Sunnyside Campground about 6:00 p.m.—a relatively easy descent. Then I walked to see the Lower Yosemite Falls before taking the shuttle bus back to Upper Pines.

After dinner, we attended a campfire program at the Lower Pines Campground Amphitheater.

So Near, Yet So Far

Since Yoke-Sim and Junius missed the view of the valley from the top of Upper Yosemite Falls, the next day we decided to get a panoramic view of the Yosemite Valley and the eastern Sierra from the lofty heights of Glacier Point (7,214 ft or 2,200 m), only 4.8 miles (7.1 km) on the Four Mile Trail or 8.5 miles (13.6 km) on the Panorama Trail. However, the driving distance to Glacier Point is 30 miles or 48 km (going west and south along SR41 to Wawona, and then heading east and north on Glacier Point Road). Because the climb up would be too arduous for many visitors, they have the choice of getting there by the hikers' bus ($25 one-way in 2010) and climbing down one of the trails, taking the bus both ways, or driving their own vehicle back and forth. We decided to drive.

Described as "the most awesome lookout in the Lower 48," Glacier Point enables you to view the entire Yosemite Valley 3,200 ft. (980 m) below

SHELTON A. GUNARATNE

to the north; Nevada and Vernal falls to the east; Illilouette Fall to the southeast; Half Dome to the northeast; Yosemite Falls to the northwest; El Capitan, Tunnel View, and Bridalveil Falls to the west. The Four Mile Trail, which switchbacks down to Yosemite Valley, provides "wonderful views of the Valley." The Panorama Trail provides a "close-up view of Illilouette Fall and panoramic views of eastern Yosemite Valley before joining the Mist or John Muir trails down past Vernal and Nevada falls."

After we examined the main attractions of Yosemite Valley from Glacier Point, we stopped at Washburn Point to the south to look at the surroundings from the Vernal and Nevada falls' angle. Rain delayed our next adventure: a 1.1-mile trek to Sentinel Dome (elevation 8,122 ft or 2,466 m), a granite rock. We climbed to the top of the dome with a family from Ohio to get a 360-degree view of the valley. The dead Jeffrey pine that remained on the dome during our visit was removed in 2003.

Picture 59.1 The author and his son Junius climbed to the top of the Sentinel Dome to get a 360-degree view of the valley on August 14, 1983. The dead Jeffrey pine that featured the dome during their visit was removed in 2003.

Next, we stopped at the Yosemite Pioneer History Center in Wawona, thirty miles south of Glacier Point on SR41. The center exhibits a collection of restored and authentic stagecoaches representing early travel to the Yosemite region. Its several log cabins depict living history—with living people depicting historical characters. This was a wonderful experience.

From Wawona, we drove to the Mariposa Grove of Giant Sequoias and walked a mile to see the Grizzly Giant, estimated to be eighteen hundred years old; and the California Tunnel Tree, cut in 1895 to allow horse-drawn stages to pass through.

We then heard that we couldn't get back to Yosemite Valley on SR41 because of a rockslide. The only recourse we had was to exit Yosemite from its South Entrance and reenter the park from the middle (Arch Rock) entrance. Thus, we were back on SR49 driving north from Oakhurst to Mariposa, a stretch we passed through on July 19. But every downside has its upside. In this case, the upside was that we earned the distinction of going through all three western gateways to Yosemite. And we had planned to leave Yosemite through its only eastern gateway.

We spent most of Monday (December 15) in Yosemite Valley, exploring areas we couldn't visit closer to our Upper Pines Campground over the first two days. To start with, we took the shuttle to Happy Isles, 1.2 miles southeast of Upper Pines. From there, we walked on the Fall Trail to the 317 feet Vernal Fall. On the way, we had a distant look at the 370 feet Illilouette Fall, as well. Back at Happy Isles, we visited the Nature Center, where we watched an interesting film on trees.

Around noon, we took the shuttle to Mirror Lake Junction, from where we walked a mile to Mirror Lake, 1.5 miles northeast of Upper Pines. It was fast changing into a meadow during our visit. Now, it is also called Mirror Meadow. The reflection of Mount Watkins on the lake, fed by Tenaya Creek, was beautiful. We walked quite a ways up the Mirror Lake Trail, along the creek, and ate our lunch.

Then, we returned to Curry Village and drove our car to visit Ahwhanee Hotel, Yosemite Village, and Yosemite Lodge. Thereafter, we drove further west for a stop at the El Capitan Picnic Area and the 620 ft. Bridalveil Fall.

SHELTON A. GUNARATNE

From Upper Pines to White Wolf

We left Upper Pines and the Yosemite Valley late afternoon for camping and exploration of northeast Yosemite along Tioga Pass Road (SR120), the only gateway to Yosemite from eastern Sierra. But since it started to rain on our way, we decided to camp overnight at the nearby White Wolf Campground, thirty-three miles by road from Upper Pines on SR120 but still slightly to the northwest of our former campground. Most of the camping sites were wet, and the one that we first selected turned out to be used by someone else. It was the coldest night we experienced during this tour.

Tuesday (August 16), we started on a six-mile (12-mile roundtrip) long walk on the eastern trail from White Wolf to the lookout of the Grand Canyon of the Tuolumne, starting about 9:00 a.m. and returning on the western trail about 5:30 p.m. The downpour of the previous evening had made the trail muddy. Having gotten used to walking with wet shoes, we reached the trail junction to Harden Lake close to noon. There we ran into three hikers from Santa Barbara, California, including two Iranians, who shared some camping food with us.

We ate lunch at the lookout, which shows the Hetch Hetchy Reservoir on one side and the Tuolumne River Canyon on the other. Leaving Junius and Yoke-Sim at the lookout, I walked down the trail to take a close-up photo of the canyon. When I returned to the lookout, neither Junius nor Yoke-Sim was around. Jitters went through my system. I trudged back and forth on the trail yet unable to spot them. I talked to a couple of people I had seen on the trail earlier whether they saw a boy and a Chinese woman lost in the vicinity. I was about to give up and cry, "Wolf" when I saw the duo roaming at a distance.

The relief that I experienced as I saw them was unforgettable.

Wednesday (August 17) goes down in our family annals as the day the Gunaratne family used all four gateways to the Yosemite National Park when they crossed the Tioga Pass, the highest mountain pass in California, to reach the foothills of the eastern Sierra.

Picture 59.2 Yoke-Sim and Junius at the Tuolumne Grand Canyon Lookout on August 16, 1983 just before their "vanishing act." When the author returned to the lookout, neither Junius nor Yoke-Sim was around. Jitters went through his system.

We left White Wolf at 8:00 a.m. and headed for Lukens Lake. Having parked our vehicle on the roadside, we walked on the trail to the lake watching the unmelted patches of snow, which Junius and Yoke-Sim had not seen since their brief glacier experience in New Zealand in December 1981. On our way east, we stopped at several such scenic turnouts. The scenery from Olmsted Point was pretty with Half Dome, Glacier Point, and Tunnel View clearly visible to the west. Tenaya Lake was along the way.

We visited the Tuolumne Meadows Visitors Center about 11:00 a.m. Then, we drove to see the adjoining campground. We walked on the Glen Aulin Trail up to Parson's Lodge, a historical landmark, next to Soda Springs, the water of which we tasted. We were lucky to view all these things on this occasion because normally the surrounding meadows are covered by snow most of the year. After a stop at the eight hundred feet. (240 m) Lembert Dome, we went to see the cottages at Tuolumne Lodge.

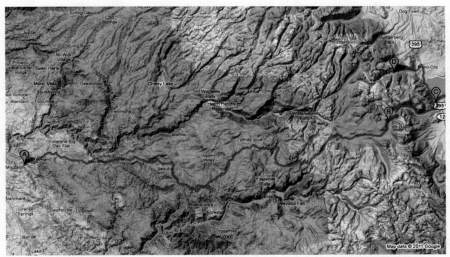

Map 59.1 Tioga Pass Road (SR 120) crossing the Yosemite National Park west to east. *A*, Moccasin; *B*, Tioga Pass; *C*, Lee Vining; *D*, Lundy.

Soon, we passed the Tioga Pass Entrance Station, eighty-three miles east of Moccasin, the northwest entry point to Yosemite on SR120. I drove down this breathtaking mountain pass with utmost trepidation. The grade down the eastern Sierra was so steep. Moreover, a downpour on the hills made the drive hazardous. So I was much relieved when I reached Lee Vining, California, the town next to Mono Lake. We visited the visitors' center and the county park.

We decided to stay overnight at the Mill Creek Campground, just east of Lundy Lake. We camped by the roaring creek. Our neighboring campers—Tim Carmody and his son from Newport Beach, California—invited us for a campfire chat and tea. Rain fell as we drank tea.

CHAPTER 60

California-Nevada: Wild West beyond Great Divide

E—YOKE-SIM, JUNIUS, AND I—enjoyed the night of camping at Lake Lundy in the idyllic foothills of the Great Divide that we decided to hang around the vicinity of the lake area for the next couple of days. Having a campfire chat while drinking hot tea with a father-and-son team of campers, whom we had never met, with the noise of the roaring creek and the sound of raindrops literally falling on our heads creating a sort of eerie lull within us, gave us spontaneous joy. We were camping directly east of Tioga Pass at an elevation of 7,858 feet (2, 395 m).

The next morning (August 18), our two neighbors—Tim Carmody and his son—left the campground before we did. Carmody, a photographer from Newport Beach, California, asked us to visit them on our return to Fullerton. We never had that opportunity.

We started the day with a visit to Lundy Lake Resort. Lundy (earlier known as Mill Creek) was founded as a mining camp in 1879. The town got its name from W. J. Lundy, who operated a sawmill in the area.

Gold and Ghost Towns

Going north, we reached Dog Town, associated with the gold rush of the eastern Sierra. Going further north, we stopped at Bridgeport (pop 817) to wash our clothes at a laundromat, purchase groceries essential for our sustenance, and fill up the tank of our gas-guzzler. While we engaged in these routine activities, Junius played in the park next to the museum. We visited the town's courthouse built in 1880.

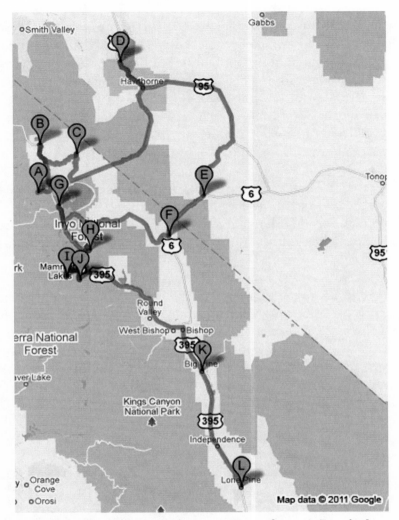

Map 60.1 The Eastern High Sierra Route from *A* (Lundy [east of Tioga Pass]) to *L* (Lone Pine [east of Mount Whitney]). *B*, Bridgeport; *C*, Brodie; *D*, Walker Lake, Nevada; *E*, Basalt, Nevada; *F*, Benton, Nevada; *G*, Mono Lake; *H*, Big Springs; *I*, Devils Postpile; *J*, Lake Mary; *K*, Big Pine.

Then we backtracked on US 395 and headed east on SR270 to see the gold-rush ghost town of Brodie, now a National Historic Landmark. Founded in 1859, it earned the reputation of being one of Californa's most lawless towns. At the time of our visit, only 5 percent of its original buildings were still standing.

Thereafter, we drove to the north shore of Mono Lake and headed northeast on SR167, which becomes SR359 at the Nevada border and terminates in Hawthorne (pop 3,300). We had driven more than 100 miles to reach Hawthorne since we left Lundy in the morning. We had to drive 16 miles further northwest on US 95 to set up tent for our overnight stay at Sportsmen's Beach on Walker Lake. Carson City, the capital of Nevada that we visited in July, was less than 100 miles to the northwest of Walker Lake, which has a surface area of 130 square km.

Having set up the tent and eaten dinner, I left Junius and Yoke-Sim at the campground to do whatever they pleased, and drove back to Hawthorne to explore the neighborhood alone. I stopped at a downtown bar and sipped a beer. Then I drove further south to Mina to stop at a casino for another beer.

When I returned to the campground about 8:30 p.m., I found our tent reeling because of heavy winds. Yoke-Sim was in an agitated condition. Luckily, two good Samaritans—an Arizona couple who identified themselves as Dee and Van (Young)—came to our rescue and helped steady the tent with supports. Thus, we learned that camping could be dangerous, as well.

Picture 60.1 Van and Dee Young from Arizona helped to steady our tent on Sportsmen's Beach at Walker Lake, Nevada, on August 18, 1983 evening. Heavy winds almost unplugged the tent while I was away visiting Hawthorne.

SHELTON A. GUNARATNE

Friday (August 19) morning, we said good-bye to Dee and Van Young who helped us the previous night and left Sportsmen's Beach about 10:00 a.m. Back in Hawthorne, we visited the Mineral County Museum and also filled up the car. The townsfolk were quite friendly. Next, past Mina, where I had been the previous evening, we left US95 heading southwest on SR360, which merged with US6 at Basalt, Nevada. Then, via the Mount Montgomery Pass, we drove past the last casino and Janie's Ranch, and crossed the Nevada border back to California. At Benton, we drove northwest on SR120 to the site of Mono Mills, where we ate lunch.

Our next stop was the south shore of Mono Lake. (We drove along its north shore the previous day.) Mono Lake is an alkaline and hypersaline lake with a surface area of sixty-nine square miles (180 square km). First, we went to the Navy Beach; then, we took the scenic trail to see the strange-looking spires and knobs called the Tufa Towers, mostly calcium carbonate. Then, we climbed the nearby Panum Crater from the top of which we picked up two pieces of obsidian.

Exp(os/lor)ing the Devil

Next, we drove on the June Lake Loop (SR 158), past Grant Lake and Silver Lake to reach the June Lake beach area, which we found to be very attractive as a holiday spot. However, we resisted the temptation to camp here and went further southeast on US395 until we turned east on Owen River Road.

We found our ideal, free campground a couple of miles away at Big Springs, just by the Deadman Creek. This is where we camped for the night, which turned out to be cold. We were just ten miles north of Mammoth Lakes.

The creek provided an abundant supply of trout for the campers to fish, cook, and relish. Our neighbors offered us several freshly caught rainbow trout, which enabled us to treat ourselves to a very delicious dinner. Yoke-Sim was elated. I wondered why people would holiday in four-star hotels, when a simple tent by a creek in the foothills of the eastern Sierra could offer more joy at a fraction of the cost.

Saturday (August 20) morning, we ate a bountiful breakfast of trout and set out to explore the area surrounding the Mammoth Scenic Loop (SR203), off to the west of US395. We received orientation information at the Mammoth Visitor Center or Ranger Station. Then, we went to Mammoth Mountain Ski Area to park our car and board a Quicksilver Lines shuttle bus ($3.50 per adult) to go to the Devils Postpile National Monument because the road beyond the Minaret summit was not open to private vehicles without permits.

We arrived at the DPNM about 11:00 a.m. and joined a ranger-conducted tour of the monument, a fine example of columnar basalt formed nearly a million years ago. DPNM was once part of Yosemite National Park, but discovery of gold near Mammoth Lakes prompted a boundary change that left the Postpile on adjacent public land. A proposal to build a hydroelectric dam later called for blasting the Postpile into the river.

(Thus, although we left Yosemite on Wednesday, we were still hanging around the northeastern Sierra, not paying enough attention to southeastern Sierra, closer to Mount Whitney.)

We climbed to the top of the Postpile to see the polished tops. From there, we walked to see the Rainbow Falls, where the Middle Fork of the San Joaquin River drops 101 feet.

From the falls, we walked up to Red's Meadow, the last shuttle stop. After returning to the ski area about 4:00 p.m., we drove to see the Mammoth earthquake fault, a fifty-feet deep split in hardened lava. Located off Hwy. 203 on the way to Mammoth Mountain, this sizable fissure is not an earthquake fault caused by a single quake. Then, we explored the lakes along Lake Mary Road starting with Twin Lakes. We decided to camp overnight at the Lake Mary Campground despite a drizzle.

In the evening, we drove to the visitors' center on Old Mammoth Road to see a slide show on Mount Whitney and Boundary Peak, which we expected to see Sunday. On our way back to the campground, we stopped at Baskin Robbins for an ice cream.

Final Day

Sunday (August 21) was the scheduled final day of our exploration of the foothills of the eastern High Sierra. By 11:00 p.m., we were back in Fullerton. The Whitney Portal Road was 105 miles south of Mammoth Lakes. And Fullerton was another 231 miles south. Driving 336 miles on a single day was feasible, but climbing up Mount Whitney was not feasible within the time constraints we had imposed on ourselves.

Before leaving Mammoth Lakes in the morning, we couldn't resist the temptation to stop at Horseshoe Lake to the northwest of our campground and to do a short walk on Old Mammoth Road, just to the northeast. Then, we headed southeast on US395 for Bishop (pop 3,500), where we turned west on SR 168 to have a glimpse of Bishop Creek Canyon, a striking example of Sierra scenery—"an alpine wonderland of pine forests, rushing streams, and deep-blue lakes surrounded by mighty mountain peaks." We also stopped at Power Station no. 4 to see the dam. After filling up the gas-guzzler yet again, we entered the premises of the Paiute-Shoshone Indian Culture Center, where we ate lunch.

Past Big Pine, we arrived in Independence (pop 600), formerly called Little Pine and Putnam's, where we tarried at the Mount Whitney Fish Hatchery, which had a Swiss Chalet-style main building, a beautiful shady place. We went to see the site of Camp Independence and also visited the Commander's House (1872) and the East California Museum. Two elderly ladies showed us around at the Commander's House. We also saw Edwards House (1865), Inyo County's Courthouse. Yoke-Sim and Junius stopped at a vacant piece of land to pick up peaches and grapes while I went to fetch the car from Dehy Park.

Our next stop was Manzanar, most widely known as the site of one of ten camps where more than one hundred and ten thousand Japanese Americans were imprisoned during World War II, less than 10 miles to the north of Lone Pine (pop 1,700). Then, at Lone Pine, we drove west on the Whitney Portal Road to see the famous Alabama Hills, an expanse of rocks with unusual shapes used as a setting for western movies. We also saw the Cottonwood Charcoal Kilns.

Picture 60.2 With Mount Whitney in the background, the writer stands along the Whitney Portal Road at Alabama Hills, Lone Pine (August 21, 1983).

One of the main objectives of our two summer trips was to see Mount Whitney, the highest peak in the Lower forty-eight states. Now, we were directly facing it from the angle of the US Inter-Agency Visitor Center in Lone Pine. Thanks, big guy. Sorry, we couldn't climb on to the top of your head!

Thus, we accomplished all our travel objectives on exploring the main features of the Sierra. This definitely called for a celebration. So as we drove further south on US395 in the Mojave Desert, we stopped for a lavish dinner at a casino named Hi Desert Inn in Adelanto, California.

CHAPTER 61

California: From Hearst Castle to Redwood Forests

OUR YOSEMITE ESCAPADES and Eastern Sierra Foothills exploits constituted the tail end of our twenty-two-day second trip that began on July 30, 1983. This travelogue focuses on our camping adventures and explorations on the West Coast from San Luis Obispo, Calif., to Corvallis, Oregon, during the two weeks before entering Yosemite on August 12.

On day one (Saturday, July 30), my wife Yoke-Sim and I, together with our three-year-old son Junius, drove from Fullerton to San Simeon, a distance of 277 miles (445 km) heading northwest, to spend the night at San Simeon State Beach Campground. Our intent was to visit the Hearst Castle, designated as a national historical landmark since 1976, Sunday.

On the morning of day one, we drove to the Hearst estate, about five miles (8 km) inland atop a hill of the Santa Lucia Range at an altitude of 1,600 feet (490 m). I was here once before in 1966 during the WPI tour of the West Coast. The current tour was for me to indulge in nostalgia and orient my wife and son to some places I particularly liked.

As a journalism scholar at the University of Oregon in 1967-1968, I became aware of how yellow journalism (sensational and exaggerated journalism lacking in veracity) emerged from the relentless circulation war between the *New York Journal* owned by William Randolph Hearst (1863-1951) and the *New York World* owned by Joseph Pulitzer (1847-1911), especially prior to and during the 1898 Spanish-American War. The most famous exemplification of the extent of exaggeration is the apocryphal story that when artist Frederic Remington telegrammed

Hearst to tell him all was quiet in Cuba and "There will be no war;" Hearst responded, "Please remain. You furnish the pictures, and I'll furnish the war."

Picture 61.1 We visited Hearst Castle in San Simeon on July 31, 1983. Yoke-Sim (center) and Junius (partly hidden) are seen with our tour group.

Hearst Castle

Now, we had camped overnight to see the palace built for the same Hearst (the semifictional *Citizen Kane* in the 1941 Orson Welles's movie, wherein "Xanadu" identifies Hearst Castle) who earned part of his wealth through yellow journalism.

SHELTON A. GUNARATNE

Our day two visit to the magnificent estate and the castle buildings that architect Julia Morgan designed and built from 1919 explained why more than a million people were attracted to see the complex every year. As Wikipedia describes, Hearst Castle featured fifty-six bedrooms, sixty-one bathrooms, nineteen sitting rooms, 127 acres (0.5 square km) of gardens, indoor and outdoor swimming pools, tennis courts, a movie theater, an airfield, and the world's largest private zoo . . . Morgan, an accomplished civil engineer, devised a gravity-based water delivery system from a nearby mountain. One highlight of the estate is the outdoor Neptune Pool, located near the edge of the hilltop, which offers an expansive vista of the mountains, ocean, and the main house. The Neptune Pool patio features an ancient Roman temple front transported wholesale from Europe and reconstructed at the site . . . As a consequence of Hearst's persistent design changes, the estate was never completed in his lifetime.

After watching the make-believe world that Hearst had created out of sheer vanity, the crux of Buddhist philosophy ran through my mind: Life is *anicca* (impermanent), *dukkha* (sorrow), and *anatta* (no-self). For sure, Hearst did not understand the first noble truth and mistook his ceaseless craving for wealth as the path to happiness.

At the Hearst Castle, the Department of Parks and Recreation gave us two complimentary tours. Janet Horton-Payne was our guide for the Enchanted Hill Tour. Hank Alviani was our guide for the La Pesa Grande Tour. They told us about the famous personalities who visited the place Hearst preferred to call "La Cuesta Encantada" or "the ranch": political heavyweights like Churchill, Coolidge, and Roosevelt; entertainment stars like Chaplin, Gable, Grant, and Hope; and other luminaries like Lindbergh.

We ate lunch after the tours. Then, we went to Sebastian's in San Simeon to buy a few mementos and headed south to the nearest city, San Luis Obispo, forty-three miles (69 km) away. We spent the afternoon visiting Mission SLO de Tolosa and County Historical Museum. We tarried at Mission Plaza, where we drank beer and listened to a singer.

We set up camp for the night at the nearby Morro Bay State Park Campground. Jim Hayes and his two youngest children, Jason and

Kelly, visited to greet us at the campground. Hayes was a contemporary of mine at the University of Minnesota. They took us to the top of Black Hill and the foot of Morro Rock.

Picture 61.2 While camping at Morro Bay State Park (July 31, 1983), the author (right) had a visit from Jim Hayes and his two youngest kids, Jason and Kelly. Hayes was a contemporary of the author at the University of Minnesota in the late 1960s.

Morro Bay to Tamalpais

Our day three destination was Mount Tamalpais State Park, 253 miles (407 km) northwest of Morro Bay. On this northward trip, we preferred to travel on US 101 or the scenic SR 1, the two coastal highways, rather than on Interstate 5, which runs through the heart of California's Central Valley.

We stopped at San Juan Bautista (pop 1,600), where we visited Mission SJB (1797), the largest Spanish mission church; and the SJB State Historic Park. We ate lunch at Santa Clara (pop 109,000), where we spent sometime at Marriott's Great America. Junius thoroughly enjoyed most things at the Kid Kingdom. Next, we stopped at the Stanford University campus in Palo Alto (pop 61,200). Then, via El Camino Real, we reached San Francisco (metro population 4.2 million) at sunset.

It was about 9:30 p.m. when we crossed the Golden Gate Bridge and entered the Pantoll Campground of Mount Tamalpais along Panoramic Highway. (I chose this campground because of my nostalgic fascination with nearby Sausalito and Mill Valley during the 1966 WPI tour.) We drove all the way up to the west peak of the mountain when a ranger led us to our campsite in very woody, scenic surroundings.

The primary feature of the park is the 2,571 ft. (784 m) Mount Tamalpais. The park contains mostly redwood and oak forests. The mountain itself covers around 25,000 acres (100 square km). The park has about 60 miles (97 km) of interconnected hiking trails.

We took it easy on Tuesday. Junius and I went for a hike along a trail close to our campsite prior to leaving the park at 11:00 a.m. Our destination for day four camping was Austin Creek State Recreation Area, about eighty-two miles (132 km) northwest on US 101.

On day four, we backtracked our way southeast to Sausalito (pop 7,400), where we visited the Bay Model Visitor Center (US Army Corps of Engineers), a three-dimensional hydraulic model of San Francisco Bay and Delta areas capable of simulating tides and currents, over 1.5 acres (6,100 sq m) in size. At Mill Valley (pop 13,600), we bought groceries and gasoline.

Around 3:00 p.m., we set off to Sonoma (pop 9,900), where we visited the Sonoma State Historic Site, including Toscano Hotel, Sonoma Barracks and Mission San Francisco Solano. In Santa Rosa (pop 154,200), we relaxed at Juilliard Park, which has a church built from a redwood tree; and walked across to see the Luther Burbank Memorial Gardens.

Then we turned west to see the extremely scenic Russian River Area on our way to the campground in Austin Creek SRA via Fulton, Trenton, Hilton, and Rio Nido. (On the elimination list for 2008 in Governor Schwarzenegger's attempts to solve California's budget crisis, ACSRA is located seven miles north of Guerneville on Armstrong Woods Road via the same entrance as Armstrong Redwoods State Natural Reserve.) We had to get to the campground through a narrow, winding, sandy road. We set up our tent facing Bullfrog Pond in a six-thousand-acre area of conifers, oaks, rolling hills, and meadows that contrasted with the dense redwood forests below. Yoke-Sim cooked a reasonable dinner. Junius and I walked around the lake.

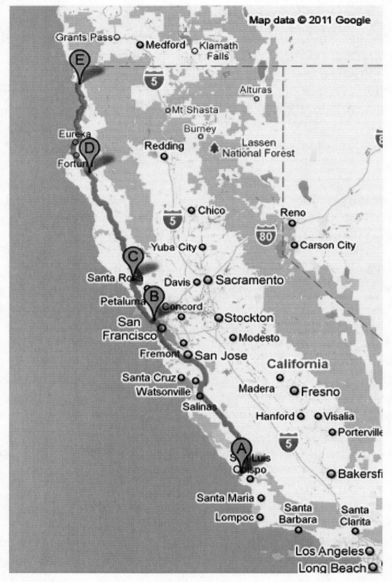

Map 61.1 Route of West Coast Tour. *A*, Morro Bay-San Simeon; *B*, Mount Tamalpais State Park; *C*, Austin Creek State Park; *D*, Burlington Campground of Humboldt Redwoods State Park; and *E*, Mill Creek Campground of Del Notre Coast Redwood State Park.

Redwoods Rendezvous

Austin Creek lies parallel to Sacramento in the Central Valley on the east. Our plan was to end day five at the Burlington Campground of the Humboldt Redwoods State Park, 208 miles (335 km) further north on US 101in Weott, California.

Having hobnobbed with the giant sequoias in the Sierras to the south, we were now encroaching into the redwood forests of California's northern coastal belt. In fact, we had just camped north of an 805-acre reserve of the Coast Redwood *(Sequoia sempervirens)*. The Parson Jones Tree is the tallest tree in the grove, measuring more than 310 feet (94 m) in height. Giant sequoias and Coast Redwood trees are closely related and they are both in the redwood family, *Taxodiaceae*. However, they are different species.

We left Austin Creek about 9:00 a.m. to absorb the scenic splendor along the Russian River resort area from Guerneville through Monte Rio to Jenner.

We stopped for rest at the Fort Ross State Historic Mark: Founded in 1812, Fort Ross was the largest single Russian trading center south of Alaska. It served as the southern headquarters for the hunting of sea otter. It also provided food supplies for the company's Alaskan operations. However, the operation never proved profitable. In 1841, John Sutter bought the fort from the Russians. Our next stop was at the Kruse Rhododendron State Reserve in Plantation. The reserve contains second-growth redwood, Douglas fir, grand firs, tanoaks, and a plethora of rhododendrons. We walked on the rhododendron loop.

We ate lunch at a vista point south of Elk (pop 208). At Little River (pop 412), we went to see the pygmy forest in Van Damme State Park where pygmy pine and cypress grow to a height of only two feet because of the nature of the infertile, acidic soil called podzol. In Mendocino (pop 824), a beautiful town with nineteenth-century architectural looks, we tarried at the Art Center on Little Lake Road. At Fort Bragg (pop 7,026), we saw the historical monument.

About 8:30 p.m., we reached the Burlington Campground of Humboldt Redwoods State Park, which lies almost parallel to Redding at the northern end of California's Central Valley. We drove the last fourteen miles from Phillipsville to our campground along the thirty-one-mile long Avenue of the Giants, which winds along the scenic Eel River and runs parallel to US 101. The two-lane avenue is renowned for its Coast redwoods that overshadow the road and surround the area.

Heading to Oregon Border

Next day (day six), we spent more time to learn about redwoods. In the morning, we went to the Humboldt RSP visitor center, where we learned that the 53,000-acre Humboldt RSP was established in 1921 with the dedication of the Raynal Bolling Memorial Grove, and that it was home to the tallest (demoted to fourth tallest in 2004) measured living redwood, the Stratosphere Giant (112.94 meters).

We set off to explore the park with a visit to the Founders Grove. Then we turned west on Creek Fats Road to Rockefeller Forest, where we walked around Flat Iron Tree, Giant Tree and Tallest Tree. (HRSP lost its 1600-year-old Dyerville Giant in March 1991.)

We continued driving north on the Avenue of the Giants and rejoined US 101 at Pepperwood. Our plan was to camp overnight at the Mill Creek Campground of Del Norte Coast Redwood State Park, 126 miles (203 km) further north, in Crescent City, close to the Oregon border. Del Norte CRSP, established in 1927, is a 6,400-acre (26 sq km) expanse with about 50 percent old-growth coast redwood and eight miles (13 km) of wild coastline. On the way to our destination, we stopped at Eureka (pop 26,100), Arcata (pop 17,300), and Klamath (pop 650).

In Eureka, we visited the Fort Humboldt State Historical Park, Clarke Memorial Museum, and Samoa Cookhouse Museum. We stopped for a late lunch at the Sequoia Park Zoo behind which was a grove of virgin redwoods.

Five miles north of Arcata, we stopped at the thirty-acre Azalea State Preserve, where we walked along a self-guided nature trail with emphasis on other plants of the north coast. We also had brief stops at Patrick's

Point State Park, from where we walked to see Mussel Rock on the beach; Dry Lagoon State Park; and Prairie Creek State Redwoods Park, where we went to see the Big Tree. At Klamath, we took a picture of the 35-foot (10-meter) statue of Babe the Blue Ox, the legendary sidekick of Paul Bunyan, at the entrance to Trees of Mystery Park. (*Note:* On November 20, 2007, the head of the statue fell off. The head has since been repaired.)

About 8:30 p.m. on day six, we reached our campground for the night at Del Norte CRSP in Crescent City. We were ready to cross the border next day for a six-day nostalgic excursion in Oregon, which was my home for more than a year in 1967-1968.

CHAPTER 62

California-Oregon: A Nostalgic Tour of the Oregon Coast

FRIDAY (AUGUST 5, 1983) morning, we—Junius, Yoke-Sim, and I—left the Mill Creek campground of Del Norte Coast Redwood State Park for our Oregon excursion. We headed nine miles (14 km) northwest to Crescent City (pop 7,300), the last California city before crossing the border to Oregon.

On the way, we stopped at the Rellim Demonstration Forest, where we walked along a nature trail to learn about plants—an activity that Junius appeared to enjoy. We learnt that Lost Monarch, the largest known Coastal redwood by volume, thrives in "The Grove of the Giants" in the nearby Jedediah Smith Redwoods State Park. But no one in our company wanted to say hello to the Lost Giant perhaps because we thought we had met bigger giants at the Kings Canyon-Sequoia National Park.

Crescent City, founded by gold-seekers in 1851, got its name from the horn-shaped bay. Point St George, the headland immediately north of the harbor, protects the town from the cold.north winds. The paddle steamer "Brother Jonathan" sank off this coast in 1885 causing the death of 265 people. We visited the Brother Jonathan Cemetery (Ninth Street, Pebble Beach), their burial place. A further disaster, a tidal wave, destroyed a large part of the town in 1964.

Before leaving Crescent City, we went to the Point St George area and drove south to get a good view of the old lighthouse at Battery Point established in 1856. The lighthouse is a forty-five-feet white cylindrical brick tower built on a square granite house.

Crossing to Oregon Coast

Only the Buddhist concept of *bhava* (re-becoming) could metaphorically convey a sense of my emotions and gratification as we passed Khoonkhwuttunne on the California border to Oregon, which was my home for more than one year from 1967 to 1968. Ensconced in the Willamette Valley, I sharpened my journalism skills at the Eugene *Register-Guard* and studied journalism to get my master's degree from the University of Oregon.

I felt that my daughter Carmel, then a fetus (to be born on January 31, 1984), was also a participant in this nostalgic excursion to Oregon. The trip offered me the opportunity to introduce my family to "my-home-away-from-home" although I had not made arrangements for meetings with old friends and acquaintances. Time was in short supply. Our schedule did not contain even an overnight stay in Eugene, where I lived both as an intern and a graduate student.

Oregon has a current population of 3.8 million although it ranks ninth in the United States in terms of land area (98,466 sq miles or 255,026 sq km). Its population in the late 1960s was about two million, which rose to 2.6 million in 1980. Thus, although Oregon increased its population by 90 percent over the last forty years, it remains a small state in terms of the total US population of 308 million.

But despite its population size, a mere 1.2 percent of the US population, Oregon has played a prominent role in federal governance because the US Senate representation allocates two seats per state irrespective of population size. Thus, I can still remember how Senator Wayne Morse from Oregon (in office from 1945 to 1969) became a national icon among those who protested against the Vietnam War in the 1960s. Morse set a record for performing the longest one-person filibuster in the history of the Senate.

I owed plenty of gratitude to Oregonians who subsidized my graduate education at the University of Oregon. I returned the favor by giving an annual donation to UO during my professorial career.

These characteristics of Oregon and much more went through my mind during this brief excursion, which I also turned into an academic excursus to attend the annual convention of the Association for Education in Journalism and Mass Communication at the Oregon State University in Corvallis, August 7-9, 1983. Thus, as usual, I combined business with pleasure (camping and recreation).

On the Oregon Coast

This was my first experience of travelling to Oregon through its southwestern coastal belt route on US101. I took a photo of the border crossing and wrote in my diary, "Oregon always seems to be friendlier." The first Oregon coastal town to greet us was Brookings (pop 6,500), where we stopped at the (US Forest Service) Chetco Ranger Station for Siskiyou National Forest (renamed Rogue River-Siskiyou National Forest in 2004). We learned that the 55.5-mile long Chetco Wild and Scenic River drops from 3,700 ft to sea level before it empties into the Pacific Ocean between Brookings and Harbor.

From Brookings, we proceeded northwest to Harris Beach State Park to eat our lunch while looking at Goat Island, a sanctuary for migratory birds.

Driving further north, just south of the town of Gold Beach (pop 1,900), we stopped at Cape Sebastian State Park, a precipitous headland rising 700 ft above tide. It provided great scenic vistas. The sheer beauty of the spot provoked me to walk all the way down to the beach and climb up again along the winding trail. It was my adventure of the day that took more than one hour. I ate berries on the way. So I have good memories of Gold Beach.

North of Port Orford (pop 1,200), we visited Cape Blanco to observe fossilized shells for which it is well known. We saw the lighthouse, and we walked to the beach from the state park. We also stopped at the Hughes House built in 1898.

On arrival in Bandon (pop 3,235) about 7:00 p.m., we bought gasoline—much cheaper than in California—to rejuvenate our vehicle. We also bought a bottle of cold duck wine to drink with our dinner.

Then, we checked in at Bullards Beach State Park, where we set up our tent to spend the night. Yoke-Sim, now become accustomed to preparing meals that befit nomadic living, prepared a tasty dinner that went well with the cold duck.

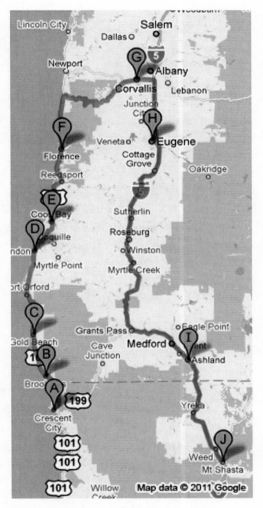

Map 62.1 Route of the Oregon excursion.

For the $9 we had to pay for our campsite (including a nonresident surcharge of $2), the facilities were much better than in the California state parks. Although we traveled only 118 miles (190 km) during the whole day, our emphasis was on leisurely enjoyment, not on the distance covered.

On Saturday (August 6) morning, we went to see the Coquille River Lighthouse, the so-called "Navigator's Nightmare," at the southern end of the spit at Bullards Beach. Then, driving twenty-seven miles (44 km) further north, off US 101 via West Beaver Road and Seven Devils Road, we reached Cape Arrago State Park, the southernmost of three contiguous state parks—with Sunset Bay in the north and Shore Acres in the middle—located in a small beautiful coastal peninsula. Cape Arrago is the recognized domain of Oregon sea lions. The beautiful botanic gardens in Shore Acres adds to the pleasure of those who visit the cape to watch the wily sea lions dance and prance in their natural habitat probably shouting "obscenities" at the gullible humans ashore. (I was on the selfsame spot sixteen years ago when a local woman, Mary Johnston, gave me a tour of the Oregon Coast. See further below.)

We left the sea lions alone to proceed twenty-five miles (40 km) further northeast via Charleston to rejoin US 101. Immediately thereafter, we stopped at North Bend (pop 9,600), where we visited the Coos-Curry Historical Museum in Simpson Park. Then, heading south to Coos Bay (pop 16,300), we joined the industrial tour of the House of Myrtlewood—a demonstration of the intricate processes involved in converting myrtle logs into a variety of sophisticated by products.

The day's adventure was our fifty-mile (80 km) roundtrip detour to Golden and Silver Falls State Park in the Coast Range. We reached the park heading northeast on Coos River Road or Highway. Hiking trails wind through scenic canyons to each of the waterfalls, which plunge over sheer rock cliffs to moss-covered boulders 100 ft below (see photo). We ate our lunch in the picnic area along the banks of the Glen and Silver creeks shaded by large alder, maple, and Oregon myrtle trees. Junius and Yoke-Sim confessed their thorough joy of hiking to the two waterfalls.

Back in Coos Bay, we headed for Florence (pop 8,300), fifty miles to the north on US 101. I reminisced nostalgically about this stretch of the highway whereon I had been before some sixteen years ago—April 1-3, 1967—when I was the guest of a Florence family, Stuart and Mary Johnston. The Johnstons were highly impressed with my views published in the Eugene *Register-Guard* that they invited me to visit with them for an in-depth conversation. Stuart, a dentist, was the mayor of Florence at the time.

Picture 62.1 Yoke-Sim watches the beauty of Silver Falls at the Golden and Silver Falls State Park, 25 miles northeast of Coos Bay on the Oregon Coast (August 6, 1983).

On that occasion, Mary Johnston took me to Coos Bay, introduced me to librarian Ruth Watson, bought me lunch at Pony Village, and took me to Shore Acres, Sunset Bay, and Cape Arrago—the identical spots that I introduced to Junius and Yoke-Sim on this trip.

On the way, we also stopped at Umpqua Lighthouse State Park, south of Reedsport (pop 4,400), to see the twenty-feet sand dunes and visit the Coastal Visitor Center.

However, I did not have the contact information on the Johnstons to arrange for a reunion. "Thank you and au revoir, Johnstons for giving me the Coos Bay experience."

Our destination for the day was Corvallis (pop 54,880), ninety-seven miles from Florence. We continued north on US 101, turned east on SR 34 at Waldport to cut through Siuslaw National Forest, and then headed northeast to reach Corvallis at 8:30 p.m.

We checked in for three nights at Bloss Hall on Oregon State University campus so I could focus on the business aspect of this trip, viz., attending the three-day AEJMC Convention, where I expected to see some of my erstwhile professors and graduate colleagues from Oregon and Minnesota. Because we missed the convention buffet, we had to eat dinner in the town. We also found out that our vehicle had run out of gas.

Corvallis lies in the Willamette Valley roughly midway between Salem (pop 54,000), the state capital; and Eugene (population 154,620), the state's second largest city. More than 42 percent of Oregon's population lives in the Portland metropolitan area.

I reminisced about the several trips I made to Corvallis and Salem with Lloyd Paseman, who covered the education beat for the *Register-Guard* in 1967.

The convention offered me the opportunity to introduce my wife and son to several of my old buddies and professors during the Minnesota and Oregon alumni receptions, the historical tour of Corvallis conducted by historian Kenneth Mumford, and at the salmon barbecue dinner for delegates at Avery Park. I was privileged to dine with my Minnesota mentor-professor emeritus (the late) Raymond B. Nixon and his wife at the salmon barbecue.

On Last Day in Oregon

Wednesday (August 10) morning, we left Corvallis for Ashland (pop 21,630), the home of the renowned Oregon Shakespeare Festival, 223 miles (360 km) south on Interstate five at the California border. We had bought tickets to see the Shakespearean play *Much Ado About Nothing* at 8:30 p.m.

Thus, when we arrived in Eugene at 9:45 a.m., I had to be very selective about people, places, and memories that I wanted my wife and son to meet, see, and remember. We planned to leave Eugene by 5:00 p.m.

My first priority was to show them the School of Journalism (the Eric W. Allen Hall), where I studied for my master's degree in journalism (see photo). Two faculty members from my era—professors (the late) Roy P. Nelson and John Crawford—chatted with us.

Picture 62.2 The writer and his son at the University of Oregon on August 10, 1983. Behind them is Eric W. Allen Hall, the location of the School of Journalism and Communication, where the writer was a graduate student in 1967-1968

My second priority was to show my family the Register-Guard office, where I did my WPI internship, in downtown Eugene. Journalist Lloyd Paseman welcomed us and explained the changes that have occurred since my internship. I also met senior journalists Ed Kenyon and Dean Rea, who was also a teacher of mine at Allen Hall.

Although I intended to give my family a good orientation to the campus, this was not possible because of the changes over the preceding fifteen years. Even with the help of a map, I was finding it difficult to find my way.

We ate lunch at the Erb Memorial Union, which had been expanded beautifully to include a skyway lounge. I did not forget to show them the library, where I spent much of my time. I also took them to the Lane County Pioneer Museum and the Chamber of Commerce in the city.

We left Eugene as scheduled, ate dinner at Roseburg, and arrived in Ashland just in time for the play. "Much Ado About Nothing" went on until 11:15 p.m., when we went to camp overnight at Glenyan KOA on SR 66. Our campsite was close to Neil Creek.

Thursday (August 11) morning, we returned to Ashland city to have a closer look at the theaters of the Oregon Shakespeare Festival, which began in 1935. Since then, it has staged Shakespeare's complete canon three times, completing the first cycle in 1958 with a production of *Troilus and Cressida* and completing the second and third cycles through the works in 1978 and 1997.

We left Ashland, Oregon, for Stockton, California, 341 miles (549 km) to the south on Interstate 5, just before noon. We drove through the northern half of the Central Valley, stopping at Shasta Lake for lunch. We reached Stockton at 6:15 p.m. and stayed overnight at Jan Mullen's home.

The next morning (Friday, August 12), we entered Yosemite National Park.

CHAPTER 63

California:
Etching Carmel in Monterey

MY MOTHER, SEVENTY, arrived in Los Angeles on December 4, 1983, after a stay with my youngest sister Nayana in London to supervise the closure of our year in Fullerton and to help out my wife Yoke-Sim, who was in the last month or two of her pregnancy. Junius, Yoke-Sim, and I were at the Los Angeles International Airport to welcome her. Mother brought gifts for each of us. We brought her home (Larry Taylor's condo in Wellesley Court, Fullerton, that we were occupying during the exchange year) about 9:30 p.m.

Mother recovered from her travel-related headache the next day. She was delighted to be in the company of her grandson Junius. Over the next few days, Junius took upon himself the task of orienting his grandma (*Aachhi*) to the layout and facilities of our enclosed community and often accompanied her to the nearby Gemco Shopping Center. One Friday night (December 9), we honored her with a dinner at Good Earth Restaurant in Brea. Three of our East Indian neighbors at Wellesley Court—Razeek and Cheryl Alibullah and Ebrahim Unwallah—joined us at the dinner.

Despite her reluctance to travel because of advancing age, I arranged in Mother's honor an excursion of Carmel and Monterey Peninsula (three nights), San Francisco and Bay Area (four nights), and Santa Barbara (one night). We had skipped these areas during our two long summer trips.

We agreed to terminate the Fullerton year step by step: Junius and Yoke-Sim would return to our home in Australia at the end of December so Yoke-Sim would encounter no problems in giving birth to Carmel the next month. Mother would stay with me until I completed the teaching session at Fullerton College and leave the United States on January 27, 1984. I would disembark in Hawaii for a weeklong excursion, while Mother would fly directly to Australia to join Junius and Yoke-Sim.

Carmel Connection

Now, let me explain how Carmel got her name.

Carmel was a fetus, just forty-five days pending her birth in Rockhampton, Australia, when we (including Junius and my mother) spent eight days in the Monterey Peninsula and Bay Area in mid-December 1983—almost at the end of our Fullerton year. I had visited the Monterey Peninsula in late 1966, during my World Press Institute year, to interview bare-footed folksinger Joan Baez at her Carmel retreat. I fell in love with the serenity, beauty, and enchantment of Carmel on that occasion. I wanted my entire family to experience a similar sensation by visiting the selfsame spot on earth.

Map 63.1 The scenic route from *A* (King City) to *C* (Carmel-by-the-Sea) via *B* (Carmel Valley). *D*, Monterey State Historical Park; *E*, Point Lobos; *F*, Big Sur.

SHELTON A. GUNARATNE

The thirty-six-mile (58-km) Carmel River, which originates in the Santa Lucia Mountains, flows northwest through the Carmel Valley and winds its way to disgorge itself to the Pacific Ocean at Carmel-by-the-Sea (simply called Carmel). Each of us experienced varying degrees of enchantment as we drove on a Saturday afternoon (December 17) along the sixty-mile stretch of County Road G16 that cuts through the Carmel Valley from just north of King City, California, to Carmel-by-the-Sea.

We reached Carmel Valley Village (pop 4,700) about 4:30 p.m., stopped at the post office, and visited the shopping square. We arrived in Carmel (current population 4,100) after dark and checked in at Motel 6 (2124 Fremont St.), just north of Monterey Pines, for three nights.

Located on the southeast corner of the Monterey Peninsula, Carmel had a reputation as an artists' colony when I first stopped there. The town has had several mayors who were artists or actors—e.g., Herbert Heron, Perry Newberry, and Clint Eastwood.

We spent most of Sunday morning assiduously attempting to see all the attractions along the Monterey Peninsula coast—Fisherman's Wharf, built in 1846; Cannery Row, made famous by novelist John Steinbeck; St Mary's-by-the-Sea, Lovers Point Park and Monarch butterfly sanctuary in Pacific Grove; Point Pinos Lighthouse Reservation, etc. Then, via Asilomar State Beach, we entered the scenic 17-Mile Drive at the Lighthouse Gate ($4 admission per car) to see the gated community—a form of residential community or housing estate containing strictly controlled entrances for pedestrians, bicycles, and automobiles—of Pebble Beach owned and operated by the Pebble Beach Corporation. Pebble Beach, with fewer than five thousand relatively affluent residents, is well known for its seven eighteen-hole golf courses. We left the 17-Mile Drive at the Carmel Gate.

We topped the day with a visit to Big Sur, forty miles south of Carmel on scenic SR1. It is the area where the St. Lucia Mountains rise abruptly from the Pacific Ocean with the Cone Peak ascending nearly a mile above sea level. We drove up to the point where landslides of 1983 blocked the highway. The awesome cliffs of Big Sur overwhelmed our senses. However, the beauty of the place came at a price—the danger of landslides.

On Monday, our third day in Carmel, we spent most the morning at the Point Lobos Ecological Reserve, a marine-protected patch of the Pacific coast just south of Carmel. It contains a number of hiking trails, many next to the ocean, and a smaller number of beaches. I walked on the North Shore Trail from Camry Point to Cypress Cove, where I saw the Old Veteran Cypress. Then all the family—Junius, Yoke-Sim, and my mother—joined me to walk on the Cypress Grove Trail and the Sea Lion Point Trail. Finally, I took the Bird Island Trail through China Cove and returned to the reserve entrance along the South Plateau Trail. The ability to exercise ourselves in scenic splendor was another positive impression of Carmel conjured in our minds.

Just north of Point Lobos, we stopped at Mission San Carlos Borromeo de Carmelo (Carmel Mission), the headquarters of the original Alta California Missions headed by the Rev. Junípero Serra from 1770 until his death in 1784. Just west of the mission, we visited the Tor House and Hawk Tower built by poet Robinson Jeffers in 1919. *The Purse Seine*, a poem written by Jeffers dwelling on the fishing industry, provides an example of the impact of Carmel on Jeffers's work. Prior to eating lunch at the Carmel Plaza in downtown Carmel, we also stopped by to appreciate the Carmel Beach City Park, Carmel Art Association and Forest Theater. In the afternoon, we delved further into the history of the area by joining a guided tour of the Monterey State Historical Park, which includes seventeen contributing buildings (e.g., Casa Sobaranes, Casa del Oro, Pacific House, Custom House, Stevenson House, etc). The site became a National Historic Landmark in 1970.

Although we had to say good-bye to Carmel on Tuesday (December 20) to tour San Francisco over the next four days, we spent most of Tuesday also in the Monterey area.

We started the day with an early visit to Jacks Peak Park, where we spent almost an hour hiking the nature trail (while my mother remained in the car). Then, we returned to the historical district for the 10:00 a.m. tour of the R. L. Stevenson House (at 530 Houston St.) R. L. Eugene, our guide, filled us with information for forty-five-minutes and ended his spiel after showing us the second-floor room that Stevenson, a Scottish writer, rented in autumn 1879 to court his future wife Mary Osbourne. While living in this room in what was then called the French Hotel,

Stevenson wrote articles for the local Monterey newspaper that captured the essence of the "Old Pacific Capital."

Thereafter, we walked to see the Royal Presidio Chapel originally built in 1770 by Padre Serra; Colton Hall, where the California constitution was written in 1849; Monterey Institute of Foreign Studies and assorted venues. At the Presidio of Monterey, we saw the remains of Fort Mervine, near the J. D. Sloat Monument. From there, we went to Dennis the Menace Playground to eat lunch and let Junius amuse himself to his heart's content.

We left for San Francisco in the afternoon thinking of Carmel as a potential retirement retreat. Since medical evidence attested that Yoke-Sim would give birth to a daughter, made in California but to be delivered in Queensland, we followed the Middle Path by naming her Carmel Maya (after Buddha's mother; Sirima [Ratwatte] was not an option) to remember one of the most enchanted spots in the world. Thereby, we artfully tried to show the potential of East-West coexistence, not antagonism.

Note: Similarly, I have explained in part 1 *Journey of a Journalist* why we gave our son the name Junius Asela (after a modern Sinhala politician who showed much promise in 1980 but disappointed his people as he grew old, and a second century BC Sinhala king).

CHAPTER 64

California:
From Monterey to San Francisco

THE SAN FRANCISCO Bay Area (comprising nine counties, 101 cities, and 8,000 sq miles or 22,000 sq km) is home to some 7.4 million people. But the combined city-county of San Francisco (occupying a land area of 47 sq miles or 121 sq km) has a population of only about 810,000. It is, therefore, the fourth most populous city in California—after Los Angeles (3.8 million), San Diego (1.3 million), and San Jose (1 million).

I first visited San Francisco in late December 1966—exactly seventeen years before—as a World Press Institute fellow. I had revisited it several times. Therefore, I arranged the current (1983) trip primarily for the benefit of Junius and Yoke-Sim. Mother would have been happier relaxing in the condo in Fullerton rather than going through the hassles of imposed sightseeing. She became a globetrotter because her children and grandchildren were dispersed in Australia, England, Germany, Sri Lanka, and the United States and not out of geographical curiosity.

On the Way

After leaving Monterey on Tuesday (December 20) afternoon, we took the coast-hugging scenic SR1 to reach San Francisco, 126 miles (203 km) northwest of Carmel. At the northern point of Monterey Bay, we stopped briefly at Capitola (pop 10,000) to admire the Begonia Gardens. Capitola is the town that thousands of birds, mostly sooty shearwaters affected by domoic acid poisoning, attacked in 1961. Alfred Hitchcock, "the Master of Suspense," who was a frequent visitor to the nearby city of Santa Cruz (pop 56,000) used this unusual attack as the factual basis for his 1963 movie, *The Birds*, overtly based on the 1952 novella *The Birds* by Daphne de Maurier.

Although the Santa Cruz Beach Boardwalk was not in operation during weekdays in winter, yet we stopped there to get a close look at California's oldest surviving amusement park dating back to 1915. The Giant Dipper roller coaster, one of the best-known wooden coasters in the world, dominates the eastern end of the boardwalk. All of us enjoyed walking on the boardwalk along Beach Street.

Map 64.1 From *A* (Monterey) to *E* (San Francisco) via *B* (Capitola), *C* (Santa Cruz), and *D* (Half Moon Bay). Return to Fullerton via *F* (Salinas) and *G* (Santa Barbara).

Picture 64.1 The Giant Dipper roller coaster, one of the best-known wooden coasters in the world, dominates the eastern end of the boardwalk. All of us—including the author, his mother, and son (pictured)—enjoyed walking on the boardwalk along Beach Street (December 20 1983).

Back on SR1, we drove fifty miles further north to Half Moon Bay (pop 11,400), and another thirty miles (48 km) to San Francisco, which we reached about 6:00 p.m. We had booked accommodation with Trinity Inn. However, when we tried to register, a man told us that the inn has closed down and directed us to Adelaide Inn (5 Adelaide Place). We complied. The charge was $35 per night with $3.50 extra to park our car at the Turk Street Garage. (Located close to Union Square, the inn bears the current name Adelaide Hostel and the address 5, Isadora Duncan Lane.)

Thumbnail of Frisco

Wikipedia gives the following thumbnail sketch of San Francisco (derided as Frisco):*San Francisco is a popular international tourist destination renowned for its steep rolling hills, eclectic mix of Victorian and modern architecture, and famous landmarks, including the Golden Gate Bridge, Alcatraz Island, the cable cars, Coit Tower, and Chinatown. The city is*

SHELTON A. GUNARATNE

also known for its diverse, cosmopolitan population, including large and long-established Asian American and LGBT communities. It is the second most densely populated city in the United States, behind only New York City and from the time of the Gold Rush until the 1920s it was the largest city in California in terms of population. It was also one of the first cities in California to be incorporated, and is the only consolidated city-county in the state of California.

Wikipedia, launched on January 15, 2001, is a creation of this century. But its sketch of the city is applicable to what San Francisco was like in 1983, as well. During our five-day sojourn, we managed to uncover most of the unique features and characteristics of the city adumbrated above. Except on day one (Wednesday, December 21), when Mother and Junius decided to rest in the hotel room, all of us together uncovered the city.

While fact-checking this essay, I noticed a glaring discrepancy between everyone's desire to make San Francisco his or her preferred habitat and the city's loss of some 45,000 residents between my first visit in 1966 and the current in 1983.

Uncovering Northeast

On day one (Wednesday), when Yoke-Sim and I set off on a self-guided walking tour, what we basically did was to orient ourselves to the northeast section of San Francisco that included Union Square, Chinatown, Jackson Street Historical District, North Beach (tenderloin area), Telegraph Hill (Coit Tower), Fisherman's Wharf, and Embarcadero (the eastern waterfront road of the Port of San Francisco, along the San Francisco Bay; roughly meaning "place of embarkation").

Because climbing up Telegraph Hill would have been too tedious, we took a no. 39 bus from Washington Square to Pioneer Park atop Telegraph Hill, where Lillie Hitchcock Coit built the Coit Tower in 1933. Architects Arthur Brown Jr. and Henry Howard designed the art deco tower, 210 feet (64 m) of unpainted reinforced concrete, with murals by twenty-six different artists and numerous assistants. We had a 360-degree view of San Francisco from the tower.

Fisherman's Wharf is another indispensable landmark of San Francisco. It is best known for being the location of Pier 39, San Francisco Maritime National Historical Park, the Cannery Shopping Center, Ghirardelli Square, a Ripley's Believe it or Not museum, the Musée Mécanique, the Wax Museum at Fisherman's Wharf, Forbes Island and restaurants, and stands that serve fresh seafood, most notably Dungeness crab and clam chowder served in a sourdough bread bowl.

Picture 64.2: Fisherman's Wharf is another indispensable landmark of San Francisco. Yoke-Sim stands at the entrance to the wharf (December 21, 1983).

Alcatraz Island (The Rock) lies in the San Francisco Bay, 1.5 miles (2.4 km) offshore from San Francisco. It has served as a lighthouse, a military fortification, a military prison, and a federal prison until 1963. Later, in 1972, Alcatraz became a national recreation area and received land-marking designations in 1976 and 1986. Now, the National Park Service operates the island as a historic part of the Golden Gate National Recreation Area. Although we did not take the ferry ride to Alcatraz, we viewed it from the museum ship Eureka when we visited the Hyde Street Pier off the Embarcadero.

Family Waking Tour

On day two (Thursday), all of us went on a walking tour of the city in spite of the continual drizzle and the grey skies. The highlight was a tour of the Old US Mint, which opened in 1854 to accommodate the Gold Rush (1848-1855) and moved into the current premises in 1974. My mother was extraordinarily impressed with the visual delight of hobnobbing with stacks of gold bars. At the Civic Center, we joined a tour of the magnificent City Hall (1915) with its soaring rotunda constructed of California granite to look like the US Capitol. Our tour guide was a Chinese American woman, who took us to see the chamber of the board of supervisors and explained the significance of the artwork. She permitted us to peep into the opera house, the symphony hall and the civic auditorium.

We started the day with a visit to St Mary's Cathedral of the Assumption, a structure made of Italian marble, on Cathedral Hill; then tarried at the Japan Center (*Nihonmachi*). We closed the day with a car trip to Mission San Francisco de Asis (built in 1776), the oldest surviving structure in the city. We stopped at the top of Twin Peaks to see how the city looked like on a rainy evening. Then, we drove to Sacramento Street (between Broderick and Cherry) and Union Street (between Fillmore and Van Ness) to see an abundance of Victorian architecture.

To celebrate Mother's visit to San Francisco, we treated ourselves to a sumptuous Indian-style dinner at Pasand Lounge (1875 Quincy St.).

CHAPTER 65

California: Uncovering San Francisco with Family

Uncovering Golden Gate

DESPITE RAINY WEATHER, we spent most of day three (Friday) at the 1,017-acre rectangular-shaped (0.5 miles x 3 miles) Golden Gate Park, located about four miles south of the Golden Gate Bridge, a suspension bridge spanning the Golden Gate, the opening of the San Francisco Bay into the Pacific Ocean. We had already crossed this bridge on our camping trip to Mount Tamalpais in August. Built in 1937, it has been ranked fifth on the *List of America's Favorite Architecture* by the American Institute of Architects.

However, our focus on this occasion was the park, not the bridge. We visited the park's main features: Conservatory of Flowers, a glass building erected in 1879 a la Kew Gardens. (Since our visit, a severe storm shattered its glass structure in 1995. It was reopened in 2003.); Kezar Stadium, equipped with 59,000 seats, that hosted many athletic events (but since our visit, the original stadium was demolished in 1989 and replaced with a modern 9,044-seat facility.); and San Francisco Botanical Garden at Strybing Arboretum, where we went on an exploratory tour through the fifty-five-acre expanse of special collections—Demonstration Gardens, Biblical Garden, Garden of Fragrance, Zellerbach Garden of Perennials, Moon-viewing Garden, Succulent Garden, Redwood Trail, Garden of California Native Plants, Conifer Garden, and so on.

For us, the primary attraction of the park was the Music Concourse Area, particularly the California Academy of Sciences—one of the ten largest museums of natural history in the world—where we spent much of our time studying the exhibits in Wattis Hall of Man, Steinhart Aquarium, Fish Roundabout, North American Bird, and Mammal halls, Fossil Hall, Mineral Hall, Simson African Hall, Science Hall, and Lovell White Hall. (In 2010, general admission to CAS was $25 with discounts for seniors, students, and children.) We don't know to what extent Junius benefitted from these exhibits. But we certainly know that he enjoyed the visit to the nearby children's playground.

Since our visit, the park has added another main attraction: the AIDS Memorial Grove, established in 1996. Other attractions included Stow Lake, Spreckels Lake, Golden Gate Park Stadium, Bison Paddock, Windmills, Beach Chalet, and Roadways.

We left the academy at 3:00 p.m. and drove around the entire park although it was raining cats and dogs. At the western edge of the park, we turned north on Point Lobos Avenue to enter Sutro Heights Park, where we visited Cliff House to watch Seal Rocks to the west and Sutro Baths to the north.

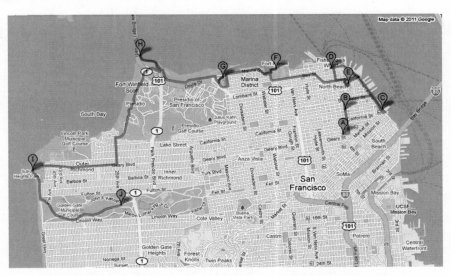

Map 65.1 Main attractions in San Francisco. *A*, Union Square; *B*, Chinatown (Buddha Lounge); *C*, Embarcadero (Ferry Building); *D*, Fisherman's Wharf; *E*, Coit Tower (Telegraph Hill); *F*, Fort Mason; *G*, Exploratorium; *H*, Fort Point National Historic Center (underneath the south-end of Golden Gate Bridge); *I*, Seal Rocks and Sutro Baths; *J*, Golden Gate Park. Alcatraz (not in the map) is visible from the north shore.

Sutro Baths were a privately owned swimming pool complex opened to the public in 1896 by entrepreneur Adolph Sutro, who was mayor of San Francisco from 1894 to 1896. He also built a seven-story Victorian chateau (nicknamed The Gingerbread Palace) on the cliffs next to the baths. But these material representations of *tanha* (desire or craving) could not defy the truths of *anicca* (impermanence) and *dukkha* (unsatisfactoriness). A fire destroyed the baths and the palace in September 1907. The rebuilt baths faced the same fate again in 1966. Only the ruins of the baths remain.

North of the baths, we drove to see the USS San Francisco Memorial at Land's End. Then, we stopped at the nearby Palace of the Legion of Honor in Lincoln Park for a quick look at the exhibits. Thereafter, we crossed San Francisco from west to east along Lincoln Boulevard and Lombard Street to see the "Crookedest (most winding) Street in the World"—the one-way section of Lombard Street on Russian Hill between Hyde and Leavenworth streets. Here, the roadway has eight sharp turns (or switchbacks) instituted in 1922 to reduce the hill's natural 27 percent grade, which was too steep for most vehicles to climb. The speed limit in this section is 5 mph (8 km/h).

Next, we stopped in Chinatown, just to the northeast of our hotel, to purchase our dinner. San Francisco's Chinatown is the oldest Chinatown in North America. Established in the 1840s, it became the starting point and home for thousands of Chinese immigrants. Its shops, restaurants, and attractions draw more tourists annually to San Francisco than the Golden Gate Bridge. On day one (Wednesday), during our (restricted to Yoke-Sim and me) self-guiding walking tour of San Francisco, we had already ambled along Grant Street to see the heart of Chinatown and visited the Chinese Culture Center and the Chinese Historical Society of America.

From Chinatown, all of us drove to Nob Hill to visit the free Cable Car Museum (1201 Mason St.) because San Francisco is synonymous with its cable cars. Cable cars are not the same as San Francisco's trolleys, which operate on Market Street. The San Francisco cable car system is the world's last permanently operational manually operated cable car system—a transport network operated by the San Francisco Municipal Railway. Cable cars operate on two routes from downtown near Union

Square to Fisherman's Wharf, and a third route along California Street. Although my mother recalled the tramcars and trolley buses that cluttered the streets of Colombo in the 1950s, she did not wish to ride a cable car in San Francisco because of the high fares.

Picture 65.1 We—including the author, his mother and son Junius (pictured)—climbed up to the top of Fort Point National Historic Site (December 24, 1983) to have a very close view of the Golden Gate Bridge, as well as of Alcatraz. This proved to be an unexpectedly interesting site and sight.

Uncovering North Side

Day 4 (Saturday) was another rainy day. Undeterred, all of us set forth to explore the north shore of San Francisco. Because no visit to San Francisco would be complete without seeing the Embarcadero,

Fisherman's Wharf, and Alcatraz, we revisited the locations to provide a sense of these features to Mother and Junius who missed them on day one. Then, we moved on to Fort Mason, since 1976 a part of the Golden Gate National Recreation Area and walked down to see the former barracks transformed into a regional cultural center. From here, we had an outer view of the Jeremiah O'Brian berthed at Pier 3.

Moving on Marine Drive, our next stop was the Palace of Fine Arts (3301 Lyon St.), the only remnant of the 1915 Panama-Pacific Exhibition. Here, we were pleased to find the delights of the Exploratorium (current general admission $14 with various discounts), a science museum with more than 500 (more than 1,000 in 2010) interactive exhibits. I was most interested in the exhibits on language development. Both Mother and Junius enjoyed the machines, the lights, and the sounds. We spent two hours in the facility, set up in 1969 at the behest of physicist Frank Oppenheimer.

Our next stop was the Presidio Army Museum housed in the Old Station Hospital, built in 1859. From there, we went to see the Fort Point National Historic Site, a granite fortification built in 1861 under the southern end of Golden Gate Bridge, along the lines of Fort Sumter. We climbed up to the top of the fort to have a very close view of the famous bridge, as well as of Alcatraz. This proved to be an unexpectedly interesting site/sight.

We left the Presidio to see Temple Emanu-el (2 Lake St.), a synagogue, built in 1925 with a 150-ft. orange-hued dome. Our last stop was Chinatown, where we bought our dinner and a few gifts.

Grand Hurrah

Our tour of San Francisco came to an end on day five (Christmas Sunday). We checked out of Adelaide Inn, which turned out to be an inexpensive lodge right in the heart of downtown. We spent the morning in Chinatown. I showed my family the location of Buddha Lounge (901 Grant St.) about which I created a ha-ho in Sri Lanka in 1966-67 because the association of Buddha with an alcoholic establishment is nothing short of sacrilege. Maybe the Rajapakse Government should take up the matter directly with San Francisco Chinatown.

Picture 65.2 The author (with his mother and son) in front of Buddha Lounge at 901 Grant St. in San Francisco's Chinatown (December 25, 1983). He asserts that the association of Buddha with an alcoholic establishment is nothing short of sacrilege.

We left Chinatown about 11:00 a.m. Overcast skies and continuing rain chased us as we drove south. We stopped in Salinas for lunch and arrived in Santa Barbara about 7:00 p.m. We ate a buffet dinner at the Holiday Inn in Goleta, where Don Voegele, a colleague of mine at Fullerton College, directed us to his brother's studio apartment (at 590 Ribera St., Goleta) to settle down for the night.

The next morning, Voegele gave us a brief tour of Santa Barbara, primarily for Mother's benefit. We left Santa Barbara for Los Angeles about 1:00.p.m. To make Mother happy, we took her to the Buddhist Vihara (1147 N. Beachwood Drive) in Los Angeles. The priests, Ahangama Dhammarama Thera and D. Gnanissara Thera welcomed us and administered *Pansil*. At the temple, I was delighted to have a conversation with Sri Lankan journalist Walter Jayawardhana.

We were back in Fullerton that evening.

CHAPTER 66

California: A Taste of San Diego—Say Hello to Wild Animals and Nudists

FULLERTON (POP 126,000) was the base for my extensive travels on the West Coast during my Fullerton year (1983 through January 1984). It was my most extensive travel year bar for 1966-67, the year of my World Press Institute Fellowship. I took advantage of my exchange year at Fullerton College to visit and enjoy almost all nooks and corners of California that I adjudged worthy of a visit.

Fullerton is twenty-five miles (40 km) southeast of downtown Los Angeles and eleven miles (18 km) north-northwest of Santa Ana, the Orange County seat.

San Diego, just hundred miles southeast of Fullerton, was a must in my travel plans. In fact, I visited San Diego four times during the Fullerton year alone: first, during the weekend of July 9-10; second, during the weekend of August 27-29; third, on our roundtrip to Baja (Lower) California, November 10-13; and fourth, on a visit to California State University on January 20, 1984. (My wife Yoke-Sim and son Junius were participants in the first three. Mother was not.)

San Diego (pop 1.3 million) is California's second most populous city, after Los Angeles. Located twenty miles north of the United States-Mexico border, the 372-square-mile city "lies on deep canyons and hills separating its mesas, creating small pockets of natural parkland scattered throughout the city and giving it a hilly geography" (Wikipedia).

San Diego has gone through a population explosion since 1950, when it had only 333,900 people. In 1983, the year of our visits, its population numbered 875,600—an increase of 162 percent over three decades. Since then, its population has gone up another 46 percent. The influx of a large number of military personnel and the attraction of year through mild sunny weather for retirees contributed to this explosion in no small measure.

We already knew the main attractions of San Diego we wanted to see: tourist attractions such as Balboa Park, Belmont amusement park, San Diego Zoo, San Diego Wild Animal Park, and SeaWorld San Diego; historic sites such as Mission San Diego de Alcala and Old Town San Diego State Historic Park.

Trip One

On trip one, we visited the San Diego Zoo (established 1915) in Balboa Park, where we spent about four hours of a Sunday afternoon. First, we joined the guided tour of the zoo, which houses more than four thousand animals of more than eight hundred species, on the upper deck of a double-decker. Then, we went to see the world's largest reptile collection before accompanying Junius to the children's zoo to have his own fun. Yoke-Sim took a picture of me with Kiri and Kalu, two boars from Sri Lanka. The 107-acre zoo contains sections to identify the origins of the animals—African Rocks, Asian Passage, Discovery Outpost, Elephant Odyssey, Lost Forest, Outback, Panda Canyon, Polar Rim, and Urban Jungle. The San Diego Zoo has been a pioneer in building "cageless" exhibits. Onya-Birri, the world's only albino koala in a zoo, was born in this facility, which is also renowned for its New Guinea singing dogs.

Established in 1868, the 1,200-acre Balboa Park is a National Historic Landmark. Besides open areas and natural vegetation, it contains a variety of cultural attractions, including museums, theaters, gardens, shops, and restaurants. Many of these attractions are located along El Prado, the long promenade running through the center of the park, just south of the zoo.

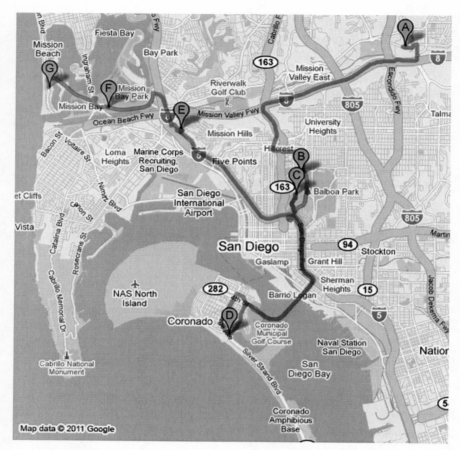

Map 66.1 Main attractions in San Diego. Wild Animal Park in Escondido, thirty-two miles northwest of *A*, Mission San Diego de Alcala; *B*, San Diego Zoo; *C*, Balboa Park; *D*, Hotel del Coronado; *E*, Old Town San Diego State Historic Park; *F*, Sea World; and *G*, Belmont (Amusement) Park.

On the first day (July 9) of trip one, we stopped at Mission San Juan Capistrano (established 1776), a place famous for its white pigeons; and Camp Pendleton, the largest Marine Corps base in the United States. Heading south, we enjoyed the beachfront at Oceanside and Carlsbad. We ate lunch at the Quail Botanic Gardens at Encinitas (pop 62,000) while feasting our eyes on the Australian and New Zealand zone. At Del Mar Heights, I drove west on Carmel Valley Road (the popularity of the name Carmel to convey a sense of scenic beauty struck me) for a short exploration of Torrey Pines State Reserve. There, I walked down a steep cliff to "discover" that Torrey Pines State Beach was actually a nudist colony.

We had reached the northern bounds of the University of California San Diego in La Jolla, where we stopped at the Scripps Aquarium and Museum. Junius was highly pleased with this diversion. Next, we visited the Sunny Jim Cave at La Jolla Caves before driving to the summit of the 823-foot (251 m) Soledad Mountain to view the surroundings.

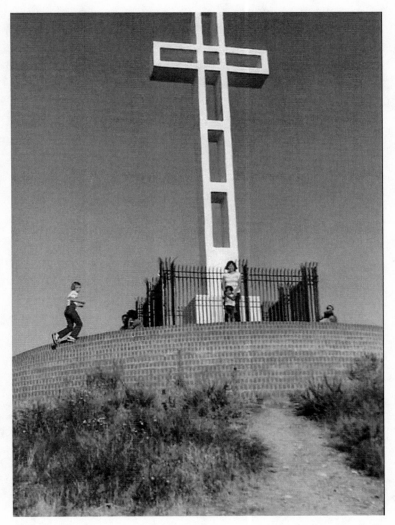

Picture 66.1 Yoke-Sim and son Junius on the summit of the 823-foot Soledad Mountain in La Jolla trying to get a good view of San Diego to the south (July 9, 1983). The Mount Soledad cross has been the subject of a continuing controversy over the involvement of religion in government.

Finally, we camped overnight at Campland on the Bay in Mission Bay Park.

The next morning, we visited Sunset Cliffs, south of Pescadero Beach, and Cabrillo National Monument in Point Loma at the southern tip of the peninsula that engulfs Coronado. However, the fog obscured our view. Next, we stopped at Shelter Island on the eastern shore of the peninsula to take pictures of the Friendship Bell. Driving along the length of Harbor Island, and passing through downtown, we reached San Diego Zoo, the major attraction of interest on this trip. Before we returned to Fullerton, we ate dinner at San Diego Pier, Inc., a restaurant built on the water of San Diego Bay.

Picture 66.2 The author and his son Junius at the Cabrillo National Monument at the southern tip of Point Loma Peninsula (July 10, 1983). It commemorates the landing of Juan Rodríguez Cabrillo at San Diego Bay on September 28, 1542.>

Trip Two

On trip two, we visited the San Diego Wild Animal Park, Sea World San Diego, and Old Town San Diego State Historic Park.

The 1,800-acre San Diego Wild Animal Park (established 1972) is located 32 miles (51 km) north from the zoo, at 15500 San Pasqual

Valley Road, east of Escondido. Currently, it houses more than three thousand animals of more than four hundred species. Arriving at the park on a Saturday, we began with the five-mile, fifty minute Wgasa (Who gives a shit anyway) Bush Line monorail tour (now discontinued) of the park's collection of wild and endangered animals. It was a pleasing experience for all of us to see the wild animals in their large and open compounds. After the tour, we stopped over to see the very popular Bird Show, which amused Junius no end, and the less impressive Cat and Canine Show. In between, we briefly attended a concert at Mahala Amphitheater. We also hiked on the Kilimanjaro Trail to get a better view of some animals. "This park was more interesting than the zoo," I wrote in my diary. We left the park at 5:00 p.m.

> The park's most famous and popular exhibits are the open-range enclosures. Visitors view various habitats representing the Asian Plains, East Africa (the largest of the enclosures; it alone is larger than the San Diego Zoo), North Africa, Asian Waterhole, Southern Africa, and the Mountain Habitat. A number of smaller enclosures visible only from the tram are home to Grevy's zebras, Somali wild asses, kiangs (one of the world's only captive populations of this endangered wild equine), Arabian oryx, gorals, Japanese serows, black rhinoceroses, bonobos, and Przewalski's wild horses. (*Source:* Wikipedia)

An update: In March 2007, in place of the discontinued monorail, the park introduced the Journey into Africa, a wheeled tram tour that brings visitors eye-to-eye with wildlife.

On this trip, we reached Escondido (pop 144,900) from Fullerton via SR 91 east and I-15 south. Our first stop was Lake Elsinore (pop 50,300) and the second Temecula (pop 102,600). The third was Lawrence Welk Theater-Museum, just eight miles north of Escondido, where we saw a thirty-minute documentary, *America's Musical Family—The Lawrence Welk Story*.

The next day (a Sunday), we visited the 189-acre Sea World San Diego (established 1964), an animal theme park, Oceanarium, and marine mammal park. On arrival at Sea World on Mission Bay, we attended the 10:00 a.m. dolphin show. Then, we joined a behind-the-scenes guided tour, which took almost ninety minutes. Thereafter, we visited the

Penguin Encounter, which features more than three hundred penguins representing eight different species; ate lunch at the Nautilus Pavilion; and attended a succession of shows: Up with People Show, Shamu Killer Whale (Orca) Show, Sparklett's Water Fantasy Show, Seal and Otter Show, and Japanese Village Pearl Diving. (These 1983 show names have gone through changes. Check the Sea World website.) We also visited the White Whale Experience, the Tide Pools, and World of the Sea and Marine aquariums. We took Junius to play at Captain Kids' World. We also saw marine mammals at Whale and dolphin pool, Sea otter exhibit, and Walrus Pool. "All in all, Sea World was better than Marineland," I wrote in my diary. We left the place about 5:00 p.m.

Our next destination was the Old Town San Diego State Historic Park, the twenty-nine-acre Old Town neighborhood of San Diego founded in 1825. There, we hiked up to the Presidio Park to see "El Charro," Fort Stockton (decommissioned in 1848), Serra Cross, and Serra Museum (2764 Presidio Drive). Thereafter, we walked down the golf course to the historical park to look at the Old Town's landmarks: Original adobe constructions like Casa de Estudillo (2744 Juan St.), Casa de Carillo, Casa de Pedrorena, Casa de Bandini, etc.; Bazaar del Mundo (4170 Taylor St.), Seeley Stables, Old Town Plaza, etc.

On trip four, I visited Mission San Diego de Alcala (established 1769), the "Mother of Alta California Missions" (10818 San Diego Mission Road). Spanish friar Junípero Serra established it as the first Franciscan mission in the Alta (Upper) California region of New Spain (viz., the official tag for colonial territories of Spain from 1535-1821). The mission and its vicinity was dedicated to Saint Didacus of Alcala, also called San Diego. The mission also marks San Diego's first Christian burial, as well its first public execution. Father Luís Jayme, "California's First Christian Martyr," lies entombed beneath the chancel floor. Angry Kumeyaay Indians from the surrounding *rancherias* killed Jayme on November 4, 1775 when they invaded the mission.

Odds and Ends

On trip two, we were the guests of John and Merle Grubb (3245 Ivy St.), who lived about a mile east of Balboa Park. We became friends with the Grubbs during our 1981 Tiki Tour of New Zealand. They quit the tour on Christmas Day 1981 when Merle hurt herself stepping off the bus at Waitomo Caves. After we reached their San Diego home about 7:00 p.m. on August 27, we joined them for a sumptuous home-cooked dinner. Yoke-Sim joined Merle to cook dinner the next day while John and I perused the album of photos of the New Zealand tour and indulged in nostalgia.

After saying good-bye to the Grubbs on August 29, we drove six miles southwest to visit Coronado (pop 29,300), a tombola joined to the mainland by a narrow ten-mile isthmus called the *Strand*. We entered the tombola from the south on SR75 and stopped at Silver Strand State Beach, Hotel del Coronado (established in 1888) and Star Park. We returned to the mainland via the 2.1-mile (3.4 km)-long Coronado Bridge in the north. On our way back to Fullerton, we visited the library of the University of California San Diego.

On trip three, our primary focus was Baja California, which will be the subject of the next travelogue.

On trip four (January 20, 1984), I was on a business trip to meet journalism faculty colleagues at CSUSD. I visited the mission because it was just west of the campus. In the afternoon, I joined a tour of Villa Montezuma (built 1887) at 1928 K St. and toured the Gaslamp Quarter of the city. Finally, I visited the Grubbs again for a farewell tea party, because I was returning to Australia the next week at the end of my Fullerton year. Back in the Fullerton condo, Mother was eagerly awaiting me.

CHAPTER 67

Mexico: A Peek into Baja (Lower) California

E VISITED BAJA (Lower) California on our trip three through San Diego, November 10-13, 1983. I first visited Mexico in 1967, from July 12-22, as a guest of the National Tourism Council (Consejo Nacional de Tourismo). On that occasion, however, we saw only the 295-km (183-mile) north-south corridor of the country from Mexico City through Cuernavaca and Taxco to Acapulco on the Pacific Coast. (More about that later.) So our 1983 foray into Baja California gave the first whiff of Mexico for my son Junius and wife Yoke-Sim, and the second for me. Mother was not a party to this trip.

Some Background

Mexico, a federation of thirty-one "free and sovereign states," has a current population of 111.3 million. Mexico City, also identified as the Federal District (Distrito Federal), is its biggest city and capital. It has a population of 8.9 million while the total metropolitan area constitutes 21.2 million. Thus, about 19 percent of Mexicans live in and around Mexico City. I spent a week in Mexico City in 1967 during the WPI tour.

Baja California, which became a state in 1953, has a population of 3.2 million, mostly Mesitzos, migrant workers from other states. It occupies an area of 62,921 square kilometers in the upper half of the BC Peninsula.

Tijuana (pop 1.6 million), the largest city in Baja California, is the third largest city in Mexico. The Tijuana metropolitan area has some 1.8 million people, the fifth largest in Mexico. An estimated annual influx of some eighty thousand people has made Tijuana one of the fastest growing cities in Mexico. We spent one night in Tijuana in 1983.

The state capital is Mexicali (pop 654,000), a border city adjacent to Calexico, California, on the eastern end of the California-Baja California border. But the municipality of Mexicali (pop 900,000) sprawls southwards to include San Felipe (pop 15,000) on the Gulf coast of the peninsula, 190 km (118 miles) from the US border. We visited neither the city nor the municipality of Mexicali in 1983.

Ensenada (pop 260,000, within the municipality 414,000) is the third largest city in the state. It is a coastal city located 114 km (70 miles) south of Tijuana. We spent two nights in Ensenada in 1983.

Other important cities include Tecate (pop 60,000, rising to 90,000 at municipal level) on the US border; and Playas de Rosarito (pop 57,000, rising to 73,000 at municipal level), a beach city 29 km (18 miles) south of Tijuana. We stopped briefly at both places in 1983.

My notes do not contain the population size of cities in Baja California in 1983, when we visited the state. The demand for Mexican labor in the United States determines the population levels of the cities along the border. The US states, along the border from west to east, are California, Arizona, New Mexico, and Texas. The Mexican states are Baja California, Sonora, Chihuahua, Coahuila, Nuevo Leon, and Tamaulipas.

The Wikipedia describes the 1,969-mile (3,169 km) United States-Mexico border thus:

> The . . . international border between Mexico and the United States runs from San Diego, California, and Tijuana, Baja California, in the west to Matamoros, Tamaulipas, and Brownsville, Texas, in the east, and traverses a variety of terrains, ranging from major urban areas to inhospitable deserts.
>
> From the Gulf of Mexico it follows the course of the Rio Grande (Río Bravo del Norte) to the border crossing at El Paso, Texas, and Ciudad Juárez, Chihuahua; westward from that binational conurbation it crosses vast tracts of the Sonoran and Chihuahuan

Desert, the Colorado River Delta, westward to the binational conurbation of San Diego and Tijuana before reaching the Pacific Ocean.

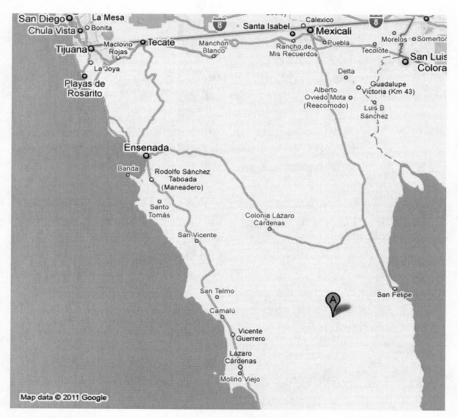

Map 67.1 *A*, Baja California Norte. The tour narrated in this article is limited to the northwest corner of the state of Baja California Norte—the triangular area connecting Tecate, Tijuana, Playas de Rosarito, and Ensenada.

Bienvenido a Mexico

After driving some 100 miles from Fullerton, we crossed the international border at San Ysidro, the world's busiest land border crossing, to Tijuana, Baja California, at 11:00 a.m. on a Thursday. About three hundred thousand visitors cross by foot or motor vehicle from the San Ysidro gateway.

SHELTON A. GUNARATNE

The shrewd Mexicans maneuvered us to commence our foray into their land by enticing us to enrich our memory cells with a dose of Mexican culture and history. They were keen to show us their latest showcase of cultural pride, the Tijuana Cultural Center (CECUT), which opened in October 1982, about a year before our visit. Located in Zona Rio district, its main attraction is the superb OMNIMAX theatre, with a 360-degree projector that gives one the illusion of being inside the movie. Popularly known as "La Bola" (the ball) because of its spherical shape, the 308-seat facility implicitly conveys the architectural genius of Pedro Ramirez Vazques and Manuel Rossen Morrison.

Picture 67.1 Popularly known as "La Bola" (the ball) because of its spherical shape, the 308-seat OMNIMAX Theater at Tijuana's CECUT implicitly conveys the architectural genius of Pedro Ramirez Vazques and Manuel Rossen Morrison. Beside "the ball," Yoke-Sim and Junius appear to be "midgets" (November 10, 1983).

We paid $2.35 each to join an almost-full house at the Omnitheater for the 2:00 p.m. show *El Pueblo del Sol*, which was made especially for the opening, a multistage movie, featuring images from the most representative regions of Mexico that received rave reviews. (Wikipedia records that the movie lasted thirteen years as the only movie showing and at full capacity. Today, the centre offers up to three different movies playing daily and it premieres an average of four movies per year.) I trace Junius's subsequent fascination with Omnimax theaters to this unforgettable experience.

Earlier, we paid an admission charge of 45 cents per person to see the center's permanent exhibition, "Museo de las Californias," which stores more than two hundred pieces and is a walk through the history of the Baja Peninsula and the state of California from the prehistoric period until the first half of the twentieth century. The exhibit also includes a pre-Hispanic garden, "Jardin Caracol" (Snail Garden), which contains sculptures from the different regions of the meso-American cultures that inhabited south Mexico before the arrival of the Spanish Army. Visitors can go through this experience while sipping a cup of coffee.

This collection introduced us to Mexican arts and crafts spanning some thirty five hundred years.

(In September 2008, on the eve of its twenty-sixth anniversary, CECUT opened its doors to a brand new building called "El Cubo" (The Cube), primarily for international exhibitions.)

We ate lunch and munched Mexican pastries at a bakery in the adjoining Plaza Rio Tijuana shopping center. Also, I bought two pairs of socks for two hundred pesos. Mexicans, however, preferred greenbacks to their own pesos. Thereafter, we checked in at Hotel El Conquistador on Boulevard Agua Caliente in Revolucion.

Later in the afternoon, we left the hotel to visit the Agua Caliente Racetrack (Hipodrome) southeast of Zona Centro, the central business district. Although I was driving on a main road, Boulevard Agua Caliente, finding my way through a clutter of roads with Spanish signs drove me crazy. However, we reached the Hipodrome safely after a few wrong turns. Opened in 1929 to cater to the gambling instincts of the Hollywood rich, the Hipodrome survived President Lázaro Cárdenas' ban on gambling in 1935 and continued to offer horse racing (now discontinued), greyhound racing and *jai alai*, a fast-moving ball game resembling a hybrid of squash and tennis that originated in Spain's Basque Country.

Early evening, we stopped for a grand dinner at Boccaccio's, near the Tijuana Country Club on Boulevard Agua Caliente. As we ate dinner, a mariachi singer volunteered to "serenade" Junius. Junius was nonplussed by this uncalled-for attention. We enjoyed both the gastronomic and acoustic dimensions of the evening (although I later reaped the results of excessive indulgence in the unpleasant form of a bellyache). We tipped the singer handsomely and paid the waiter $18.25 for food.

Next, we went on an exploratory tour of the renowned Avenida Revolucion, a must to claim that one really visited Tijuana. This long north-south avenue, the gateway to Zona Norte from Zona Centro, is the tourist center of the city, where the Caesar's Salad had its origin. It is home to several distinct attractions, from cantinas and table dance bars to numerous dance clubs and art galleries. At the night market, I bought a leather belt for $4.50. Yoke-Sim bought a leather purse for $8.50. Currently, the famous avenue is going through a major crisis with more than 80 percent of the businesses closed.

Northwest of the Avenida Revolución is the Zona Norte, the city's red light district (referred to as La Coahuila after one of the main streets in it). It "boasts a large number of legal street prostitutes as well as, in parts, a selection of strip clubs offering at least one establishment per block" (Wikipedia).

On the Way to Ensenada

Friday morning (November further exploration. We tarried at El Toreo, the (now defunct) bullring in the neighborhood of our hotel in 11), we checked out of the hotel soon after breakfast and drove to the northwestern edge of the city for the Revolucion sector. We tarried again at Parque Teniente Guerrero before proceeding west to see Plaza de Toros Monumental, the renowned bullring by the sea in Playas de Tijuana, a planned beachfront community. However, we weren't much impressed with the structure of the homes.

Picture 67.2 The author and his son at Plaza de Toros Monumental, the renowned bullring by the sea in Playas de Tijuana (November 11, 1983).

We returned to Zona Centro to visit Centro Artesenal, the retail outlet of the government-run National Fund for the Promotion of Handicrafts (FONART); and Frontón Palacio Jai Alai, a Tijuana landmark fronting nearly an entire block of Avenue Revolución. Its construction began in 1926, but wasn't completed until 1947. Forced to close down with the decline of *jai alai*, it now hosts cultural events including music and theater performances.

We ate lunch at a sidewalk café. Thereafter, we found our way with difficulty to drive almost thirty miles southwest along old Highway 1 to the beachfront resort city of Playas de Rosarito. Fascinated by the sight of some horseback riders on the beach, we stopped in Rosarito beach to watch them in action. Rosarito has been the in-place for several well-heeled Hollywood celebrities like Britney Spears, Ava Gardner, Spencer Tracy, Katherine Hepburn, Rita Hayworth, Mickey Rooney, and Orson Welles.

Driving forty miles further south along the coast (on Mexico 1D) to reach our scheduled destination, we discourteously ignored the inhabitants of Popetla, Las Gaviotas, Cantamar, and La Fonda. We stopped briefly at La Mision (pop 1,100), located on a wide, steeply walled valley on the Transpeninsular Highway. We climbed out of the valley past abrupt volcanic bluffs via a series of curves. At the village of San Miguel, we joined the new highway leading to our destination.

Finally, we reached Ensenada about 4:00 p.m., and checked in at Casa del Sol Motel (on Avenida Lopez Mateos), just south of the city center, for two nights.

In the evening, we explored the curio shops along the avenue where our motel was. We capped our day with a visit to the famous El Ray Sol French restaurant for one of the best dinners we ate recently—a remarkable gastronomic delight! Our bill exceeded $30. The pastry was superb. Most of all, I was spared another bellyache!

CHAPTER 68

Mexico: A Capital Trap

NOSTALGIA OVERWHELMED ME when I listened to Neil Diamond's famous lyric years after I first visited Ensenada in 1983:

> *In Ensenada*
> *We were running*
> *from the things that we knew best*
> *We only took the good and left the rest*
> *In Ensenada*

Small mountain ranges back the Ensenada landscape giving it much of its charm.

Ensenada lies in the heart of a wine country that many compare with the Napa Valley of California. The story goes that the first *vitis vinifera* (common grape vine) made it to the peninsula (specifically to the San Ignacio Mission) in 1703, when Jesuit Padre Juan de Ugarte planted the first vineyards there. I bet the wine we drank with our superlative dinner Friday came from a local winery.

Located in the Bahía de Todos Santos, Ensenada is formally known as Ensenada de Todos Santos. It is also the municipal seat of Ensenada Municipality and the third largest city in Baja California. It is an important commercial and fishing port as well as a cruise ship stop. Navy and Army bases and a military airfield have added to the city's economic power.

Ensenada Experience

Saturday (November 12) morning, we ate breakfast at the Best Western coffeehouse on Avenida Lopez Mateos. Then, despite a light rain, we ambled to the Tourist Information Office to plan our day. At the FONART, just across Arroyo de Ensenada, we bought an ashtray and a wall tray for 160 pesos ($10.70) because we wanted to splurge the Mexican currency we exchanged on arrival.

At 11:00 a.m., we joined a tour of the Bodegas (Winery) de Santo Tomas ($1.50 per person). Located 44 km south of Ensenada, this winery has been in operation since 1888. It is known for its Duetto, a 50-50 Santo Tomas-Wente blend, and for its Santo Tomás Reserva Unico. However, despite the availability of good wines, the average wine consumption per capita in Mexico is only two glasses a year. The Mexican government imposes a tax of 40 percent per bottle, making it hard to compete with beer and tequila.

After the tour, we drove to the hilly northern end of Avenida Moctezuma to get a good view of the bay and its surroundings. Then, we proceeded to the top of Chapultepec Hills to see the fashionable residential neighborhood.

We returned to the city center and stopped at Plaza Civica on Boulevard Costero to look at the twelve-feet-high busts of three historical figures: Benito Juarez, Miguel Hidalgo, and Venustiano Carranza. Then, we went to see the former Hotel Riviera del Pacific, a bay front casino and resort of the 1930s, now renovated as the city's cultural, arts, and convention center.

In the afternoon, we ate at a bakery on Avenida Ruiz before going on another shopping spree. At Beauty Supply, I bought two leather belts ($4.50 each) and a pair of Hines bookends ($18). At La Perla del Pacifico, I bought a pair of G. B. H. leather shoes ($38) and two pairs of socks ($2.54). At Fashions, Yoke-Sim bought a leather bag ($25) and a blanket ($13). Poor Junius bought nothing.

We ate a good seafood dinner for $21 at the seafront Restaurant Casamar (987 Blvd Costero). The day's drizzle continued even at bedtime.

Sunday (November 13) was our last day in Mexico. In the morning, we drove southwest to reach the western tip of Punta Banda to see La Bufadora, a marine geyser or Blowhole. The ocean waves and air drawn into an underwater cave point on the Cliffside creates the spout of marine water that occurs every minute or so to varying degrees of height. The trapped air and water then explode upwards.

Picture 68.1 We drove southwest of Ensenada to reach the western tip of Punta Banda to see La Bufadora, a marine geyser or Blowhole. The camera distracted Yoke-Sim while Junius got an eyeful of La Bufadora (November 13 1983).

On the return journey, we stopped at the resort on Estero Beach and walked on the large expanse of sand. Back in Ensenada, we checked out of our motel at noon and stepped into Casamar no. 2 (at the bay end of Avenida Macheros) to eat shrimp and crab salad for lunch. At Robert's Gifts (on Avenida Lopez Mateos), I purchased a Padito's goatskin jacket ($68) while Yoke-Sim bought a sheet ($14).

Having disposed of our greenbacks in almost one fell sweep, we said *despedida* to Ensenada at 2:00 p.m. We traveled more than 100 km (66 miles) north on Mexico three to the border city of Tecate. On the way, we passed El Sauzal; Guadalupe, where I climbed up to see the site of Mission Nuestra Senora de Guadalupe (1834), El Testerazo, where we saw cottonwood carvings, and Valle de Las Palmas.

Picture 68.2 We stopped at El Testerazo, where we saw cottonwood carvings. The author hobnobs with several carved characters (November 13, 1983).

Tecate is a small city best known outside of its region as the home of Tecate beer and author Daniel Reveles, a fictional writer. Tecate border crossing is much less crowded than San Ysidro (Tijuana) or Mexicali. We tarried at Parque Hidalgo and at FONART and bought some pastry at a Tecate bakery before we crossed the border to the United States at 5:00 p.m.

We ate Kentucky Fried Chicken for dinner at San Clemente, the home base of disgraced US President Richard Nixon. We were back in Fullerton at 9:00 p.m. But we couldn't immediately get into Larry's condo because our remote control gadget in the car failed to open the garage door.

Recalling Mexico 1967

The US State Department's intermittent warnings about the dangers of touring Tijuana and many other Mexican cities are not based on hearsay alone. I became the victim of a tourist swindle on my first visit to Mexico City in 1967 as the Ceylon member of that year's World Press Institute's group of journalists. (All of the 1966-1967 WPI journalists, except the late Kebede Anissa from Ethiopia, visited Mexico on the invitation of Consejo Nacional de Turismo even though we clearly understood this to be a public relations exercise of the Mexican government.)

We arrived in Mexico City on a Wednesday (July 12) evening by Aeronaves de Mexico from New York. CNT officials welcomed us and took us to Hotel Del Prado on Avenida Juarez. Ben Antao (India) and I set off to explore the streets when a fellow approached us and volunteered to take us to a private club.

Thursday (July 13) morning, CNT folks showed us the Olympic installations. Robert Kenny, the director of special events, told us about the arrangements made to cover events. The Committee of the Olympic games gave us a luncheon at the Bay Horse Inn on Avenida Conscripto with folk singers and banjo players in the background. In the evening, I explored the streets to the west of our hotel.

We visited the National Museum of Anthropology and History Friday (July 14) morning. Then, we paid a courtesy call on Mexico President Miguel Aleman Valdez (1946-1952), who headed the CNT during our visit. We toured the Chapultepec Park before attending a luncheon at the Presidents Hotel. In the evening, the International Press Club invited us for cocktails at the Continental Hilton, where I chatted with Turkish journalist Rosita "Debra" Saalie.

On Saturday (July 15), we went on a tour of the Three Cultures Square and the archeological zone of Teotihuacán, about thirty-two miles northeast of Distrito Federal.

- The square contains the remains of Aztec temples and is flanked by the Catholic church of Santiago Tlatelolco and a massive housing complex built in 1964. The former headquarters of the Secretariat of Foreign Affairs are now a memorial museum to remember the 1968 Mexican student demonstrations and the Tlatelolco Massacre victims and survivors. The name "Three Cultures" is in recognition of the three periods of Mexican history reflected by those buildings: pre-Columbian, Spanish colonial, and the independent "Mesitzo" nation. (Wikipedia)

SHELTON A. GUNARATNE

- *Teotihuacan* is an enormous archaeological site in the Basin of Mexico, containing some of the largest pyramidal structures built in the pre-Columbian Americas (c. 200 BCE). Apart from the pyramidal structures, Teotihuacan is also known for its large residential complexes, the Avenue of the Dead, and numerous colorful, well-preserved murals. (Wikipedia)

On Sunday (July 16) about 11:00 a.m., I was walking on Paseo de La Reforma, when an elderly man claiming to be a rich rancher from Sonora stopped me and wanted to know how he could change the $100 bills he had in his pocket. Just at the moment, the old man accosted another passer-by with whom he spoke in Spanish ostensibly making the same inquiry. The newcomer translated to me in English what the old man told him in Spanish. This developed into a friendly conversation, and the pair invited me to join them for a tour of the vicinity. In my mind, the old man appeared to be lost in the big city and in need of some help. Despite my extensive travels in the big cities in the United States, not the faintest suspicion arose in my mind when I said OK.

We got into the passer's-by car, which he stopped at a waterhole with a billiard room. The "rancher" and the "good Samaritan" got cozy at playing billiards with the "rancher" betting his $100 bills. The "rancher" bungled the games badly and lost a couple of times. The winner egged me on to play with the "rancher," who again bungled the game against a billiards novice of my dubious caliber. Suspicion began to stir in my mind when the pair asked me to bet my camera and wristwatch, in addition to my original bet for hundred pesos. The bungling rancher instantly turned into a master player of billiards claiming possession of all the material wealth I carried.

My gut instincts turned on at top gear as I told the bunch of swindlers that I was in Mexico as the guest of President Aleman and the CNT, who must be already looking for me. Then, I grabbed hold of my camera and the wristwatch and dashed out of the billiards room out into the streets against all the threats. I lost only the hundred pesos. Nobody shot at me or followed me. Nevertheless, it was an incredible risk.

That evening, I joined the WPI group to see the Ballet Folklorico de Mexico at Palacio de Bellas Artes.

On Tuesday (July 18) morning, we left Mexico City for Taxco (pop 50,000), where we stayed overnight at Posada de La Mision. On the way, fifty-three miles (85 km) south of DF, we stopped at Cuernavaca (pop 350,000), the capital and the largest city of the state of Morelos, where we spent some time at Cortes' Palace and the Central Square.

Map 68.1 The 1967 WPI tour route of Mexico. From *A* = Ciudad de Mexico [Mexico City] to Acapulco through Cuernavaca, Taxco and Chilpancingo.

SHELTON A. GUNARATNE

Taxco, located in the north-central part of the state of Guerrero (about 170 km or 105 miles southwest of DF), is a colonial monument town with twisting cobble-stoned streets and steep hills dotted with tile-roofed houses displaying sixteenth-century architecture. Taxco is famous for silver. We spent the entire evening walking on winding streets and the market center facing the church of Santa Pisca. Taxco is unique, just beautiful and peaceful.

Wednesday through Friday (July 19-21), we had an uninterrupted vacation at the Las Brisas resort in Acapulco (pop 617,000), a coastal city in the state of Guerrero 300 km or 186 miles southwest of DF. My diary entry for Friday reads: I spent the morning swimming in the pool. I didn't join the group who went yachting. I had a hearty meal in the open-air dining area near the pool and the cabanas. In the evening, we went to see the divers in action at La Quebrada. Diving into the sea from the steep hill seemed to be a marvelous feat. A few of us spent the rest of the night at Dali Bar at the hotel.

Saturday (July 22) morning, Arturo von Vacano Alberta, the WPI journalist from Bolivia, helped me write in Spanish my letter of resignation from Lake House. At noon, we left Acapulco to return to Mexico City, DF. We stopped for food at Chilpancingo (pop 167,000), the capital of Guerrero located 130 km or 83 miles north of Acapulco. Back in DF, we checked in again at Hotel Del Prado. Two Mexican socialites, Anna Luisa and Mercedes, joined me for dinner.

Sunday (July 23) at 9:30 a.m., we left our hotel for the return flight to New York. A few journalists decided to fly directly to their home counties. Only Ko Shioya (Japan), Veikko Pajunen (Finland), Hector Olave Vallejos (Chile), Pietro Banas (Italy), Ted Miller (our WPI minder), Ben, Arturo, and myself were on Flight AF-700.

A story about us (the WPI group) appeared in the *News*, a Mexican publication in English. It included a photo of mine.

CHAPTER 69

California: Making the Best out of Greater Los Angeles

LOS ANGELES IS big and sprawling both in terms of population and area. If you are talking about Greater Los Angeles, also called the Southland, you are referring to the large urbanized area comprising five counties—Los Angeles (88 cities with 9.9 million people), Orange (thirty-four cities with 3 million people), Riverside (twenty-seven cities and 2.1 million people), San Bernardino (twenty-five cities and 2.1 million people), and Ventura (ten cities and 753,200 people)—with a total population of 17.8 million in an area covering 35,316 square miles. (Holy Cow, the whole of Sri Lanka covers a mere 25,333 square miles!)

The Los Angeles Metropolitan Area refers to the area covered by the adjacent Los Angeles and Orange counties with a joint population of 12.9 million.

The Los Angeles County of 9.9 million people spans an area of 4,752 square miles.

The smallest unit is the city of Los Angeles encompassing an area of almost 500 square miles with a population of 3.8 million.

Recapitulation

I quote from chapter 57:

> I was an exchange instructor at Fullerton College in 1983 occupying the residence of my exchange partner, Larry Taylor, at 2903 Wellesley Court, Fullerton, a suburb of Los Angeles. I arrived

with my family in California on February 2, 1983, and we decided to make use of our weekends and the summer break to explore the West Coast to the fullest.

Chapter 13 (part 1) of this book also mentions my exchange year in Fullerton, which ended in January 1984. However, none of the previous chapters revealed the story of how we explored Greater Los Angeles during holidays and weekends throughout our stay in Southland.

We landed in Los Angeles on a Wednesday ahead of the Air New Zealand's scheduled 5:00 p.m. arrival time. Gail Nagel (Larry's partner) and her daughter Lisa were at the airport to welcome us despite the rain and cold weather. We could not get out of the airport's car park for nearly forty-five minutes because of a traffic jam. We stopped to eat dinner at a MacDonald's before Gail and Lisa brought us to Fullerton and let us in to settle down at Larry's condo at 2903 Wellesley Court.

Picture 69.1 The author and his son Junius, three, in front of Larry Taylor's condominium (2903 Wellesley Court, Fullerton), which became their home for one year (April 1983).

Next morning, Don DePuy (chairman) and Paul Kelly of Fullerton College's Division of Communication visited us and took us to the campus to show us the facilities in the Applied Arts Building and to introduce us to relevant personnel. They also took us out for lunch at the nearby Big Boy restaurant. Then, DePuy conducted us to FC Administration and introduced us to President Philip Borst and deans Jane Armstrong and Robert Gates. Jan Ballard, the divisional secretary, gave me the keys to my office (room 513) and the classrooms. At the end of all the formalities, DePuy brought us back to the condo. That evening, we shopped at the University Shopping Center (then popularly called Gemco), a hop-step-and-a-jump north of the condo, for groceries. The Crossroads Shopping Center was a block away to the east. Adjoining it was Placentia Town Center Shopping Center.

The next day (Friday), accompanied by Yoke-Sim and Junius, I drove the five miles from Larry's condo (south on North Placentia Avenue and west on East Chapman Ave.) to FC campus in Larry's Volvo with trepidation. I had to overcome the psychological block of getting used to driving on American freeways. I spent the weekend at the condo preparing for the courses assigned to me for teaching in the spring semester—Reporting and Writing, Magazine Production, Mass Media Survey, and Public Relations and Publicity. The classes began on Monday (February 7). Toni Schrotberger, a graduate intern from California State University Fullerton, helped me as my teaching assistant in the Reporting and Writing class (on Tuesday nights) and the PR class (on Wednesday nights).

Exploring Locality

Fullerton (pop 126,000) is a twenty-two-square-mile city in northern Orange County, twenty-five miles (40 km) southeast of Los Angeles city. It shares borders with La Habra and Brea on the north, La Mirada on the northwest, Buena Park on the west, Anaheim on the south, and Placentia on the east.

Geographically, Fullerton's northern and western reaches are dominated by the Coyote Hills, a low-lying mountain range divided into the East Coyote Hills and West Coyote Hills; the lands nestled to their south and west are known as Sunny Hills. For most of the city's history these areas were groves of citrus trees, open scrubland, and oil fields (Wikipedia).

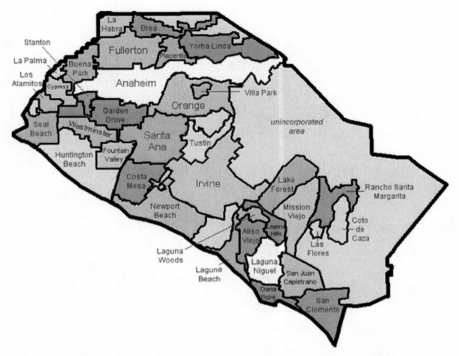

Map 69.1 Cities comprising Orange County, California. (*Source:* Wikimedia Commons)

Fullerton oversees more than fifty city parks, including Hillcrest Park, the Craig Regional Park, and Ralph B. Clark Regional Park. The Fullerton Arboretum (adjoining CSUF campus) comprises twenty-six acres of sculpted gardens and unusual plants in northeastern Fullerton. Additionally, the city features about two hundred acres of recreational land in the Brea Dam Recreational Area (about a mile northwest of FC campus), plus an equestrian center and trails, two golf courses, a tennis center located south of St. Jude Medical Center, and the Janet Evans Swim Complex (Wikipedia).

I was happy that I could use the rubberized athletic track of Fullerton College to do my afternoon jogging.

Fullerton has also the distinction of being the birthplace of Kim Chambers, the famous blue movie star.

Neighborhood First

Our exploration of Greater Los Angeles began with our immediate surroundings in Fullerton and its border cities. I visited the CSUF campus, a stone's throw on the southwest of Larry's condo, and Cypress College campus, fourteen miles to the west, during the first week to get an idea of the vicinity and to get rid of my freeway phobia. (I had to drive on three freeways—Orange, Riverside, and Artesia—to get to Cypress.) I had not driven on an American freeway since I left the United States early 1974. On Saturday (February 12), Yoke-Sim also gained the experience of American freeway driving, when she drove home from Cypress College, where she attended a course on data processing. That experience nearly gave her a "heart attack," she confessed.

I got my California driver's license on March 3. Yoke-Sim got hers a week later.

Having got used to local driving conditions over a month, we—Junius, Yoke-Sim, and I—made our first joint trip to downtown Los Angles on Friday, March 4. The purpose was to exercise our right to participate in the Australian federal election. Our polling booth was the office of the Australian Consulate-General in Los Angeles. After voting, we toured the city's Chinatown, where Yoke-Sim purchased a bagful of groceries essential for our survival.

Larry Taylor's condo, Fullerton College, and AAA provided me all the facilities and information I needed to plan my regular explorations of Greater Los Angeles and beyond.

Our methodical forays into specific parts of GLA for exploration began on Saturday, March 12, with northwestern Orange County as our target. We drove east all the way to Yorba Linda (pop 59,0000) and beyond, along the boulevard bearing the same name; then, we headed northeast on Esperanza Road to explore the Hidden Hills area on the Eastern edge of Yorba Linda. The most visited and well-known site in Yorba Linda is the Richard Nixon Presidential Library and Museum (18001 Yorba Linda Blvd.). The graves of Nixon and the First Lady, as well as Nixon's birthplace, are in the premises.

Picture 69.2 Junius Gunaratne, three, relaxes on a chair by a Jacuzzi in the Wellesley Court pool garden on a sunny day during the Gunaratne family's year in Fullerton (April 1983).

Then, we drove southwest to Anaheim Hills and circled around the country club along Nohl Ranch Road, Serrano Avenue, and Canyon Rim Road with a stop at the Plaza Shopping Center. Finally, we went north on Imperial Highway, Valencia Avenue, and Carbon Canyon Road to Sleepy Hollow (pop 400) in San Bernardino County, where we walked leisurely on Oakway Lane to observe the dilapidated homes in the terraced area. On the way back, we stopped at La Vida Mineral Springs and the Olinda village in Brea.

Our second foray was an exploratory tour of central coastal Orange County on Sunday, March 27. Our first stop was the Laguna Hills Mall, off Interstate 5. Then, via El Toro Road and Laguna Canyon Road, we came to Laguna Beach (pop 24,000), where we stopped at Irvine Bowl, Main Beach, Heisler Park, Art Museum, and Village Fair. Then, we headed north on Coast Highway to Balboa Island (in Newport Beach), where we stopped for refreshments and walked on Park Avenue to get the feel of the place. The streets on the island were narrow and quaint.

We left the place at 5:00 p.m. to return home stopping in Placentia (pop 47,000) for dinner.

We went back to Newport Beach (pop 87,000) again on Saturday, April 2, to find bumper-to-bumper traffic in the beach area. Unable to park, we drove to the eastern tip of Balboa Peninsula at Channel Road and looked across at Corona del Mar. Then, we came back on Ocean Front Boulevard to Balboa Pier and ate a mud pie at Ruby's. Thereafter, we crossed over to Edgewater Avenue to see the boats and the ferry to Balboa Island. We also drove around Lido Isle. On the way back home, we tarried at the South Coast Plaza for more than an hour. We capped the day with a family dinner at the Sizzler Family Steak House, close to our condo.

Two days later, on April 4, Junius started his preschooling at the Ivy Crest Montessori Private School (still in operation at 2025 E. Chapman Ave.). The arrangement was for me to deposit Junius at the school on my way to office in the morning and to pick him up at 3:30 p.m. on my way back to the condo.

CHAPTER 70

California: Memories of Los Angeles's Marineland and Movieland Wax Museum

IN THIS CHAPTER, I shall first focus on the category of much ballyhooed popular attractions that failed; then, move on to the category of esoteric attractions that thrive in obscure silence in offbeat locations.

For sure, everything is impermanent (*anicca*). Yet sorrow (*dukkha*) overwhelmed me when I heard about the demise of two Metropolitan Los Angeles themed attractions, which we—the Gunaratne family—visited and thoroughly enjoyed in 1983, our Fullerton year: one was Marineland of the Pacific; the other was Six Flags Movieland Wax Museum.

Map 70.1 Greater Los Angeles.

Marineland of the Pacific

We visited Marineland of the Pacific on the Palos Verdes Peninsula on a Saturday (June 18), two months before we visited its counterpart SeaWorld in San Diego. It opened as a public oceanarium in 1954 and closed its doors in 1987—four years after our visit.

I had fond memories of my first visit to Marineland in 1966 (December 23, a Saturday again!), when Ted Miller (our WPI minder), Pietro Banas (Italy), Arturo von Vacano Alborta (Peru), and Idoan rented a car to explore Los Angeles County and ended up in Rancho Palos Verdes, where we stopped at Marineland to see its then renowned Whale Show and Seal-and-Porpoise Show, among other things.

On this occasion, we reached Long Point, the location of Marineland, from Fullerton via Hermosa Beach (pop 18,600) and Redondo Beach (pop 63,300), where we stopped to visit "Seaport Village" on the marina-harbor-pier complex to witness its array of Korean seafood eateries, waterholes, boutiques, and the arcade. We hoped that by introducing Junius to Marineland, we could expand his interest in the oceanic life world.

In Marineland, we joined Junius to watch the Great American High Dive Team (in action), Dolphin Show, Sea Lion Show, Pilot Whale Show, and Killer Whale Show.

We bought Junius a Marineland cap to remember the trip. Before leaving the facility, we walked around the Oval Tank and the Passages beneath the Sea.

Today, Terranea, a large resort in Rancho Palos Verdes (pop 41,200), occupies the site of Marineland that we visited. San Diego SeaWorld, which bought Marineland in 1987, shifted all popular shows of the latter to the San Diego enterprise.

About a mile east of Marineland, we stopped at the Wayfarers Chapel (built c. 1951) designed by the American architect Frank Lloyd Wright. Also called "The Glass Church," the chapel features geometric designs and incorporates the natural landscape into the design.

SHELTON A. GUNARATNE

Driving further southeast, we reached Point Fermin Park and Lighthouse; then, we headed north to San Pedro, the port neighborhood of the city of Los Angeles. A thin strip of land called the "Harbor Gateway" connects San Pedro with the city. Driving a short distance east, we reached the "Ports O' Call" tourist village (built in 1963), where we enjoyed walking around the gas-lit streets, restaurants, and shops along the main channel of Los Angles Harbor.

We decided to eat dinner at Jo Ann's Chili Bordello, where the menu included Madame Hot Pants and Madame Sheryl R. We were served a drink called Naked Lady—Chablis, fresh melon, and Pina Colada. (For us, this was an off-the-beaten path "discovery.")

We talked about the dinner all the way back to Larry's condo in Fullerton.

Picture 70.1 The author with his son Junius at now defunct Marineland (June 18, 1983).

Movieland Wax Museum

We visited the Six Flags Movieland Wax Museum in Buena Park on another Saturday (September10). Allen Parkinson established the museum in 1962 on Buena Park's E-Zone district along Beach Boulevard, which was also home to Knott's Berry Farm and its sister water park Knott's Soak City (opened in 1999), Pirate's Dinner Adventure Show, and Medieval Times dinner show.

Parkinson sold the Movieland Wax Museum, one of the largest of its kind in the world, to Six Flags Corporation in 1970. Just across the street was one of the thirty-five Ripley's Believe It or Not! museums. A Japanese Village and Deer Park also operated on Knott Avenue but folded in the mid-1970s.

In 1983, at the time of our visit, the Six Flags Movieland Wax Museum displayed more than two hundred figures of movie and TV stars in authentically replicated sets. This was the largest wax museum in the United States "with over three hundred wax figures in 150 sets," Wikipedia claims. It goes on to say:

Several actors and actresses attended the unveilings of their wax likenesses, and even went so far as to donate costumes to be worn by their likenesses, accompanied with sets replicated from well-known movie scenes. Movie themes and sound effects also added to the authenticity of the museum. A clapboard on each set included the name of the wax figures and facts about the movie, props, costume, and the person whom the wax figure was modeled on.

The two hours we spent at the museum was insufficient to pay attention to each of the wax figures. Among the figures that we admired were those of Elizabeth Taylor, Elvis Presley, Shirley Temple, Sammy Davis Jr., and Marilyn Monroe.

While at the Movieland Wax Museum, we took Junius into the Black Box for a horror-movie-set experience. Junius hung on to me and kept his eyes shut.

After lunch, we crossed over Beach Road to the Kingdom of Dancing Stallions for the 2:00 p.m. show. The forty-five-minute dancing show of Andalusian horses put Junius to sleep. I regretted the money spent on his ticket.

The Movieland Wax Museum closed its doors to the public in 2004 after Six Flags Corporation sold it to the new owners in 1985. Buena Park's Believe it or Not! closed in 2009. It occurred to me that the law of the fish (the stronger devouring the weaker) applies well to American capitalism.

Queen Mary and Spruce Goose

On another weekend (Saturday, September 3), we drove to Long Beach (current pop. 493,000), the fifth largest city in California located twenty miles or 32 km south of downtown Los Angeles on the border of Orange County, to visit two offbeat attractions: Queen Mary and Spruce Goose.

The population of Long Beach has increased 43 percent since our 1983 visit.

- The RMS [Royal Mail Ship] *Queen Mary* is a 1936 art deco ocean liner permanently docked at Pier 5 of the port of Long Beach. Wikipedia elaborates: "Roughly 200 ft (61 m) longer than the Titanic, the former Cunard Liner is famous for being the fastest in the world from 1936 to 1952, for its distinctive art deco design and for its use during World War II as a troop transport." The city of Long Beach purchased it in 1967 for conversion to a hotel and maritime museum. *Queen Mary* reputedly crossed the Atlantic 1001 times.
- *Spruce Goose* is the nickname cynics gave the first Hughes H-4 Hercules flying boat that Howard Hughes flew on a trial run on November 2, 1947. In 1983, when we visited, it was exhibited in a dome next to *Queen Mary*. We had to wait in long line for almost one hour to get into the flying boat, which was the forerunner of the modern aircraft industry. Since 1993, it has been housed at the Evergreen Aviation Museum in McMinnville, Oregon.

After leaving the exhibits, we drove twelve miles northeast along the southeastern edge of the CSU Long Beach campus to El Dorado Park, where Junius had a lot of fun chasing the ducks prancing around the lakes. We returned to Fullerton about 7:00 p.m.

Update: Queen Mary (1126 Queen's Highway: Admission $30), which has been open to the public since 1971, faced near-bankruptcy in the late 1980s and early 1990s. It shut its doors to the public at the end of 1992 but reopened in February 1993. Delaware North Companies of Buffalo, New York, took over the management of the ocean liner in September 2009.

Long Beach has added several new attractions since our 1983 visit, e.g. the Aquarium of the Pacific (opened in 1998 on Rainbow Harbor) was perhaps intended as a replacement for the defunct Marineland in nearby Rancho Palos Verdes. The aquarium features a collection of some 12,500 animals representing 550 different species.

Another new attraction is Walter Pyramid (opened in 1994), formerly known as Long Beach Pyramid—a five thousand-seat, indoor multipurpose stadium on the campus of California State University, Long Beach.

CHAPTER 71

California: En Route to Camping in San Gabriel Wilderness

THOSE WHO WANT to escape the hustle and bustle of sprawling Greater Los Angeles from time to time can do so by retreating to the Chilao Campground in the Angeles National Forest, an open space of one thousand square miles, lying amidst the San Gabriel Mountains. The campground, located along the sixty-six-mile-long Angeles Crest Highway (SR 2), is just forty miles northeast of downtown Los Angeles (or about seventy miles north of Fullerton, where we lived in 1983).

Having had the experience of two long-durée camping trips in July and August, we—my three-year-old son Junius, wife Yoke-Sim, and I—decided to try out Chilao on a late October weekend (29-30). We entered the Angeles Crest Highway from its western terminus (I-210 in La Cañada Flintridge), and drove northeast toward its eastern terminus (Mountain Top Junction at SR138 in Wrightwood). Chilao Campground lies just twenty-six miles from La Cañada Flintridge.

Wikipedia clarifies that the Angeles Crest Highway was originally envisioned in 1912 as "the most scenic and picturesque mountain road in the state [California]," but the need for a road for fire fighting was at least equally important. "Funds were allocated beginning in 1919. Construction began in 1929, continuing piece by piece until 1956." One good reason to spend a weekend in Chilao is to explore the scenic splendor that SR 2 itself has to offer. However, it is typically closed to car traffic and unplowed between Islip Saddle and Big Pines, a sixteen-mile stretch some fifteen miles east of Chilao Campground, after the first snowfall (typically October through December) until May or June.

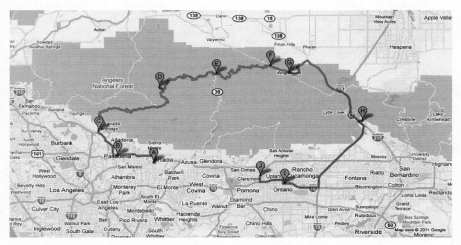

Map 71.1 Angeles Crest Highway and its vicinity. *A*, Arcadia; *B*, Pasadena; *C*, La Canada Flintridge; *D*, Chilao Campground; *E*, Islip Saddle; *F* Big Pines; *G*, Wrightwood; *H*, Devore Heights; *I*, Ontario; and *J*, Claremont.

On Angeles Crest Highway

Upon entering the Angeles National Forest on a Saturday (October 29) afternoon, we visited the Mount Wilson Observatory located on the 5,715 foot (1,742 m) peak bearing the same name, Founded by George E. Hale circa 1904, the observatory housed the sixty-inch (1.5 m) reflector, which "became one of the most productive and successful telescopes in astronomical history. Its design and light-gathering power allowed the pioneering of spectroscopic analysis, parallax measurements, nebula photography, and photometric photography. Though surpassed in size by the Hooker telescope nine years later, the Hale telescope remained one of the largest in use for decade" (Wikipedia)

Mount Wilson also accommodates the Hooker Telescope Infrared Spatial Interferometer and CHARA array. We visited the small astronomical museum, as well as the adjacent Skyline Park.

Camping overnight at the Lower Chilao Campground cost us a mere $5. Today, the facility offers 110 sites located on three loops. The National Forrest Service has increased the site fee to $12. My diary entry for that night says, "Except for some loud music from the neighboring tent, we enjoyed the serenity of the San Gabriel Wilderness."

Picture 71.1 Angeles Crest Highway (SR2) on San Gabriel Mountains. (*Source:* Wikimedia Commons)

Sunday (October 30) morning, when we stopped by at the Chilao Visitor Center, we tried out a little bit of hiking on the very tempting Silver Moccasin trail. Then, we proceeded driving eastward to complete the scenic tour of the entire Angeles Crest Highway stopping at outstanding scenic spots to pay our obeisance.

We stopped at Inspiration Point to get a closer look at Mount Barden-Powell and Mount San Antonio (Old Baldy Peak). We also stopped at the Big Pines Visitor Center perched on the highest point (6,862 ft.) along the San Andreas Fault. We walked through the nature trail behind the visitor center. I noticed the verse or words "In the Pines" (attributed to one William Bristol) on the large rock tower.

We crossed Los Angeles County into San Bernardino County as we entered the settlement of Wrightwood (pop 4,000), just to the east of which is Mountain High Ski Resort, the most-visited resort in Southern California.

Onto Ontario

Then, we left the National Forest to visit several offbeat attractions in two cities on the southern rim of the forest.

First, we drove on I-15 and I-10 to Ontario (pop 170,400), a city in San Bernardino County, where we stopped for an industrial tour of The Graber Olive House (315 E. Fourth St.) a producer of olives. The place is a city historical landmark and one of the oldest institutions in Ontario. We watched the canning of olives.

Claremont

Then, we crossed back to Los Angeles County to visit two places in Claremont (pop 37,400), nicknamed the "City of Trees and PhDs" because of its tree-lined streets and the seven top-notch higher-education institutions.

A six-mile drive northwest from Graber Olive House brought us to the first place of our interest: Rancho Santa Ana Botanic Garden (RSABG), an eighty-six-acre garden devoted to California native plants (currently some seventy thousand representing two thousand species). Admission to RSABG was free for fifty-eight years until 2009.

Then, we drove south to visit the second place of our interest: the Claremont Colleges—a consortium of seven schools of higher education, viz. Pomona College, Claremont McKenna College, Scripps College, Harvey Mudd College, Pitzer College, Keck Graduate Institute, and Claremont Graduate University. The British Oxford model inspired the consortium. Each college is independent in the sense that each college has its separate administration and admissions departments; and students receive their degrees from the one college in which they are enrolled. However, they all share the large or expensive facilities and programs. We strolled on the impressive one-square mile of campuses for more than thirty minutes.

Pasadena

We planned the Chilao camping trip so that we could also visit the super attractions in Pasadena (pop 150,200), the cultural center of San

Gabriel Valley. So we spent a good part of the preceding day (October 29) in Pasadena, located just six miles southeast of the western terminus of Angeles Crest Highway, on our way to Chilao.

To cite Wikipedia: "Famous for hosting the annual Rose Bowl football game and the Tournament of Roses Parade, Pasadena is the home of many leading scientific and cultural institutions, including the California Institute of Technology (Caltech), Pasadena City College (PCC), NASA's Jet Propulsion Laboratory (JPL), Art Center College of Design the Pasadena Playhouse, California School of Culinary Arts Pasadena, the Norton Simon Museum of Art, and the Pacific Asia Museum."

Pcture 71.2 Tournament House in Pasadena, California (*Source: Wikimedia Commons*)

Our first stop was to see Tournament House (391 S. Orange Grove Blvd.) in Wrigley Garden. Once owned by the Wrigley family of chewing gum fame, this Italian Renaissance style mansion (built in 1914) was ceded to Pasadena city in 1958. It is the operational headquarters of the Tournament of Roses Association. This is the starting point of the annual Parade of Roses on New Year's Day that started in 1890.

Our second stop was the Ambassador Auditorium (300 W Green St.) on the campus of what was then called Ambassador College (1947-1997) operated by the Radio or Worldwide Church of God until a doctrinal split caused its demise 1997. Built under the guidance of radio evangelist Herbert W. Armstrong, the 1,262 capacity auditorium was used for religious services and concert performances. The architecture resembled that of a Jewish temple.

Our next stop was the Rose Bowl stadium, where a large crowd was waiting to watch the football game between UCLA and Washington. Opened in 1922, it became the site of the annual college football bowl game, the Rose Bowl, held on New Year's Day. In 1982, it became the home field of the UCLA Bruins college football team of the Pac-10 Conference. The Tournament of Roses reports the stadium's capacity at 92,542.

After leaving Pasadena, we visited the 150-acre Descanso (Botanic) Garden in La Cañada Flintridge. E. Manchester Boddy, owner of the *Los Angeles Daily News*, ceded the premises he started as a commercial camellia garden to Los Angeles County in 1953. The county developed the property to include a Rosarium, a Japanese teahouse, a lilac garden, a bird sanctuary, and a Xeriscape (to emphasize landscaping possibilities with drought-resistant plants to promote water conservation). Its Enchanted Railroad takes the visitors to a section of the gardens in a diesel train.

Arcadia

We had already explored the two main attractions of the "rim" city of Arcadia (pop 53,100), just east of Pasadena, two weeks before (October 15) the Chilao trip. Today, the city has gone through a remarkable demographic change from an almost-all-white community three decades ago to one with 45 percent Asian Americans. We visited the following places:

- The 320-acre Santa Anita Park, which opened in 1934 for thoroughbred horse racing. It is the oldest racetrack in Southern California. Its 1,100-foot-long grandstand is a historic landmark that seats 26,000 guests. The grandstand bears an Art Deco style and is the original facade from the 1930s. Moreover, its sixty-one barns accommodate more than two thousand horses eligible for treatment at the equine hospital on the premises.

- The 127-acre Los Angeles State and County Arboretum (301 N. Baldwyn Ave.) jointly operated by California State and LA County since its inception in 1954. Plants in the arboretum are grouped by geography with gardens for South American, Mediterranean, South African, Australian and Asiatic-North American plants.

The arboretum or botanic garden, neighboring Santa Anita Park, kept us busy for hours. Yoke-Sim was enamored by the Sunset demonstration home gardens and the plant displays at Ayers Hall. We passed through Garden for All Seasons, Greenleaves, Herb Garden, and Aquatic Garden; we liked the serenity of the man-made waterfall and the two lagoons next to Meadowbrook. In the historical area, we visited the Queen Anne Cottage, the Hugo Reid Adobe, the Corn Barn, the Indian Wickiups, and the Santa Anita Depot. Finally, we went through the Prehistoric and Jungle Garden.

CHAPTER 72

California: Hollywood Is More Than a Place

I FIRST VISITED Hollywood on December 22, 1966 (a Thursday), during the West Coast tour of the World Press Institute fellows. I was impressed by the gigantic sign that spelled out *Hollywood* in forty-five-foot-tall, pure-white caps in the Hollywood Hills area of Mount Lee on Griffith Park. Although the sign is visible from most parts of the city, insiders say that the view from Griffith Observatory is the best. It's this landmark (established in 1923) that races into my mind whenever I hear or read the word Hollywood. Wow!

I have not yet attained the meditative state needed to analyze this particular outcome of the interaction of codependent variables upon the "stream of consciousness" that constitutes me.

In 1966, Clarke Wales, public relations director of the Motion Picture Producers Association, welcomed the WPI journalists, including me, to Hollywood. He gave us the basic facts and figures on the film industry. Then, off we went for a tour of 20th Century Fox Studios, where Don Prince, a studio representative, showed us the shooting of films, and took us for lunch at the studio restaurant. We saw Jayne Mansfield, among other celebrities. We also visited the Hollywood Bowl, the Griffith Observatory, and Grauman's Chinese Theater.

Hollywood 1983

On September 4 1983 (a Sunday), my son Junius and wife Yoke-Sim joined me to pay obeisance to the famous Hollywood Sign yet again. It was the day we chose for our foray into Hollywood in the narrow geopolitical sense. Our focus was the neighborhood commonly identified as Hollywood lying to the west-northwest of downtown Los Angeles. For all its fame, Hollywood is not a separate city although it has an honorary mayor appointed by the Hollywood Chamber of Commerce.

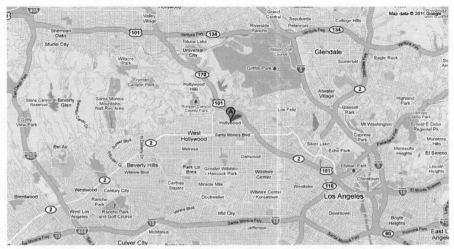

Map 72.1 Hollywood and its vicinity.

(In 2006, Hollywood was recognized as a district of Los Angeles City with defined boundaries encompassing twenty-five square miles with a population of 124,000. Wikipedia describes the border loosely as the area east of Beverly Hills and West Hollywood; south of Mulholland Drive, Laurel Canyon, Cahuenga Boulevard, and Barham Boulevard, and the cities of Burbank and Glendale; north of Melrose Avenue; and west of the Golden State Freeway (I-5) and Hyperion Avenue. This includes all of Griffith Park and Los Feliz—two areas that were hitherto generally considered separate from Hollywood.)

However, sometimes, what the world calls Hollywood goes well beyond this geographical patch of twenty-five square miles with popular landmarks such as:

- John Anson Ford Theater, established in 1920 (2580 E. Cahuenga Blvd.). We watched the rehearsal of a French play here.
- Hollywood Bowl (2301 N. Highland Ave.), which can seat 17,376 people. The Bowl was built in 1919 in a natural amphitheater/canyon, which was called "Daisy Dell." Opened in 1922, it has been the host of hundreds of musical events every year.

- Grauman's Chinese Theater (6925 Hollywood Blvd.), opened in 1926, along the Hollywood Walk of Fame, where we matched our feet to the footprints of the stars. The concrete in the theater's forecourt contains almost two hundred celebrity footprints, handprints, and autographs.
- Ripley's Believe It or Not! Odditorium on Hollywood Boulevard.
- Hollywood Wax Museum (6767 Hollywood Blvd.), opened in 1965 by "Spoony" Singh.
- The Lot (former Warner Hollywood Studios) at 7200 Santa Monica Blvd.
- Hollywood Center Studios (1040 N. Las Palmas Ave.)
- Red (former Ren-Mar) Studios (846 N. Cahuenga Blvd.).
- Paramount Studios (5555 Melrose Ave.)

Picture 72.1 Yoke-Sim and Junius at the Hollywood Bowl (September 4, 1983).

Hollywood has two other wider meanings: Many people use the term Hollywood to refer to Greater Los Angeles in general. Others use Hollywood as a metonymy of American cinema. Wikipedia explains:

The nicknames "Star Struck Town" and "Tinsel Town" refer to Hollywood and its movie industry. Today, much of the movie industry has dispersed into surrounding areas such as the Westside neighborhood, but significant auxiliary industries, such as editing, effects, props, post-production and lighting companies remain in Hollywood, as does the backlot of Paramount Pictures.

On this tour, we paid little attention to the Westside area, which has now absorbed a large portion of the entertainment industry. Wikipedia says that Century City, a major business hub of the Westside, contains many major production corporations, film studios, commercial effects houses, talent agencies, and entertainment law firms. Other important entertainment industry centers are Santa Monica, Venice, Beverly Hills, and new developments near Los Angeles Airport.

American pianist and comedian Oscar Levant (1906-1972) once described Hollywood in a nutshell: "Strip away the false tinsel from Hollywood, and you find the real tinsel inside." So the glamour, celebrity, and wealth associated with Hollywood, thanks to its movie industry, is a façade or illusion (*maya*) behind which lies a life world of suffering (*dukkha*). Another quote from Levant highlights one aspect of that suffering: "Everyone in Hollywood is gay, except Gabby Hayes—and that's because he is a transvestite."

Extending the "tinsel" metaphor to Mumbai (Bombay) motion picture industry, the term Bollywood—a portmanteau of Bombay and Hollywood—came into widespread use in the 1970s, when India overtook America as the world's largest film producer.

At Universal Studios

We visited Universal Studios Hollywood (owned by National Broadcasting Co.) on a subsequent Saturday (October 8, 1983). Located in Universal City, an unincorporated area of sixty-five square miles, Universal Studios operates both as a theme park (with sixteen rides) and as a movie studio. (Discounted admission cost us $18 in 1983, with no charge for Junius. General admission in 2010: $70.)

We spent the first couple of hours touring the Backlot by train and foot. We saw costumes and props, sound stages and sets, drawing rooms, etc. We entered Studio 32 to see a demonstration of special effects.

We found the train tour very daring and exciting—going through a bridge that almost fell apart; through a snow tunnel that nearly turned us around; and through the edge of a lake into which we almost fell while a shark came screaming toward us!

Having ascertained that we survived our derring-do for sure, we went on a self-guided tour of the Entertainment Center (Upper Lot and Lower Lot).

First, we attended the "Adventures of Conan: A Sword and Sorcery Spectacular," which had its run from 1983 to 1992. Its current replacement is "Creature from the Black Lagoon: The Musical," which began in 2009 for one year only.

Second, we attended the "Screen Test Comedy Theater." Its current successor (since 2004) is "Shrek 3-D."

Third, we attended the "Wild Wild West Stunt Show," which had its run from the 1980s to 2002. Another stunt show, "The A-Team Live Stunt Show" (1984-1987) has been replaced by "Waterworld: A Live Sea War Spectacular," which began in 1995.

Fourth, we saw action on the "Animal Actors School Stage," which had its run from the 1970s to 2001. Its current replacement (since 2007) is "Universal's Animal Actors."

We also visited the World of Woody Woodpecker and the Motion Picture and Television Museum. Woodpecker is Universal's mascot. He walks around the park with other costumed characters such as Andy Panda, Scooby Doo, Dracula, Beetlejuice, and Crash Bandicoot.

At NBC Studios

We devoted another Saturday (November 5, 1983) morning to join the ten o'clock walking tour of the NBC Studios in Burbank (3000 W. Alameda Ave.). Burbank is just six miles northeast of Universal City.

Overall, the tour was a disappointment. Our guide, Brian D., took us to the mini-studio, where we saw ourselves on camera. Brian showed us several studios and sets used by celebrity news anchors and stars. Earlier, we visited the NBC employees' arts and crafts fair.

Picture 72.2 Author and his son Junius at the NBC Studios in Burbank (November 5, 1983).

Burbank had struck a chord in my mind because comedians Dan Rowan and Dick Martin, my favorite TV starts in my graduate-student days, used to constantly brag about "beautiful Burbank" in their popular "Laugh-in" from 1968 to 1973. But the tour failed to show me the memorabilia associated with the two comedians.

NBC Studios refer to the company's TV studio facilities in Burbank, as well as its TV studio facilities in New York City, where the company headquarters are located. NBC has a third production facility in Chicago called the NBC Tower.

In mid-October 2007, NBC announced its plan to move most of its operations by 2011 from Burbank to a new complex across the street from Universal Studios in Universal City. It intended to retain only an office presence at the current Burbank site.

CHAPTER 73

California: Holidaying in Santa Barbara, "the American Riviera"

ON VOEGELE, WHO hailed from Santa Barbara, was an adjunct instructor at Fullerton College in 1983, the year I spent in California as an exchange instructor. Although he was not from the Division of Communications, he made it his business to get acquainted with us for the simple reason that we came from Down Under. A card-carrying member of the Sierra Club, he was perhaps enamored by Australia's open country façade.

Many locals knew our alien presence on FC campus within a couple of months after our arrival because of good publicity we received from the college and local press. The May 25, edition of the (Fullerton) *Daily News-Tribune*, for example, carried a half-page news feature written by Mary Edwards on me and my family (illustrated with a large family photo) headlined "From Fullerton to Down Under and Vice Versa." It also carried a column written by my exchange partner Larry Taylor.

After the initial overtures of getting to know each other, Voegele joined us for dinner on a Saturday (June 4) at Richard Jones Pit BBQ (5781 Santa Ana Canyon Road) in Anaheim Hills. We ate Texas-style hickory-smoked BBQ featuring pork spare ribs, smoked beef briskets, ham and chicken—all for just $25! Voegele visited us at our condo before the dinner and suggested that we visit Santa Barbara, where he and his brother John shared a studio apartment in Summerland, during a weekend.

By this time, Yoke-Sim and I had got into the habit of splurging money on restaurants during weekends in our quest for gustatory variety with Junius as the beneficiary. For example, two Saturdays earlier (21 May), we ate dinner at Sengoka Sushi Bar (1490 N. Kraemer) in Placentia. Yoke-Sim ate a platter of seafood—scallops, oysters, fresh fish, and shrimp tempura—while I ate an early bird special—vegetable tempura, chicken teriyaki, beef teriyaki, Japanese cucumber, soup, and rice. We topped all that with *Chawanmushi*—Japanese egg custard soup—for just $23!

Incidentally, the preceding Friday (May 20), I ate lunch at El Paso Cantina (on Nutwood Avenue in Fullerton) with another visiting instructor from Australia at CSU Fullerton, Peter W. Mehra, a lecturer in marketing at NSWIT in Sydney.

Let me leave this digression on dining to return to Voegele's invitation.

En Route to Santa Barbara

After we enthusiastically accepted Voegele's invitation to visit his hometown, we agreed to schedule our tour for the last weekend of June. He volunteered to accompany us on the trip. He was willing to do some of the driving as well.

Picking Voegele on the FC campus, we left Fullerton on a Friday (June 24) morning for Santa Barbara, located 120 miles to the northwest. However, we chose to travel on the coastal scenic route (SR 1), which increased the distance by about ten miles. We drove west on SR 91 (Artesia Fwy. or Blvd.) to Manhattan Beach (pop 34,000), where we joined SR 1 heading northwest. Then, past Westchester (L. A. Airport area), we reached Santa Monica (pop 88,000), which is known for its landmark pier and the stretch of coastal greenery called Palisades Park. Proceeding ahead, we entered the Los Angels district of Pacific Palisades (pop 27,000); and Malibu (pop 13,000), an elite city carved out of a twenty-one-mile (34 km) strip of Pacific coastline to meet the whims and fancies of the filthy rich associated with the Hollywood film industry. It is a beachfront community known for its warm, sandy beaches, and for being the home of many movie stars and their sidekicks.

(We were destined to return to this area on October 22, to explore the J Paul Getty Museum at its original location on SR 1. I shall keep the details of that enjoyable excursion for the grist of another installment.)

We visited the beautiful 830-acre Malibu campus of Pepperdine University, established in 1937 by the Churches of Christ. The Princeton Review ranked Pepperdine on the list of colleges with "Dorms Like Palaces" in 2004 and 2007 and no.1 under "Most Beautiful Campus" in 2006 and 2007.

Santa Barbara 101

Santa Barbara was another sixty-five miles northwest from Malibu. However, Voegele began his Introduction to Santa Barbara as we moved from Los Angeles County to Ventura County, but still within the western territorial boundary of Greater Los Angeles. (The eastern boundary of Santa Barbara County marks the western edge of GLA.) He determined the course of the journey from here onwards.

To show us the scenery surrounding the campus, Voegele took us on a drive along the Coral Canyon Road. Back o SR 1, he took us to Point Mugu, an unincorporated area in Ventura County. This is the location of Naval Base Ventura County Point Mugu (NBVC). The "Mugu Rock" is a landmark in the area. Our next stop was the US Navy "Seabee" Museum in Port Hueneme (pop 22,000), a 4.6 square-mile charter city almost surrounded by Oxnard (pop 200,000), the largest city in Ventura County.

Then, via Channel Islands Boulevard and Harbor Boulevard, we entered the Channel Islands National Park Headquarters' visitor center, where we paused to relax and eat our lunch. The park consists of five of the eight Channel Islands off the Southern California coast from Point Conception near Santa Barbara to San Pedro near the port of Los Angeles. At the visitor center, we watched a movie on the Channel Islands.

Next, we moved on to the city of Ventura (pop 107,000), the county seat and the location of Mission San Buenaventura (or Ventura for short). We visited the premises of the mission that Father Junípero Serra founded in 1782. We saw a fascinating slide show at the adjoining small museum, which displays Chumash Indian artifacts and mission-era items.

When we reached the oceanside city of Carpinteria (pop 15,000), Voegele treated us to a round of Thrifty ice cream, his favorite, to celebrate our arrival in Santa Barbara County. We walked to the Carpinteria State Beach. Finally, we arrived in Voegele's official residence in Santa Barbara—2185 Lillie Avenue, Summerland.

Picture 73.1 Don Voegele plays with Junius who hangs on to the author's back at Mission San Buenaventura in Ventura (June 24, 1983).

Summerland (pop 1,600), an area encompassing two square miles, is on the coast directly east of the city of Santa Barbara and west-northwest of Carpinteria, and is almost entirely surrounded by the unincorporated community of Montecito (pop 10,000).

Later in the evening, Voegele and I joined a Sierra Club walking tour of the San Ysidro Canyon Trail, north of Montecito. Following this rejuvenating exercise, all the hikers repaired to Rusty's Pizza Parlor to eat supper. We had a good time.

Santa Barbara bears the nickname "American Riviera," but to which Santa Barbara does it refer—the city (pop 93,000), the contiguous urban area (pop 220,000), or the county (pop 422,000)? (The SB urban area includes the cities of Goleta on the west and Carpinteria on the east, along with the unincorporated regions of Isla Vista, Montecito, Mission

Canyon, Hope Ranch, Summerland, and others). I think the nickname applies to the contiguous urban area because the entire horizontal coastal stretch lies between the rising hills of Santa Ynez Mountains (in the Los Padres National Forest) and the Pacific.

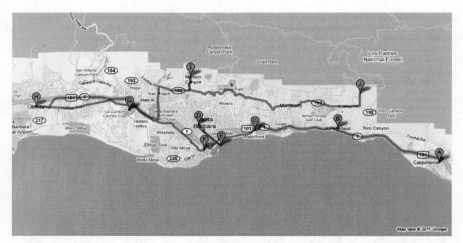

Map 73.1 Places of interest in Santa Barbara: *A*, Carpinteria; *B*, Summerland; *C*, Bird Refuge and Zoo; *D*, Downtown Santa Barbara; *E*, Stearns Wharf; *F*, SB City College; *G*, Hope Ranch; *H*, Goleta and UCSB; *I*, SB Botanic Gardens; *J*, Vedanta Temple.

Day 2 in Santa Barbara

Yoke-Sim and I decided that we (including Junius) should self-explore the attractions of Santa Barbara so that Voegele and his brother John could attend to their respective chores. Thus, the next morning, we headed west to downtown SB along the coastal Channel Drive and Cabrillo Boulevard.

From the Stearns Wharf in the southeast, the downtown extends northwestwards for a mile along State Street, its backbone. We visited the quaint El Paseo Plaza in Old Town; El Cuartel, the remnants of a two-room soldiers' quarters in the El Presidio de Santa Barbara State Historic Park; the Historical Society Museum; the Moreton Bay Fig Tree (believed to have been shipped from Australia and planted in 1877) on Chapala Street; the County Courthouse; the Museum of Art; and the

Alice Keck Park. We also had a good look at Piccadilly Square, Lobero Theatre, and Victoria Court.

In the afternoon, we visited Mission Santa Barbara (Queen of the Alta California Missions) founded in 1786 by Father Fermin Lasuen for the religious conversion of the Chumash tribe. Just north of the mission, we explored the Museum of Natural History before our final destination for the day—the Botanic Gardens on Mission Canyon Road, where we walked on the trails. Finally, we drove back to Summerland on the hilly scenic drive admiring some of the magnificent homes in Montecito along the way. We celebrated the day with a family-style dinner at the nearby Big Yellow House.

Day 3 in Santa Barbara

Sunday morning, the Voegele brothers—Don and John—joined us for breakfast at the Omelet Parlor in Summerland. Then, we took off again for self-exploration. We drove west on East Cabrillo Boulevard to see the Andree Clark Bird Refuge, adjoining the SB Zoological Gardens; the Stearns Wharf, south of downtown; the Sunday Market, east of State Street on Cabrillo Boulevard; and the nearby Santa Barbara City College.

Because we were curious to know more about how the wealthy folks splurged their greenbacks on prime property, we proceeded further west to the unincorporated area called Hope Ranch (popualtion 2,200), one of the wealthiest areas in California. (The median home price in Hope Ranch was $2.61 million in 2006.) We drove on hilly streets (like Via Laguna and Lago Drive) feasting our eyes on homes we could only dream about, when we saw a cricket game in full swing at the park on Via Rosita—an oddity in America! However, the players were mostly East and West Indians.

Being homesick for cricket, we watched the game for quite a while before going further west to Goleta (pop 55,200; it became a city in 2002) to visit the University of California Santa Barbara—our last stop on this excursion. We read the *Weekend Australian* in the library and then walked along the north shore of the campus lagoon.

We were back in Summerland by 5:00 p.m. ready for the return journey to Fullerton. With Don Voegele as driver, we left Summerland an hour later. He started the journey with a five-mile trip north to show us the Vedanta Temple in Montecito (927 Ladera Lane). The temple was established in 1956 on a thirty-acre property (later expanded to forty-five acres) donated in 1944 by Spencer Kellogg to the Vedanta Society of Southern California.

Picture 73.2 Junius with his father and mother at the Vedanta Temple at 927 Ladera Lane, Santa Barbara (June 26, 1983).

Run by a convent of seven nuns, the temple's activities include daily worship, meditation and vesper services, Sunday lectures, and *pujas* (special worship services).

After leaving the temple, via Toro Canyon Road, Voegele got on to the freeway US 101and drove all the way east to Sherman Oaks, where we ate a late dinner at Carl's Jr. We reached Fullerton about 11:00 p.m.

SHELTON A. GUNARATNE

CHAPTER 74

California: Visiting Getty Villa and Crossing LA's Mulholland Drive

HEN WE PASSED through the scenic coastal highway from Santa Monica to Malibu on our way to Santa Barbara in mid-1983, we were intrigued by the impressive architecture of the J. Paul Getty Museum we sighted in the proximity of Topanga Canyon. Although we were not fans of art museums, the novelty and the architectural elegance of the building enticed us to put it on our "must-visit" list.

Four months later, we did indeed visit the Getty Villa, the art museum located at 17985 Pacific Coast Highway, in Pacific Palisades, a mile east of Malibu. In short, it is within the city limits of Los Angeles. What originally impressed us was the classical European-style museum building with an extremely beautiful main peristyle garden.

Minnesota-born oil tycoon J. Paul Getty (1892-1975) originally opened a gallery adjacent to his home in Pacific Palisades. When his expanding collection of cultural artifacts exceeded the storage capacity of his home, he opened a second museum on the property in 1974. This is the Getty Villa that attracted our attention on our way to Santa Barbara on June 24, 1983.

Docent Betty K. Asher, who gave us an orientation to the one and only J. Paul Getty Museum at the time of our visit on October 22, explained that the Villa of the Papyri at Herculaneum inspired the model of Getty Villa. The building also incorporated additional details from several other ancient sites. I discerned an inexplicable affinity between Getty Villa and Hearst Castle, which we visited on July 30.

The mission of the museum was "to further knowledge of the visual arts and to nurture critical seeing by collecting, preserving, exhibiting, and interpreting works of art of the highest quality." The mission inspired us, the visitors, to take a deeper interest in what the museum had so carefully selected for public exhibition charging no admission for the privilege (except $15 for parking).

At the Main Level of the museum, we visited the classical collection in the Hall of Aphrodite; then, we moved on to the Greek Masterpieces, Atrium, Attic, Memorial Sculpture, Late Classical and Hellenic Sculpture, Room of Colored Marbles, Etruscan Vestibule, and Basilica Temple of Heralds and Mosaics.

At the Upper Level, we saw numerous classical paintings—Dutch, Flemish, Italian Renaissance, and Baroque. We also visited the Regence Period Room, the Rococo Period Room, and the Neoclassical Period Room. Finally, we saw a changing exhibit—Renaissance Painting in Manuscript from the British Library. We also went to see the Garden Tea Room and the Herb Garden. It was a wonderful educational experience for Junius, Yoke-Sim, and me. We spent three hours at the museum.

Picture 74.1 The author, with Junius in his arms, reads a brochure on J Paul Getty Museum in front of what is now called Getty Villa (October 23, 1983).

In 1997, fourteen years after our visit, the magnificent Getty Villa was closed for renovation and a small part of the museum's collection was moved to the Getty Center in nearby Brentwood. Getty Villa reopened on January 28, 2006. Wikipedia provides the following update:

> Getty Villa once again holds Greek and Roman sculptures some of which were housed in the interim at the Getty Center and the large part in storage for the duration of the Villa's closure. The Greek, Roman, and Etruscan antiquities are arranged by themes e.g. *Gods and Goddesses*, *Dionysos and the Theater* and *Stories of the Trojan War*, housed within Roman-inspired architecture and surrounded by Roman-style gardens.

Machado and Silvetti Associates conceived the new architectural plan surrounding the Villa, which houses some forty-four thousand works of art although only twelve hundred are on display.

Visitors to the Villa now gather in an open-air Entry Pavilion, then walk along a scenic pathway to the heart of the site, the 450-seat Barbara and Lawrence Fleischman Theater (an outdoor classical theater), which links the new Cafe, Museum Store, and Auditorium to the J. Paul Getty Museum entrance.

Back to Santa Barbara

Junius, Yoke-Sim, and I returned to Santa Barbara the weekend after our first visit. On this occasion, we drove on a different route. Starting from Fullerton, we drove on Orange (SR 57) and Pomona (SR 60) freeways to downtown Los Angeles, where we turned northwest on to El Camino Real or Hollywood Freeway (US 101).

At Hollywood Hills, we tuned west to drive along the fourteen-mile long eastern stretch of the scenic and winding Mulholland Drive, which loosely follows the ridgeline of Hollywood Hills and Santa Monica Mountains offering spectacular vistas of the San Fernando Valley. Along the way, we stopped at the Fryman Canyon Overlook; and again at Franklin Canyon Ranch, where we hiked the 2.3-mile roundtrip Hastain Trail on the Santa Monica Mountains. We had a foggy view of the city from the summit (elevation 980 feet).

Map 74.1 An offbeat (124-mile) route from Mulholland Drive (Los Angeles) to Summerland (Santa Barbara). *A*, Eastern terminus of Mulholland Drive in Hollywood Hills; *B*, "Dirt Mulholland" at Water and Power Pole Road; *C*, Western terminus of Mulholland Drive, which turns into Mulholland Highway; *D*, Canoga Park; *E*, Simi Valley; *F*, Moorpark; *G*, Fillmore; *H*, Santa Paula; *I*, Ojai; *J*, Lake Casitas; *K*, Summerland; *Red A*, Getty Villa, Pacific Palisades.

We tarried at the Tree People Nursery on the way back to Mulholland Drive, which turns into a dirt road on reaching the Water and Power Pole Road in Topanga State Park, a few miles to the west after it crosses the San Diego Freeway (Interstate 405). Because the "Dirt Mulholland" was not open for vehicles, we decided to skirt around it to reach the western terminus of Mulholland Drive. Turning itself into Mulholland Highway, it then heads southwest to join the Pacific Coast Highway, west of Malibu.

Exploring the enigma of Mulholland Drive was the highlight of the day. (David Lynch's 2001 movie *Mulholland Dr.* centers around a woman who turns amnesic after a car wreck on this road.

We turned north on Topanga Canyon Boulevard to visit the western Los Angeles communities of Woodland Hills (pop 67,000) and Canoga Park (pop 53,300). We gawked at the Canoga. Mission Gallery (23130 Sherman Way, West Hills), a former stable built in the Mission Revival style in 1936 by actor Francis Lederer.

Then, we crossed over the southeastern limits of Ventura County to enter the city of Simi Valley (pop 119,000), seventeen miles northwest of Canoga Park. Surrounded by the Santa Susana Mountain Range and the Simi Hills, it has provided the enchanting backdrop for several movies and TV shows. As fans of Steven Spielberg's 1982 blockbuster *E.T. the Extra-Terrestrial*, we were naturally interested in seeing the Simi Valley landscape captured in the movie to thrill thousands of its fans. We drove along Los Angeles Avenue between Yosemite Avenue and First Street. We also stopped at a farmers' market to buy some nectarines.

Then, we headed nine miles further west to Moorpark (pop 47,500). Our focus was the 134-acre scenic campus of Moorpark College (estbd. 1967) with a current student enrollment of 16,600. Students call the college "Kraproom" ("Moorpark" spelled backwards).

We really left the beaten track, when we drove eleven miles north of Moorpark on SR 23 to visit the 2.8 square mile city of Fillmore (pop 13,700). Wikipedia says: Fillmore has classic "turn of the century" downtown architecture, a one-screen theater, a historic train depot (the Fillmore and Western Railway), a much photographed city hall, and many unique shops and businesses, including a local winery operation.

Nine miles further to the southwest, we visited Santa Paula (pop 28,600). Dubbed the "Citrus Capital of the World," the city was one of the early centers of California's oil industry. Wikipedia describes Santa Paula "as a quaint town, boasting a main street reminiscent of Middle America but with a Mexican flavor." We visited the Oil Museum.

We were again off the beaten path, when we visited Ojai (pop 8,000), a 4.4 square-mile city surrounded by hills and mountains of the Ojai Valley. Lying seventeen miles to the northwest of Santa Paula, Ojai is well known for its Film Festival, Music Festival, and Poetry Festival.

Our final stop in Ventura County was Lake Casitas Recreation Area, seven miles southwest of Ojai. Summerland in Santa Barbara was another twenty-two miles southwest of Lake Casitas.

After settling down again at the Voegele brothers' pad in Summerland, Yoke-Sim cooked a simple dinner. Don Voegele joined us for the meal, while we related our day's adventures.

Sunday (July 3, 1983)

This morning, all of us joined a four-hour hike, with Don as leader, up on Romero Canyon Trail, north of Summerland. It turned out to be a strenuous hike. I had to carry Junius some of the way. Yoke-Sim followed with some difficulty. John, who brought his dog named "Lady" with him, sighted three snakes.

In the afternoon, we explored another part of Santa Ynez. Bernadette Bauer, a friend of Don's, joined us. Don took us to La Cumbre Peak (elev. 3,985 ft.), from where we had a good view of the valley below. We also stopped to see the ruins of the Knapp Castle, the Painted Village, and Jane Fonda's Ranch at Laurel Springs.

We ate dinner at Skandia Buffet in Santa Barbara.

Monday (July 4, 1983)

It being Independence Day, we left the Voegele brothers alone, and set forth to explore more offbeat attractions in Santa Barbara in the vicinity of SR 192 (Foothills Road) and SR154 (San Marcos Pass Road). Our first stop was Westmont College in Montecito, and the second was Cold Spring Tavern (5995 Stagecoach Road), fourteen miles northwest of the city. Then, we went to see the Bradbury Dam on Lake Cachuma.

The community of Santa Ynez (pop 5,600) named after Saint Agnes, and located forty miles north of Santa Barbara, was our next target. We walked along Sagunto Street, which resembled the Old West. Proceeding further, we reached the community of Los Olivos (pop 1,000), renowned for its wineries and tasting rooms. We stopped at Mattie's Tavern (2350 Railway Ave.), a stagecoach inn built in 1886, and at Firestone Vineyard (5000 Zaca Station Road). But both were closed.

At Los Olivos, the northern terminus of SR 154, we turned south on US 101 to return to Santa Barbara. We stopped at the McDonalds in Buellton (pop 3,900) for lunch; and also at Pea Soup Anderson's for desert.

Then, we reached our main destination for the day: Solvang (pop 5,400), a city of 2.5 square miles founded in 1911 by a group of Danish educators. The city's architecture, its Hans Christian Andersen statue, its restaurants, bakeries, shops, and museums are all designed to promote its essential pride in all things Danish.

We returned to Summerland about 7:00 p.m. after three more short stops at Alisal Guest Ranch (in Solvang), Nojoqui Falls County Park, and the hot springs in Gaviota State Park.

Later in the evening, Don Voegele took me to visit with his mother, Lorraine Myers, at her elegant home in the Riviera. The next morning, Voegele joined us on our return journey to Fullerton.

Picture 74. 2 The author and his son Junius enjoy their visit to the County Courthouse in Santa Barbara (June 25, 1983).

Postscript

Before the end of my Fullerton Year, we spent another night at Voegeles' pad (new location: 590 Ribera St., Goleta)—on Christmas Day on our return trip from San Francisco with my mother. I have already dwelled on it in chapter 65.

Although Voegele had a few steady female friends, he remained single. He was a nomad of sorts who taught as an adjunct in several two-year colleges. While on a camping trip in the Midwest, he and his significant other, Julia Christy, visited us in Minnesota. But they preferred to sleep in their campervan rather than in the guest room we offered.

CHAPTER 75

California: Palm Springs, The City of Celebrities

WE—JUNIUS, YOKE-SIM, AND I—spent a Saturday (November 26, 1983) in Palm Springs, the fashionable resort in the Upper Colorado Desert on the eastern foothills of San Jacinto Peak (elev. 10,804 ft.). The city of Palm Springs (pop 48,000), which occupies an area of ninety-five square miles in the Coachella Valley in Riverside County, is well known for its 125 golf courses and its connections with numerous celebrities.

Celebrity Connections

Let me illustrate these connections with the following examples gleaned from Wikipedia:

- Entertainer Sonny Bono (1935-1998) ran a restaurant in downtown Palm Springs. Frustrated by the lack of cooperation he faced from the city council over a new sign for the restaurant, he took matters into his own hands and ran for mayor. With Marshall Gilbert, the conservative talk radio host on KNWQ, as his campaign manager, Bono won the mayoral election in 1988. Having put himself back in the public eye, Bono won a seat in the US House of Representatives in 1994, a position he held until his death in a skiing accident in 1998. His widow, Mary, filled the vacancy.
- The legendary animation genius Walt Disney (1901-1966), who owned the Smoke Tree Ranch in Palm Springs, was so proud of his property that he had the ranch's brand embroidered on all of his neckties. Disney reluctantly sold the property to help finance the construction of Disneyland. *The Partners*, bronze sculptures

of Disney standing next to Mickey Mouse in each of the Disney theme parks clearly show the brand on Disney's tie.

- Since the 1930s, Palm Springs has been a magnet for many Hollywood stars. Bing Crosby (1903-1977); Charles Farrell (1901-1990), who was elected mayor of Palm Springs in 1953 and held that office for seven years; and Ralph Bellamy (1904-1991) founded the first tennis club in Palm Springs. Crosby also started the Blue Skies Trailer Park in Rancho Mirage. Other 1930s and 1940s celebrities who frequented Palm Springs included Humphrey Bogart (1899-1957), John Barrymore (1882-1942), Douglas Fairbanks Jr. (1909-2000), Mary Pickford (1882-1979), and Judy Garland (1922-1967).
- Elvis Presley (1935-1977), who frequently visited Coachella Valley, honeymooned in Palm Springs in 1967. Frank Sinatra (1915-1998), Bob Hope (1903-2003), and Dinah Shore (1916-1994), who resided in the valley, helped create three major golf tournaments.
- President Gerald Ford (1913-2006), who was a longtime Rancho Mirage resident, became a benefactor of the substance abuse center that bears his wife's name, the Betty Ford Center. Lucille Ball (1911-1989) and Desi Arnaz (1917-1986) were instrumental in forming the exclusive Thunderbird Heights gated hillside in Rancho Mirage, where some of the rich and famous live in homes valued at between $1 million and $10 million.

Location and Population

We travelled ninety miles east of Fullerton to reach Palm Springs. Riverside (pop 316,000), the county seat of the eponymous county, is located fifty-six miles west of Palm Springs.

Between the twenty-five-mile north-south geographical stretch between Palm Springs and La Quinta (pop 43,200) lie four other resort cities: Cathedral City (popualton 54,200), Rancho Mirage (pop 13,300), Palm Desert (pop 50,800) and Indian Wells (pop 5,200). The community of Bermuda Dunes (pop 7,000), and the cities of Indio (pop 83,000) and Coachella (pop 33,800) lie further to the east. People use the name Palm Springs to connote all the contiguous cities listed in this paragraph.

More than two million people live in Riverside County, which is part of Greater Los Angeles. The county's population has increased by more than 200 percent since I visited its most famous city (Palm Springs) and its county seat (Riverside) in 1983. Over the same time span, the population of Palm Springs has increased by 48 percent while that of Riverside city by 85 percent.

The reason for the expansion of Riverside population is the exodus of people from Metropolitan Los Angeles to the outskirts for cheaper housing. The cities of Murrieta (pop 100,200; established in 1991) and its neighbor Temecula (pop 105,000; established in 1989) accounted for 20 percent of the county's population growth since 2000.

Map 75.1 In Orange County. *A*, Bowers Museum, Santa Ana; *B*, Crystal Cathedral, Garden Grove (in Riverside city area, Riverside County); *C*, Mount Rubidoux Park; *D*, Mission Inn; *E*, UCR Botanic Gardens; *F*, March AFB. (In Palm Springs area, Riverside County); *G*, Palm Springs Aerial Tramway; *H*, Agua Caliente Indian Reservation; *I*, Cathedral City; *J*, Rancho Mirage; *K*, Palm Desert; *L*, La Quinta.

Palm Springs 1983

Our first stop in Palm Springs was the Valley Station (elev. 2,643 ft. or 806 m) in Chino Canyon from where we took the Palm Springs Aerial Tramway to Mountain Station (elev. 8,516 ft. or 2,596 m) on the eastern edge of Long Valley in the San Jacinto Wilderness. Opened in 1963, this tramway claims to be the largest of the three rotating aerial tramway in the world. (The other two "Rotair" aerial trams are in Cape Town, South Africa, and Titlis, Switzerland.) The 2.5-mile ride passes up North America's sheerest mountain face through several life zones on its way providing breathtaking views, which amply compensated the $9 we each paid for the ride.

A freezing temperature (22 degrees F) greeted us at the top. Mountain Station area was covered with snow. Although we were not prepared for freezing weather conditions, we tried to walk on the Dessert View Trail. Junius hung on to me and cried most of the way because of the intense cold. We returned to the Valley Station before 2:00 p.m.

Our next stop was Palm Canyon on the Agua Caliente Indian Reservation. (Admission cost us $2.50 per adult.) Founded in 1896 to accommodate the Cahuilla Indians, the reservation occupies 31,610 acres, of which 6,700 come within the Palm Springs city limits. I walked about a mile along the beautiful canyon through the numerous Washingtonian palms, about 1,500 to 2,000 years old.

Picture 75.1 Junius in the company of a cluster of Washingtonian palms at the Agua Caliente Indian Reservation in Palm Springs (November 26, 1983).

We also drove to Andreas Canyon and walked along the terrain past unusual rock formations.

We returned to downtown Palm Springs via Murray Canyon Drive and Sunrise Way. We stopped by at the Village Green Heritage Center and walked up Palm Canyon Drive to window shop. Then, we stopped at Louise's Pantry to eat a home-style-cooked dinner.

On this trip to Palm Springs, we did not run into any of the celebrities who inhabit this city of conspicuous consumption, nor did we go looking for them.

Visiting Riverside City

The next day (Sunday, November 27, 1983), we made an exploratory tour of the city of Riverside. Our starting point was Mount Rubidoux (elev. 1,329 ft. or 405 m) in the San Bernardino Mountains. This 161-acre park is a Riverside landmark, which provides numerous dirt hiking-trails—a delight for those addicted to self-propulsion. The Santa Ana River winds its way at the foothills of the peak. Junius was highly thrilled to travel the very narrow, winding road up and down the peak, where a cross dedicated to Father Junípero Serra stands. An outstanding feature of Mount Rubidoux is the World Peace Tower and Bridge. Riverside celebrated the 100th anniversary of the Easter Sunrise service at the summit of Mount Rubidoux on April 12, 2009.

Mission Inn (3649 Mission Inn Ave.) was the second Riverside landmark we chose to visit. Christopher Columbus Miller built a two-story, twelve-room adobe building called "Glenwood Cottage" in 1876. In 1902, Miller's son Frank changed its name to "Mission Inn" and started expanding it in a wild variety of shapes until he died in 1935. Our guide Barbara showed us the St Francis Chapel, Santa Cecelia Chapel, International Shrine of Aviators, President Taft's Chair, and other antiques. She said that President Nixon married his wife Pat at one of the two wedding chapels; that President Reagan and his wife Nancy honeymooned there; and that several other presidents (e.g., Harrison, McKinley, Roosevelt, Taft, Hoover, Kennedy, and Ford) had visited the inn. We climbed up to see the rooms where famous writers stayed. Overall, we were very much impressed with what we saw.

Then, we crossed over to spend some time at the Riverside Municipal Museum (3720 Orange St.), which was getting ready to celebrate the city's centenary. Next, we stopped at the forty-acre Botanic Gardens of the University of California, Riverside. Located in the eastern foothills of Box Spring Mountain, the gardens contain more than thirty-five hundred plant species from around the world. It has seven collections organized by species and six organized by geographical origin.

Then, via the Riverside International Raceway, we drove to March Air Force Base, but its museum display of some seventy aircrafts was closed. Thus, we decided to spend the rest of the day at the Riverside Plaza Mall.

Picture 75.2 Junius was not inclined to use his energy for self-propulsion on the day we visited the World Peace Tower and Bridge at Mount Rubidoux Park in Riverside. Yoke-Sim had to carry Junius (November 27, 1983).

SHELTON A. GUNARATNE

Back to Orange County

The previous Friday (November 25, 1983), we visited two offbeat attractions in Orange County that we wanted to see before the end of my Fullerton Year:

- Bowers Museum in Santa Ana (2002 N. Main St.), a cultural art repository, was founded in 1936 with the guiding philosophy of helping people learn about other cultures through their arts, and offering "a greater understanding of ourselves and appreciation of the world in which we live." Since our visit to the museum in 1983, it has gone through two renovations and expansions in 1992 and 2007 respectively. Its permanent collection comprises more than one hundred thousand items focusing on several areas, such as African, South Pacific, Asian, Native American, Pre-Columbian art, and California plein-air painting. It balances Getty Villa's European bias.
- Crystal Cathedral in Garden Grove (12141 Louis St.), a mega church of the Reformed Church in America, was designed by architect Philip Johnson to seat 2,736 people in the main sanctuary. The builder used a silicone-based glue to tie together more than ten thousand rectangular panes of glass. The Rev. Robert H. Schuler founded the church in 1955. The high quality of its music program and the eclectic variety of its musical guests has contributed to its success.

CHAPTER 76

California: Watts Goes Latino but Remains Poor

THE WATTS RIOTS of 1965 were fresh in my memory when I first visited Los Angeles in December 1966 as a World Press Institute fellow. The WPI journalists visited the home of author Budd Schulberg (1914-2009) in Beverly Hills (1666 Beverly Drive) for a conversation with the man who wrote the 1941 novel *What makes Sammy run?* and other literary works and was also instrumental in forming the Watts Writers Workshop intended as an artistic outlet for promising black youth who were frustrated because of alleged "police brutality."

The five days of Watts Riots (August 11-15, 1965) followed the arrest of black youth Marquette Frye by white highway patrolman Lee Minikus for alleged drunk driving. The toll: 34 people killed; 2,032 people injured; 3,952 people arrested; and $40 million in damage to property.

Our conversation with Schulberg and several members of the Watts Writers Workshop on December 26, 1966, more than one year after the riots, enabled us to assess the extent of racial tension afflicting Los Angeles in the mid-1960s in the stories we wrote for our home country media. The story I wrote, *Schulberg on Watts*, appeared in the January 13, 1967 edition of *CDN*.

During my Fullerton Year (1983), we—Junius, Yoke-Sim, and I—decided to explore the Watts area and the vicinity one Saturday (September 17) so we could see the changes eighteen years after the riots. We reached Watts, thirty-five miles northwest of Fullerton, via Norwalk, Downey, and South Gate.

Watts (current population 35,000) is a mostly residential neighborhood of the city of Los Angeles, located about twelve miles south of downtown. From 1907 to 1926, Watts Station was a separate city, where the Mexican railroad workers had settled down. Watts became predominantly black only in the 1940s when thousands of blacks left the segregated Deep South to settle down in Southern California. The black influx resulted in a white flight out of areas like Watts in the 1960s.

The city set up three public housing schemes to help the working class residents of Watts:

- Nickerson Gardens (estbd. 1955), a 1,054-unit apartment complex (in 156 buildings) at 1590 E. 114th Street.
- Jordan Downs (estbd. 1955), a seven hundred-unit apartment complex (in 103 buildings) in a block bounded by Grape, 97th, Alameda and 103rd streets.
- Imperial Courts (estbd. 1944), a 498-unit complex at 11541 Croesus Ave. on Imperial Highway between Grape Street and Mona Boulevard.

By the mid-1960s, these housing schemes had turned into almost 100 percent black ghettos.

The 2000 census showed that 61 percent of Watts' residents were Latino (mostly Mexican, Guatemalan, Honduran, and Salvadoran immigrants) and only 38 percent black (mostly African American). However, with almost one-half of its residents living below the poverty line, Watts remain one of the poorest neighborhoods of Los Angeles.

During our 1983 visit, we sensed the increasing tension between the blacks and the Latinos. We heard about the emergence of gang violence in the wake of Watts Riots.

Today, the percentage of African American residents in South Los Angeles is about half of what it was in the 1970s.

Map 76.1 The boundaries of Watts: *A/F-B*, Imperial Highway; *B-C*, Alameda Street; *C-D*, Firestone Boulevard; and *D-F*, Central Avenue; *E* (Exposition Park) is five miles north of *D*.

Impact of Workshop

I was curious to know whether Schulberg's Watts Writers Workshop, a creative writing group composed primarily of young African Americans in Watts and the surrounding neighborhoods, had made a noticeable impact on the community. Rockefeller Foundation had helped the group expand its facilities and activities over the ensuing years. Investigative reporting later revealed that the FBI had targeted the Workshop for covert operations. However, several well-known writers emerged from the Workshop: Poet Quincy Troupe (b. 1939), music and cultural critic Stanley Crouch (b. 1945) and Herbert Simmons, as well as the poetry group Watts Prophets (a group formed in 1967 comprising Richard Dedeaux, Father Amde Hamilton, and Otis O'Solomon). FBI informant Darthard Perry burned down the Workshop in 1975 after spending his own money to keep the facility going following the cut-off federal funding.

In 1983, I was unable to contact any of the Workshop participants—Leumas Sirran, Harry Doland and James Jackson—whom we interviewed at Schulberg's home in 1966. Their view then was that things were getting better although they complained about unemployment and poor transportation.

Although the Workshop was intended to redress the frustrations of the black youth in South Los Angeles, methinks it was not an adequate solution to divert their attention to positive community building. Instead, the black frustrations fostered a fertile ground for increased gang activity and crime. Following four years of peace negotiations, four of Watts' influential gangs—Watts Cirkle City Piru Bloods, Grape Street Watts Crips, Bounty Hunter Watts Bloods, and PJ Watts Crips—formed a Peace Treaty agreement in 1992.

However, these developments could not prevent the eruption of the 1992 Los Angeles Riots sparked by the decision of a jury to acquit four LAPD officers accused of beating Rodney King, a black motorist. The toll of the six-day riot that began on April 29 was as follows: fifty-three people killed, thousands injured and arrested, and US$1 billion in property damage.

Blacks still form the largest ethnic group in the southwestern portion of South Los Angeles. Violent crime in this region, although still high, has been decreasing since 1992. In recent years, there has been an influx of white and Asian families to some communities of South Los Angeles because of gentrification and revitalization, particularly around the West Adams and Jefferson Park districts (Wikipedia). Gentrification is a process that engenders sociocultural changes in a neighborhood following the purchase of property in depressed areas by the wealthy or by the exodus of residents with rising incomes to settle down in more affluent areas.

Watts Towers

We stopped to see the Watts Towers (Towers of Simon Rodia at 1765 E. 10th St.), a collection of seventeen interconnected structures, two of which reach heights exceeding 97 feet or 30 m. An Italian immigrant construction worker, Sabato ("Sam" or "Simon") Rodia, built them in his spare time over a period of thirteen years, from 1921 to 1954. The towers, which exemplify non-traditional vernacular architecture, became a National Historic Mark in 1990. The documentary "Build the Tower" unfolds the story of Rodia.

Exposition Park

We spent the rest of the day at the Exposition Park, ten miles northwest of Watts and just southwest of downtown Los Angeles. It was our pleasure to explore the park's best two attractions:

- Museum of Science and Industry (renovated and renamed the California Science Center in 1998); it consists of the IMAX Theater, the Sketch Foundation Gallery—Air and Space Exhibits (formerly Aerospace Hall) and the Science Center itself—including the March 2010 opening of the Ecosystems exhibition wing.
- Natural History Museum of Los Angeles County, the largest of its kind in the western United States. Its collections include nearly thirty-three million specimens and artifacts and cover 4.5 billion years of history.

Picture 76.1 Junius and Yoke-Sim at the Watts Towers, a National Historic Landmark (September 17, 1983).

Picture 76.2 Junius "rides" the giant tortoise or turtle or terrapin outside the Los Angeles County Museum of Natural History (September 17, 1983).

There was so much to do at these two sites that we had to hurry through many of the exhibits. "Excellent value for the time spent," I wrote in my diary. The 160-acre park also contained several other attractions, such as,

- Los Angeles Memorial Coliseum,
- Los Angeles Memorial Sports Arena,
- Exposition Park Rose Garden, and
- EXPO Center.

Finally, we crossed the park to visit the University of Southern California, where we stopped at the Annenberg School of Communication. I also paid a visit to the office of the School of Journalism. Then, we walked around the nearby Shrine Auditorium after a quick stop at the Fisher Art Gallery.

Before returning to Fullerton, we decided to splurge on a Japanese style dinner. So we repaired to Little Tokyo village in downtown Los Angeles to eat dinner at Mitsuru Café although Yoke-Sim was worried about "the riffraff" on Main Street.

CHAPTER 77

California: Thugs Vandalize Vehicle in Downtown Los Angeles

AS MY FULLERTON Year (1983) was rapidly coming to a close, I realized that we—Junius, Yoke-Sim, and I—had not spent much time exploring the multitude of attractions available in downtown Los Angeles even though we had been to numerous nooks and corners of California that many an inveterate native would have missed. The last twenty chapters have focused on California. To play "catch up," I made four additional forays to downtown on three Saturdays (November 19, December 3, and January 18) and a Wednesday (November 23) afternoon.

Thugs "Hurt" Volvo

My exchange partner Larry Taylor's Volvo, which we used for all our local travel, withstood all the rigors of our two long camping trips and sundry trips to San Diego, Santa Barbara and San Francisco until the Saturday (December 3) morning, when we parked it in downtown Los Angeles at Fifth Street and Maple, close to Fire Station 23.

Having parked the car and making sure that it was safely locked with nothing visible to invite attention, we set off on a walking tour of the attractions in the vicinity. We stopped to see:

- The Coca Cola Building (1334 S. Central Ave.) with the appearance of a ship with portholes, catwalk and a bridge from five existing industrial buildings (1939)

- The Herald-Examiner Building (1111 S. Broadway), which is used nearly exclusively as a film location since the Hearst-owned Herald Examiner folded in 1989. It brought memories of Hearst Castle, which we visited on July 31.
- The Flower Market (Seventh and Wall)
- Fire Station No. 23 (225 E. Fifth St.), the "Taj Mahal" of firehouses, 1910-1960
- The Stock Exchange (618 S. Spring St.) (Closed)
- The Los Angeles Theater (615 S. Broadway) (Closed)
- Clifton's (terrazzo) Sidewalk (648 S. Broadway), which depicts Los Angeles area highlights and
- The James Oviatt Building (617 S. Olive St.), an Art Deco high-rise (1928)

Picture 77.1 Los Angeles Fire Station No. 23 Historic Site, where shady characters were apparently conniving to break into our vehicle on the Saturday (December 3, 1983) morning when we visited the site. We had parked the car on East Fifth at Maple, close to the site. Yoke-Sim and Junius are at the entrance.

Next, we spent some time at Arco Plaza; then, crossed over to Westin Bonaventure Hotel when it started raining. We took the lift to the hotel's revolving restaurant at the top. Then, we crossed over to the World Trade Center and the Security Pacific Plaza. From there, I walked in the rain to the spot where we parked the Volvo.

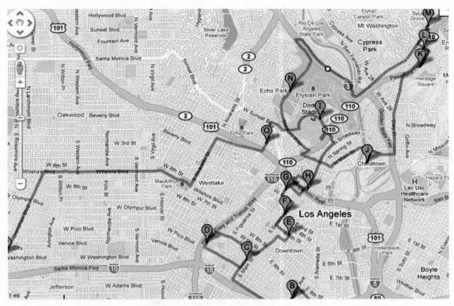

Map 77.1 Selected attractions in downtown Los Angeles and its vicinity. *A*, Farmer John Pig Mural; *B*, Coca Cola Building; *C*, Herald-Examiner Building; *D*, Los Angeles Convention Center; *E*, Fire Station No. 23; *F*, Bradbury Building; *G*, LA Music Center; *H*, El Pueblo de Los Angeles State Historic Park; *I*, Dodger Stadium; *J*, San Antonio Winery and Chinatown; *K*, Heritage Square; *L*, Lummis Home and Gardens; *M*, Southwest Museum; *N*, Echo Park; *O*, 1300 bloc Carroll Street (fashionable Victorian-style homes); and *P*, Dharma Vijaya Buddhist Temple.

To my utter dismay, I found the Volvo "in pain." A Los Angeles thug had smashed its right-hand rear passenger window. We still don't know what "booty" he took away from the vehicle. However, we recalled the uncomfortable feeling we had at the fire-station stop because of the body language of the shady characters hobnobbing there.

We promptly reported the matter to LAPD, which took it as a routine incident. The officer blamed us for parking the car in a downtown street.

We drove to the Heritage School (450 N. Grant), where we ate our picnic lunch in the rain. Then, we proceeded to Hammond Park to visit the Southwest Museum, Casa de Adobe, Lummis Home, and Heritage Square. We reviewed the Dodger Stadium from Elysian Park. Finally, we drove to the Farmers Market to eat dinner at Peking Kitchen.

Becoming Hog Friendly

If you want to appreciate the lifestyle of a hog and like the smell of bacon, stop by at Clougherty Meat Packing Co., just to the south of downtown Los Angeles, to see the *Farmer John Pig Mural* (3049 E. Vernon Ave., Vernon). That's exactly what we did on another Saturday (November 19) morning on our way to downtown exploration.

Picture 77.2 A scene from the *Farmer John Pig Mural* in Vernon, three miles southeast of downtown Los Angeles. Yoke-Sim and Junius are trying to hobnob with the hogs. The smell of bacon added to flavor of the mural (November 19, 1983).

The mural, which surrounds the entire building, basically depicts farm landscapes—fields, trees, corn, barns, etc., and of course, lots of pigs, big and small. It reflects the artistic talent of Hollywood painter Les Grimes, who approached Barney Clougherty, then owner of "Farmer John" brand

SHELTON A. GUNARATNE

meat-packing company, to decorate the outside of his building. In 1957, with Clougherty's blessing, Grimes started work on the massive mural and spent the next eleven years working on his "masterpiece." Unfortunately, Grimes died in a fall from the fifty-feet-high scaffolding he was using to paint a portion of the sky on the mural. Then, Clougherty hired Arno Jordan to finish the mural.

Niche for Performing Arts

In spite of its negative reputation for crime, we found downtown Los Angeles a haven for those who appreciate the performing arts. The testimony is in the success of the Music Center (135 N. Grand Ave.). Located in an eleven-acre area, it comprises four venues: Dorothy Chandler Pavilion (3,197 seats), Ahmanson Theatre (1,600 to 2,007 seats), Mark Taper Forum (745 seats), and (the 2003 addition) Walt Disney Concert Hall (2,265 seats). The complex is officially called the Performing Arts Center of Los Angeles County, and it attracts some 1.3 million visitors annually. We saw the center from outside because none of the venues was open on the Saturday morning we visited.

For History Lovers

Our main destination of the day was El Pueblo de Los Angeles State Historic Park, where we gathered at the Old Plaza Firehouse (1884). Docent Grace King took us on a walking tour of the forty-four-acre park from noon to 1:30 p.m.

King showed us the Avila Adobe (1818), the oldest existing house in Los Angeles; the Old Plaza Church (1822), the oldest church in the city; the Masonic Hall (1858); the Sepulveda House (1884); the Merced Theater; and the Pico House.

The Avila Adobe was the residence of Francisco Avila, a wealthy ranchero and alcalde (mayor) of the pueblo of Los Angeles (1810-1811). Today, only one wing of the original eighteen-room mansion remains. The adobe contained three-feet-thick cottonwood timber walls. Originally built with packed earth floors, it now contains plank wood floors. King also explained the other buildings on Olvera Street, one of the oldest streets in the city considered the home to Mexican culture.

After the tour, we visited the St Vibiana Cathedral (1876). Then, we went to the Grand Central Public Market, where we ate a late lunch at China Café.

Refreshed, we crossed the road to see the Bradbury Building (304 S. Broadway), an architectural landmark built in 1893. Silver mining millionaire Lewis Bradbury hired architect George Wyman, who gave the building an Italian Renaissance-style exterior façade. "But the magnificence of the building is the interior: reached through the entrance, with its low ceiling and minimal light, it opens into a bright naturally lit great center court" (Wikipedia).

We stopped briefly at Pershing Square before visiting Biltmore Hotel (1923). Our final tour stops for the day were the Central Library and the shopping area of Westin Bonaventure Hotel (1976).

Value-Added Wednesday

On a Wednesday (December 23) afternoon, Yoke-Sim and I added a few more downtown-area attractions to our "brag list" on our way to Burbank (pop 108,000) for a two-hour tour The Burbank Studios or TBS (4000 Warner Blvd.), the home of Warner Bros. and Columbia Pictures. (We left Junius with a babysitter in Fullerton.) Dick Mason, an eighteen-year veteran of TBS, gave us an introductory talk and assigned us to a female guide who bundled us into an open vehicle to explain what was going on within the 108-acre premises of the studios. We saw the actual filming of *Black Thunder* and *Falcon Crest*.

The value-added attractions we visited on this trip were as follows:

- San Antonio Winery (737 Lamar St.), founded in 1917. It is Los Angeles' oldest winery still in operation. We bought a bottle of red wine for subsequent consumption.
- Echo Park, a hilly neighborhood northwest of downtown. I walked along the lagoon enjoying the downtown Los Angeles skyline in the background.
- Angelina Heights, where we saw the once fashionable Victorian neighborhood (the 1300 block of Carroll Ave.) dating back to 1886.

Junius and Yoke-Sim left for Australia on January 1, 1984. My mother accompanied me on my Fullerton Year's final foray into downtown Los Angeles on January 14 The important attractions we visited included the Convention Center, the Variety Arts Theater (940 S. Figueroa St.), the Otis Art Institute (2401 Wiltshire Blvd.), the Wiltshire Boulevard (Jewish) Temple, the Mormon Temple (10777 Santa Monica Blvd.) and the Dharma Vijaya Buddhist Vihara (1847 Crenshaw Blvd.).

CHAPTER 78

California: Huntington, a Scholars' Dream, Has Quaint Vicinity

JUNIUS, YOKE-SIM, AND I visited The Huntington Library, Art Galleries and Botanical Gardens (1151 Oxford Road, San Marino), also known as The Huntington, on a Sunday afternoon (November 6, 1983). Located in the San Rafael Hills in the vicinity of Pasadena, it shares with Hearst Castle and Getty Villa the extraordinary attributes of scenic splendor and exuberant ambience. We spent about 2.5 hours to get a feel of the Huntington legacy.

The Huntington (estbd. 1928) was the first public art gallery opened in Southern California. When railroad magnate Henry E. Huntington died at the age of seventy-seven in 1927 (three years after the death of his second wife Arabella Yarrington), the mansion they lived became the centerpiece of the art gallery and the library.

Picture 78.1 The Huntington in San Marino. (*Source:* Wikimedia Commons)

Library and Art Collection

Arabella Huntington, who died at the age of seventy-four in 1924, is acknowledged "the force behind the art collection" at The Huntington. She was a collector of art, jewelry, antiques, and other luxury items.

Her particular interests were in old masters, Medieval and Renaissance devotional images, and Louis XIV Louis XV furniture and decorative arts.

The Huntington library, Wikipedia elaborates, stands out because:

- It holds an extensive collection of rare books and manuscripts, which include a Gutenberg Bible, the Ellesmere manuscript of Chaucer, and thousands of historical documents about Abraham Lincoln, including the papers of his bodyguard, Ward Hill Lamon.
- It holds some 6.5 million manuscripts and more than a million rare books, which are among the most heavily used in the United States. Every year, more than seventeen hundred scholars come from all over the world to study these rare materials.
- It is the only library in the world with the first two quartos of *Hamlet*, as well as the manuscript of Benjamin Franklin's autobiography, the first seven drafts of Henry David Thoreau's *Walden*, the double-elephant folio edition of John James Audubon's *Birds of America*, a collection of manuscripts and first editions of the works of Charles Bukowski, and many other great treasures.

In 2010, the library acquired thirty-five personal letters, twenty-eight of which never published, written by Charles Dickens (1812-1870), my favorite British author. The Huntington already holds about a thousand letters by Dickens, as well as other manuscripts relating to his work and forty-nine original drawings by "Phiz" for Dickens' *Nicholas Nickleby*.

Botanical Gardens

The 120-acre botanical gardens of The Huntington follow the same theme approach that we saw at the USCR Botanic Gardens in Riverside and the Los Angeles State and County Arboretum in Arcadia. The gardens exhibit some fourteen thousand different varieties of plants in more than a dozen themed sections: Australian Garden, Camellia Collection, Children's Garden, Chinese Garden, Cycads (largest collection of the sculptural and "palm-like" cycads in the United States), Desert Garden and Conservatory, Herb Garden, Japanese Garden and

Zen Garden, Lily Pond, North Vista, Palm Garden, Rose Garden, Rose Hill Foundation Conservatory for Botanical Science, Shakespeare Garden, and Subtropical and Jungle Garden.

Admission to The Huntington is free to all visitors on the first Thursday of every month. General admission on weekdays is $15; and on weekends $20, and closed on Tuesdays.

Picture 78.2 Junius expresses his satisfaction with the visit to the Japanese Gardens of The Huntington (November 6, 1983).

In the Vicinity

We also stopped at several offbeat attractions in the vicinity of The Huntington within an area ranging from thirty miles west of the library to twenty miles southeast:

- *M*, Will Rogers State Historic Park (14253 Sunset Blvd., Pacific Palisades), which we visited on a Saturday (October 22, 1983). (Use key to locate attraction in Map 1)

SHELTON A. GUNARATNE

Located six miles northeast of the Getty Villa, the park is 30 miles southwest of The Huntington. This is the 186-acre property that Will Rogers (1879-1935), the American trick-roper "cowboy philosopher," purchased in 1922 to establish his thirty-one-room ranch home, which includes eleven baths and seven fireplaces. Surrounding the home are a stable, corrals, riding ring, roping arena, golf course, polo field, and riding and hiking trails.

Picture 78.3 Yoke-Sim guides Junius at the Will Rogers State Historic Park in Pacific Palisades (October 23, 1983).

Rogers, his wife Betty and their three children—Will Jr., Mary, and James—lived here. The ranch became a state park in 1944 after the death of Betty Rogers.

Rogers wrote his most famous epigram—his epitaph—in 1930. It reads as follows:

> When I die, my epitaph or whatever you call those signs on gravestones is going to read: "I joked about every prominent man of my time, but I never met a man I didn't like."

I am so proud of that I can hardly wait to die so it can be carved. And when you come to my grave you will find me sitting there, proudly reading it.

We toured the patio and the north and south wings of the ranch house. However, we were allowed only into the living room. We walked a mile to the Inspiration Point on Santa Monica Mountains to see the layout of the entire property, including the polo field to the south.

- *L*, Forest Lawn at Hollywood Hills (6300 Forest Lawn Drive). We visited this and the next attractions on a Saturday (November 5, 1983). (*L* is twenty-two miles north and east of *M*.)

Part of the Forest Lawn chain of six privately owned cemeteries in Southern California, many famous people are buried or entombed here. Its three main features are the Court of Liberty, Lincoln Terrace, and Plaza of Mesoamerican Heritage. In the court, we saw the Hall of Liberty American History Museum, the Old North Church; the *Birth of Liberty* mosaic; and the statues of Washington and Jefferson.

- *K*, Forest Lawn Memorial Park at Glendale (1712 S. Glendale Ave.). (*K* is about eight miles east and southeast of *L*.)

This is the original location of the Forest Lawn chain of privately owned cemeteries founded in 1906 by a group of businessmen from San Francisco. The group hired Dr. Hubert Eaton, a firm believer in a joyous life after death, to create a cemetery complex that reflected his optimistic Christian beliefs.

Here we saw the stained-glass recreation of Leonardo da Vinci's *The Last Supper* at the Memorial Court of Honor. In the Hall of the Crucifixion-Resurrection, we saw Polish artist Jan Styka's 45 195 feet *Crucifixion* and its companion, the 51 70 feet *Resurrection*. At the adjoining museum, we saw Lorenzo Ghiberti's *Paradise Doors* and a gem collection. The park contains a major collection of white Carrara (Italy) marble statuary. We also visited the Freedom Mausoleum, the Court of Freedom, the Mystery of Life, the Court of David, and the Court of Christos.

The private entombing of Michael Jackson in the privacy of Holly Terrace in the Great Mausoleum received much media attention in 2009.

- *J*, Church of the Angels (1050 N Ave. 64, Pasadena). Junius, Yoke-Sim, and I visited this and the next five attractions on a Sunday (November 6, 1983). (*J* is four miles east and northeast of *K*.)

This picturesque Episcopalian church encompasses an area that was once part of the Rancho San Rafael property. Frances, the wife of Alexander Robert Campbell-Johnson, built it to honor her husband. It is one of the oldest stone buildings in the area and has an imported, stained-glass masterpiece above the altar. The priest stopped to talk to us just after the service.

- *I*, Gamble House (4 Westmoreland Place, Pasadena). (*I* is two or three miles northeast of *J*.)

David B. Gamble House, another National Historic Landmark constructed in 1908/9, is an outstanding example of American Arts and Crafts style architecture that focuses on use of natural materials, attention to detail, aesthetics, and craftsmanship. Following the deaths of David and Mary Gamble in the mid-1920s, the Gamble family ceded the property to the city of Pasadena in 1944. The house and its garage served as the exterior of Doc Brown's mansion in the 1985 film trilogy *Back to the Future*, an American science-fiction adventure comedy.

- *H*, Pacific Asia Museum (46 N. Los Robles Ave.) (*H* is 1.5 miles east of *I*.)

This museum, specializing in Asian art, occupies the Nicholson Building, a National Historic Landmark constructed in 1924-1926. Grace Nicholson, a dealer in Native American and Asian art and antiques, founded the museum. A 2009 exhibit focused on the mash-up of Chinese calligraphy and American graffiti. One of its current exhibits is titled *Visualizing Faith: Buddhist Art in Thailand*.

- (*G, The Huntington*, is three miles east and south of *H*.)

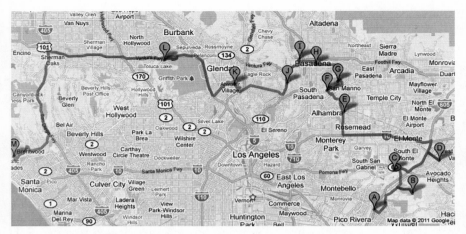

Map 78.1 Select offbeat attractions around *G* (The Huntington). The text identifies each attraction by its key.

- *F*, El Molino Viejo (1120 Old Mill Road, San Marino). (*F* is two miles southwest of *G*.)

Father José Maria de Zalvidea from the Mission San Gabriel Arcángel (San Gabriel Mission) built El Molino Viejo (the Old Mill) in 1816. (According to legend, the priest used Indian labor to build the water-powered gristmill on the burial spot of Catalina, a sixteen-year-old Indian, who died of sorrow when handsome Jose did not return after a two-year stint on a ship. Catalina had offered roses to Virgin Mary in hopes of Jose's return but turned her back on Virgin Mary when Jose decided not to return. The water gushing out of the mill's natural spring is Catalina's stream of tears!) It is the oldest commercial building in Southern California and a historic landmark.

- *E*, Mission San Gabriel Arcángel (428 S. Mission Drive, San Gabriel). (*E* is three miles southeast of *F*.)

Father Juniper Serra founded the Roman Catholic mission in San Gabriel (current population 40,000) in 1771 as the fourth of the twenty-one Spanish missions in California. Its aim was to convert the area's Tongva native tribe. Father Antonio Cruzado from Cordoba (Spain) designed the mission to give it a Moorish architectural look. Its capped buttresses and the tall, narrow windows are unique among the California missions. (*Note:* Asians make up 49 percent of the city's population compared with 33.4 percent white.)

- *D*, Industry Hills Expo Center (*D* is ten miles south and southeast of *E*.)

This is a multipurpose arena in the city of Industry (pop 777 in 2000). Built in 1981, it seats more than five thousand spectators. It is home to the Los Angeles Lynx of the National Indoor Football League. It also houses the Ralph W. Miller Memorial Golf Library. Industry is home to more than twenty-two hundred businesses and is almost entirely industrial.

- *C*, Whittier Narrows Nature Center (South El Monte). My mother and I visited this attraction and the next two on a Saturday (January 21 1984). (*C* is 4.5 miles southwest of *D*.)

Located in South El Monte (pop 21,200), this multiuse facility contains North Lake, Center Lake, and Legg Lake (where visitors can operate radio-controlled model speedboats, a rifle—and pistol-shooting range, numerous softball and soccer fields with picnic tables, a paved airstrip for radio-controlled hobby aircraft, and a connector trail between the Class I Rio Hondo bicycle path, and the San Gabriel River bicycle path.

- *B*, Rose Hills Memorial Park (Whittier). (*B* is three miles southeast of *C*.)

This is the largest cemetery in the United States. It features three mausoleums: Whittier Heights Mausoleum (built in 1917), El Portal de la Paz or Doorway of Peace (dedicated in 1930) and The Buddhist Columbarium (built in 1999). The columbarium is located on 2.5 acres at the highest elevation of Rose Hills, the largest Buddhist pagoda in the United States.

- *A*, Pio Pico State Historic Park (6003 Pioneer Blvd., Whittier). (*A* is 5.5 miles southwest of *A*.)

This is the site of "El Ranchito," also known as the Pio Pico Adobe or Pio Pico Mansion, the final home of Pío de Jesus Pico (1801-1894), the last governor of Alta California under Mexican Rule and a pivotal figure in early California history.

CHAPTER 79

California: "Rim of the World" in San Bernardino Mountains

I STARTED MY focus on California and West Coast travel adventures for three months after writing the chapter on mingling with giant sequoias (chapter 57). In the travelogues that followed, I attempted to dramatize the vast experience I gathered as an inveterate traveler in 1983, the year I spent in California as an exchange instructor at Fullerton College.

In 1966-1967, my first year of worldwide travel experience as a fellow of the World Press Institute, I was more a participant than a travel planner. In 1983, I was the master of my own (and my family's) destiny. Writing about these travels in 2009-2010 presented another challenge—the need to update what I had noted down in my diaries. Willy-nilly, I had to do the research and check the accuracy of spelling of names, distances, directions, and developments. I relied heavily on the Wikipedia and the Google maps. Time available to me after my retirement enabled me to develop twenty-three composite or separate stories related to my Fullerton Year.

Chapter 80 will conclude my focus on California that began with an explanation on the five-county Greater Los Angeles. However, I failed to focus on San Bernardino County, except for mentioning our stopovers in two places on its western border: Sleepy Hollow (chapter 69) and Ontario (chapter 71).

Focus on San Bernardino

Yoke-Sim and Junius left for Australia on January 1, 1984 leaving me and my mother to fend for ourselves in Fullerton for the rest of January. This allowed us the rare opportunity to indulge in nostalgic conversation about my childhood days in Pathegama, my birthplace in southern Sri Lanka.

On the day I turned forty-four (Sunday, January 22, 1984), exactly a week before the end of my Fullerton exchange, Mother treated me to a traditional village breakfast of *kiri bath* (milk-rice). To celebrate the occasion, I took my mother, then seventy, on a daylong 210-mile roundtrip excursion to San Bernardino Mountains.

(*Background:* San Bernardino County, which is part of Greater Los Angeles, is home to more than 2.1 million people spread out in an area of 20,105 square miles. In geographical size, it is the largest county in the "Lower 48" states of the United States. It has twenty-five incorporated communities, of which the largest is the eighty-two-square-mile city of San Bernardino [population. 205,000], the county seat. The next five largest cities are Fontana [population 180,700], Rancho Cucamonga [population 174,300], Ontario [population 172,700], Victorville [population 102,600], and Rialto [population 100,000]. All the big cities lie closer to the border of Los Angeles County again indicating the population exodus from Los Angeles metropolitan area to San Bernardino and Riverside counties, the so-called inland empire, for cheaper housing.

The city of San Bernardino lies about fifty miles northeast of Fullerton via Corona and Riverside. It is the home of the University of California San Bernardino. Its various attractions include the Fox Performing Arts Center, the California Theatre, the Robert V. Fullerton Museum of Art, Route 66-McDonald's Museum, the Santa Fe Rail Road Museum, and the Arrowhead Springs Resort and Hotel.)

When we arrived in San Bernardino on January 22 (Sunday), we used the city only as a gateway to the eponymous mountains. My mother had no cultural interest in visiting any of the listed attractions. Therefore, immediately after arrival in the city, I headed north on Waterman Avenue, which turns into the Rim of the World Highway (SR 18) as it enters the mountains in the San Bernardino National Forest. Crestline (pop 10,300) lies around Lake Gregory at the north end of the initial sixteen-mile stretch of the Rim of the World. Then, the highway takes a sharp turn east to zigzag its way to other points of interest.

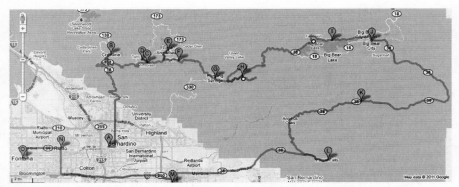

Map 79.1 Rim of the World Highway from *A* (San Bernardino) to *J* (Big Bear City). Other codes: *B*, Crestline; *C*, Rainforest; *D*, Strawberry Lookout; *E*, Lake Arrowhead; *F*, Skyforest (Santa's Village); *G*, Running Springs; *H*, National Children's Forest; *I*, North Shore/Big Bear Lake; *J*, Big Bear City; *K*, Barton Flats; *L*, Forest Falls; *M*, Redlands; *N*, Rialto; *O*, Fontana. Distance from *A-O* is 142 miles.

Just three months earlier, on another Sunday (October 30, 1983), Junius, Yoke-Sim, and I had been within twenty to thirty miles northwest of Crestline as we crossed the national forest from Los Angeles County to San Bernardino County at Wrightwood on our drive through Angeles Crest Highway (SR 2), which terminates at its junction with SR 138. Heading southeast from the junction, SR 138 links Angeles Crest Highway (SR 2) with Rim of the World Highway (SR 18) at Crestline. So it seemed to me, that Mother and I were continuing to explore the crest of the same chain of mountains.

No visitor to San Bernardino Valley can miss the immense Arrowhead geological landmark on the side of the San Bernardino Mountains stretching some 60 miles in an east-west direction. I have it on authority that the face of the arrowhead consists of light quartz, supporting a growth of short white sage; and that this lighter vegetation shows in sharp contrast to the surrounding chaparral and greasewood. The native Indians in the San Bernardino Valley considered the vicinity holy ground because they believed that the arrowhead pointed the way to the hot mineral springs below, with healing qualities.

At Rimforest, we drove two miles northwest on Bear Springs Road to reach the lookout to view Strawberry Peak (elevation: 6,155 feet or 1,876.04

m). Then, back on SR 18, we came to Crest Park, where we turned north on SR 173 and drove less than two miles to reach Lake Arrowhead (population 9,000), named after the renowned geographical landmark. Located twenty-three miles north and northeast of San Bernardino, the unincorporated community of Lake Arrowhead depends almost entirely on tourism. About four million people visited the area in 2009. The adjacent 780-acre Lake Arrowhead Reservoir is an artificial lake.

Picture 79.1 Driving up to the mountain community of Crestline surrounding Lake Gregory, one can see the natural geographical landmark resembling an arrowhead on the side of a mountain peak. Legend has it that this large arrowhead guided the Indians to the springs. The landmark void of natural vegetation has been visible for hundreds of years. (*Source:* Wikimedia Commons)

Mother and I walked around the shopping village and refreshed ourselves with junk food from the MacDonald's.

Next, back on SR 18, we visited the now-defunct Santa's Village, a popular theme park from 1959-1998, near Skyforest. Another attraction was the nearby Heaps Peak Arboretum. Communities in the vicinity include Cedar Glen, Blue Jay, Rimforest, Deer Lodge Park, and Agua Fria. We drove past Running Springs (population 5,200), the junction where SR 330 provides a short cut to return to San Bernardino via Highland.

Heading further east on SR 18, we took Keller Peak Road to visit the National Children's Forest. The drive involved a steep climb from 6,000 ft. to 7,882 ft. along a smooth, paved, two-lane road to the top of Keller Peak. The view from the peak was breathtaking. Created in the wake of the 1970 Bear Fire, the National Children's Forest—thirty-four hundred acres of forest nestled between Rim of the World Highway and Keller Peak Road—is a unique forest-fire study area dedicated to thousands of children nationwide who have helped reforest the country's burned timber. It was here that my mother touched and tasted snow for the first time in her life.

Then, past the scenic Lake View Point (elev. 7,207 ft.), we headed toward Big Bear Lake (population 5,500), the largest recreation lake in Southern California. SR 18 continues along the seven-mile length of the South Shore of the reservoir while its North Shore (SR 38) begins at the Dam Junction of SR 18. We took the North Shore route, which travels east past the historic location of Gray's Landing, a famous 1920s fishing camp. It turns north around Grout Bay and travels through the small unincorporated town of Fawnskin. The road meanders across North Shore through Forestry lands, past the Big Bear Solar Observatory, Big Bear Discovery Center, the Serrano Campground (USFS) and Stanfield Cutoff, and continues into Big Bear City.

After stopping at the solar observatory, we drove a few miles north on a dirt road to Holcomb Valley, where we saw the sites of Wilker's Grave, Two Gun Bill's Saloon, and Hangman's Tree, all associated with California's Gold Rush days. Back on SR 38, we drove to Big Bear City, where SR 18 crosses over to the north and goes northeast for a short distance before taking a northwestern direction all the way to Victorville; and SR 38 crosses over to the south and goes southeast for quite a distance before taking a south-westward direction all the way to Redlands.

We drove on SR 38 for our return journey. Our next stop was Barton Flats, which is directly south of Big Bear Lake although we had to drive twenty-one miles to get there. The purpose of the stop was for me to try out walking through the Ponderosa Nature Trail and the Whispering Pines Trail.

Picture 79.2 The author and his mother at the Japan Center in San Francisco—a month before their visit to the San Bernardino Mountains.

Meanwhile, my mother was getting impatient as it was getting dark. She had little interest in the activities I was enjoying. Darkness set in as we reached Forest Falls, sixteen miles further southwest. To make matters worse, our vehicle skidded on an icy patch of the highway. Although two good Samaritans came to our rescue and helped me straighten up the car for safe driving, the incident aggravated my mother's anxiety to get back home. I had no option but to return to Fullerton, a distance of seventy miles from Forrest Falls via Redlands.

We reached our Fullerton condo before 7:30 p.m. Despite the vehicle mishap, I enjoyed my forty-fourth birthday exploring another scenic spot of the world. Moreover, on this trip, I saw the joy of my mother—the erstwhile Punchi Hamine from the village of Pathegama in the Deep South of Sri Lanka—as she touched and tasted some snow for the first time in her life!

CHAPTER 80

California: County Fair that's a Fair for All

WE—JUNIUS, YOKE-SIM, AND I—had "a very enjoyable day" at the Los Angeles County Fair on a Saturday (September 24, 1983). We arrived on the fairgrounds in Pomona at 10:00 a.m. and engaged ourselves in an abundance of activities that appealed to our basic senses and detained us at the fair until 9:00 p.m. Normally, I loathe to spend more than a couple of hours at any event. But the X factor (or *emergence*) that the fair engendered exceeding the sum of its parts appeared to induce the visitors to linger longer.

Bill Arballo, the media information coordinator for the fair, gave me all the background information I needed for writing the following story, which appeared in the Australian daily the *Mercury* (Hobart) on October 7, 1983 (with revisions and updates in square brackets):

Picture 80.1 The 2009 Los Angeles County Fair. (*Source:* Wikimedia Commons)

The *Mercury* Story

For the first time in my life, I spent more than 10 hours at a fair and still couldn't visit everything I wanted to see. The Los Angeles County Fair, which ran for 18 days and nights from 15 Sept. until 2 Oct., was just too big to handle on a single day and night. [This year's fair will run from 4 Sept to 3 Oct. 2010. The fair began as an annual event on 17 Oct. 1922, and ran for five days through 21 Oct. Highlights of the inaugural event were harness racing, chariot races and an airplane wing-walking exhibition.]

The fairgrounds in Pomona, 30 miles east of Los Angles, cover 487 acres with 1.5 million square feet of exhibit space and 18 exhibit buildings. A record 1.38 million people visited the fair in 1981; but that number dropped by about 162,000 [in 1982]. [Fair attendance has topped 1 million people in every year but one since 1948.]

The Los Angeles County Fair Association calls this the largest county fair in North America. But in terms of 1982 attendance, it ranked ninth of all fairs and expositions behind Columbus, Dallas, Toronto, Oklahoma City, St. Paul, Vancouver, Indianapolis and Tulsa. [More than 1.37 million people attended the LA County Fair in 2009—about the same number as in 1981; and it ranked fourth of all fairs and exhibitions behind Houston, Dallas and St. Paul.]

For someone used to the annual fairs in Brisbane and Rockhampton [in Australia], the LA County Fair strikes not only as big in size but also in imagination and variety.

The fair's theme [for 1983] was "fair for all." And it certainly had a variety of imaginative things to occupy the interests of almost every visitor who cared to pay $5 to get in. [Admission to the fair has gone up more than twofold to $12 (regular) and $9 (senior) on weekdays. Add $5 extra to these prices for weekends. Among the promotions at the Los Angeles County Fair for 2010 is a season pass for $24.95, about half of last year's $49.95 price tag.]

One has to remember that in Southern California a fair has to compete with an assortment of famous amusement parks and other attractions to get a share of the audience.

Thus, unlike in most American cities where fairs can become the major draw cards for their duration, the LA County Fair has to go on the offensive to grab attention and to provide attractions that can bring in a diverse audience. [Each of the counties constituting Greater Los Angeles—LA, Orange, Riverside, San Bernardino and Ventura—has its own annual fair. But the midgets concede the dominance of giant LA]

How does it do it?

It attracts a large number of racing fans by holding daily 12 races with *pari-mutuel* wagering, a form of betting in which winners divide losers' stakes. [In 1983], every day during the fair there was one Appaloosa, two quarter horse and nine thoroughbred events. The fair's grandstand accommodated 20,000 spectators. And the general admission to the track was included in the admission ticket to the fair.

Racing is the No. 1 spectator sport in the United States—larger than baseball and football. Thus the LA County Fair has had horseracing as a major attraction for forty-five years.

To go with horseracing are the horse shows presented in Carnation Arena and Equestrian Center. Highlights [in 1983] were the draft and mule show and the Budweiser Clydesdale performances. [This was our last stopover for the day. We crossed the pedestrian tunnel to the stables to have a glimpse of Carnation Arena, etc., before leaving the fair.]

The fair attracts a large number of parents who have small children. It does so by providing free admission to children under 6 and by giving them a full complement of kiddy rides in two locations called Kiddieland [where Junius and Yoke-Sim took a ride on the merry-go-round].

[In 1983, the fair facilitated the children to] also enjoy the "hands-on" exhibit of barnyard animals in Storybook Farm, where they [could] meet Peter Cottontail, Three Little Pigs, the Cow that Jumped Over the Moon and even some of the animals from Old McDonald's Farm. [Junius had the pleasure of meeting these characters in the afternoon.]

SHELTON A. GUNARATNE

Picture 80.2 Plaza of the States at the 1983 Los Angeles County Fair.

Kids and their parents [could] then go to see the model trains in the railroad village that had rolling stock moving all over a California diorama. [After visiting the Model Train Village and the Plaza of the States, we walked to the Picnic Hill to enjoy our drinks.]

Or they [could] go to a circus under a Big Top featuring animals, high wire acts, clowns, jugglers and trapeze artists. [We visited the Big Top Circus.]

Or they [could] go down a simulated shaft to see a replica of the Golden Empire Mine in Grass Valley. [We visited the replica, the Flower and Garden Pavilion. Then, we passed through the Education Expo to the carnival area. It being about 7:30 p.m., we stopped at the Red Barn Café to eat a special chicken dinner.]

And if the youngsters [were] tired, they [could] be left at a childcare center—a professionally staffed nursery.

The fair includes a number of features to attract the youth as well. They had their own Youth in Action Pavilion in which the theme [appeared to] be "anything adult exhibitors do we also can do." Just to the south was the Youth Plaza where they put on various events. [After lunch, we visited the Kitchen Karnival and Youth in Action Exhibit. We stopped for drinks at the Youth Plaza.]

A further attraction for the youth was the evening performance of superstars from stage, screen and television. [In 1983] the fair featured Barbara Mandrell and her Do-Rites group, the Beach Boys and Eddie Rabbitt. Another attraction for them was the championship rodeo held on five consecutive evenings.

The youth were also catered for in the Education Expo, featuring industrial education exhibits and displays from various school districts.

The fair had set apart pavilions to feature the needs of special interest groups in the areas of agriculture, home arts, livestock, poultry, pigeon, rabbits and cavies [guinea pigs], flowers and gardens. After all, [the fair was incorporated] "primarily for the promotion of the agricultural, horticultural and animal husbandry interests of the great South West."

The Agricultural Pavilion is a massive exhibition hall refurbished [in the early 1980s] at a cost of $4.4 million. This is where California's various counties try to promote themselves with some of the most imaginative and original exhibits. This is what I enjoyed most.

[We entered the fair through the C Gate and started our walking tour through the World Bazaar. Then, we entered the Agricultural Pavilion, where promoters gave us a surfeit of delicious yogurt to consume on the spot free of charge. This pavilion is a haven for those who like giveaway food samples.]

[In 1983] the fair also featured a first-of-its-kind—African Images in the New World, an effort to show the African influence upon the arts and crafts of South America. Artists from Surinam and Brazil demonstrated their work in person. Adjoining was an international exhibition of photography. [We visited these exhibits after leaving the Agricultural Pavilion.]

For the train buffs, the fair had an exhibition of historical locomotives, including the "Big Boy," the steam-powered locomotive weighing 1 million pounds.

And for the general public, the fair's amphitheater presented community programs, concerts, dance exhibitions and contests; its Mexican Village presented artisans, entertainers and exhibitors; its carnival presented more than 60 rides, including a dozen "screamers;" and its neatly landscaped Picnic Hill gave a place to relax and unwind.

CHAPTER 81

Hawaii: Craters Humble Nosy Writer by Soaking Him in Rainwater

Sidebar: Exit Fullerton

MY MOTHER AND I left California on the last Friday of January 1984. It was the last day of my Fullerton Year.

I handed all my grade sheets to Admissions and Records at Fullerton College and said goodbye to many colleagues and friends over the preceding two days.

Larry Taylor, my exchange partner, had returned from Australia Wednesday and paid me a surprise visit Friday morning. I returned the keys to his beloved Volvo. He refunded me the money I spent on car repairs.

Ebrahim Unwallah, a resident at Wellesley Court, took me out for Friday lunch at Kentucky Fried Chicken. Later, we had tea at his condo, where mother joined us.

About 4 p.m., Unwallah took us to the airport bus service terminal at Disneyland Hotel in Anaheim, where we said our goodbyes. Mother and I arrived at the L.A. International Airport about 6.50 p.m.

Although mother and I were both returning to Australia, we had two different travel schedules. I went with mother to Terminal 6, where she boarded the Continental Airlines flight to Sydney. After disembarking in Sydney, she would connect with a domestic flight to Rockhampton.

Thereafter, I took the shuttle to Terminal 2 to board the Air New Zealand flight to Hawaii, where I planned to explore the "Big Island" for the next three days.

When I disembarked in Honolulu, it was past 11 p.m. Hawaii time. I met mother again at the Honolulu Airport, where I said goodbye to her.

I had informed a Sri Lankan colleague of mine living in Honolulu about my arrival. His absence at the airport sent me the implicit message that he was too busy to meet with me although he had once visited me in Sri Lanka to ask for a favor. I decided to rough out the wee hours of Saturday morning at the Honolulu Airport until my 6 o'clock flight to Hilo. I put my luggage in a rented locker and caught some sleep on a lounge chair.

Big Hawaii

When I toured the "Big Island," the largest island in the state of Hawaii, for four days at the end of January 1984, the state's population was 30 percent lower than its current estimate of 1.2 million. The "Big Island," however, has only a population of 150,000 in contrast to the smaller Oahu island's 877,000.

But the "Big Island" can be a joy for those who tend to be nature lovers and epicureans. The epicureans converge on the western Kohala Coast to enjoy the luxury of hotels such as the classic Mauna Kea.

Nature lovers can explore some of the earth's most prodigious volcanic formations or seek the peace of the magnificent Waipio Valley." You can see Hilo in less than a day," a Californian told me just before I flew into the Hawaiian archipelago.

At the time of my visit, some 35,300 people inhabited Hilo, the big city in the "Big Island." (Hilo's population was 40,759 at 2000 census.)

The flight from Honolulu to Hilo (370 km) took about forty minutes. The "Big Island" is almost twice the (land) size of all the other islands (in the archipelago) combined.

The most efficient and cheapest way to explore t he island is by car.

Perhaps the best way to get acquainted with the "Big Island" is to spend the first day sightseeing in Hilo.

Exploring Hilo

That's what I did. After landing at Hilo airport on a Saturday (January 28) early morning, I stopped at Phillips' U-Drive Inc. and rented a Toyota compact, which I used as storage for my baggage, as well as a temporary shelter for myself, as I explored the island with the help of a map. I first headed three miles northwest to the Uncle Billy's Hilo Bay Hotel (at 87 Banyan Drive), where I had booked accommodation so I could do my ablutions and rest for a while. But the receptionist was reluctant to let me in that early. A heated exchange of words resulted in my favor.

A good starting point is the 20-ha Lili'uokalani Park and Gardens (300 Wai Nani Way, Hilo) with its Japanese Garden and the bridge to Coconut Island. It's on Banyan Drive overlooking Hilo Bay. The gardens contain the Waihonu Pond, as well as bridges, koi ponds, pagodas, statues, and a Japanese teahouse.

After eating breakfast at the hotel, I decided to explore the city right away despite the continual rain. And Lili'uokalani was just to the southwest of my hotel. There, I crossed the bridge to Moku Ola (Coconut Island), a popular picnic spot that provides spectacular views of Hilo Bay front, downtown Hilo, and the rest of Hilo Bay. The massive breakwater protecting Hilo Bay lies to the east.

Next, I stopped at Lyman Museum and Mission (at 276 Haili St.). An associate of the Smithsonian Institution since 2002, the museum has extensive displays on Hawaiian culture. It "is renowned for its collection of shells and minerals, including a specimen of orlymanite, named for Orlando Hammond Lyman (1903-1986), the museum's founder and great grandson of David and Sarah Lyman" (Wikipedia). The Lyman family built the mission house in 1838. In 1978, it received recognition as a national historic site. (The current general admission to the museum is $10, which includes a conducted tour of the galleries. In 1984, I paid $3.50 for admission.)

Next, the nearby Hilo Public Library (300 Waianuenue Ave.) attracted my attention. The 2,000 -lb. Naha Stone, which the Hawaiian King Kamehameha I (ca. 1758-May 8, 1819) supposedly lifted at the age of fourteen, rests in front of the library.

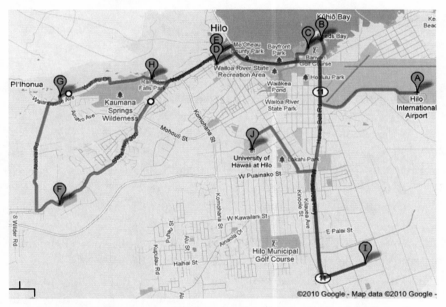

Map 81.1: Day 1 tour of Hilo. *A*, Hilo Airport; *B*, Uncle Billy's; *C*, Lili'uokalani Park and Gardens; *D*, Lyman Museum and Mission; *E*, Public Library; *F*, Kaumana Caves; *G*, Boiling Pots; *H*, Rainbow Falls; *I*, Nani Mau Gardens; *J*, University of Hawaii at Hilo.

Then, off I went to see the Kaumana Caves, actually a large lava tube formed during the 1881 eruption of Mauna Loa. I drove further north to see the Boiling Pots, a series of small falls and pools on the twenty-six-mile Wailuku River, the longest river in Hawaii. About a mile to the east, I stopped at the eighty-feet Rainbow (Waianuenue) Falls, which cascades over a natural lava cave, the mythological home to Hawaiian goddess Hina, the Mother of Maui. Concealed by the mist of the falls, she beat and dried her *kapa* in the sun each day.

My next stop was the magnificent twenty-acre Nani Mau (Forever Beautiful) Gardens (421Makalika St.), which claim to "contain more than 2,000 plant varieties, with approximately 225 types of flowering plants, including 100 species of fruit trees; and over 2,300 orchids. Major garden features include an anthurium grove, Japanese-style bell tower (built from 20,000 boards without nails or screws), botanical museum, butterfly house, European garden, fruit orchard, ginger garden, hibiscus garden, Japanese gardens, orchid display, palms and coconut trees, and water garden" (Wikipedia).

Before returning to the hotel, I tarried for a while at the main campus of the University of Hawaii Hilo (200 W. Kawili St.)

Day 2: Tour of Volcanoes National Park

I spent the whole day, in spite of the inclement weather, exploring the 330,000-acre (134,760-hectare) Hawaii Volcano National Park on the southwestern part of the "Big Island." Established as a national park in 1916, it offered two of the world's most active volcanoes: Kilauea (4,096 ft.) to the east and Mauna Loa (13,679 ft.) to the west.

Lava flows from the 1983-present eruption at Kilauea volcano have overrun more than two hundred structures, including the Wahaula Heiau and Visitor Center, which succumbed in June 1989, just five years after my visit. However, flowing at an average rate of 800-1,300 gallons (3,000-4,920 liters) per second from vents on the east rift zone, the lava has added more than five-hundred acres (two hundred hectares) of new land to the island.

In the morning, I drove 24 miles southeast from my hotel in Hilo to see the Lava Tree State Monument (in the Nanawale Forest Reserve), which preserves lava molds of the tree trunks formed in 1790 when a lava flow swept through the area. Driving five miles further east toward the coast, I reached the Kapoho Cone (in the Puna District), which I readily climbed to observe the destruction wrought on Kapoho by the 1960 Kilauea eruption, which "swallowed" the town on January 28.

SHELTON A. GUNARATNE

Picture 81.1: The Kilauea Shield Volcano in Hawaii Volcanoes National Park (2011). After eruption, the Puu Oo vent of the volcano has been oozing out liquid lava (Source: USGS photo in Wikimedia Commons.)

Driving south and west on the Kapoho-Kalapana Road (a nineteen-mile stretch), I stopped at the Isaac Hale Park and MacKenzie State Park along the southern coast to absorb the scenery. I treated myself to a Hawaiian lunch at Kaimu before I proceeded to Kalapana, where the Kaimu-Chain of Craters Road served as the southeastern entry point to the Hawaii Volcanoes National Park via the Wahaula Heiau (Temple of the Red Mouth) and Visitor Center. The 1990 Kilauea lava flow from the Kupaianaha vent destroyed and partly buried both Kaimu and Kalapana. Now, they lie buried beneath more than fifty feet of lava.

Chain of Craters Road is a twenty-three-mile winding paved road through the East Rift Zone and coastal area. The road has paths and road offshoots that allow access to various volcanic views such as pit craters, active and dormant lava flows, plumes from lava tubes, and various geographic sites that can be accessed by trails from the road. It follows a line of pit craters and descends 3,700 feet into twenty-three miles and ends where a 2003 lava flow crossed the road. The Kaimu-Chain of

Craters link road that I drove on in 1984 might be buried under the lava flow spewed out by the Kilauea shield volcano. I have fond memories of driving on the Chain of Craters stopping at narrow places to read signs, explaining various lava formations. I also stopped to see several pit craters along the way.

The ten-mile (16 km) paved Crater Rim Drive circles the Kilauea Caldera, starting from the Visitor Center, where I viewed a ten-minute documentary on the surrounding volcanoes. I took the short paved road, off the Crater Rim Drive, to get a close look at the Kilauea Iki Crater, the origin of the 1995 eruption that closed the Chain of Craters Road. I drove through the Tree Fern Fungi to see the Thurston Lava Tube. After a stopover at the Volcano House, I went to see the Tree Molds on the Mauna Loa Road. Thereafter, I walked on the mile-long trail in the Kipuka Puaulu (Bird Park).

Despite the heavy rain, I stopped at the Volcano Observatory to look at the Kilauea Caldera. I also stopped to have a closer look at the Halemaumau Crater. But because of torrential rain, I could not complete the walk on the Devastation Trail. What gave me the greatest excitement was the steam rising from the Halemaumau Fire Pit, the principal vent of Kilauea Caldera, and the legendary home of Pele, the goddess of fire.

I left the Volcanoes National Park about 6:00 p.m. I was soaking wet when I returned to Uncle Billy's in Hilo to rest and sleep.

(The *Straits Times* (Singapore) published the original version of this story on July 13, 1985 under the headline "Hawaii in Four Days.")

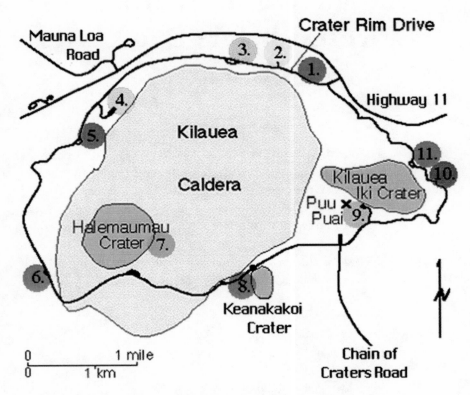

Map 81.2 The ten-mile Crater Rim Drive circles the Kilauea Caldera. The twenty-three-mile Chain of Craters Road joins it from the southeast. 1, Kilauea Visitor Center; 2, Steam Vents, Steaming Buffs, and Sulfur Banks; 3, Kilauea Overlook; 4, Jaggar Museum; 5, Southwest Rift Zone; 6, Halemaumau Crater; 7, Devastation Trail; 8, Keanakakoi Crater; 9, Puu Puai Overlook; 10, Thurston Lava Tube; 11, Kilauea Iki Overlook. (*Source:* National Park Service)

CHAPTER 82

Hawaii: Carmel Arrives in Capricornia before Dad Leaves Pu'Uhonua

MY FASCINATION WITH volcanoes did not end with my near-encounter with Pele, the goddess of fire, at the entrance to her abode in the awesome fire pit called Halemaumau Crater. She accelerated the velocity of the downpour that soaked me when I was about to enter her doorstep. I surrendered by turning back.

In the poem *Looking at Kilauea*, Asian poet Garrett Hongo (born 1951 in Volcano, next to the Kilauea Volcano) wrote that he saw,

> solidified eddies of *paho'eho'e*
> swirled like fans of pandanus leaves
> inundating Highway 130 near Kaimu;
> or a frozen cascade of lava
> sluiced over a low, dun-colored bluff
> that foregrounds a deep-focus panorama over the sublime,
> shades of gray and black plain of Ka'u Desert,
> the mother's breast of my universe.

Hongo's poem provides a perspective of a phenomenon that is still shrouded in mystery.

I decided to skip the trail leading to the summit of Mauna Loa, the world's largest volcano, because I thought I had already seen enough of the molten magma, lava, cones, craters, and calderas associated with volcanic activity. Experts say that about six hundred volcanoes have had known eruptions in recorded history, while about fifty to seventy volcanoes are active each year. An average of twenty volcanoes erupt per year.

Day 3: Hāmākua and Kohala Coasts

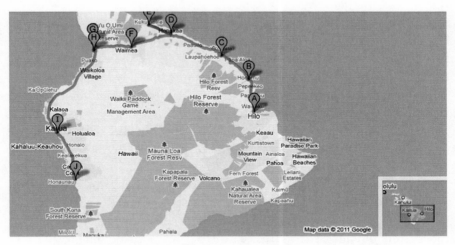

Map 82.1 My travel route on day three and day four—(anticlockwise) from Hilo to Captain Cook. Note the highway offshoot from Honoka'a to the idyllic Waipi'o Valley. *A*, Hilo; *B*, Honomu (Akaka Falls); *C*, Laupahoehoe; *D*, Honoka'a; *E*, Waipi'o Valley (Kukuihaele); *F*, Waimea (Kamuela); *G*, Kawaihae; *H*, Mauna Kea Beach Hotel and Resort; *I*, Uncle Billy's Kona Bay Hotel (Kailua-Kona); *J*, Pu'uhonua o Hōnaunau National Historical Park (Captain Cook).

Monday (January 30) morning, I checked out of Uncle Billy's Hilo Bay Hotel and headed for Uncle Billy's Kona Bay Hotel on the opposite (west) coast—some sixty-three miles by plane or ninety miles by road via Saddle Road and Hawaii Belt Road. However, I chose to drive on the longer semicircular west-north-east route, a driving distance of 122 miles.

First, I drove fourteen miles northward along the Hilo Bay and stopped at the Akaka Falls State Park, a twenty-seven-hectare tropical garden in Honomu (pop 541) noted for its two waterfalls—Akaka Falls on Kolekole Stream that drops 422 feet and Kahuna Falls that drops 100 feet further to the north. A scenic one-mile loop trail takes the visitor to both waterfalls.

Legend has it that Akaka Falls (masculine energy) marked the spot where God Akaka fell 422 feet to his death as he ran away from his wife when she found him with his mistress. Thereupon, the mistress created the Kahuna Falls (feminine energy) so the two falls represented the yang and the yin of Oriental lore.

Back on the coastal highway, I stopped at the Honomu Plantation Store to purchase a few odds and ends. Then, I visited the nearby Kolekole ("raw" or "scarred") Beach Park to enjoy some of the goodies I bought at the store. Another thirteen miles to the north along the Hāmākua Coast, I stopped at the Laupahoehoe (leaf lava) Point County Park, where a memorial recalls the 1946 "April Fools Day" tsunami that caused the deaths of twenty students and four teachers in the area.

The quiet, historic town of Honoka'a (pop 2,233), another nineteen miles to the northwest, was my lunch stop. Originally settled by the Chinese, Honoka'a was the center of the island's sugar industry. With the decline of sugar, the Hāmākua district has seen better prospects in other crops such as pineapples, coffee, papaya, macadamia nuts, and tea. I visited the Hawaiian Holiday Macadamia Nut Plant and the Kama'aina Woods Factory.

Picture 82.1 View from the Waipi'o Valley Lookout (August 19 2006). (Photo by Paul Hirst, Wikimedia Commons)

Waipi'o (curved water) Valley, one of nature's magnificent masterpieces, lies nine miles to the northwest of Honoka'a. It was the capital and permanent residence of many early Hawaiian kings (*ali'i*) up until the time of King "Umi-a-Liola (1510-1525). There also stood the ancient grass palace of the kings of yore. The lookout point, located on the top of the southern wall of the valley past the Last Chance Store in Kukuihaele, provides spectacular views of the idyllic surroundings, which no nature-lover can afford to miss. The view of the massive cliffs, which reach up to 2,490 feet (760 m) alongside the coast, is a rare treat. These cliffs are ribboned with waterfalls in rainy seasons. Wild pigs, pheasants, turkeys, and peacocks abound the valley, which has lush vegetation, taro fields, and fish ponds. To explore beyond the lookout, one needs a four-wheeler or resort to self-propulsion.

I backtracked to the main highway to continue my journey westward. My next stop was Waimea or Kamuela (pop 9,241), fifteen miles west of Honoka'a. I was now in Hawaii's *paniolo* (cowboy) country; so I paid a short visit to the 135,000-acre Parker Ranch (established 1847), once superlatively called the largest privately owned cattle ranch in the United States. It has more than fifty thousand head of cattle and five hundred horses. The ranch is the venue of the annual Fourth of July rodeo. Waimea is also the headquarters of two astronomical observatories standing on Mauna Kea: the W. M. Keck Observatory and the Canada-France-Hawaii Telescope. I also had a casual stop at the Kamuela Museum (now defunct). After leaving the ranch, I drove 13 miles west to Kawaihae, an unincorporated village on the Kohala Coast, from where the Parker Ranch ships its cattle to feedlots in Oahu.

First, I stopped at the eighty-six-acre Pu'ukohola Heiau (Temple on the Hill of the Whale) National Historic Site exhibiting the ruins of the temple that Kamehameha I built and dedicated in 1791. Second, I relaxed at the adjoining Samuel M. Spencer Beach Park, just to the southwest of the heiau, simply trying to figure out the reason why the white sand of the Kohala Coast has become such a magnet for the epicureans.

As I cruised along the Mauna Kea Beach Drive, a couple of miles to the south, I found that one of the draw cards was the magnificent setting of the Mauna Kea Beach Hotel, where I tarried to vicariously experience the splendid luxury of conspicuous consumption without necessarily splurging my "wealth." When Mauna Kea opened in July 1965 (with 154 guestrooms compared with the current 258), travel writers considered it the most expensive luxury hotel ever built, at $15 million. It was closed twice—once from 1994-1995 and again from 2006-2008—for renovations. It pampers its guests with its coastal golf course, thirteen tennis courts, as well as all sorts of amenities and recreational activities.

The Pavilion at Manta Ray Point, noted for its architecture inspired by eighteenth-century Buddhist temples, offers a selection of food to please the taste of all epicureans.

After waking up from reverie at Mauna Kea, I drove the last thirty-four miles south along the coastal road and reached Kailua-Kona (pop 9,870) about 7:00 p.m. I ate a light dinner at McDonald's and checked in at Uncle Billy's Kona Bay Hotel where I spent the night in Room 1023 with absolutely no clue that my daughter Carmel would come out of her mother's womb in less than three hours—at 9:52 p.m., Hawaii time.

Day 4: Final Exploits

I decided to celebrate my final day (Tuesday, January 31, 1984) in Hawaii by treating myself to a Royal Hawaiian Breakfast and to rest in the hotel until 10:00 a.m. Because I had arranged to leave the "Big Island" from the Kona Airport at Keahole for Honolulu (to board my flight to Australia) in the evening, I had almost an entire day for further exploration.

All the spots that I planned to visit were located no more than thirty miles south of Kailua-Kona along the coastal road named Ali'i ("Grand") Drive. The parallel highway SR11 was for those in a hurry.

First, I drove past all the resort hotels to Kahalu'u Beach Park, north of the Kona Country Club. Enticed by the greenery around me, I gave in to my temptation for self-propulsion so I could establish greater intimacy with the place. I walked southwest to the Sheraton Keauhou Bay Resort, another haven for the epicureans. In the vicinity, I also paid homage to the birthplace of Kamehameha III (1825-1854), who was born on August 11, 1813.

Picture 82.2 The Daifukuji Soto Mission, a Zen Buddhist temple in Honalo, Hawaii (August 18, 2009). (Photo by W. Nowicki, Wikimedia Commons)

Second, I visited the Daifukuji (The Temple of Great Happiness) on Hooper Villa Road (facing Cahill Drive) in Honalo. I had some difficulty locating this Zen Buddhist temple standing to the north of the Daifukuji Soto Mission. Backtracking on Ali'i Drive, I turned north on Kamehameha III Road, and then south on SR11 until I came to the intersection with Hooper Villa Road. The Ven. Kaiseki Kodama, a Japanese monk, founded the temple in 1915. He walked around the island twice to collect the donations for its construction. The Japanese community, associated with the area's coffee and macadamia plantations, rebuilt the temple in 1921. The architects applied an eclectic blend of Western and traditional Japanese forms to the new structure. Following the bombing of Pearl Harbor in 1941, the temple was forced to close until 1944.

The main hall highlighted the historical Buddha. To his right was the seated figure of Zen Master Dogen and to the left was Zen Master Keizan. In the alcove to the right of the main altar were two more figures: Bodhidharma Daishi, who carried the Teachings from India to China, and Daigen Shuri Bosatsu, another great bodhisattva. I entered the hall, chanted the precepts and the prayers just as I was wont to do at Aggrabodhi Vihara in Weligama (Sri Lanka) under my mother's guidance. That the Zen masters had replaced the disciples of the Buddha and the Hindu gods did not concern me the least.

Third, I went to see the Captain James Cook Monument in the Kealaketua Bay Historical Park. Hawaiian tradition says that a chief named Kalanimanokahoowaha killed British explorer Cook (1728-1779), who was on his third voyage, at this spot on February 14, 1779. Four of the Marines with Cook were also killed. The Hawaiians dragged Cook's body away.

After leaving the temple, I drove further south on SR11 to Kealaketua, where I stopped to buy some luncheon food and visit the Ken Hamilton Macadamia Nut Co. At Captain Cook, I left SR11 to reach Kealaketua Bay, where I ate my lunch. On the way, I stopped to buy a pound of Kona coffee to take home to Australia. At the bay, I also visited the Hikiau Heiau in the vicinity.

Fourth, I drove four miles further south on the narrow coastal road to see what turned out to be the star attraction of the day—*Pu'uhonua o Hōnaunau* (Place of Refuge) National Historical Park. As the Wikipedia explains, the park

> preserves the site where, up until the early 19th century, Hawaiians who broke a *kapu* (one of the ancient laws) could avoid certain death by fleeing to this place of refuge or *pu'uhonua*. The offender would be absolved by a priest and freed to leave. Defeated warriors and non-combatants could also find refuge here during times of battle. The grounds just outside the Great Wall that encloses the *pu'uhonua* were home to several generations of powerful chiefs.

The concept of refuge associated with the park seemed to me so Buddhistic because it is so close to the *abhaya bhumi* privilege mentioned in Buddhist literature. I will leave further discussion of it to another occasion.

I left the refuge to return to Kailua-Kona, where I returned the rented car at the airport and got on the evening flight to Honolulu.

Sidebar: *Enter Carmel*

My wife Yoke-Sim, who left for Australia with Junius on 1 Jan. 1984, was expecting to give birth to our daughter within a matter of days. Our friends in Rockhampton, Qld., were willing to take care of Yoke-Sim if she were to deliver her second child before mother and I returned to Australia.

Carmel, in her typical obstinate way, decided to arrive in this world before my mother or I could arrive in Rockhampton. Carmel was born at 5.52 p.m. Tuesday, 31 Jan. 1984, Queensland time, at the Mater Hospital.

At the particular moment when Carmel's birth was being witnessed by nurse Diane Black and Dr. John Birks, it was 9.52 p.m. Monday, 30 Jan., Hawaii time. I was spending the night in Room No. 1023 at Kona Bay (Uncle Billy's) Hotel, Kailua-Kona, unaware of my daughter's birth. I was relaxing after a 100-mile exploratory excursion from Hilo to Kailua Kona on Highway 19.

As I later gathered:

- Yoke-Sim felt contractions about 6.30 a.m. She rang Mater Hospital about 9 a.m.
- Kathy Cant accompanied Yoke-Sim to Mater Hospital about 10.30 a.m.
- Yoke-Sim was in labor from 11 a.m.
- Yoke-Sim gave birth to Carmel (7 lbs 10.5 oz.) at 5.52 p.m.

My mother arrived in Rockhampton Wednesday (1 Feb.) after a stopover with relatives in Sydney.

I arrived in Rockhampton Thursday (2 Feb.). Dentist Robert Kwong, a friend, gave me a ride from the airport to our home in Frenchville, North Rockhampton, where my mother was looking after Junius.

Thereafter, Kwong took me to Mater Hospital, where Yoke-Sim was doing well with the latest addition to the family.

CHAPTER 83

Montana-Idaho-Wyoming:

President Roosevelt Interrupts our Journey to Yellowstone National Park

RED LODGE, MONTANA, is the starting point of the Beartooth Highway, which the late CBS correspondent Charles Kuralt called "the most beautiful drive in America." The highway straddles the Montana-Wyoming border as it wiggles its way to the northeast entrance to Yellowstone National Park (YNP), and is situated about 670 miles (1,076 km) southwest of the Fargo-Moorhead Metropolitan Area, where we live.

In July 1996, we—daughter Carmel, twelve; son Junius, sixteen; wife Yoke-Sim; and I—planned an excursion that would include the Theodore Roosevelt National Park (TRNP) in the Badlands of North Dakota; the Yellowstone National Park in Wyoming; and the Mount Rushmore National Memorial (MRNM), near Keystone, South Dakota. This excursion was doubly important to Junius because it gave him the opportunity to prove his ability for driving long distances on the freeway.

Another couple, faculty colleague Henry Chan and his wife Janet, joined us in another car on the forward journey to YNP. Two visiting females from Canada related to Janet accompanied them.

We began our long journey at 7:45 a.m. on a Thursday (July 4), which was also the nation's Independence Day. After I drove the first hundred miles on Interstate 94 to Jamestown, N.D., Junius took over driving all the way to the rest area near Richardton, North Dakota, where we ate lunch. He drove almost 170 miles! Then, Yoke-Sim took over and drove us to Medora, North Dakota, the gateway to TRNP, another sixty miles west.

The TRNP

(We recalled the marathon drive on the same freeway, I-94, we made seven years earlier, on July 17, 1989, when we drove from Moorhead to Billings (pop 105,845), Montana's largest city, a distance of 610 miles, on my way to Longview, Washington, to take up an internship with the *Daily News*. On that particular Monday, we stopped for a hurried tour of Bismarck, the capital of North Dakota, and ate lunch at Medora after a stopover at the Painted Canyon Visitor Center to get a glimpse of the Badlands. We stayed overnight at Billings' Sheraton Hotel, where Carmel and Junius played in the hotel's pool to their hearts' content. We also climbed up Pompey's Pillar to see the site of a famous natural landmark where explorer William Clark had inscribed his name in July 1806. Two years earlier, on July 31, 1987, we had stopped overnight in Bismarck, wherefrom we drove as far as Dickinson, North Dakota, just thirty-seven miles east of Medora, on a weeklong camping excursion to the Black Hills on the border of South Dakota and Wyoming.)

Now, in 1996, we were back, repeating history, on the same spot—the Painted Canyon Visitor Center! We intended to see more of the park this time. The TRNP, established in 1947 to honor President Theodore Roosevelt's achievements in conservation as president (1901-1909) and for the landscape's influence on his life, covers 110 square miles (285 sq. km) of land in three sections: the smaller North Unit, the larger South Unit, and the Elkhorn Ranch Unit in-between. The 96-mile Maah Daah Hey ("area that has been/will be in existence for long") Trail and the Little Missouri River connect the three units.

We skipped the North Unit because its entrance was another 80 miles north of the South Unit on US-85.

Wildlife viewing is a popular activity in the TRNP, which is home to a wide variety of Great Plains wildlife: e.g., bison, feral horses, elk, bighorn sheep, white-tailed deer, and mule deer, prairie dogs, and at least 186 species of birds including golden eagles, sharp-tailed grouse, and wild turkeys.

TR came to the North Dakota Badlands in September 1883 to hunt buffalo. By the end of his hunting trip he had become the owner of the Chimney Butte Ranch, also called the Maltese Cross Ranch, about seven miles south of Medora. In 1884, Roosevelt purchased the Elkhorn Ranch, about thirty-five miles north of Medora, accessible by gravel roads. At Elkhorn, Roosevelt, as confessed in his later works particularly, enjoyed sitting in the veranda in a rocking chair, reading in the shade of the cottonwood trees.

We entered the TRNP from the Medora Visitor Center, seven miles northwest of the Painted Canyon. As we entered the park, TR "himself" spoke to us at his Maltese Cross cabin. (In my public relations classes, I had learnt that TR was a very PR conscious president who greeted every one who visited him by the visitor's name. TR studied the visitor's profile the night before the meeting.).

We decided to drive through the thirty-six-mile Scenic Loop Drive in the South Unit. Driving anticlockwise, first, we stopped at the Scoria Point Overlook. Then, we stopped to go for a short walk on Ridgeline Trail. Next, we climbed the 2,855-feet Buck Hill overlooking the Painted Canyon to get "the best view of the park." Heading northwest, we stopped at the Boicourt Overlook. Finally, driving southward, we stopped at Beef Corral Pullout. We were fascinated to observe the several prairie dog towns scattered all along the scenic loop.

After leaving the TRNP, Yoke-Sim drove us sixty miles to Glendive, Montana. Junius drove the next eighty miles to Miles City, where we stayed overnight at Motel 6. We regrouped with the Chans as we ate dinner at 4 B's Family Restaurant.

The next (July 5, 1996) morning, we left Miles City and drove another 146 miles west on I-94 to Billings, where we had stayed overnight in 1989.

The YNP—Day 1

Interstate 94 crosses North Dakota like a straight horizontal line into Glendive, Montana; then heads southwest through Billings, where I-94 merges into I-90. Our destination for the day was Gardiner, the north entry gate to the YNP, which we could have reached by heading westward on I-90 all the way to Livingston and turning south on US 89.

But as we reached Billings, we decided to leave the Interstate freeway and drive sixty miles southwest to Red Lodge (pop 2,200), Montana, on the more scenic and slower US 212. In 1896, Red Lodge, a coalmining town, had twenty saloons, and earned a reputation for riotous and violent living. By 1906 its population had grown to four thousand and by 1911 to five thousand. The Great Depression forced the closure of many of its coalmines. We stopped at the public library and ate a picnic lunch on the banks of the Rock Creek.

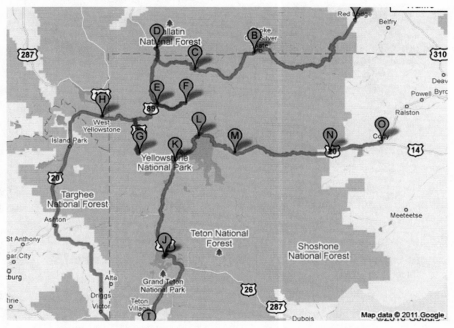

Map 83.1 Our Tour Route in Yellowstone National Park.
A, Red Lodge, MT; *B*, Cooke City or Silver Gate, MT (Northeast entrance); *C*, Tower Junction, WY; *D*, Gardiner, MT (North entrance); *E*, Norris, WY; *F*, Canyon Village, WY; *G*, Old Faithful, WY; *H*, West Yellowstone, MT (West entrance); *I*, Jackson, WY; *J*, Colter Bay/Moran, WY (South entrance); *K*, West Thumb, WY; *L*, Lake, WY; *M*, Sylvan Pass, WY; *N*, Wipiti, WY; *O*, Cody, WY (East entrance).

Picture 83.1 Beartooth Highway, near Beartooth Pass (May 26, 2006). (Photo by Phil Armitage. *Source:* Wikimedia Commons)

In 1938, the Beartooth Highway opened linking the town with the YNP. Yoke-Sim bravely took over driving from Junius to guide us through this sixty-nine-mile long Beartooth, which begins at 5,650 ft. and rises to the 10,974-feet-high Beartooth Pass via a series of steep zigzags and switchbacks through portions of the Custer National Forest and Shoshone National Forest along the Montana-Wyoming border. We stopped at lookouts to enjoy breathtaking views of idyllic scenery, including snowfields, little lakes, and flower patches. Then, we descended in to the dense pine forest and stopped to see the Hazardous Fall. We entered the Yellowstone National Park officially (current park fee is $25 per car) through its northeast entry point—Cooke City or Silver Gate (pop 140), Montana. The Yellowstone National Park's primary home is Wyoming but with extensions into Idaho and Montana (see map).

Mudslides and rockslides forced the closure of the Beartooth Highway in 2005. Because of the dangers of slides, the highway is open only part of the year.

From the northeast entry point, we drove twenty-nine miles to Tower Junction, where we visited the Roosevelt Lodge, where we recalled our

SHELTON A. GUNARATNE

chat with TR the day before at the TRNP. We also made short trips to see the Tower Fall (132 ft.), the Calcite Springs Overlook and the Petrified Tree. We drove further west to Mammoth Hot Springs and then north to Gardiner (pop 851), Montana, where we spent the night at the Town Motel.

Picture 83.2 The author (left) with his son Junius, 16, and daughter Carmel, 12, on the Lower Terrace, close to Albright Visitor Center and Museum located at Mammoth Hot Springs, five miles south of Gardiner (July 6, 1996).

Gardiner has been the main entrance to the Yellowstone National Park since 1872. In 2005, Gardiner became the venue for the Yellowstone National Park Heritage and Research Center.

The Yellowstone National Park—Day 2

Yellowstone, which spans an area of 3,472 square miles (8,992 square km), was the first national park in the world and is known for its wildlife and its many geothermal features, especially Old Faithful Geyser, one of the most popular features in the park. It has many types of ecosystems, but the subalpine forest is dominant.

Almost 3.3 million people visited the Yellowstone National Park in 2009 to see its lakes, canyons, rivers, and mountain ranges. Yellowstone Lake, centered over the Yellowstone Caldera—the largest super volcano on the continent, is one of the largest high-altitude lakes in North America. The caldera, an active volcano, has erupted with tremendous force several times in the last two million years. Wikipedia asserts that half of the world's geothermal features are in Yellowstone, fueled by this ongoing volcanism. "Lava flows and rocks from volcanic eruptions covered most of the land area of Yellowstone. The park is the centerpiece of the Greater Yellowstone Ecosystem, the largest remaining, nearly intact ecosystem in the Earth's northern temperate zone."

The Grand Loop Road provides access to the major features of the park, including the Upper, Midway and Lower geyser basins, Mammoth Hot Springs, Tower Fall, the Grand Canyon of the Yellowstone, and Lake Yellowstone.

Although we traveled only 144 miles Saturday (July 6), we learned much about the park's geothermal undercurrents as we drove along southward on the Upper Grand Loop in the morning starting with the Mammoth Hot Springs. We passed landmarks such as Golden Gate, Sheepeater Cliff, Indian Basin, and Roaring Mountain. We stopped at Norris Geyser Basin, the Yellowstone National Park's hottest geyser basin, to see the Steamboat Geyser and the numerous geysers along the Back Basin Tray.

Thereafter, we drove thirteen miles east to Canyon Village, where we walked around and ate our lunch in the vicinity of the Canyon Visitor Education Center. Along the North Rim Drive, we stopped at several lookouts—Inspiration Point, Grand View Point, Lookout Point, Lower Falls, and Upper Falls—to view the canyon. Along the South Rim Drive, we enjoyed the canyon views from Uncle Tom's Parking Area and Artist Point. We left the canyon area bout 4:00 p.m.

We stopped at Sulphur Caldron, one of Yellowstone National Park's most acid hot springs; and at the Mud Volume area as we continued driving south to Yellowstone Lake. We ate dinner at the Lake Lodge in Lake Village. (Splurging $31 was well worth the dinner considering the state of our unfed belies, which were making ugly noises.)

Picture 83.3 Junius and Carmel inspired by the Inspiration Point view of the 23 mile-long Grand Canyon of the Yellowstone as we toured the North Rim Drive of the Grand Loop (July 6, 1996).

Our final stop for the day was the cone geyser Old Faithful, the first geyser to receive a name in 1870, during the Washburn-Langford-Doane Expedition. Wikipedia says:

> Eruptions can shoot 3,700 to 8,400 US gallons (14,000 to 32,000 l) of boiling water to a height of 106 to 185 feet (32 to 56 m) lasting from 1.5 to five minutes. The average height of an eruption is 145 feet (44 m). The highest recorded eruption was 185 feet (56 m) high. Intervals between eruptions can range from 45 to 125 minutes, averaging 66.5 minutes in 1939, slowly increasing to an average of ninety minutes apart today.

We watched the 7:55 p.m. (July 6, 1996) eruption of Old Faithful. Then, we walked on the boardwalks to explore the Upper Geyser Basin. We paid particular attention to Geyser Hill and Castle-Grand Group. We left the basin at 9:00 p.m.

We arrived in West Yellowstone, Montana, at 10:00 p.m. and checked in at His Westward Ho Motel, where we spent the night.

CHAPTER 84

South Dakota: Avatars of Four Presidents Greet Us in Black Hills

WHEN WE LEFT West Yellowstone, Montana, Sunday (July 7, 1996), our intention was to explore the southeastern section of Yellowstone from Moran (pop 414) to Cody (pop 8,835). In the morning, we drove 127 miles south from West Yellowstone (pop 1,177) to Jackson (pop 8,647), Wyoming, via US 20 (then SR 32 and SR 33) along the eastern border of Idaho. Jackson is a major gateway for millions of tourists visiting nearby Grand Teton National Park, Yellowstone National Park, and the National Elk Refuge.

Our aim was to see at least the northern end of the Grand Teton National Park, Yellowstone National Park's immediate neighbor to the south, on this tour.

The Grand Teton NP, established in 1929, covers an area of 484 sq. miles. It's named after the Grand Teton, the tallest mountain (13,770 ft.) in the Teton Range. As we reached the top of Teton Pass on SR 33, we had an excellent view of the Idaho countryside. We stopped at the Jackson Visitor Center to get information on the Grand Teton National Park.

Then, along the Jackson Hole Valley, we headed to the Moose Visitor Center, where we ate our lunch. Our next stop was South Jenny Lake, where we walked to see the lakeshore. Moving northeast, we went to the top of Signal Mountain to get a good view of Jackson Lake and the Teton Range to the west. Our last stop in the Grand Teton National Park was the Colter Bay Visitor Center/Moran, the south entry point to the Yellowstone National Park.

Back in Yellowstone, we drove past Lewis Lake for a stop at the Grant Village Visitor Center (named after President Ulysses S. Grant, who signed the bill that created the Yellowstone National Park in 1872), where we saw a documentary on the 1988 Yellowstone fires. Then, we stopped at the West Thumb Geyser Basin for a last look at the geysers. Yellowstone's geyser basins reminded me of my 1984 near-encounter with Pele, the goddess of fire, at the Halemaumau Crater in Hawaii. She was kinder to me on this occasion.

It was past 7:00 p.m. when we came to the Fishing Bridge Visitor Center from where we saw the Lake Lodge where we ate dinner the previous day (Saturday July 6).

We left the Grand Loop Road on the north shore of the Yellowstone Lake and followed the Eastern Entrance Road (closed in the winter) to Cody, a stretch of seventy miles that was in "very poor shape" in the Sylvan Pass area. Yoke-Sim did all the hazardous driving past Pahaska Tepee and Wapiti all the way to Cody, where we arrived at 8:00 p.m. and checked into Big Bear Motel. We ate a modest dinner at Kentucky Fried Chicken. Overall, we covered a distance of 333 miles for the day.

Cody is named after William F. "Buffalo Bill" Cody (1846-1917), who received the Medal of Honor, the highest military honor awarded by the US government, in 1872. He was one of the most colorful figures of the American Old West. The Buffalo Bill Historical Center, located near the center of the city, contains five museums in one—Buffalo Bill Museum, Plains Indians Museum, Whitney Gallery of Western Art, Cody Firearms Museum, and Draper Museum of Natural History.

After spending three nights in the Yellowstone National Park, we were ready to say good-bye to "Old Faithful," Pele, and their associated progeny to reexplore an area along the Wyoming-South Dakota border that all four of us had visited nine years before, in 1987—the Black Hills.

Onto Black Hills

Monday (July 8) morning, we left Cody for Rapid City, South Dakota, 419 miles to the east. On the way, along US 14, we stopped to visit the museum in Greybull (pop 1,815); crossed the Bighorn Scenic Byway (from Shell to Dayton) through the Bighorn National Forest to view the Shell Canyon and the Granite Pass (8,950 ft.); and stopped to visit the Connor Battlefield (where the 1865 Battle of the Tongue River took place) at Ranchester, Wyoming (132 miles northeast of Cody), almost on the Montana border, before getting on to Interstate 90 to head further east to South Dakota.

On I-90, Junius took over driving from Sheridan to Moorcroft, a stretch of 135 miles.

We reached the rest area in Moorcroft about 5:00 p.m. Over refreshments, we reminisced how we camped at the KOA campground nine years ago on our visit to Devils's Tower on the eastern border of Wyoming on a Saturday (August 1, 1987), just thirty-two miles northeast of where we were.

"Carmel, Junius, and I swam in the pool [of the KOA Campground] to refresh ourselves," I had written in my diary (August 1, 1987). "And we walked to Belle Fourche River to look at the red rock at the front of the Devils's Tower." The two kids could barely remember what we did on that visit. Wikipedia says that the tower, which the Lakota Indians called *Mato Tipila* (Bear Lodge) rises 1,267 ft above the surrounding terrain, and that its summit is 5,112 ft above sea level. The so-called tower is a volcanic neck (or the core of a volcano exposed from erosion). President Theodore Roosevelt declared it a national monument in 1906. It lies in the northern Black Hills between Hulett (pop 408) and Sundance (pop 1,161) in northeastern Wyoming, above the Belle Fourche River. Several fascinating legends explain the origin of Devils Tower.

One story traces the tower to seven little girls who were playing outdoors when they spotted several giant bears heading toward them. The hapless girls climbed up a rock and invoked the help of the great spirit, who raised the rock from the ground toward the heavens to save the girls from the bears, which left deep claw marks when they attempted to climb the steep rock. (Those are the marks that appear today on the sides of Devils Tower.) When the girls reached the sky, the great spirit turned them into the Pleiades star constellation.

SHELTON A. GUNARATNE

Picture 84.1 The Devils Tower (2006). (*Source:* Wikimedia Commons. Photo by Colin Faulkingham)

Another legend centers on a Native American who decided to sleep overnight at the base of Bear Lodge, next to a buffalo head. In the morning, he found that the Great Medicine had transported both himself (the sleeper) and the buffalo head to the top of the rock with no way down. He spent another day and night on the rock with no food or water. After he had prayed all day and then gone to sleep, he awoke to find that the Great Medicine had brought him back down to the ground, but left the buffalo head at the top near the edge.

In 1987, we reached the Black Hills by traveling west on I-94 all the way to Belfield, North Dakota, just east of the Theodore Roosevelt National Park, and then turning south on US 85 to enter South Dakota at Ludlow. From there, we proceeded further south through Buffalo to experience the "Geographical Center of United States of America" in Butte County. My diary entry for August 1, 1987 records: "We climbed up the hill to find nothing impressive except the sign that said the center shifted from Kansas in 1959 with the addition of Hawaii and Alaska." Then, we crossed over to Wyoming on SR 34 to get to Devils Tower, which brought in memories of our (sans Carmel's) visit to the Devils Postpile National Monument in Mammoth Lakes, California, in 1983.

The next (Sunday) morning, National Park Service ranger David Thomas took us on a one-hour tour to explain the natural phenomena along the Tower Trail, where we saw another prairie dog colony. (Prairie dogs are small woodchucks whose bark resembles that of a dog.) Soon after, we drove on US 14 to reach Sundance, the town associated with horse thief Harry Longabaugh, also known as the "Sundance Kid." The 1969 motion picture *Butch Cassidy and the Sundance Kid* starring Robert Redford (as Longabaugh) made the town well known.

Whereas we couldn't see the Crook County Museum and Art Gallery in 1987 because of Sunday closure, its doors were open to us in 1996.

On the current (1996) trip, we stopped at Spearfish (pop 8,606), South Dakota, to eat dinner at Cedar House Family Restaurant. About 9:00 p.m., we arrived in downtown Rapid City (pop 59,607), also known as the "Star of the West" and the "Gateway to the Black Hills," where we checked in at the Family Inn (3727 Sturgis Road) to spend the night.

We met the Chans and their Canadian travel companions, whom we had missed for two days, at the Family Inn the next (Tuesday July 9, 1996) morning as we left to revisit the Mount Rushmore National Memorial (MRNM), which we first visited (on August 5, 1987) when Carmel was three and Junius was seven.

Revisiting Mount Rushmore

MRNM is a sculpture carved into the granite face of Mount Rushmore, near Keystone, in the Black Hills of South Dakota. The sculpture is the work of Gutzon Borglum (1867-1941) and his son Lincoln Borglum (1912-1986). The superlative memorial features sixty-foot (18 m) sculptures of the heads of four former US presidents—the country's first nonparty president, George Washington (1789-1797); third president, Thomas Jefferson (1801-1809), a Democratic-Republican; twenty-sixth president, Theodore Roosevelt (1901-1909), a Republican; and sixteenth president, Abraham Lincoln (1865-1869), a Republican. The entire memorial covers 1,278.45 acres (5.17 sq. km) and is 5,725 feet (1,745 m) above sea level.

Picture 84.2 Borglum's sculpture of four presidents at Mount Rushmore. (From left) George Washington, Thomas Jefferson, Theodore Roosevelt, and Abraham Lincoln. (*Source:* Wikimedia Commons. Photo by Dean Franklin)

Backed by federal funding, Borglum started work on the memorial in 1927 and completed the job between 1934 and 1939. Borglum selected the presidents on the basis of their role in preserving the republic and expanding its territory. The entire project cost a total of $990,000. More than 2.7 million people visited MRNM in 2006.

We reached Mount Rushmore, only twenty-four miles southwest of Rapid City, along US 16. We took the Skyline Drive to the Dinosaur Park, which the kids enjoyed very much, before visiting the MRNM to introduce Carmel and Junius to the sculpture of the Borglums. There, we joined a ranger's guided tour from the orientation centre to the sculptors' studios. On our first visit to MRNM in 1987, we camped overnight in nearby Keystone to see the magnificence of the lighted faces of the four presidents at night.

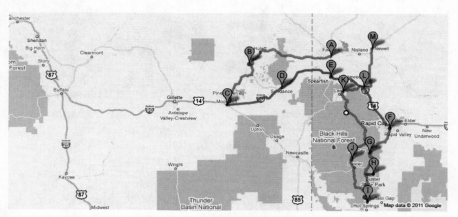

Map 84.1 Tour of the Black Hills 1987 and 1996.
A, Geographical Center of USA on US85, SD; *B*, Devils Tower
National Monument, WY; *C*, Moorcroft, WY; *D*, Sundance, WY;
E, Spearfish, SD; *F*, Rapid City, SD; *G*, Mount Rushmore National
Memorial or Keystone, SD; *H*, Custer State Park; *I*, Wind Cave
National Park; *J*, Crazy Horse Memorial; *K*, Deadwood, SD; *L*,
Sturgis, SD; *M*, Newell, SD (exit to Faith).

CHAPTER 85

South Dakota: Jitters and Joys of Camping in and Around Black Hills

ON TUESDAY (JULY 9, 1996), we left the four presidents in Mount Rushmore meet and greet their thousands of other fans who kept on flocking, while we continued our adventures in the Black Hills (*Pahá Sápa* in Lakota) National Forest. We spent most of the next morning with *Crazy Horse* (ca.1840-1877), an Oglala Lakota warrior who took up arms against the US federal government to fight against encroachments on the territories and way of life of the Lakota people.

Crazy Horse led the Battle of Little Bighorn in 1876. His father was *Waglula* (Worm) and his mother *Rattling Blanket Woman*. *Crazy Horse* had three wives—*Black Buffalo Woman*, *Black Shawl Woman*, and *Nellie* Laravie.

Sculptor Korczak Ziółkowski (1908-1982), who had worked with Gutzon Borglum on the Mount Rushmore memorial, began the *Crazy Horse* sculpture in 1948 after consultations with Chief Henry Standing Bear and his fellow chiefs. When completed, it would be 641 ft (195 m) wide and 563 ft (172 m) high. The head of *Crazy Horse* would be eighty-seven feet (27 m) high compared with sixty feet (18 m) height of each presidential head. On the death of Ziółkowski, his wife, Ruth and seven of their ten children continued with the completion of the project as a nonprofit enterprise. They have refused federal funding for the project. We spent most of our time in the Indian museum and took a bus tour to see the first level of the nine-storey high face of *Crazy Horse*.

From the Wind Cave National Park, we drove northwest on US 385 to visit the *Crazy Horse* Memorial, consisting of the incomplete carving (monument) of *Crazy Horse* on Mount Thunderbird, the Indian Museum of North America, and the Native American Cultural Center. It is located in Berne, seventeen miles southwest of Mount Rushmore, between Custer and Hill City.

The Black Hills are a small, isolated mountain range rising from the Great Plains in western South Dakota and extending into Wyoming. It is the location of the tallest peaks of continental North America east of the Rockies, e.g., Harney (7,244 ft.), Odakota (7,205 ft.), and Bear (7,166 ft). This mountain range encompasses the 1.25 million-acre Black Hills National Forest managed by the US Forest Service. The National Park Service administers the national parks, monuments, and memorials.

Wikipedia describes Black Hills as "a very spread-out urban area" with a population of 250,000. Important Black Hills cities and towns include Hot Springs (pop 4,129), an old resort town in the southern Hills; Custer (pop 1,860), a mining and tourism town and headquarters for Black Hills National Forest; Keystone (pop 311), gateway to Mount Rushmore; Hill City (pop 780), a timber and tourism town in the center of the Hills; Lead (pop 3,087), home of the defunct Homestake (Gold) Mine; Deadwood (pop 1,380), a historic and well-preserved gambling mecca; Spearfish (pop 8,606), home of Black Hills State University; Sturgis (pop 6,642), the seat of Meade County originally a military town now famous for one of the largest motorcycle rallies in the world; Belle Fourche (pop 4,565), a ranching town; and Newcastle (pop 3,065) in Wyoming, now the center of the Black Hills petroleum production.

Needles Highway

In 1996, we drove west from Keystone on SR 244 and south on SR 87—the so-called "Needles Highway"—to visit the seventy-one-thousand-acre Custer State Park, South Dakota's first and largest state park. On SR 87, we stopped at Sylvan Lake, just to the southwest of Harney Peak, to absorb the fascinating beauty of the tallest mountains in the Midwest. We walked along the lake to the dam, where the four-mile

Sunday Gulch Foot Trail starts. We recalled our walk along the trail on a Wednesday (August 5) in 1987. On this occasion, however, we found the trail closed. The drive along the fourteen-mile Needles Highway brought memories of our drive through the Tioga Pass in Yosemite and the more recent experience of our drive through the Beartooth Pass in Yellowstone.

Picture 85.1 The Needle's Eye Tunnel on the Needles Highway in the Black Hills (2010). (*Source:* Wikimedia Commons)

We passed the Needles and Cathedral rock formations, as well as the Woodpecker Ridge to reach Legion Lake, where we stopped to walk along the lake looking for the Badger Hole, the home of poet laureate Charles Badger Clark (1883-1957), which we visited in 1987 but eluded us on this occasion. We also drove briefly on the eighteen-mile Wildlife Loop Road to visit a prairie dog town, where we met "the friendliest prairie dogs" we encountered. Some of the park's wild "begging" burros (donkeys) live at the southernmost end of this road, which follows the varied landscape offering views of the higher portions of the Black Hills, badlands, endless sky and lush streambeds.

Picture 85.2 Along the Wildlife Loop Road in Custer State Park, we met "the friendliest prairie dogs" we encountered. Carmel, twelve (seated), hobnobbed with a couple of prairie dogs (July 9, 1996).

The seventy-one-thousand-acre Custer State Park is named after Lt. Col. George Armstrong Custer (1839-1876), a hero of the Civil War. The park is famous for its scenery and its herd of fifteen hundred free roaming bison. Its other wildlife include elk, mule deer, white-tailed deer, mountain goats, bighorn sheep, pronghorn antelope, mountain lions, and feral burros. (In 1987, we camped at Grace Coolidge Campground at Custer State Park.)

Joys of Camping

Our destination for the day was the 28,295-acre Wind Cave National Park, south of the Custer State Park. We stopped at the Visitor Center and Cave Entrance, where we bought tickets to join the 6:00 p.m. cave tour, which turned out to be "too bland." The cave is notable for its displays of the calcite formation known as boxwork. Theodore Roosevelt declared it a national park in 1903.

After dinner, we repaired to the amphitheater to join a program titled *The Experiences of a Cave Explorer.* Participating in programs arranged by the park rangers was one of the joys of camping. We camped overnight at the Elk Mountain Campground.

Wednesday (July 10, 1996) morning, we ate breakfast, folded our tent, and went for a walk along the Elk Mountain Nature Trail. For us, trail walking was another joy of camping. It always reminded me of my boyhood exploits in the woods of Pathegama.

Other joys of camping, as I have recorded in previous tales of my travels, include the feeling of oneness with nature; the ability to adjust to ongoing changes in habitat; learning the value of good neighborliness; and the joy of experiencing the interconnection of *anatta, anicca,* and *dukkha*—the three signs of existence.

Jitters of Camping

We learned on our extended Black Hills camping trip in 1987 that the joys of camping do not come without accompanying jitters. We set up our tent at an idyllic spot called the Trout Haven Resort and Campgrounds (vaunted as "fifteen acres of paradise") on US 385 on a Monday (August 3) evening after we toured the historically notorious towns of Deadwood and Lead. The resort (some thirty-three miles north of Crazy Horse; or some nineteen miles south of Deadwood) provides two ponds full of trout and sells the fish to the catcher on a per-inch charge. Cleaning is free but cooking costs extra. We felt joy when Junius caught a trout or two without any ado, and Yoke-Sim cooked the "expensive" fish for our dinner. I collected firewood for a campfire. More joy!

But our joy didn't last that long. Fear gripped us when a storm of rain and hail pelted on our tent and almost blew it away. I had to hold on to it with all my might. Fortunately, Carmel, three, who was fast a sleep did not wake up to see the scary commotion.

We had similar jitters on the night we camped on Sportsmen's Beach, Lake Walker, Nevada, in summer 1983—August 18—five months before Carmel's birth. Rain and strong winds almost unplugged our tent on that day too (see travels-19). I have recorded another kind of jitters I experienced at Hetch Hetchy in Yosemite in mid-August 1983 (see travels-20).

As we passed Trout Haven in 1996 on our revisit to Deadwood, we reminisced over the jitters once again. In Deadwood, we bought food at a supermarket and ate a picnic-style lunch at the city park on Sherman Street. In 1987, we explored the historic Main Street and learned about "Calamity Jane," "Madame Dixie," and their charges at the Green Door. And in Lead, Junius and I joined a tour of the historic Homestake Mine. In 1987 (on Sunday August 2), we camped overnight at the city campground in Spearfish as well. We attended the 8:15 p.m. performance of the Black Hills Passion Play in an open-air amphitheatre (seating seven thousand), with masses of evergreens and the towering Lookout Mountain as a backdrop. Despite thunder, lightning, and rain, the play went on. It was a joy to get back into our tent and fall sound asleep.

Until its last performance on August 31, 2008, the show was produced under the auspices of Passion Player Josef Meier's daughter Johanna, a world-famous opera singer who had her debut in the play at the age of five weeks.

We drove a distance of 1,330 miles in our Toyota Camry wagon to complete our 1987 Black Hills camping excursion. Our more ambitious 1996 tour of Yellowstone and Back Hills on the same vehicle covered a distance 2,453 miles.

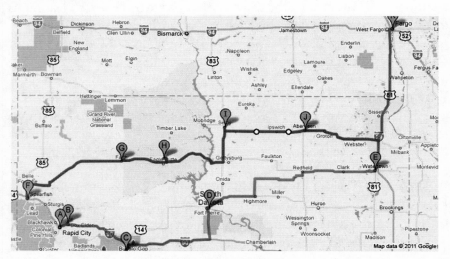

Map 85.1 From Black Hills to Fargo-Moorhead.

1996 Trip—*F*, Deadwood and Spearfish; *G*, Faith; *H*, Cheyenne River Indian Reservation; *I*, Selby; *J*, Aberdeen; *K*, Fargo. 1987 Trip—*A*, Rapid City; *B*, Ellsworth AFB; *C*, Badlands National Park; *D*, Pierre; *E*, Watertown; *K*, Fargo.

SHELTON A. GUNARATNE

Return Trip Jitters

Our return trips from the Black Hills, both in 1987 and 1996 (see Map 1) gave us both joy and jitters. In 1996, we left Deadwood about 3:00 p.m. (Wednesday July 10), and Junius drove us some 114 miles to Faith on US 212. Yoke-Sim continued driving east on US 212 the next hundred miles through the Cheyenne River Indian Reservation to the Missouri River crossing, near Gettysburg. We stopped at the enchanting rest area on a hill overlooking the river to eat dinner disregarding the loss of one hour as we shifted to Central time at the crossing. Our joy blinded us to the approaching winds and the onset of gloaming. I took over driving and headed north on US 83, then east on US 12. By the time I reached Ipswich, after driving ninety-three miles, I could hardly see the road because of winds and dark clouds. Junius emerged as a sixteen-year-old heroic boy who took over driving from me at Ipswich, filled up the car at Aberdeen, some thirty miles ahead, and drove us all the way to Fargo Moorhead—a distance of 215 miles. We reached home at 2:00 a.m. on Thursday.

In 1987, we took two days after leaving Black Hills to reach Fargo-Moorhead. We spent Thursday (August 6) visiting several museums—the Museum of Geology, Dahl Fine Arts Center, the Sioux Indian Museum, and the Minnilusa Pioneer Museum. We stopped at Storybook Island (on Sheridan Lake Road) and Dinosaur Park (on Skyline Drive) to provide amusement to Carmel, three, and Junius, seven. We camped overnight at the Lake Park Campground, on the western shore of Canyon Lake in Rapid City.

Friday (August 7) morning, we left the campground early because of impending rain. Yoke-Sim cooked our breakfast at a way shelter in Canyon Lake Park on the western shore of the lake. Then, we left the Black Hills on I-90 to visit the Ellsworth Air Force Base, about thirteen miles to the east. We joined the 9:20 a.m. guided tour of the base and browsed the South Dakota Air and Space Museum. Next, we drove seventy-six miles southeast to visit the 244,000-acre Badlands National Park, which we entered at Wall on SR 240. Despite the rain, we covered the entire Badlands Loop to see the "spectacular examples of weathering and erosion." We ate lunch at the Cedar Pass Visitor Center and left the park about 4:00 p.m. We had to drive another 124 miles east and north (on I-90 and US 83) to reach Pierre (pop 14,072), the capital of South Dakota, at 8:00 p.m.

We camped overnight at the free campground (facing the Missouri River) at Griffin Park in Pierre, some seventy miles southwest of the Missouri crossing where we stopped for dinner on our 1996 tour. Junius was highly thrilled when we crossed the time zone to Central. A free campsite facing the river was almost a dream come true! Yoke-Sim cooked our dinner without delay on the spot.

Picture 85.3 Carmel, twelve, and Junius, sixteen, play with a green dinosaur at the Dinosaur Park, Rapid City, South Dakota (July 9, 1996).

Because of overnight rain, we got up late Saturday (August 8) morning. After breakfast, we left the campground to visit the Oahe Dam (in North Stanley), where we joined a one-hour guided tour of "the world's second largest rolled earth-fill dam." Back in Pierre, we toured the state Capitol and the Robinson State Museum. We ate lunch at the Pierre Mall, which we left at 2:00 p.m. We reached Watertown (pop 20,247), 190 miles further east, about 6:00 p.m. There, we allowed Carmel and Junius to have all the fun they needed at the Bramble Park Zoo. We ate dinner at the employee-owned Hy Vee.

Yoke-Sim and I shared the 146-mile driving distance between Watertown and Fargo. I drove the final leg of our return trip "even though I found driving in the gloaming somewhat discomfiting." Jitters of camping!

CHAPTER 86

Minnesota: Camping in Voyageurs National Park on the Canadian Border

WHEREAS THE MAIN access to most national parks is by automobile or by foot, the primary access to the 218,054-acre Voyageurs National Park is via water. Because Voyageurs NP lies to the west of the famous Boundary Waters Canoe Area Wilderness (BWCAW) in Minnesota, "the Land of 10,000 Lakes," this peculiar feature should come as no surprise. Many people visited the park by canoe and kayak.

These canoeists, kayakers, other boaters, and fishermen found the park an aquatic haven. The (Sinhala-sounding) Kabetogama Peninsula, which lies entirely within the park and makes up most of its land area, is accessible only by boat. Others rented houseboats. Established as a national park in 1975, the *Voyageurs* (named after the French-Canadian fur traders) attracted an estimated 220,650 people in 2007.

In the late summer of 1988 (August 11-20), Carmel, four, Junius, eight, Yoke-Sim and I set forth on a ten-day camping excursion of the Voyageurs National Park, Zippel Bay State Park, and Two Harbors (in northern Minnesota), as well as four provincial parks—Rushing River, Blue Lake, Kakabeka Falls, and Pigeon River Falls (in southern Ontario, Canada). Having had her first major camping experience in the Black Hills at the age of three, Carmel was humming to the tune of "Twinkle Twinkle," something like the following:

> *I'm going camping, yes sirree!*
> *I'm going camping, won't you come with me?*

First we'll pitch our tent on the ground,
Then make a fire as we all gather round.

And camping we did go, covering a roundtrip driving distance of some 1,722 miles.

Day 1 (Thursday)

We left Fargo-Moorhead at 8:30 a.m. and arrived at the Kabetogama Lake Visitor Center at 3:30 p.m. with stops at Mahnomen (pop 2,052), Bemidji (pop 13,419), and Blackduck (pop 696).

(The entire Mahnomen County is part of the White Earth Indian Reservation [*Gaa-waabaabiganikaag*]. Bemidji is the central hub of the Red Lake Indian Reservation, White Earth Indian Reservation and the Leech Lake Indian Reservation. Eight miles outside of Blackduck is Camp Rabideau, which Franklin Roosevelt set up as part of his New Deal to give jobs to young people.)

After driving 272 miles to reach Voyageurs National Park, we parked our Toyota Camry wagon at the Kabetogama Lake Visitor Center because vehicles did not have access to the campgrounds. We set up tent at the Woodenfrog State Forest Campground (current site fee is $12 per night) to enjoy the park's facilities for the next two days. We ate dinner seated around a campfire. The highlight of the evening was a program on water the park rangers presented at the interpretive center.

Day 2 (Friday)

In the morning, while Yoke-Sim and the two kids went to International Falls (pop 12,000)—located northwest of the national park on the Rainy River directly across from Fort Frances, Ontario—to explore the Koochiching County Historical Museum, I joined a six-hour (10:00 a.m. to 4:00 p.m.) fifty-mile roundtrip cruise on lakes Kabetogama and Namakan aboard the Betsy Anna with Dean Litwiller of Voyageur Park Lodge as the captain and tour guide.

The highlights of the Litwiller cruise were the short stops at the Hoist Bay logging camp (in southwest Namakan Lake) and at the Mica Island's abandoned mica mine (in the Namakan Narrows). Hoist Bay is named for the machinery used to *hoist* floating logs out of the lake. Mica Island got its name when two prospectors discovered a rich vein of mica on the island in 1895.

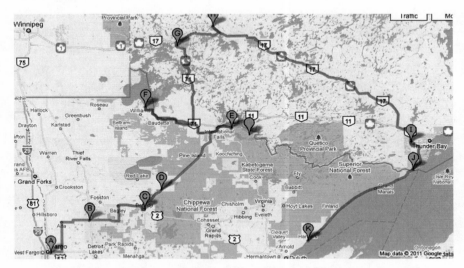

Map 86.1 Where we camped around Minnesota-Ontario boundary.
E, Voyageurs National Park (Red Arrow denotes Woodenfrog campground); *F*, Zippel Bay State Park in Williams, Minnesota; *G*, Rushing River Provincial Park in Kenora, Ontario; *H*, Blue Lake Provincial Park in Dryden, Ontario; *I*, Kakabeka Provincial Park, west of Thunder Bay, Ontario; *J*, Pigeon River Provincial Park in Ontario; *K*, Burlington Bay Campground in Two Harbors, Minnesota.
Other Places on the Way
A, Fargo-Moorhead; *B*, Mahnomen, Minnesota; *C*, Bemidji, Minnesota; *D*, Blackduck, Minnesota.

I felt the ninety-minute stop at the historic Kettle Falls Hotel was way too long. No roads lead to Kettle Falls. Ed Rose, a lumber baron, built the hotel, now a national historical marker, between 1910 and 1913 to accommodate assorted lumberjacks, gold prospectors, sportsmen, and bootleggers.

(Eating my $5 hamburger on the go, I crossed the Kettle Falls Dam southward over to Kettle Island in Ontario with no hassles of border crossing. It was my briefest visit to Canada!)

At the dam, I watched the waterfall ten feet from Namakan Lake to Rainy Lake. However, the high degree of excitement I expected from this cruise did not materialize. The three eagle nests that I saw on three of the more than two hundred islands dotting the lakes and a glimpse of the Ash River camping area were hardly sufficient to raise even a minor eye brow.

Yoke-Sim and the kids also had joined a short afternoon (2:00 p.m. to 4:30 p.m.) cruise of the Rainy Lake at the Rainy Lake Visitor Center, located twelve miles (19 km) east of International Falls. They came to pick me up at the Kabetogama Lake Visitor Center, located on the southwestern edge of the park, at 5:30 p.m. (A third facility, the Ash River Visitor Center, is located on the southern boundary of the park.) The park encompasses the entire Lake Kabetogama and one-half the waters of the three lakes—Rainy, Namakan, and Sandy Point—that straddle the Ontario-Minnesota boundary.

Day 3 (Saturday)

This morning, we left the Woodenfrog campgrounds for International Falls, which still promoted itself as the "Icebox of the Nation" after Fraser, Colorado, failed to substantiate in court its claim to be the superlative "Icebox." The US Patent and Trademark Office officially registered the slogan with International Falls on January 29, 2008. Frostbite Falls, the fictional hometown of Squirrel and Moose in "The Rocky and Bullwinkle Show" of the early 1960s was a spoof of the real-life International Falls.

We drove on the eleven-mile stretch of SR 11 from the visitor center to the route's eastern terminus at Island View on Rainy Lake to observe the northern bounds of the Voyageurs National Park. On the way, we stopped at Ranier to see the City Beach.

Then, we crossed the International (Toll) Bridge to Fort Frances (pop 8,103). We spent more than four hours on Canadian soil visiting the components of the Fort Frances Museum and Cultural Center: Lookout Tower Museum, a hundred-feet (33 m) tower moved from Atkikokan in 1972; The Hallet, a sixty-feet logging tugboat, which was "the largest and most powerful boat on Rainy Lake;" and Fort St. Pierre—all located in the Pither's Point Park, where we ate lunch. Next, we island hopped along the Noden Causeway on our way back to the United States. (This was the first taste of Canada for Carmel, Junius, and Yoke-Sim. I first visited Canada in 1967 (July 7-9) to attend the Montreal Exposition.)

Yoke-Sim bought some wild rice and groceries at the International Mall to prepare dinner at the Zippel Bay State Park on the southeastern shore of the Lake of the Woods, eighty-nine miles west of International Falls.

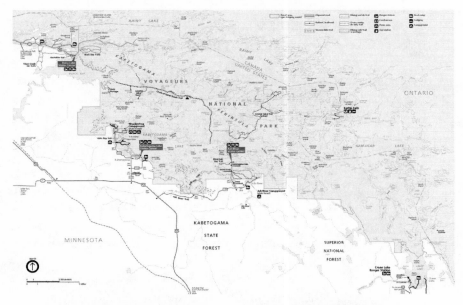

Map 86.2 Enlarged Map of Voyageurs National Park, Kabetogama Peninsula—surrounded by Rainy Lake, Namakan Lake, and Kabetogama Lake—is accessible only by water. (*Source*: National Park Service. Wikimedia Commons)

Heavy rain in the afternoon and evening marred our exploratory instincts a great deal although we did stop at the Grand Mound Interpretive Center and walked on the trail to see the prehistoric Indian burial grounds. Bad weather also connived with twilight to prevent us from absorbing the scenic abundance the Lake of the Woods would have provided at sunset on a sunny day. We set up our tent in the Lakeview Campground, ate our (wild rice) dinner, and planned our daring explorations for Sunday.

Day 4 (Sunday)

We got up late this morning because rain had drained our energy. We left the state park about 10:30 a.m. after a walk along the magnificent Zippel Bay to replace some of the lost energy.

Because my septuagenarian barber used to brag about his fishing exploits on Lake of the Woods, I had developed a craving to see this huge freshwater lake up close. It is more than seventy miles long and wide, and it accommodates more than 14,552 islands and 65,000 miles (105,000 km) of shoreline. The state of Minnesota (in the United States) and the provinces of Ontario and Manitoba (in Canada) shared the lake.

We decided to rough it out by following a route closest to the southeastern shore of Lake of the Woods. To do so, we backtracked twenty miles to Baudette, crossed the Rainy River on the toll bridge ($1.45 in 1988) to Canada and headed another thirty-eight miles north on ON-600N (via Harris Hill) and ON-621N (via Bergland) to Morson, from where one could see the Lake of the Woods Provincial Park located on Bigsby and Dawson islands just a boat ride away. We ate lunch on the beach across the Birch Campground. We also went to see the day-users' area of the campground before cruising in the vicinity to see more of the lake. Then, by chance, we ran into an Indian powwow at the Big Grassy Indian Reserve.

Soon, we had to face the consequences of choosing to drive on unpaved dirt roads for the day's explorations. Yoke-Sim's initiation into driving in Canada began on the 55 miles of rough roads (along ON-621S to Minahico, ON-619E and S to Cozy Corners, and ON-600E and S to Deerlock and Black Hawk) linking Morson with Trans-Canada 71N. We suffered enormous *dukkha* trying to brave our way through this "driving nightmare."

We found common cause with an Ontario family who were driving behind us with a high noise level because the exhaust pipe of their car had come apart in the rough and tumble of negotiating bumpy roads. Thus, we felt ecstatic on reaching Trans-Canada 71, a very scenic highway winding along the eastern shore of Lake of the Woods from Caliper Lake (parallel to Morson), where I took over driving from Yoke-Sim.

I stopped four miles north at the picturesque Nestor Falls to capture the storybook scenery. For the next sixty miles up to the Rushing River Provincial Park, which we reached at 7:00 p.m., Trans-Canada 71 snaked through the eastern edge of Lake of the Woods to mesmerize all of us with spectacular panoramas of the sunset.

After driving 196 miles for the day entailing some of the roughest roads in Ontario, we were happy to find solace in the enchanting Rushing River Provincial Park straddling the Dogtooth Lake. After selecting an idyllic campsite facing the lake, Carmel, Junius, and I dipped into the soothing waters of the lake. Yoke-Sim preferred to go to the shower. We ate a hearty dinner and went to bed by 9:00 p.m.

CHAPTER 87

Minnesota and Ontario: Go Past "Devils Gap" and Greet "Husky Muskie," "Max Moose," and "Sleeping Giant" on the Way

I DID NOT err when I said (in the last chapter) that we visited the eastern shore of Lake of the Woods Provincial Park in 1988. But the offshore area in the vicinity of Morson that we had the honor to visit currently answers to the name Assabaska Ojibway Heritage Park—a fact that even the ubiquitous Wikipedia has failed to pick up.

Ontario Parks—a branch of the Natural Resource Management Division of the Ministry of Natural Resources—clarifies that the renamed park, "formerly part of Lake of the Woods Provincial Park," is located off Highway 621, near Morson, (and) managed by the Anishinabe First Nation under the direction of the Ministry of Natural Resources. The Anishinabe had reclaimed the park as "part of on-going Treaty No. 3 land claim negotiations." Cultural activities, like the powwow we attended, rock painting, and traditional games are among the park's attractions.

Ontario claims world expertise in developing park systems. Currently, Ontario (pop 13.2 million) has thirty-nine national parks, 330 provincial parks, and 292 conservation reserves. Fees for camping vary according to the facilities and services provided.

Ontario Parks has classified the provincial parks into six categories: 65 Recreational parks, six Cultural Heritage parks, 80 Natural Environment parks, 109 Nature Reserve parks, 62 Waterway parks, and

8eight Wilderness parks. Current campsite fee per night (including the harmonized sales tax of 13 percent) varies from $15 to $46 depending on three levels of facilities—low, middle, and premium.

Lake of the Woods PP (classified Natural Environment) on Dawson and Bigsby islands, which we saw Sunday, attracts people who enjoy wildlife viewing, trails, boating, and swimming. Bird species in the park include pelicans, yellow-headed blackbirds, scarlet tanagers, and redheaded woodpeckers.

The 340-hectare Rushing River PP (established in 1958 and classified as recreational), where we camped Sunday (August 14, 1988) night, gets its name from the small river that runs between Dogtooth and Blindfold lakes. It offers a variety of nature-based activities between July and August designed for young people. They learn about bugs, bats, wolves, canoeing, and more through active, sensory-oriented activities.

Day 5 (Monday)

Monday morning, we got up early to use the park's showers for a thorough wash. After breakfast, we walked through the park's Beaver Pond Trail, returned to the campsite to pack up, and then took off to explore the park's scenic environment further. Next, we headed twenty miles northwest to Kenora (pop 15,177), which was originally known as Rat Portage, the hub of Ontario's northwest. It lies on the plethora of islands constituting the northern end of Lake of the Woods.

We stopped at the Lovepax Pottery village before we went to the waterfront to join the eight-mile, two-hour cruise on board MS *Kenora* to view the myriad islands of Lake of the Woods, including the mystical "Devils Gap"—a deep-water channel guarded by the Spirit Rock first painted in the late 1800s with the face of a devil. (Aboriginals believe that spirits inhabit the rocks on the lake resembling creatures or beings.) The cruise took us past Coney Island's public beach and through the circle route of the picturesque channels and bays that gave us a peek into the private summer mansions of the famous and the "filthy rich," as well as a view of the "peaceful, unspoiled wilderness." Built in 1968 to accommodate two hundred passengers, MS *Kenora*'s current family package (for two adults and two kids) is $69, including the 13 percent

HST. In 1988, the same package cost us $18. "We enjoyed the cruise very much," I wrote in my diary.

We also visited McLeod Park to introduce Carmel and Junius to "Husky the Muskie," the forty-feet-tall effigy of a muskellunge, a relatively uncommon freshwater fish, constructed in 1967 as a potential Canadian Centennial project by Jules Horvath and Bob Selway. At nearby Keewatin, we visited the Mather-Walls Home (1116 Ottawa St.) and the rock potholes on a hilltop, as well as the beach. Finally, we got onto Trans-Canada 17 and drove east to Vermillion Bay (pop 1,200), where we turned northwest on ON-647 for camping the night at the 2,314-hectare Blue Lake Provincial Park classified as Natural Environment.

The driving distance for the day was one hundred miles. "The attendant at the office was unfriendly," I wrote in my diary. Ignoring his annoying disposition, we set up our tent on one of the park's 198 campsites. Then, we went for a dip in the magnificent Blue Lake. Alas, beauty came with a dose of agony inflicted by the stinging flies of the park!

Day 6 (Tuesday)

I got up at six in the morning to take the family for a hike on the park's Spruce Bog Trail and the Boulder Ridge Trail. Hiking the trails gave us superlative joy. We marveled at the crystal clear water of Blue Lake that allowed us to see the lake's bottom at twenty feet (six meters) all along its long, sandy beach. We passed through a swamp of spruce, stands of jack pine, red pine, white birch, and poplar—the natural habitat of several bird species (like the hairy woodpecker, ruffed grouse, spruce rouse, and flicker), as well as of other fauna (like the chipmunk, the squirrel, the red fox, and the hare). We feasted our eyes on the gardens of orchids and other delicate starflowers. We controlled our temptation to invade the patches of red bunchberries and wild blueberries. In short, we thoroughly enjoyed the Boreal forest surrounding the lake.

We left the Blue Lake (and its stinging flies!) at about 8:30 a.m. and headed southeast on Trans-Canada 17. Our destination for the day was the five-hundred-hectare Kakabeka Falls Provincial Park in the municipality of Oliver Paipoonge, west of Thunder Bay. The distance between the two parks is 237 miles.

Picture 87.1 The stinging flies of Blue Lake Provincial Park in Ontario marred the idyllic beauty of its scenery. (*Source:* Ontario Parks

On the way, our first stop was Egli's Sheep Farm and Animal Park in Minnitaki. There, Carmel and Junius had a chance to hobnob with the sheep. We introduced the kids to "Max the Moose" at Dryden (pop 8,195) on the north shore of Wabigoon Lake, our second stop. Max is the city's 5.6-meter high mascot, who plays an important role at Dryden's annual Moosetest Festival. "We found the people [of Dryden] extremely friendly," I noted down. Our third stop, this time for refreshments after driving for almost fifty miles, was the 117-hectare Aaron Provincial Park (classified as Recreational) on Thunder Lake, an offshoot of the larger Wabigoon on its eastern shore.

Our fourth stop was Ignace (pop 1,431), almost sixty miles further southeast from Aaron Provincial Park, just before the junction where ON-599 begins its 181-mile (292-km) journey from Trans-Canada 17 to Pickle Lake (pop 479) in north Ontario. Therefore, ON-599 is "the longest secondary highway in Ontario" and also "the northernmost highway in Ontario." We stopped at the public library and the tourist office in Ignace to check the facts. The tourist office encouraged us to visit the 8,053-hectare Sandbar Lake Provincial Park (classified as Natural Environment) located just ten miles north on ON-599 to get a taste of the renowned unpaved highway. Thus, we ended up eating our lunch at Sandbar Lake PP just for the record.

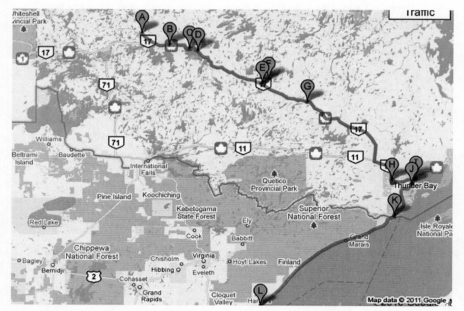

Map 87.1 From Blue Lake, Ontario, to Two Harbors, Minnesota.
A, Blue Lake PP; *B*, Minnitaki; *C*, Dryden (on Wabigoon Lake); *D*, Aaron PP (on Thunder Lake); *E*, Ignace; *F*, Sandbar Lake PP (gateway to Ontario 599); *G*, English River; *H*, Kakabeka Falls PP; *I*, Thunder Bay; *J*, Old Fort William; *K*, Pigeon River PP (all in Ontario); *L*, Two Harbors (in Minnesota) Note the voyageurs' trade route along the Pigeon River (*K*) from Lake Superior to Lake of the Woods.

Yoke-Sim and I shared driving the remaining 150 miles to Kakabeka Falls Provincial Park, which we reached at 6:30 p.m. Eastern time. Yoke-Sim drove up to English River from where I took over. The intermittent drizzle turned into rain in the late afternoon. We set up our tent on a campsite close to the falls, where we ate dinner. Then, I walked along the Kaministiquia River to watch Kakabeka Falls plunge 131 ft (40 m) over sheer cliffs. Some call it the Niagara of the North. The combined forces of rain, thunder, and lightning gave us jitters the entire night.

Day 7 (Wednesday)

This morning, we wanted to absorb the scenic splendor of the Kakabeka Falls once more and to get a feel of its spray as its endless waters fall forty meters down on to the rocks below. Junius and I also walked the Mountain

Portage Trail to the Kaministiquia River as we drove on the Circle Trail around the upper campground before our foray into Thunder Bay (city pop 109,140; metro pop 122,907), nineteen miles further east.

Picture 87.2 Kakabeka Falls, west of Thunder Bay (2005). (*Source:* Wikimedia Commons)

The cities of Port Arthur and Fort William merged in 1970 to form the city of Thunder Bay, often referred to as the "Lakehead" or "Canadian Lakehead" because of its location at the end of Great Lakes navigation. We started our tour of the city from the northside's Terry Fox Monument, a memorial dedicated to a cancer research activist who participated in the 1980 Marathon of Hope.

Carmel and Junius found supreme bliss in the playground area and the children's small animal farm of the sixty-seven-hectare Centennial Park. All of us enjoyed its 1910 Logging Camp and Museum. The park has a chalet with a concession and indoor picnic area. A number of recreation trails follow the Current River through Centennial and Trowbridge Falls parks to join the Cascades Conservation Area. Other city attractions we explored during the day included the following:

- The seventy-four-hectare Boulevard Lake Park (located on the west shore of the southern portion of Boulevard Lake) that includes a playground and facilities for supervised sand beach canoeing, kayaking, and various other water sports.

- The Hillcrest Park—which provides the finest scenic views of the city, the harbor, and the Sleeping Giant—also features a unique Sunken Gardens, with more than seventy varieties of flowers. (Sleeping Giant is a formation of mesas and sills on Sibley Peninsula that resembles a giant lying on its back when viewed from the city's west to north-northwest.)
- The Canada Games Complex (located at 420 Winnipeg Ave.) built at a cost of $7.1 million to host the aquatic events of the 1981 Canada Summer Games. The facilities include a swimming pool, indoor fitness areas, a fitness testing area, and an indoor running track.
- The International Peace Garden (located at the south end of Chapples Park), which showcases unique monuments representing eighteen ethnic groups in the Thunder Bay area in a fifteeen-acre setting featuring man-made ponds, floral displays, picnic tables, benches, and walking trails.

We capped the day's explorations with a visit to Fort William Historical Park (known as Old Fort William in 1988), a reconstruction of the Fort William fur trade, as it existed in 1815. Located west of the Thunder Bay International Airport and operated by the Ontario government, it is one of Canada's top ten tourist attractions. Historical interpreters represent the many roles and cultures involved in the fur trade, including Scottish fur traders (people of capital); French Canadian voyageurs and workers; and native hunters and trappers. In 2008, the fort built an amphitheatre designed to host multiple events with audience sizes up to fifty thousand.

"We bought a loaf of Fort William bread [before we left the fort]," I wrote down. We simply couldn't resist the temptation to taste bread presumably baked by the 1815 pioneers right in front of our eyes!

From Thunder Bay, we drove forty miles southwest to the Ontario-Minnesota border to spend our final night in Canada at the 949-hectare Pigeon River Provincial Park (classified as Natural Environment). We camped on one of the twenty-two non-serviced campsites in the Middle Falls Campground. (This park is not officially open for overnight camping.)

Pigeon River, which flows eastward some fifty miles from the BWCAW, drains into Lake Superior at the southern boundary of the park. The river serves as the northern boundary of Minnesota. The 113-hectare Grand Portage State Park, the US counterpart of the Pigeon River Provincial Park, occupies the south side of the river. Both parks have an abundance of bur oak, red maple, black ash, and white elm mingling with the predominant species of the boreal forest.

Large mammals like moose, white-tailed deer, black bear, and wolves coexist with the more frequently seen red squirrels and chipmunks in the vicinity of the two parks. Downy woodpeckers and yellow-shafted flickers add variety to the fauna.

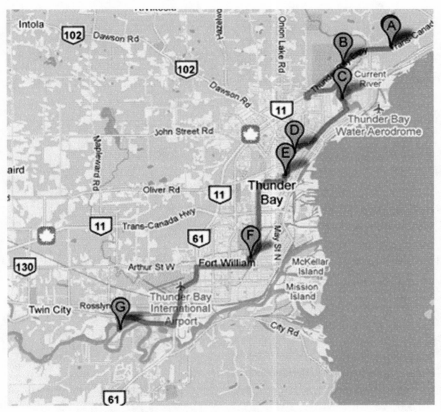

Map 87.2 Our Tour of Thunder Bay in 1988. *A*, Terry Fox National Historic Person Plaque; *B*, Centennial Park; *C*, Boulevard Lake; *D*, Hillcrest Park; *E*, Canada Games Complex; *F*, International Friendship Gardens; *G*, Fort William Historical Park.

CHAPTER 88

Minnesota: Border-X-Ing Brings Memories of BWCA Camping Trip in Mid-1960s

CONTINUE FROM the last chapter.

Day 8 (Thursday, August 18, 1988)

We left the Pigeon River Provincial Park Thursday (August 18, 1988) morning, crossed over to US territory, and entered Grand Portage (pop 557). The Grand Portage State Park did not exist then. Opened in 1989, its focal point became the 120-feet (37-meter) Pigeon Falls, known locally as High Falls. The mile of frontage along the Pigeon River offered views of the falls and river gorge from rustic outlooks. Ernest Hemingway nicknamed Grand Portage "the Big Wild."

The Department of Natural Resources promotes the High Falls as "the highest in the state" although it cannot match the 131-feet (40-meter) Kakabeka Falls in nearby Ontario. The Native Americans and the voyageurs found the gorge of the Pigeon River and its two falls—high and middle—as formidable obstacles for river travel between Lake Superior and Lake of the Woods. Thus, they created an 8.5-mile (13.7 km) footpath to bypass the waterfalls and rapids on the last 20 miles (32 km) of the Pigeon River. Called the Grand Portage (carrying place), it is part of the historic trade route of the French-Canadian voyageurs. This footpath was designated the Grand Portage National Monument in 1960.

Furthermore, it was elevated as the Grand Portage National Monument Heritage Center in 2007 to pay tribute to the Anishinabe Ojibway heritage.

The previous night, I took Carmel and Junius to see the Middle Falls and the Grand Portage from the Canadian side, where rural ON-593 hugs the Pigeon River. However, the High Falls was visible only from the US side.

Now, we were at the eastern end of the vast circle of wilderness surrounding the Minnesota-Ontario border, which we commenced exploring a week before at Voyageurs National Park. We visited the national monument and listened to the historical accounts narrated by the interpretive staff. Then Junius and I walked 0.7 miles on the Grand Portage to Fort Charlotte on the Pigeon River. The trail's high point is the head of a drainage flowing to the Pigeon River at Fort Charlotte.

About thirty-five miles southwest of Grand Portage, we stopped at Grand Marais (pop 1,353) to refill the car, eat our lunch and take a peek at the famous Gunflint Trail.

WPI Memories of 1966

I was familiar with Grand Marais. I had first visited the town on a weekend (September 9-10, 1966), twenty-two years earlier, as a World Press Institute (WPI) journalist. Let me reminisce what happened on that remarkable weekend.

Michael Johnson, then a WPI assistant director, and Dave McKenna, then a Macalester College student, drove the fourteen WPI journalists (including a woman) on the WPI minibus from our headquarters in Saint Paul to Grand Marais (Great Marsh in French), the seat of Cook County, for their very first camping and fishing expedition in the Superior National Forest in northeast Minnesota. We, the journalists, had no clue about the hazards and joys of camping in the wilderness, which we roughly knew as the Superior National Forest.

It turned out that we had to stop at Grand Marais to rent our camping and fishing gear; and to pick up our guide, Jack Underwood, who would lead us in "portaging" off the famous Gunflint Trail (County Road 12) to the camping grounds on the shores of Duncan Lake and Rose Lake (see Map 1). The Gunflint Trail is a fifty-seven-mile (92 km) paved roadway that begins in Grand Marais, and ends at Saganaga Lake in the Boundary Waters Canoe Area Wilderness (BWCA).

We got off the minibus halfway through the Gunflint Trail, thirty miles north of Grand Marais. From there, we had to "portage" our belongings, canoes, and other gear to the Hungry Jack Lodge and Campground, near Duncan Lake; and the adjacent Camp Menogyn, near Rose Lake.

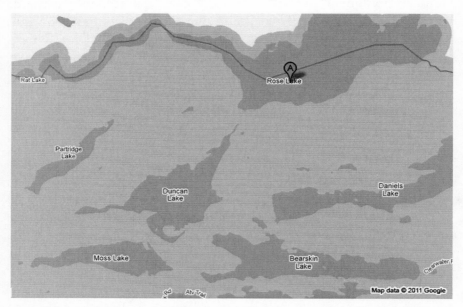

Map 88.1 The 1966-1967 group of WPI journalists camped and fished in Rose Lake and Duncan Lake on the Minnesota-Ontario border. This two-day experience (September 9-10, 1966) perhaps was the focal factor that sparked my lifelong craving for camping thereafter.

The *Ceylon Daily News* published the feature I wrote under the tile "Camping in Canoe Country." A few excerpts are as follows:

"Having traveled [more than 30 miles] on the Gunflint Trail, we turned to a path that led us to the West Bearskin Lake on the other side of the

SHELTON A. GUNARATNE

Hungry Jack Lake. The canoes were ready for us on the shore. We got into the canoes, two in each with all our camping material and crossed the West Bearskin Lake.

"From this point on, we had to carry [portage] all our belongings . . ."

It is noon. But the sky is gloomy and the wind is chilly. Even with a pullover and a jacket on, I am almost shivering. So is Arturo [von Vacano from Peru], who is seated in the middle of the canoe. Not Jack [Underwood] anyway. He has only a thick shirt on and he bears the cold smartly.

"Perched on a spot by the cliff, Veikko [Pajunen from Finland] is reading a book . . . [A journalist with the Helsinkin Sanomat, he is addicted to the *New York Times*.]"

Beneath the cedar, pine and fir trees, a fire is aflame. It is the fire with which Dick is cooking our midday meal of macaroni and beans . . . I begin to wonder how we managed to carry all this material to the camping site . . .

"It is night. Dick is playing a musical instrument. Others sing. We are seated around a fire [singing to fit Dick's music or telling yarns]. We go into our tents quite late. I get into my sleeping bag and bend like a millipede for warmth . . . But Mike [Johnson] comes and wakes us up to see the northern lights.

"The morning is colder. The wind is heavy . . . I cannot wash my face with the ice-cold water . . . [I see] Roy [Bull from England] crossing the Rose Lake in a canoe. He is determined to land on Canadian territory!"

Back to 1988

I narrated my 1966 adventures to Carmel, Junius, and Yoke-Sim as we ate lunch at the South of the Border Restaurant. I told them that as a rural boy raised in poor Ceylon, I had never dreamed of canoeing, camping, or portaging. I embellished my story further as I took them to see the Cook County Historical Museum (5 S. Broadway). Then, I treated them with a tour of six miles into the Gunflint Trail.

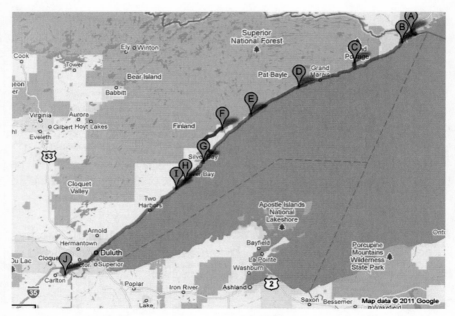

Map 88.2 Enchanting State Parks on Minnesota's North Shore.
A, Grand Portage State Park. Its main attraction is High Falls on the
Pigeon River; *B*, Grand Portage National Monument and Heritage
Center, a reconstruction of the "carrying path" (portage) of the
fur traders and the Ojibway tribe; *C*, Judge C. R. Magney State
Park. Its main attraction is the Devils Kettle waterfall on the Brule
River; *D*, Cascade River State Park. Its main attraction is the seven
cascading waterfalls; *E*, Temperance River State Park. The falls along
the Temperance River are its main attraction; *F*, George H. Crosby
Manitou State Park, the only state park on North Shore that offers
"backpacking" campsites; *G*, Tettegouche State Park. The high
cliffs overlooking Lake Superior are its main attraction; *H*, Split
Rock Lighthouse State Park. Its main attraction is the lighthouse;
I, Gooseberry Falls State Park. Its main attractions are the five falls
on the Gooseberry River and the Gitchi Gummy Trail; *J*, Jay Cooke
State Park on the Saint Louis River.

From Grand Marais, we continued driving southwest on SR 61
sandwiched between the North Shore of Lake Superior and the eastern
edge of Superior National Forest. Commonly known as the North Shore,
SR61 runs a length of 180 miles (290 km) from the north terminus of
Interstate 35 in Duluth to the Grand Portage on the Ontario boundary.
Some of Minnesota's most enchanting state parks are located on SR

Shelton A. Gunaratne

61 (see Map 2). Camping facilities are available in all except the two in Grand Portage. But on this particular Thursday in mid-August, we couldn't find a single campsite to stay overnight. We stopped to admire the scenic beauty of the Cascade River and the Temperance River state parks. We drove to the township of Lusten (pop 360) to see the operational mechanics of its chairlift to the mountains. Curiosity took us to see three other state parks—Tettegouche, Split Rock Lighthouse, and Gooseberry Falls.

Because all the campgrounds in the state parks were full, we had no choice but to accept the offer of one of the 112 campsites at the Burlington Bay Campground, a municipal facility in Two Harbors (pop 3,613), once known as Agate Bay.

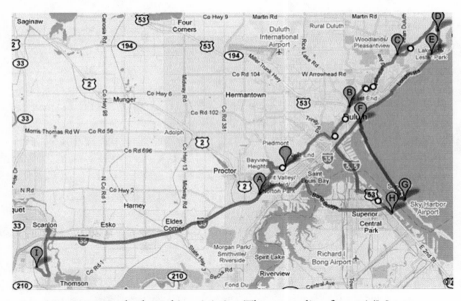

Map 88.3 Duluth and its vicinity. The upper line from *A* (Magney Park and Thompson Hill) to *E* (Lester Park) approximates the Skyline Parkway. The parkway disappears from *B* to *C* (UMD campus area) and reappears before *D* (Amity Park). *F* (Canal Park), where the Aerial Lift Bridge provides entry to *G* (Minnesota Point and Point Park on the sand strip). The Harbor Basin lies to the west of Canal Park. *H* (Barkers Island) in Wisconsin is just a hoot from Point Park. *I* (KOA Campground in Cloquet, Minnesota,) where we camped.

Day 9 (Friday)

Two Harbors is known for its annual Folk Festival in the final week of January. It also plays a pivotal role in the John Beargrease Sled Dog Marathon, an annual four-hundred-mile race on the North Shore starting in the port city of Duluth (pop 84,419). Our destination for the day was Duluth, thirty miles further to the southwest.

We left the campground in the morning to see the giant loading locks on Agate Bay, immediately to the south of Burlington Bay. Then, as we headed toward Duluth, we stopped to let Carmel and Junius enjoy the French River Coldwater Fish Hatchery, a facility of the Department of Natural Resources.

Duluth has some twenty-three thousand fewer people than in 1960. However, the population of Duluth MSA (known as the Twin Ports), which includes the adjoining Wisconsin city of Superior, stood at.276,368).

We wanted to enter Duluth through the Skyline Parkway, a somewhat disconnected 30-mile roadway that extends from the Lester River Neighborhood on the east side of the city to Thompson Hill, "West Duluth" near Interstate 35. Skyline Parkway crosses nearly the entire length of Duluth and affords breathtaking views of the famous Aerial Lift Bridge, and Canal Park to the many industries in and around the port. However, finding the eastern gateway to the parkway was not easy.

Our first stop after we entered East Skyline Parkway, which disappeared at Glenwood Street, was the Tweed Museum of Art located on the campus of the University of Minnesota Duluth. The museum has a permanent collection of more than six thousand works "covering a range of periods and cultures in art history, with particular strengths in American landscape painting."

After rediscovering East Skyline Parkway, we drove on it up to North Lake Street, from where the parkway turns in to West Skyline Parkway. One feature of the skyline is that "from high on the bow of the hill," it offers magnificent views of the tip of Lake Superior. We decided to drive down the steep hill on Lake Street to the Harbor Basin south of

I-35—"largely a conversion of an old warehouse district into restaurants, shops (especially those dealing in antiques and other novelties), cafés, and hotels" (Wikipedia).

Picture 88.1 The Aerial Lift Bridge is a landmark in Duluth. (Photo by Alfred Essa. Wikimedia Commons, 2007)

The area has become an entertainment venue with events such as is the annual Bayfront Blues Festival and Grandma's Marathon. The Harbor Basin's attractions include a three-mile long lake walk, the Duluth Entertainment Convention Center, a lighthouse pier, Lake Superior Maritime Visitor Center, Great Lakes Aquarium, and the William A Irvin floating ship museum.

On this visit, we took Carmel and Junius to see the Canal Park Marine Museum. Next to the Canal Park, we crossed the Aerial Lift Bridge (originally built in 1905) and drove on Minnesota Avenue all the way to Minnesota Point, also called Point Park, where we ate our lunch. Located seven miles away on the narrow sand spit on Superior Bay demarcating the boundary between Minnesota and Wisconsin, it was a dream spot to look around. We enjoyed the majestic view of the Interstate 535 bridge crossing over from Duluth, Minnesota, to Superior, Wisconsin, high above us on to the northwest.

Next, we retraced the sand spit back to the Canal Park to visit the 1988 star attraction, the Depot (at 506 W. Michigan St.). Built in 1892, it served seven different rail lines and accommodated five thousand passengers. It reopened in 1973, housing the Duluth Art Institute, Duluth Children's Museum, Lake Superior Railroad Museum, St. Louis County Historical Society Museum, North Shore Scenic Railroad, and five performing arts organizations. (Its current admission is $12 per adult)

Thereafter, we crossed the border to Wisconsin on I-535 Bridge, which we saw from the sand spit below earlier. On Wisconsin territory, we visited the Barkers Island from where we saw Park Point, our lunch spot. We drove past the Marina and the Old Firehouse and Police Museum (built in 1898) in Superior.

Back in Duluth, we decided to explore the West Skyline Parkway that we missed in the morning. We had no difficulty finding the western gateway to the skyline. We had a magnificent view of the city from the Enger Park Observation Tower along the parkway.

We wanted to camp overnight at the renowned Jay Cooke State Park. Because it was already packed, we had to settle for the KOA Campground in Cloquet.

On day 10 (Saturday, August 20, 1988), we crossed Minnesota from east to west. We reached Moorhead at 6:30 p.m.

CHAPTER 89

Washington: From Midwest to Pacific Northwest on American "Nullarbor"

I T TOOK US three days in summer 1989 to drive the 1,630-mile distance from Fargo-Moorhead in the Midwest to Longview-Kelso in the Pacific Northwest. I have already mentioned the first leg of this journey (in chapter 83).

The second leg of the tour took us from Billings, Montana, to Spokane, Washington—a distance of 583 miles. We left Billings (pop 105,845) somewhat late in the morning because we decided to drive through the scenic Black Otter Trail (US 318) to see the city from the northern outlooks. Along the way, we saw the grave of Luther Savage "Yellowstone" Kelly (1848-1928), an American soldier, hunter, scout, adventurer, and administrator. (Kelly joined the army in 1865 by lying about his age. After the Civil War, Kelly established himself as "one of the greatest hunters, trappers, and Indian scouts" of the American West.)

Also, along the way, we stopped at the Boothill Cemetery, the burial place of those who "have died with their boots on" or met with violent deaths. Muggins Taylor, the scout who carried the news of Custer's Last Stand to the world, is the most famous person buried here. The last burial at Boothill was in 1882.

Then, we drove south on Zimmerman Trail to the Rimrock Mall and joined the westbound traffic flow on I-90 heading toward Bozeman (pop 39,282), 144 miles away, where we stopped to eat lunch at Cooper Park, a four-acre expanse with picnic tables and grills. It occurred to me that crossing the seemingly endless prairies of Montana—some 665 miles from east to west—was much like crossing Peter Pan's Never-Never-Land, the fictional creation of J. M. Barrie. It was so boring that I felt enormously relieved when we reached Butte (pop 33,967), another eighty-five miles to the west. Butte is the gateway to Helena (pop 29,939), the capital of Montana, located almost eighty miles to the northeast. (Perhaps, I am slightly exaggerating here. Nothing can surpass the boredom of crossing the 684-mile Nullarbor Plain in Australia, as I had documented in chapter 50.) We stopped at an ice cream parlor at 2:15 p.m. It enabled us to break the monotony of travel boredom with a dash of sweetness. I was glad that Yoke-Sim took over driving the next 114 miles to Missoula (pop 68,876), close to the Idaho border.

Picture 89.1 Billings, Mont., city line (March 2008) (*Source:* Wikimedia Commons)

Because of travel fatigue, we weren't in a mood to explore any attractions in Bozeman (such as the Montana Arboretum and Garden, the Museum of the Rockies, the American Computer Museum, and the Gallatin Historical Society-Pioneer Museum) or in Butte (such as the Berkeley Pit, the World Museum of Mining, the Venus Alley, the Copper King Mansion, and the Arts Chateau). In Missoula, however, we stopped at the Chamber of Commerce, and all of us walked on a footbridge to the University of Montana campus.

Thereafter, Yoke-Sim drove us through the northern Idaho Panhandle city of Coeur d'Alene (pop 43,683) into the eastern borderline of Washington. Coeur d'Alene is the home of Snake Pit Derby Dames, an all-female flat track roller derby league.

We arrived in Spokane (pop 205,900), the second largest city in the state of Washington, about 8:30 p.m., PDT. We checked in at the Best Western Tradewinds Motel (907 W. Third Ave.), and we ate dinner at the nearby Burger King.

The third and final leg of our journey began Wednesday (July 19) afternoon.

We spent the morning exploring the city of Spokane. We stopped at the Automobile Association (1717 W. Fourth Ave.) to get the maps and tour advice before we commenced sightseeing. Then, we visited the Smithsonian-affiliated Cheney Cowles Memorial Museum (2316 W. First Ave.). Renamed the Northwest Museum of Arts and Culture, it is the largest cultural organization in the Inland Northwest with five underground galleries, an orientation gallery, café, store, education center, community room, and the Center for Plateau Cultural Studies. The MAC also includes the historic 1898 Campbell House designed by architect Kirtland Cutter. The museum's exhibits and programs focus on American Indian and other cultures, regional history, and visual art.

Next, we visited the Episcopal Cathedral of Saint John (127 E. Twelfth Ave.), an example of Gothic architecture. Work on the cathedral began in 1925.

Thereafter, we stopped for rest at the ninety-acre Manito Park and Botanical Gardens (1702 S. Grand Blvd.), which features the Finch Arboretum, the Gaiser Conservatory, the Duncan Garden, the Nishinomiya Japanese Garden, the Rose Hill, the Lilac Garden and the Ferris Perennial Garden. We also visited the hundred-acre Riverfront Park (along the Spokane River), the site of the Expo '74 World's Fair. The defining feature of the park is the Pavilion, which is marked by a 145-feet-tall (44 m) metal frame and wire shell that formed the US Pavilion during the Expo. We capped our tour of Spokane with a visit to the Crosby Library, which contains a collection of American singer Bing Crosby's (1903-1977) records and other memorabilia, at Gonzaga University, a private Catholic institution founded in 1887. We ate our lunch on the Gonzaga campus.

We left Spokane about 2:00 p.m. and drove sixty miles southwestward on I-90 to Ritzville (pop 1,736), which has four individual structures on the National Register of Historic Places—the Dr. Frank R. Burroughs's House on Main Street, the Nelson H. Greene's House on South Adams Street, the Ritzville Carnegie Library on West Main Street, and the Ritzville High School.

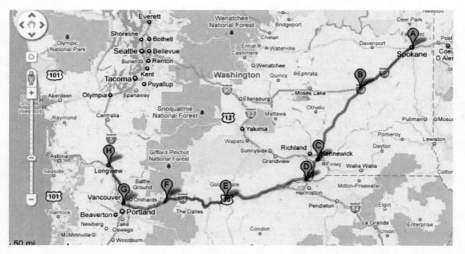

Map 89.1 The Route we took from Spokane to Longview in July 1989 (398 miles). *A*, Spokane; *B*, Ritzville; *C*, Kennewick (Tri-Cities); *D*, Plymouth (east terminus SR 14); *E*, Maryhill; *F*, Stevenson; *G*, Vancouver (west terminus SR 14); *H*, Longview.

Then, we drove eighty miles further southwest on US 395 to Kennewick (pop 67,180), where we stopped for refreshments. Located near the Hanford nuclear site, Kennewick, and the adjoining cities of Pasco (pop 55,490) and Richland (pop 47,410) formed the Tri-Cities. Kennewick lies along the southwest bank of the Columbia River, opposite Pasco and just south of the confluence of the Columbia and Yakima Rivers.

From the Tri-Cities, we drove a few miles south to Plymouth (unincorporated) to head westward on the scenic State Route 14 (also called the Lewis and Clark Highway) for some 180 miles along the north shore of the Columbia River, which separates Washington from Oregon. Its western terminus is its junction with Interstate 5 in Vancouver, Washington.

We chose SR 14 as the preferred route to reach Longview even though we could have saved about thirty miles had we continued on I-90 at Ritzville. The reason—we wanted to see the scenic splendor of the sunset as we drove westward on the serene SR 14 along the river. The colors in the sky dazzled us. We were amply rewarded by nature's own open-air theater.

Driving from Plymouth to Mayhill (pop 98) in Klickitat County, I thoroughly enjoyed the changing colors of the sky through the gloaming. A full-size astronomically aligned replica of Stonehenge stands here as a memorial to those who died in World War I. The credit goes to Sam Hill, the Quaker, who commissioned it. The replica was completed in 1929.

Picture 89.2 Replica of Stonehenge in Maryhill, Washington. (*Source:* Wikimedia Commons)

Yoke-Sim steered us for the next sixty-six miles to Stevenson (pop 1,200) in Skamania County, home to the Columbia Gorge Interpretive Center, which focuses on several tribes who inhabited the vicinity. Our two kids Carmel and Junius, who were quite used to the outdoor way of life, did not complain about their hunger pangs. I noticed, however, that they perked up after we ate our dinner in Stevenson.

I took over the wheel for the final eighty-seven mile drive to Longview, Washington, which we reached at 11:00 p.m. We checked in at the Hudson Manor Motel (166 Hudson St.) for a week.

On Tuesday (July 25, 1989), we left the motel to settle down in an apartment at 1108 Seventeenth Avenue, Longview. The same day, my elder sister Rani and my mother arrived to stay with us in Longview.

For the next month, I was back at work as a *Daily News* reporter.

CHAPTER 90

Washington: Pele Keeps Her Grudge Even at Mount St. Helens

I AM A shameless volcano buff. That's why I spent an entire day in the Volcano National Park on the Big Island late January 1984 despite the fury that Pele, the goddess of fire, unleashed on me (see chapter 82). I tried to be chummy with Pele again on a Saturday in late July 1989 during my stint with the (Longview, Washington) *Daily News* from July 10 to August 25

Longview (pop 34,660) with its twin city of Kelso (pop 11,895), located on the north-south Interstate 5, was comparable in population size to Moorhead, Minnesota (pop 32,177) with its twin city of Fargo, North Dakota (pop 95,556), located on east-west Interstate 94. However, my research revealed that the crime rate in Longview was almost double that of Moorhead because of several interconnected reasons. A major reason was that many more criminals traversed the I-5 than the I-94. An interconnected reason was the year-through warmer weather conditions in the Pacific Northwest in contrast to the cold winters in the Midwest.

Despite the adverse crime situation in Longview, I brought my entire family—Carmel (five), Junius (nine), and spouse Yoke-Sim—with me to Longview for the six-week stint. In addition, my mother, then seventy-six, and my elder sister Rani kept us company for most of our stay. All six of us joined forces on most of my exploratory forays in Washington State.

One memorable adventure was our foray into the 45,000-hectare Mount St. Helens National Volcanic Monument (MSHNVM) established in 1982 in the aftermath of the 1980 eruption of Mount St. Helens volcano in Skamania County.

Picture 90.1 A 360-degree panorama from the summit of Mount St. Helens (October 11, 2009). The ice-covered crater rim is in the foreground. (Photo by Gregg M. Erickson. *Source:* Wikimedia Commons)

The volcano (picture 90.1) is located in the Cascade Range and is part of the Cascade Volcanic Arc, a segment of the Pacific Ring of Fire that includes more than 160 active volcanoes. The Cascade Volcanic Arc includes nearly twenty major volcanoes, among a total of more than four thousand separate volcanic vents.

In 1980, on the morning of May 18, a 5.1 magnitude (Richter sale) earthquake triggered a massive landslide on the north face of Mount St. Helens (a stratovolcano—meaning, a tall conical composite volcano built up by many layers of hardened lava, tephra, pumice, and volcanic ash). The north slope avalanche of rock debris spread over and destroyed an area extending to some 15 miles (25 km) from the volcano's summit (elevation = 8,365 ft.; prominence = 4,605 ft.). It killed 57 people, destroyed 250 homes, 47 bridges, 15 miles of railways, and 185 miles of highway. Wikipedia says it was "the deadliest and most economically destructive volcanic event in the history of the United States."

Nine years later, we decided to see for ourselves the devastation the volcano inflicted on the surrounding area. So on Saturday July 29, all of us got into my Toyota Camry wagon and set forth on our 246-mile tour of the MSHNVM (Mount St. Helens National Volcanic Monument).

From Longview, we headed thirteen miles north to Castle Rock, WA (pop 2,130), the gateway to Mount St. Helens. There, we turned east on SR 504, which the state government named Spirit Lake Memorial Highway in 1982 in honor of Spirit Lake and the fifty-seven people killed by the eruption. Normally, SR 504 is a fifty-two mile stretch of secondary highway connecting Castle Rock with the MSHNVM and Spirit Lake recreation areas. Castle Rock derives its name after a 190-feet-high volcanic rock formation resembling a castle.

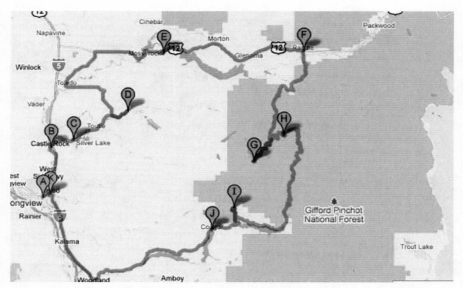

Map 90.1 Roundtrip Route from Longview-Kelso (*A-K*) to Mount St. Helens National Volcanic Monument (*G*) (246 miles). *A*, Longview, WA; *B*, Castle Rock, WA; *C*, Silver Lake, WA (Mount St. Helens Visitor Center on SR 504); *D*, Kid Valley, WA; *E*, Mossyrock, WA; *F*, Randle, WA; *G*, Mount St. Helens National Volcanic Monument; *H*, Bear Meadow, WA; *I*, Ape Cave, WA; *J*, Cougar, WA; *K*, Kelso, WA.

But on the day we traveled, we could drive only nineteen miles up to Kid Valley on SR 504 because the rest of the highway, some thirty-three miles, was closed for reconstruction following the destruction the massive avalanche caused. Thus, we missed visits to the Coldwater Ridge Visitor Center (opened in 1993 but permanently closed in August 2010) and the Johnston Ridge Observatory, which were also under restoration at the terminus of SR 504. Literature attests that a half-mile trail from the observatory provides views of the lava dome, crater, pumice plain, and landslide deposits. We also missed the Forest Learning Center located inside the blast zone of Mount St. Helens on SR 504.

For the time being, we were satisfied with the view of the visible volcanic destruction that Kid Valley offered. We had to retrace our way and take the longer northerly route via SR 505 (north) and US 12 (east) to reach the national volcanic monument.

SHELTON A. GUNARATNE

However, our first stopover was about five miles east of Castle Rock on SR 504, the Mount St. Helens Visitor Center (opened in 1987), amply prepared us to visualize the degree of destruction. Built in the Cascade-style architectural mode, the center's large glass windows and sweeping upward lines exposed the visitors to panoramic views of the Cascade Range. In addition to the various exhibits on display at the center, we saw a movie and a slideshow on the 1980 volcanic eruption. More than three hundred thousand people visit the center every year.

(In 2000, the 192-hectare Seaquest State Park absorbed the visitor center, which lies across the road from the park entrance. The park offers more than a mile of Silver Lake shoreline, as well as six miles of woodland trails for hiking and bicycling.)

Nine years after our tour, former pastor Lloyd Anderson and his spouse Doris set up another museum in Silver Lake (4749 Spirit Lake Highway) called The Seven Wonders Museum of Mount St. Helens. The Andersons claim that it offers creation evidence to support the Bible as "without error in the original writing."

From Kid Valley, we drove forty miles northeast to Mossyrock, Washington (pop 486), a logging town in Lewis County. On the way to Mossyrock, we stopped at Saint Francis Mission in Toledo, Lewis and Clark State Park, and the adjoining Jackson Court House State Park in Chehalis (all on SR 505). After turning east on US 12, we tarried at three more recreational areas—Mayfield Lake Park, Ike Kinswa State Park, and the Hopkins Hill Viewpoint. Located about five miles off Mossyrock, the crest of Hopkins Hill offered all of us a chance to see the ferocious volcano twenty-five miles to the south.

From Mossyrock, we drove another thirty miles east to Randle, Washington (pop 2,813), the northern entry point to MSHNVM—a part of the Gifford Pinchot National Forest established in 1908.

It was 3:00 p.m. when we reached the Quartz Creek Big Tree interpretive site, ten miles southwest of Randle, on Forest Road 25. (Within the boundaries of the national forest, only forest roads exist for travel.) We ate a late lunch, relaxing in the shade of the giant Douglas-fir trees, some ten feet across (diameter at breast height) and up to 750 years old. Walking through this cool, dark forest, we found it difficult to believe Quartz Creek is just one mile from the devastated forest in the volcanic blast area.

Map 90.2: Mount St. Helens Recreation Area (Source: USDA Forest Service)

SHELTON A. GUNARATNE

I had hopes of a friendly welcome by Pele now that we were once again so close to the crater of a volcano. We decided to hike the 2.25-mile trail to Norway Pass on the north side of Spirit Lake. Forest Road 99 connected the points of interest studded along the eastern shore of Spirit Lake, for example, Meta Lake, Cascade Peaks Viewpoint, Independence Pass, Harmony, Donnybrook, Smith Creek, and Windy Ridge. The volcano lay further to the southwest of Windy Ridge.

My mother was too frail to do the arduous hiking. The rest of us—Carmel, Junius, Yoke-Sim, Rani, and I—let my mother mind the car and took off on the hike to Norway Pass, where we were able to explore Spirit Lake at close range. However, we could not see the crater because of the thick cover of "floating ash" surrounding it. Obviously, Pele was unwilling to welcome me on this occasion either.

So the question of climbing Mount St. Helens to see its crater did not arise. It took us two hours to complete our hike and return to the car park. However, Rani, who was unaccustomed to outdoor recreation, let us know about her unhappiness for putting her through this miserable experience!

We left the Quartz Creek interpretive site about 5:00 p.m. Then, we drove south on FR 25, and turned west into FR 99 at Bear Meadow to drive past Meta Lake and Independence Pass, all the way to Windy Ridge, where we arrived at about 6:45 p.m. Now, we were just five miles from the volcano; yet the "floating ash" continued to hide the crater from our prying eyes. Because FR 99 terminated at Windy Ridge, we had to backtrack to Bear Meadow to join FR 25 and drive further south until it joined FR 90 West.

Before leaving the MSHNM, Carmel, Junius, and I wanted to visit the Ape Cave on the south side of the volcano. Driving west on FR 90, we reached Ape Cave (off to the north on FR 83) about 9:00 p.m. We explored the cave, a lava tube, with help of torchlight after eating a late dinner on the roadside. In terms of passageway length, it is the longest continuous lava tube in the continental United States at 13,042 feet (3,975 m).

We said good-bye to Pele and the MSHNVM as we left the monument on SR 503 via Cougar, Washington (pop 122).

We had to drive another fifty miles to reach Longview. Both Rani and my mother were relieved that the "ordeal" was over when we reached home.

Picture 90.2 We visited the Ape Cave on the south side of Mount St. Helens just before leaving MSHNVM. (Photo by Iwona Erskine-Kellie, 2009. Wikimedia Commons)

CHAPTER 91

Washington: Exploring Offbeat Attractions

ON THE FIRST Saturday (July 22, 1989) after our arrival in Longview, Junius, nine, and I went to the adjoining city of Kelso, where I purchased a Timberline-4 tent for $151 (including sales tax) at the Outdoors Store (110 S. Pacific Ave.). On previous camping trips, I used tents rented from the outdoors facility of the Moorhead State University (as my university was known then) Students' Union. Now that I had become the proud owner of a high-quality tent, I could use it on our return trip to Minnesota at the end of August for nifty camping at exotic and enchanting sites. Such was my reasoning.

Moreover, Carmel, five, was also gung-ho about camping. Our family of four clicked together. I often marveled at the fact that all four of us being born between January 19 and January 31 had anything to do with our penchant for camping. When we adopted a fox terrier as our family pet, the breeder who sold Cosmo to us for $625 intimated that the lovable creature was born on January 13, 2007. My father was a strong believer in astrology. I too have a degree of faith in the potential influence of star clusters on all sentient beings.

Apart from our excursion to Mount St. Helens National Volcanic Monument (chapter 90), we visited several other offbeat attractions during our stay in Washington.

Thursday (July 27, 1989): All of us visited St. Helens, Oregon (pop 2,000), the county seat of Columbia, twenty-four miles south of Longview, Washington, on Columbia River Highway (US 30). Cathy Zimmerman, features editor of the *Daily News*, had assigned me to write a profile of Agnes Petersen, a well-known attorney in St. Helens. The purpose of this visit was to gather background information on Petersen, so I would be adequately prepared before I met with her for a journalistic chitchat.

Having gone through all the past clippings related to Petersen in the "morgue," I wanted to sound a couple of sources who knew her well—Robert P. Van Natta, Petersen's law partner and Greg Cohen, editor of *The Chronicle*, the local rag. After interviewing these two sources, I stopped by at the People's Utility District, where Petersen was a director. PUD's Betty Lang gave me an article that Petersen had written. [Exactly a week later, I returned to St. Helens to meet with Petersen, then fifty-three, for a journalistic conversation that enabled me to write the feature titled "'Life Is a Banquet': Attorney Relishes Motherhood and Public Office," published in the *Daily News* on Friday, August 11. I have already described my newspaper internship with the Longview daily in part 1 of this book (chapter 16).]

On the way to St. Helens, we stopped at the Trojan Visitors Information Center in Rainier, Oregon (pop 1,687), and the waterfront Pixie Park, across the Cables House Museum, in Columbia City, Oregon (pop 1,955).

Rainier (earlier known as Eminence and Fox's Landing) was home to Trojan Nuclear Power Plant, the only commercial nuclear reactor in Oregon. It supplied electricity to Portland and its suburbs starting in March 1976. Because of structural problems, this reactor was closed periodically. In January 1993, it was decommissioned after cracks developed in the steam tubes. On May 21, 2006, the cooling tower was demolished. The Cables House Museum is a two-story structure built in 1870 by Charles Green Cables.

Saturday (July 29): We spent the entire day exploring the MSHNVM. I have already reported this excursion in detail in chapter 90.

July 27, 1989 trip: *A,* Longview, WA; *B,* Rainier, OR; *C,* Columbia City, OR; *D,* St. Helens, OR.

July 30, 1989 trip: *E,* Log Pond, WA; *F,* Kalama, WA; *G,* Woodland, WA; *H,* Ridgefield National Wildlife Refuge, WA.

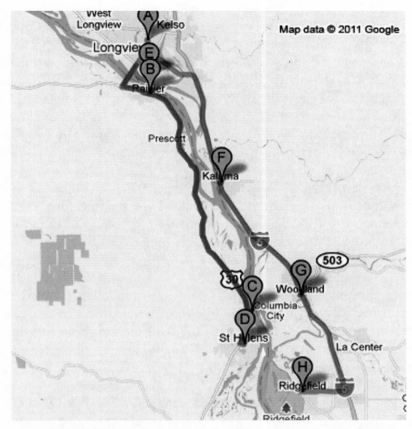

Map 91.1 Offbeat places along Columbia River, south of Longview, Washington.

Sunday (July 30): All of us spent the afternoon exploring the neighboring communities to the south of Longview along the Washington side of the Columbia River. Whereas we drove on the Oregon side of the river on our way to St. Helens on July 27, we were driving on this occasion on I-5 that runs parallel to US 30.

Our first stop was a spot south of the Log Pond (in Cowlitz County) on the east bank of the Columbia River, about four miles from Longview. From there, we had a good view of the iconic 499-feet-tall cooling tower of the controversial $500 million Trojan Nuclear Plant in Rainier, Oregon, on the opposite side of the river. Portland General Electric (PGE), which operated the plant, shut it down almost twenty years before the end of its design lifetime.

In 2005, PGE removed the reactor vessel and other radioactive equipment from the Trojan plant, "encased in concrete foam, shrink-wrapped, and transported intact by barge along the Columbia River to Hanford Nuclear Reservation (near the Tri-Cities), where it was buried in a forty-five foot-deep (14 m) pit and covered with six inches (150 mm) of gravel, which made it the first commercial reactor to be moved and buried whole" (Wikipedia). The PGE stored the spent fuel onsite in thirty-four dry casks, awaiting transport to the Yucca Mountain Repository.

I distinctly remembered the fierce public debates on nuclear energy in the late seventies and the eighties when I served as a freelance public affairs reporter for *The* (Rockhampton, Qld.) *Morning Bulletin*. Therefore, I was very much interested in learning about the Trojan project while I was back as a journalist in Longview.

Moving further south, we stopped at Kalama (pop 1,783), named after the Kalama River in Cowlitz County. We visited the city's Riverside Park, which has the "world's tallest (105 ft.) single-strand totem pole." Kalama was the northern terminus of a railroad ferry operated by the Northern Pacific Railway from Goble, Oregon.

Then, we drove to Woodland (pop 4,843), a city incorporated in 1906 by Finnish settlers. Straddling Clark and Cowlitz counties in Washington, Woodland is the home of the seven-acre Hulda Klager Lilac Gardens (115 S. Perkin Road). Klager (1863-1960) eventually hybridized more than 250 varieties of lilacs. The Lilac Society, which saved Klager's house and gardens from turning into an industrial site in 1964, administers the property as a state and National Historic Landmark. We also made a short stop at the Horse Shoe Lake Park. The Cedar Creek Grist Mill, another National Historic Landmark, is located near Woodland.

Our final stop was Ridgefield (pop 4,314), originally called Union Ridge, a trading post inhabited by Chinook Indians and associated with the Lewis and Clark Expedition of 1804-1806. Incorporated in 1909 as Ridgefield, it is the gateway to the 5,150-acre Ridgefield National Wildlife Refuge, a primary reserve for migrating waterfowl on the Pacific Flyway.

© Lyn Topinka, 2006

Picture 91.1 Cooling Tower of the Trojan Nuclear Plant in Rainier, Oregon (May 20, 2006). The Trojan Decommissioning Alliance organized several direct action protests in the seventies. Dynamite implosion demolished the tower on May 21, 2006, the day after the photographer took this picture. (*Source:* Wikimedia Commons)

While visiting the refuge, Carmel, Junius, Yoke-Sim, and I decided to hike the two-mile-long Oaks to Wetlands Wildlife Foot Trail. Leaving my mother and my sister Rani in the car at the parking lot, the four of us started to walk. On the way, I started jogging leaving the other three behind until I lost sight of them. When I returned to the parking lot, I was surprised to find that Yoke-Sim and the two kids had not returned. Jitters went through my system just like in mid-August 1983 when Junius and Yoke-Sim got lost in Hetch Hetchy (see chapter 59). In panic, I drove to the city and sought police assistance to find the trio.

Yoke-Sim and the kids reappeared in the parking lot just before the cops arrived. I could not fathom how they managed to duck me when I backtracked the foot trail.

CHAPTER 92

Oregon: Attractions in Portland and Riparian Splendor

IN SPITE OF continual rain, on Tuesday (August 1, 1989) afternoon, my family—wife Yoke-Sim, son Junius, and daughter Carmel—and I went on a 134-mile roundtrip tour from Longview to explore the attractions in Portland (pop 582,130), the administrative seat of Multnomah County. Portland is the third most populous city in the Pacific Northwest after Seattle, Washington, and Vancouver, British Columbia. The Portland Metropolitan Area has a population of 2.2 million.

I organized this half-day tour to suit the interests and tastes of my mother, then seventy-six, and my elder sister Rani that were visiting us. I was keen to take them sightseeing in Oregon and Washington as much as I could during their short stay.

After reaching Portland, we began our exploration with a visit to the sixty-two-acre National Sanctuary of Our Sorrowful Mother, popularly known as "The Grotto" (8840 Skidmore St.). Run by the Order of Friar Servants of Mary, United States Province, it strives "to provide a welcoming presence and a beautiful environment conducive to peace, quiet, and spiritual inspiration." The term *sanctuary* was what attracted me to this Catholic Shrine that some two hundred thousand people visit every year.

The heart of the shrine is Our Lady's Grotto, a rock cave carved into the base of a 110-foot cliff. Its center features a life-sized marble replica of Michelangelo's *Pietà*. The upper level of the Grotto introduces the visitors to manicured gardens, religious artwork, and beautiful panoramic views of the Columbia River Valley, the Cascades, and Mount St. Helens. The Grotto was opened in 1924.

Map 92.1 Attractions we visited in Portland, Oregon (August 1, 1989). *A*, Downtown Portland; *B*, "The Grotto"; *C*, Mount Tabor City Park; *D*, Leach Botanical Garden; *E*, Crystal Springs Rhododendron Garden; *F*, Washington Park.

Our second stop was the 196-acre Mount Tabor Park, designed and built ca. 1903 around a dormant volcanic cinder cone. It was Portland's largest park until 1947 when the newly created Mount Forest with its 5,100-acre size, grabbed that distinction. The peak of Mount Tabor lies at an elevation of 636 feet. The Tabor cinder cone is part of the Boring Lava Field, which has been dormant for more than three hundred thousand years. The park administration has cut away a hefty chunk of the cinder cone at the peak to facilitate a basketball field and an amphitheater with the associated parking space. Mount Tabor is also known for its reservoirs (built from 1894 to 1911), three of which qualified to get into the National Register of Historic Places in 2004.

From the dormant volcano, we drove to the sixteen-acre Leach Botanical Garden (6704 SE 122nd Ave.). Established in 1931 as "Sleepy Hollow," the garden exhibits some "two thousand hybrids, cultivars, and native and non-native plants, including alpines, medicinal herbs, rock garden plants, camellias, and forty genera and over 125 species of ferns." The garden began as landscaping for the private home of botanist Lilla Leach and pharmacist John Leach.

Our next stop was the 9.5-acre Crystal Springs Rhododendron Garden (Southeast Woodstock Blvd.). The garden exhibits "more than twenty-five hundred rhododendrons, azaleas, and other plants in a setting of small lakes, paved and unpaved paths, fountains, and small waterfalls." We found this spot, near Reed College, to be a delightful place with lots of ducks on the lake. Carmel and Junius enjoyed chasing and racing with the ducks. The garden originated in 1950 as a rhododendron test project.

Picture 92.1 A panorama of the International Rose Test Garden in Portland, Oregon. (Photo by Piccolo Namek. *Source:* Wikimedia Commons, January 7, 2010)

Washington Park (West Burnside St.), southwest of downtown, was our final stop. All of us found the park's 4.5-acre International Rose Test Garden a joy to behold. It contains some seven thousand rose plants of about 550 varieties. Opened in 1917, its rose collections include the Shakespeare Garden, the Gold Medal Garden, the Royal Rosarian Garden, and the Miniature Rose Garden. Carmel and Junius found happiness in the Penguinarium of the Washington Park Zoo, which we had already visited on July 25—the day we came to Portland airport to pick up my mother and my sister.

All in all, we found Portland to be a green-conscious city. We deliberately focused on a surfeit of botanic gardens at the expense of a multitude of other attractions. Washington Park itself is a 410-acre expanse of mostly steep wooded hillsides with numerous other features.

Riparian Splendor

We spent an entire Saturday (August 5, 1989) doing what I dreamed of since my internship at the Eugene (Oregon) *Register-Guard* in 1967—to

SHELTON A. GUNARATNE

experience the riparian splendor on a drive along the Lower Columbia River Highway No. 2 W (or US 30).

We left Longview at 9:00 a.m., crossed the Columbia River over to the Oregon border, and headed west along the south shore of the self-same river.

Along the forty-mile stretch from Clatskanie (pop 1,710) to Astoria (pop 10,045), US 30 and Columbia run parallel to each other like the proverbial yin and yang. This is the "stretch of riparian splendor" in my parlance. At Clatskanie, a town of Scandinavian people incorporated in 1891, we saw the Flippin Castle. Thomas J. Flippin who commissioned this castle atop the city hill in 1898 is supposed to have said, "A man's home is his castle, and so I built mine to look like one." Flippin was an early day "gypo" logger and sawmill owner.

We released all the riparian energy we accumulated through the stretch of riparian splendor when we reached Astoria, where the Columbia River releases its flow into the Pacific Ocean after a 1,243-mile journey from the Rocky Mountains of British Columbia. The river also demarcates most of the boundary between Washington and Oregon.

We visited three star attractions in Astoria—Columbia River Maritime Museum, Astoria Column, and Fort Clatsop National Memorial.

Astoria, incorporated in 1876 and named after millionaire Joseph J. Astor, is the administrative seat of Clatsop County. Rolf Klep, an avid collector of marine artifacts, founded the museum (now located at 1792 Marine Drive) in 1962. The museum's collection, made up of artifacts collected since its opening, has grown to more than thirty thousand objects, twenty thousand photographs, and a ten thousand-volume research library.

Astoria Column (located at 2199 Coxcomb Drive), a 125-feet concrete-and-steel structure built in 1926, stands on the six hundred-feet Coxcomb Hill overlooking the mouth of the Columbia River. A 164-step interior spiral staircase leads to the observation deck at the top. However, because the column was under repair during our visit, we could not climb to the observation deck. The column commands a panoramic view of the ocean, rivers and mountains.

Picture 92.2 Panorama of the Astoria-Megler Bridge and twilight-shrouded Astoria, Oregon (December 7, 1989). Looking southward from Point Ellice on the Washington side Astoria Column lit with holiday lights is on the left. Saddle Mountain is visible just right of the column. The sky displays hues of pink and purple in this early-December photo. (Photo by Gregg M. Erickson. *Source:* Wikimedia Commons)

We ate lunch at Fort Clatsop, the site where the thirty-three member Lewis and Clark Expedition wintered from December 7, 1805 until March 23, 1806. To get to the fort on the Washington border, we followed Route 30 to its western terminus and joined the Oregon Coast Highway (US 101), which climbs a 360-degree access road onto the Astoria-Megler Bridge over the Columbia River and crossed into the state of Washington. The scenic beauty that nature unfolded for us as we crossed the bridge gave us untold pleasure.

Next, after we returned to Oregon, we turned south on US 101, crossed the bridge over Youngs Bay to Warrenton and further south to Seaside (pop 5,900), Oregon's largest and oldest holiday resort. Railroad magnate Ben Holladay built a summer resort named Seaside House in the vicinity in the 1870s. The city derived its name from Seaside House and was incorporated as such in 1899. On our stopover in Seaside, we enjoyed our walk on the boardwalk along the wide beach, which we reached via Broadway, the city's main drag.

About sixty-two miles south of Astoria along US 101, we stopped at Tillamook (pop 4,675), where we visited the cheese factory of the Tillamook County Creamery Association. We were delighted to taste samples of its cheddar, gourmet ice cream, and yogurt, just like the million others who visit the factory every year.

From Tillamook, we drove west on SR 131 (Cape Meares Loop or Three Capes Scenic Route) to fulfill our desire to eat dinner in the scenic splendor of the Cape Meares State Park, which we reached via Netarts and Oceanside—a drive of twelve miles on the west loop. SR 131 indeed was an astoundingly scenic route. At the state park, Carmel and Junius paid particular attention to the Octopus Tree—"a massive Sitka spruce with branches growing like giant tentacles from its fifty-foot base"—and the Cape Meares Lighthouse.

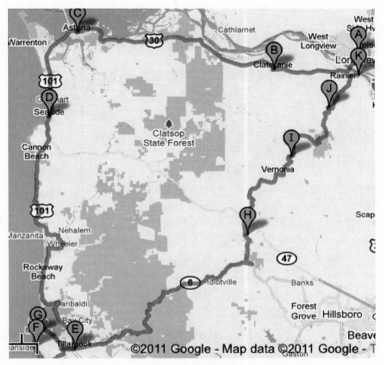

Map 92.2 Our tour of Northwest Oregon (August 5, 1989). *A*, Longview, WA; *B*, Clatskanie; *C*, Astoria; *D*, Seaside; *E*, Tillamook; *F*, Oceanside; *G*, Cape Meares; *H*, Timber; *I*, Pittsburg; *J*, Apiary; *K*, Rainier (all in NW Oregon). Distance covered is 260 miles.

My mother and Rani were getting uneasy as the nightfall darkened the skies. So we returned to Tillamook and drove northwest on SR 6 (Wilson River Highway 37) through numerous twists, turns, and steep slopes. We continued along the curvy road that connects the towns of Timber, Pittsburg, and Apiary to reach Rainier, Oregon, on Interstate 5. Yoke-Sim did most of the arduous driving on the risky SR 6 well known for its traffic accidents. When we returned to Longview, Washington, after the day's 260-mile excursion, it was past 11:00 p.m. Everyone was tired. No one cared to complain. We went to bed straight away to rest and recuperate.

CHAPTER 93

Washington: Rebuff by Canada Consul Helps Family Explore More of Seattle

ON FRIDAY (AUGUST 11, 1989), my mother and my elder sister Rani joined us—Carmel, Junius, Yoke-Sim, and me—to explore Seattle (pop 630,320), the most populous city in the Pacific Northwest, 128 miles north of Longview. Because Rani expressed a wish to see a "little bit of Canada" before her departure back to Sri Lanka on Monday (August 14), we thought of crossing over to Vancouver, British Columbia, as well.

However, being a Sri Lanka passport holder, Rani had to get a visa to visit Canada. I thought getting a visa for a day trip to Canada would pose no problem. But when we stopped by at the Canadian consulate general in Seattle at 8:30 a.m., the consular official refused her a visa on suspicion that ours was a ploy to deposit Rani in Canada as a refugee seeking "permanent" residence. The official refused to budge even when I, in my capacity as a permanent resident of the United States, agreed to guarantee her return with us on the same day. (Apparently, the Tamil exodus from Sri Lanka to Canada claiming refugee status had triggered the suspicion of the consular general.)

We promptly decided to change our plans and spend the day exploring the city of Seattle, the administrative seat of King County, located on a narrow isthmus between Puget Sound (Pacific Ocean) and Lake Washington. The much larger Seattle Metropolitan Area (pop 3.4 million) consists of King and Snohomish counties (covering the tri-city division of Seattle, Bellevue, and Everett) and Pierce County (covering the Tacoma division).

Because my mother wanted to see an American public market, we began our exploration of Seattle with a visit to the Pike Place Market (85 Pike St.), a Seattle landmark, created in 1907 in the northwest section of downtown between Belltown and Elliott Bay. Built on the edge of a steep hill, the upper street level of the market accommodates fishmongers, fresh produce stands, and craft stalls operating in the covered arcades. The market also has several lower levels, located below the main level, each of which featuring a variety of unique shops—antique dealers, comic book sellers, and small family-owned restaurants (Wikipedia). The site still has one of Seattle's few remaining head shops (retail outlets for New Age herbs and drug paraphernalia).

My sister, who had never visited the world outside Sri Lanka before her current US visit, immediately perceived the spontaneous mayhem of the Dehiwala public market, not too far from our one-time home on Terrence Avenue, Mount Lavinia, and the managed mayhem at Pike Place Market. My mother was equally delighted to imagine herself "teleported" to an environment similar to that of Sri Lanka.

From Pike Place, we crossed the Alaskan Way Viaduct over to Pier 59 adjoining the Waterfront Park. Carmel and Junius insisted on visiting the Seattle Aquarium on Pier 59. The city of Seattle opened the aquarium in 1977 (the year that Seattle Marine Aquarium on Pier 56 ceased to exist) as "a vital force for marine conservation." (The non-profit Seattle Aquarium Society took over the management of the facility in 2010. The current admission to the aquarium is $19 with concessions allowed for students.) While Carmel and Junius explored the aquarium, the rest of us enjoyed the picnic facilities and the fountain in the adjoining Waterfront Park, which extends from the privately owned Pier 57 to Pier 59—the area once known as Schwabacher Wharf or Dock. The US military used this spot during World War II. A larger-than-life bronze statue of Christopher Columbus graced the sound or ocean end of the park.

We had to choose among the many attractions in and around Downtown Seattle. (We agreed to skip the Museum of History and Industry, Museum of Flight, and Thomas Burke Memorial Washington State Museum.)

Our choice for a visit was the free Coast Guard Museum of the Northwest (1519 Alaskan Way South), about 1.6 miles from Pier 59 along Puget

Sound. It houses more than three thousand books and periodicals on US Coast Guard and Pacific Northwest maritime history; more than twenty-five hundred historical documents, clippings, and vessel plans; and more than fifteen thousand photographs (Wikipedia). It illustrates the numerous roles that the Coast Guard plays using a variety of artifacts ranging from life-saving stations to rescue boats; from buoy tenders to icebreakers and weather ships; and from modern aircraft to patrol boats and cutters.

Picture 93.1 A 1917 photo of Pioneer Square by C. F. Todd. Smith Tower and (below it) Seattle Hotel are on the far right. Pioneer Building is on the left. (*Source:* Wikimedia Commons)

SHELTON A. GUNARATNE

Driving back toward the southwest corner of downtown, we stopped at the Pioneer Square-Skid Road Historic District, where the pioneer folks of Seattle settled in 1852 after entrepreneur Henry Yester set up his lumber mill on Elliott Bay. The area south of Yester Way (originally called Mill Street) became, in the words of historian Henry Broderick, a restricted area of "a massive collection of the *demimonde.*" The neighborhood had "parlor houses" with marqueses and celebrity madames—among them Lou Graham, Lila Young, and Raw McRoberts—and piano "professors." The city was tolerant of scrupulous parlor houses but failed to deal with the far more controversial "crib houses" such as the Midway, the Paris, and Dreamland. As Wikipedia describes, "Besides the brothels there were 'an ungodly mixture of dives, dumps . . . pawnshops, hash houses, dope parlors and . . . the et cetera that kept the police guessing.' Box houses prospered—part theater, part bar, part brothel, as did all sorts of gambling."

The Great Seattle Fire of 1889 destroyed the Pioneer Square settlement of wooden structures. Late Victorian-style and Romanesque Revival brick and stone buildings replaced the burnt wooden structures. The prospectors involved in the Klondike Gold Rush (1897-1898) used Seattle as a center for travel to Alaska and helped the rebuilding of Pioneer Square.

Seattleites still regard Pioneer Square as the center of the city's nightlife.

Our exploration of Seattle included visits to the Pioneer Square unit of the Klondike Gold Rush Historic Park (free admission) and the Smith Tower, the oldest skyscraper in Seattle, located at 506 Second Avenue and named after the firearm and typewriter magnate Lyman Cornelius Smith, who built it in 1914. The thirty-eight-story tower has a pinnacle height of 489 feet. (General admission is $7.50.)

We ate lunch at the nearby Occidental Park. We cruised through The Chinatown-International District (dubbed "Little Saigon"), one of the oldest sections of Seattle, on the eastern side of Pioneer Square. A notable landmark in the area is *Uwajimaya*, the family-owned Asian-food supermarket founded in 1928 by Fujimatsu Moriguchi.

After lunch, we explored the seventy-four-acre Seattle Center, a park and arts-and-entertainment center north of downtown. Although admission to the park is free, not all of its attractions are free. The center's array of attractions include the International Fountain, the Space Needle, the Monorail terminus, and the Food Circus (later named Center House) with a repertory theater and a children's museum, the Science Fiction Museum (the Experience Music Project), the Fisher Pavilion, the Kobe Bell, the Mercer Arena, the Northwest Rooms, and the Seattle Center Pavilion.

Seattle built the International Fountain (305 Harrison St.) for the 1962 World's Fair. With more than twenty spouts, the fountain goes through programmed cycles of shooting water patterns, accompanied by recorded world music.

Our focus was its star attraction, the towering 605-feet-high Space Needle (400 Broad St.), built as the centerpiece for the 1962 World's Fair. Its width at the broadest point is 138 feet. An observation deck at the 520-feet level provides panoramic views of the city. It has the capacity to withstand winds up to 200 mph and earthquakes up to 9.1 magnitudes. Its twenty-five lightning rods at the top provide protection against lightning damage. The current general admission to the Space Needle is $18.

The Monorail terminus also dates back to 1962 World's Fair. The cost of a roundtrip ride from Seattle Center to the Westlake Central is $4. Each trip takes two minutes to cover the one-mile route.

The Center House was built in 1939 to accommodate the old Armory. During the 1962 World Fair, it was converted to the Food Court. In the early 1970s, the Food Circus was renamed Center House after some minor renovations. In 1985, the Children's Museum moved into the first floor of the building and expanded its space in 1995, building a giant toy mountain for the Alhadeff Exhibit Center. Today, more than three thousand free public performances occur in Center House each year.

Because we were running out of time to explore other attractions in Seattle Center, we decided to drive northward through the stately Queen Anne Hill neighborhood, on our way to visit the 534-acre Discovery Park in the Magnolia Peninsula in northwest Seattle.

Seattle's early economic and cultural elite splurged their wealth to build their mansions on the hill. A sharp incline of the hill separates and segregates the elites ensconced in the Upper Queen Anne from the hoi polloi of the Lower Queen Anne (also known as Uptown) inhabiting the area immediately to the west and north of Seattle Center. Architects originally designed, but failed to complete, the Queen Anne Boulevard as a three-mile loop around the crown of the hill. Examples of the many mansions on Queen Anne Hill are the Gable House on West Highland Drive and George Kinnear's home at 809 Queen Anne Avenue North.

From Seattle Center, we drove north on Queen Anne Avenue North and then turned northwest at North Queen Anne to reach Discovery Park, six miles or so away. Built on the historic grounds of Fort Lawton, the park contains the historic West Point Lighthouse as well. It is also the home of the Daybreak Star Cultural Center of the United Indians of All Tribes. Its twelve miles of hiking trails are a bonanza for the outdoor enthusiasts.

Picture 93.2 An aerial view of Hiram M. Chittenden Locks and Lake Washington Ship Canal (January 1, 1995). (Photo by US Army Corps of Engineers. *Source:* Wikimedia Commons)

We left the park after a stop at the visitors' center to get to our star attraction of the day—Lake Washington Ship Canal and Hiram Chittenden Locks, about 1.5 miles north of Discovery Park. Located on the west end of Salmon Bay, the Ballard Locks, as they are locally known, prevent the saltwater intrusion of Lake Washington and other freshwater lakes and facilitate the movement of boats from the water levels of the lakes to the water level of Puget Sound. They also maintain the fresh water level of the lakes at twenty to twenty-two feet above sea level. The US Army Corps of Engineers has operated the complex of two locks, a spillway, and a fish ladder since 1906. The corps used the spillway dam with tainter gates to regulate the freshwater levels of the ship canal and lakes. We gathered alongside the fish ladder to observe the movement of salmon. We also watched the operation of the locks with keen interest. For Carmel and Junius, this was the star attraction of the day.

We crossed the Lake Washington Ship Canal to visit the Woodland Park Rose Garden (750 N. Fiftieth St.), north of Fremont. The ninety-one-acre park is split in the middle by Aurora Avenue North with the western half occupying the Woodland Park Zoo. All of us loved the peacefulness of this All-American Rose Selection test garden. The wonderful perfume of roses enamored us. Roses of every color—miniatures, hybrid tea roses, bush roses, tree roses, and a large test garden—reminded us of our visit to the International Rose Test Garden in Portland, Oregon.

Driving further north, we cruised along the western and northern shore of the glacial Green Lake. Then, we drove south and east to the two-hundred-acre Washington Park, where we ate dinner at the arboretum. The greenery surrounding us stimulated us to ruminate on the variety of experiences we had since the Canada consul's rebuff in the morning.

We topped our travel adventures of the day by crossing Lake Washington to Mercer Island on the floating bridge—Lacey V. Murrow Memorial Bridge—the western terminus of Interstate 90. Yoke-Sim and I drove our car back to Longview, where we arrived at midnight. All the four passengers in the car had fallen asleep during the 126-mile drive to Longview on I-5.

SHELTON A. GUNARATNE

Map 93.1 Our Tour Route of Seattle (August 11 1989). *A*, Pike Place Market; B=Pier 59/Waterfront Park; C=Coast Guard Museum NW; *D*, Pioneer Square-Skid Row Historical District or Occidental Park; *E*, Smith Tower or International District; *F*, Seattle Center (International Fountain, Space Needle, Monorail, Center House, etc.); *G*, Queen Anne Avenue North; *H*, North Queen Anne; *I*, Discovery Park; *J*, Lake Washington Ship Canal or Hiram Chittenden Locks; *K*, Woodland Park Rose Garden; *L*, Green Lake; *M*, Washington Park Arboretum; *N*, Lacey V. Murrow Memorial or Floating Bridge. (Route distance is 34 miles.)

CHAPTER 94

Washington: Rural Life in Southwest Fails to Impress My Mother and My Sister

ON SATURDAY (AUGUST 12, 1989), the day after our tiring tour of Seattle, we were back on the road exploring the backwoods of southwest Washington State along what I designated as the "Willapa Loop"—a route exceeding 250 miles, not counting the side trips. The reason for this insane hurry was the pressure of time to show my mother and my sister a wide spectrum of life in the US before they returned to their respective countries of residence. Sister Rani was to depart from Portland, Oregon, Monday (August 14) and my mother the next Monday (August 21).

I have no record of the time we started. I suppose we set forth late morning considering that we needed several hours of sleep after the midnight arrival from Seattle. About fifteen miles west of Longview, on the scenic Ocean Beach Highway (also called SR 4), we stopped at the US Fish and Wildlife Service (1440 Abernathy Creek Road). But the fish hatchery, which the kids in particular wanted to see, was closed.

Ergo, we drove a further fifteen miles south and northwest on SR 4, almost hugging the Columbia River on the Washington side, to Cathlamet (pop 600), the administrative seat of Wahkiakum County. The greenery of the Douglas-firs and other flora on this stretch of the road along the river, the counterpart of US 30 on the Oregon side, was astonishing. The (Longview) *Daily News* had already sent me to Cathlamet on a Wednesday (August 2) to interview Wahkiakum County Councilor Linda Elliott and retired resident Jerry Johnson to write a feature on the six-spot Shay locomotive at the County Historical Museum. The *Daily*

News carried the story on August 14 under the headline "Old Logging Locomotive Sashays to New Home." I was proud to show the museum to my mother and my sister on this occasion.

I also decided to expand our tour with a visit to Puget Island, an unincorporated rural community of 798 people on the Columbia River. The Julia Butler Hansen Bridge, built in 1938, connects Cathlamet with the 4,785-acre island. We crossed the bridge on SR 409, which enters the island's northeast and terminates at the Cathlamet-Westport ferry connection on the southwest. The island has a preserve for an endangered species of Columbian white-tailed deer.

Back on the tour route, we stopped for refreshments at Vista Park in Skamokawa (pop 449), an unincorporated rural village settled by Scandinavian immigrants. It is a local center for fishing and kayaking in Wahkiakum County. Because I had visited this idyllic village ten days earlier to interview Sharon Hart, director of the Lower Columbia Development Council, I thought it fit to expound my knowledge of the vicinity to my mother and my sister who appeared to be totally unimpressed with my attempts to enlighten them.

For the next twelve miles, SR 4 skirted the Lutes Mountain (1,089 ft.) and Elk Mountain (1,486 ft.) in a northwest direction until it reached Grays River, a small community in the western edge of Wahkiakum County that brags of itself as "the home of the oldest covered bridge in the state that still carries a public highway." Built in 1906, the 155-feet Howe truss timber bridge we saw, however, was uncovered and under restoration.

From thereon, SR 4 follows the contours of the hilly terrain for the next thirteen miles. SR 4 descends southward to Grays Bay on the Columbia estuary and then rises northwest to Naselle (pop 377), a logging town in Pacific County. We visited the fish hatchery in Naselle. Then we left SR 4 and drove on spur road 401, a twelve-mile stretch snaking southward along the cliffs of Bear Mountain (1,010 ft.) and then southwest along the northern shore of the Columbia estuary up to the north terminus of the Astoria-Megler Bridge, which we crossed on August 1, on our tour of Northwest Oregon. It was lunchtime when we reached the Dismal Nitch rest area, very close to US 101.

As I watched the mouth of the Columbia River at the intersection of spur road 401 with US 101, I congratulated myself for exploring the riparian beauty of this magnificent river from Plymouth, Washington, in the east to its confluence in Astoria-Megler area over an approximate distance of 280 miles. Moreover, I had seen the scenic splendor of Columbia River's final seventy miles from the Oregon angle, as well as the Washington angle.

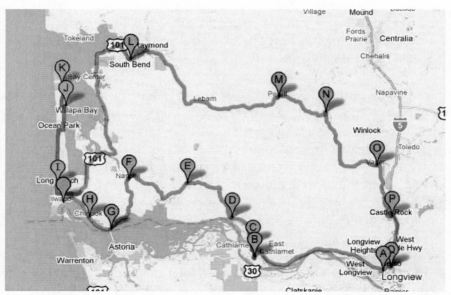

Map 94.1 The "Willapa Loop" Tour Route of Southwest Washington (August 12, 1989). *A*, Longview; *B*, Puget Island; *C*, Cathlamet; *D*, Skamokawa; *E*, Grays River; *F*, Naselle; *G*, Dismal Nitch Rest Area on SR 401, near Astoria-Megler Bridge; *H*, Chinook or Fort Columbia State Park Red arrow, Willapa National Wildlife Refuge (surrounding Willapa Bay) with headquarters at Ilwaco and Cape Disappointment State Park *I*, Long Beach; *J*, Oysterville; *K*, Leadbetter Point State Park; *L*, South Bend; *M*, Pe Ell; *N*, Boistfort; *O*, Vader; *P*, Castle Rock; *Q*, Kelso.

These thoughts nudged me to move on with our tour plan and continue on US 101 to visit several historical places commonly identified as the Lewis and Clark National and State Historical Parks—two on the Washington side of the Columbia River Confluence and three on the Oregon side.

SHELTON A. GUNARATNE

The first of these we visited was the 593-acre Fort Columbia State Park, off Chinook (pop 457). Chinook was once well known for its salmon harvest. The park includes the national historical landmark Point Chinook, from where Captain Robert Gray spotted the Columbia River in 1792. Fort Columbia is an old coastal artillery post.

The second of these we visited was the 1,882-acre Cape Disappointment State Park (formerly called the Fort Canby State Park) on the Long Beach Peninsula, south of Ilwaco (pop 950). Its facilities include two lighthouses, hiking trails, twenty-seven miles of ocean beach, and an interpretive center. It was good exercise for all of us to walk uphill to reach the interpretive center and the nearest lighthouse. The name of the cape is associated with the disappointment of John Meares, a British fur trader, who missed the credit for sighting the Columbia River because a storm forced his ship to turn around in the vicinity of the cape during one of his scouting forays in search of trade in April 1788.

Picture 94.1 Cape Disappointment Lighthouse as seen from the North Jetty, Cape Disappointment State Park, near Ilwaco, Washington. (Photo by Loren T. Vine, January 27, 2007. *Source:* Wikimedia Commons)

Next, we drove five miles north to Long Beach (pop 1,283) at the foot of the Long Beach Peninsula. The town's wide stretch of beach was agog with people of all ages who had come to enjoy the sunset. Kids were flying kites and engaged in numerous modes of play. Soon, we too merged into the beach "gang." A Good Samaritan, who took pity on Carmel and Junius, passed on a kite to them so they could also enjoy their evening on the beach. Even though it was 6:00 p.m., we let our two kids fly their bonanza kite until they were tired.

Picture 94.2 The coast of Long Beach, Washington (June 13, 2007). (*Source:* Creative Commons)

From Long Beach, we drove almost twenty miles north on the obelisk-shaped peninsula, along the Pacific Way and Ocean Beach Highway, past Ocean Park (pop 1,459) and Oysterville (unincorporated) to the Leadbetter Point State Park, south of the Willapa National Wildlife Refuge.

The refuge (with headquarters in Ilwaco on US 101) comprises more than fifteen thousand acres of tidelands, temperate rain forest, ocean beaches, and small streams. It also includes several rare remnants of old-growth coastal cedar forest. The US Fish and Wildlife Service says that the Willapa refuge preserves the habitat for spawning wild salmon, hundreds of thousands of migrating shorebirds, and threatened and endangered species such as the marbled murrelet. The refuge includes two other components outside the peninsula: Puget Island preserve and some twenty islands stretching over twenty-seven miles along the Columbia River from its confluence.

Because the tip of the peninsula was not connected to the mainland by road or ferry across the Willapa Bay, which forms the northern and eastern boundary of the refuge, we had to return to the foot of the peninsula to rejoin US 101 on the "Willapa Loop" (map 94.1).

Fortunately, the charm the excellent scenery that the highway offered all along the Willapa Bay drive from Chetlo Harbor at the mouth of Naselle River to Bay Center at the mouth of Nawakum River kept us all in happy chatter. We saw another view of the Leadbetter Point and the Willapa refuge on the peninsula from the mainland side as our route took a northeast turn at the mouth of Bone River and then a sharp southeastern turn to reach South Bend (pop 1,807), the county seat of Pacific County.

The summer dusk had set in.

Yoke-Sim, who took over driving at this point, continued along US 101 along the Willapa River to Raymond (pop, 2,895), five miles to the northeast. Then, she turned southeast on SR 6 heading for Pe Ell (pop 657) in Lewis County, roughly thirty miles away. Vader (pop 590), the next town in Lewis County, was another twenty-six miles to the southeast. Between the two towns, we could see the Boistfort Peak (3,120 ft.), the highest point of the Willapa Hills range, to our right.

The "Willapa Loop," which we traversed on August 12, 1989, covered a south-north distance of sixty-three miles from Columbia River (south) to Olympic Mountains (north); and a west-east distance of sixty miles from Pacific Ocean (west) to Cascade Range (east). We returned to Longview through Castle Rock (pop 2,130) in Cowlitz County.

Postscript

Two days later, my sister Rani left us on her return trip to Sri Lanka. I still don't know whether she enjoyed the US sightseeing excursions I had put her through.

Rani cried when she had to say good-bye to our mother and members of my family. After depositing Rani at the Portland Airport, the rest of us stopped at the Gig Creek Rest Area for coffee on the way back to Longview.

The next chapter (chapter 95) will narrate my mother's first experience in overnight outdoor camping at the age of seventy-six.

Washington: Mother, 76, Camps at Illahee State Park in Bremerton

THE SEVENTY-FIVE-ACRE *ILLAHEE State Park,* a waterfront recreational area that offers camping, hiking, and boating to the public, is located in the unincorporated hamlet of Illahee, just north of East Bremerton, on Port Orchard Bay area of the Puget Sound. The park is known for one of its proud possessions—a four-hundred-year-old evergreen conifer called the Pacific Yew (*Taxus brevifolia*). "Illahee" means *earth* or *country* in the Native American tradition. Washington State purchased the land for the park in seven parcels between 1934 and 1954. Illahee is also home to the 450-acre Illahee Preserve, as well as the 110-acre Rolling Hills golf course.

For me, this scenic spot has significance beyond measure because it was here that my mother, then seventy-six, had her first life experience in outdoor camping.

Illahee (Bremerton) lies about twenty miles directly to the west of Seattle, which we explored eight days before. Puget Sound and Port Orchard Bay separated the two cities with Bainbridge Island in the middle. The Seattle (main)-Bremerton Ferry connected the east-west ends of SR 304 across the sound. The ferry charge makes SR 304 a toll road.

My mother was not the least bit concerned with any of these geographical details or trivia. Junius and I were very keen to share with her an unforgettable camping experience in our Timberline-4 tent, which we purchased in Kelso (see chapter 91).

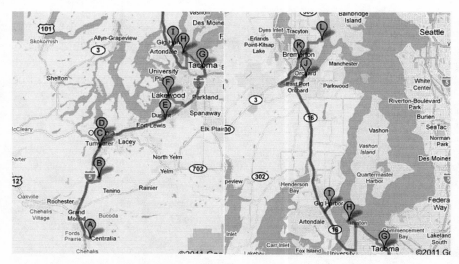

Map 95.1 Route from Centralia to Illahee State Park (Bremerton). *A*, Centralia; *B*, Millersylvania State Park or Deep Lake; *C*, Tumwater; *D*, Capitol Campus or Olympia; *E*, Fort Lewis Military Museum; *F*, Steilacoom; *G*, Wright Park or Tacoma . . . (continued right) *H*, Point Defiance Park/Tacoma; *I*, Gig Harbor; *J*, Port Orchard; *K*, Bremerton; *L*, Illahee State Park/Bremerton.

As it turned out, my mother (who was well known as "Punchi Hamine" in our native village of Pathegama in the Deep South of Sri Lanka) liked her first-ever outdoor camping experience—the when and where of it didn't matter to her. (She died in Brisbane in her avatar as an Australian citizen at the age of ninety-six in 2009.) It is for this reason that I opened this essay with a thumbnail sketch of Illahee in the vicinity of Bremerton, Washington (pop 37,259) in Kitsap County/Peninsula.

Mother joined us—Carmel, Junius, Yoke-Sim, and I—on this camping trip on a Saturday (August 19, 1989), just two days before she left on her return trip to Australia. We left Longview at 6:30 a.m. Bremerton was 127 miles to the north in Lewis County.

About forty-five miles north of Longview on Interstate 5, we decided to stop at Centralia (pop 15,699), a town founded by a black slave named George Washington (1817-1915). A white couple, James and Anna Cochran, adopted Washington, who was born in Virginia. The Cochrans moved west and successfully invoked a Missouri special right for a black to become a citizen on grounds of his literacy and special skills. Washington was a master rifleman. Subsequently, they moved to Oregon Territory, where Washington was able to purchase land, using the Cochrans as proxies, at the junction of the Skookumchuck and Chehalis Rivers. In early 1875, Washington and his wife Mary Jane formally platted the town of Centerville, which was later renamed Centralia.

Picture 95.1 Illahee State Park in the Puget Sound (June 26, 2004). (Source: Wikimedia Commons)

Then, we drove another twenty-five miles north to explore several attractions in and around Olympia (pop 42,514), the capital of Washington State and the administrative seat of Thurston County. Lushootseed-speaking Native Americans occupied this area for thousands of years before the Europeans arrived in the 1790s. In 1851, Olympia became the customs house for the Customs District of Puget Sound for Washington Territory (originally part of Oregon Territory). Because of the area's view of the Olympic Mountains to the northwest, the city was named Olympia on the suggestion a resident. Washington became a state in 1889.

SHELTON A. GUNARATNE

We went past the 842-acre Millersylvania State Park, located ten miles south of Olympia. Deep Lake, a sixty-six-acre freshwater expanse that the Native Americans had named CoKaine Lake, is a big attraction of the park, which provides camping facilities and six miles of trails in the shade of old-growth cedar and fir trees.

In Tumwater (pop 12, 698), we joined a tour of the Olympia Brewing Company "that we all enjoyed." Olympia beer was the product that came out of the complex that Leopold Schmidt built in 1896—a four-storey wooden brew house, a five-storey cellar building, a one-storey ice factory powered by the lower falls, and a bottling and keg plant. In 1902, the complex adopted the name Olympia Brewing Company. The Schmidts sold the company in 1982. SABMiller eventually purchased the company. However, Miller closed the plant in 2003. Ag Energy Resources, Inc., which purchased the machinery of the defunct company, has transformed the paraphernalia for ethanol production.

Picture 95.2 The Olympia Brewery in Tumwater, Washington (near Olympia) in 1989. (*Source:* Wikimedia Commons)

We also visited the Tumwater Historical Park located at the bottom of Capitol Lake about 2.5 miles south of the capital. The Schmidt House (330 Schmidt Place SW), the home of the beer magnate, is part of this complex.

Thereafter, we drove further north to the city for a quick tour of the Washington State Capitol Historic District. Unlike in most of the states, the executive, legislative, and judicial branches of government are not housed in a single Capitol building here. A campus of separate buildings houses the three branches in Olympia.

Our next stop was the Fort Lewis Military Museum, about fifteen miles northeast of Olympia. The museum, housed in what was once the Red Shield Inn built in 1919, displayed several collections of uniforms and equipment. A variety of military equipment and weapons occupied the surrounding grounds.

Here, we left I-5 for a five-mile-north drive to visit the coastal town of Steilacoom (pop 6,049) in Pierce County. Our purpose was to see a 1906 soda fountain at the Blair Drug and Hardware Store (1617 Lafayette St.) built in 1895. Founded by Lafayette Balch, a sea captain from Maine, Steilacoom was officially incorporated in 1854—the oldest incorporated town in Washington.

Back on I-5, we headed northeast to Wright Park in Tacoma (pop 199.638)—seventeen miles from Steilacoom. Designed by Bavarian architect Edward Otto Schwageral, this twenty-seven-acre park includes an arboretum and the Seymour Botanical Conservatory, a Victorian-style structure built in 1907. We deemed it apt to be in such pleasant surroundings to savor our late picnic-style lunch,

Then, along the northwest shore of Commencement Bay, we drove six miles to the 702-acre Point Defiance Park, which, all of us agreed, was the star attraction of the vicinity. Just as we saw in similar parks in Portland and Seattle, Point Defiance Park also offered its visitors—more than 2 million annually—its own Japanese Garden, Rose Garden, Rhododendron Garden, and Dahlia gardens. The gardens are located near the park's main entrance on the approach to the zoo and aquarium.

Zoos and aquaria naturally attracted Carmel and Junius. We ambled in the park touching, admiring, and smelling the flowers. My mother perked up considerably after this exercise of hobnobbing with nature.

The park also accommodates mule deer, red foxes, pleated woodpeckers, Douglas squirrels, and raccoons. So did Carmel and Junius by spotting wildlife as we explored the entire park by driving on the Five-Mile Road loop. From the cliffs overlooking Gig Harbor, we saw bald eagles swooping down on the salmon runs in the Puget Sound Narrows.

Picture 95.3 Panoramic view of the Kitsap Peninsula from a lookout on the western cliffs of Point Defiance Park (December 7, 2009). The Tacoma Narrows suspension double bridge is on the far left. On to the right are the silhouettes of Olympic Mountains above Gig Harbor. (Photo by Gregg M. Erickson. *Source:* Wikimedia Commons)

We also explored the Fort Nisqually living history museum comprising Factor's House and the Granary, as well as a trade store, working blacksmith shop, laborers dwelling house, demonstration kitchen, and kitchen garden. This reconstructed fort reminded us of our visit to Fort William Historical Park in Thunder Bay (see chapter 87).

We left the park and crossed the Narrows Tacoma Bridge—a pair of twin suspension bridges opened in 1950—to sprawling Kitsap Peninsula on SR 16, which took us northward via Gig Harbor (pop 7,240) to Port Orchard (pop 7,953). We rested for a while to view the Port Orchard Marina. I walked in the vicinity visiting several antique and specialty shops.

It was late in the day when we arrived in the shipyard city of Bremerton. We drove around the city to get our bearings and found the ideal spot for overnight camping at the Illahee State Park. Junius and I set up the tent on our site and invited my mother to grace it with her presence. She was all too willing—like Barkis—to lie down after a drive of 176 miles all the way from Longview with many sightseeing stops along the way.

Yoke-Sim prepared a tasty dinner, which we gobbled up seated around the campfire. My mother learnt the pros and cons of using the common rest-room facilities in a public campground. I walked downhill along the shore to enjoy the beach after dark while others got ready to sleep in the tent in their sleeping bags. I chose to sleep in my station wagon so Mother could have more tent space.

My mother confessed next morning that she had difficulty having a good night's sleep in the tent although she relished the overall camping experience.

Shelton A. Gunaratne

CHAPTER 96

Washington: Journey to Port Townsend and Return Trip On US 101

ON SUNDAY (AUGUST 20, 1989) morning, all of us got up early to beat the rush for public washrooms at the Illahee State Park's campgrounds. My mother said she relished sleeping in the tent flanked by her grandchildren Carmel, five, and Junius, nine, just as our extended family did back in Sri Lanka. She confessed, however, that she did not have a good night's rest because of the novelty of lying on the ground in a sleeping bag.

(Currently, the Illahee State Park offers sixty-two standard campsites, forty-one utility campsites, showers, picnic areas, play area, game courts, swimming beach, boat launches, dock, hiking trails, and bike trails.)

We ate a quick campsite breakfast that Yoke-Sim served, dismantled and packed our tent paraphernalia, and left the park about 8:00 a.m. bound north to Port Townsend (pop 8,334) in Jefferson County on the Canadian border, some 65-70 miles from Illahee, at the mouth of the Puget Sound. The idea of exploring the Puget Sound terrain up to Townsend was mine. Junius, who was able to read maps, also relished geographical exploration. The others passively agreed to let the chief navigator decide what they ought to see.

From Kitsap to Olympic

We drove through the unincorporated residential communities of Brownsville and Keyport to the Nordic town of Poulsbo (pop 6,318) on Liberty Bay, where we stopped for refreshments and shopped for groceries at Anderson's Supermarket. Known for its Poulsbo Bread, originally baked in the local bakery, its shops and restaurants maintain a Scandinavian theme. Jorgen Eliason, a Norwegian immigrant, founded the city in the 1880s. Incorporated in 1907, Poulsbo derived its name from the village of Paulsbo (meaning "Paul's place") in Norway. Poulsbo reminded me of Solvang, a similar-sized community founded by Danish settlers in Santa Barbara (see chapter 74).

Next, driving six or seven miles along Liberty Bay in a southeast-northeast direction, we reached Suquamish (pop 3,510), the burial place of Chief Seattle (1780-1866) of the Duwamish tribe, who pursued a path of accommodation with the European settlers. David Swinson "Doc" Maynard, Seattle city's primary founding father, was a "special" friend of Chief Seattle.

Old Man House, the "big house" that was home to both Chief Seattle and Chief Kitsap, lies just to the south of Suquamish on Agate Pass. Chief Seattle's gravesite is in the Port Madison Indian Reservation. Maynard was instrumental in naming the city of Seattle to honor Chief Seattle.

Picture 96.1 Tombstone of Chief Seattle in Suquamish (June 20, 2008). (Photo by Daniel M. Short. *Source:* Wikimedia Commons)

Map 96.1 Our August 20-21, 1989 tour route from Bremerton to Port Townsend and the return trip to Centralia and Longview on US101. *A*, Illahee State Park; *B*, Poulsbo; *C*, Suquamish; *D*, Kingston; *E*, Port Gamble; *F*, Old Fort Townsend State Park; *G*, Port Townsend; *H*, Quilcene; *I*, Shelton; *J*, Centralia.

(Note: The scales used in the top and bottom parts of this composite map are not the same.)

About eight miles northeast from Suquamish, we stopped at Kingston (pop 1,811) on Apple Tree Cove, the western terminus of the Kingston-Edmonds Ferry that crosses the Puget Sound Narrows. More than 4 million passengers per year make use of this major ferry service.

Another eight miles west and north, we arrived in Port Gamble (an unincorporated community) at the northwestern edge of Kitsap Peninsula. A nineteenth century logging town with more than thirty Victorian-style homes, Port Gamble represents one of the few remaining examples of company towns. Before we crossed the long and narrow Hood Canal Floating Bridge that connects Kitsap Peninsula with Olympic Peninsula, we visited the Of Sea and Shore Museum in the town's General Store Building. The museum displayed a huge collection of shells from around the world.

Port and Fort Townsend

Then, off we drove some twenty-seven miles north of the canal to Port Townsend at the northeastern tip of Olympic Peninsula. Port Townsend is adjacent to the Admiralty Inlet and a trio of state parks built on retired artillery installations—Fort Worden (immediately to the north of Port Townsend), Fort Casey (on Whidbey Island) and Fort Flagler (at the northern tip of Marrowstone Island)—for the protection of the entrance to Puget Sound.

We visited the 433-acre Fort Worden State Park, where we saw several restored buildings, including the Bell Tower, Manresa Castle, City Hall, the Courthouse, and the Post Office. We took pictures in front of the architecturally eclectic Jefferson County Courthouse.

With map in hand, I understood that at Fort Worden we were looking north at the ninety-five mile-long Strait of Juan de Fuca that connected both Georgia Strait and Puget Sound to the Pacific Ocean while also separating Canada from the United States. (De Fuca was the Greek navigator who sailed in a Spanish expedition in 1592 to seek the fabled Strait of Anián.) The scene was entirely different from what I observed at the mouth of Milford Sound in New Zealand in 1981 (chapter 54).

Picture 96.2 Historic buildings at Fort Worden in Port Townsend. (Photo by Joe Mabel. *Source:* Wikimedia Commons)

As Wikipedia puts it, in addition to its natural scenery at the northeast tip of the Olympic Peninsula, "the city [of Port Townsend] is also known for the many Victorian buildings, numerous annual cultural events and as a maritime center for independent boat builders and related industries and crafts."

We walked in downtown Port Townsend to see the century-old Tree of Heaven and the Victorian buildings. We saw some of the historic homes such as the 1868 Greek Revival-style Rothschild House and the 1889 Victorian-style Ann Starrrett House (744 Clay St.) from the outside.

Port Townsend is also accessible via ferry from the Keystone ferry terminal on Whidbey Island, on the east side of Puget Sound.

Return Journey

Having seen the Canadian border from the northeastern tip of the Olympic Peninsula, we had to backtrack five miles southward on SR 20 to get back to the serene surroundings of the 367-acre Old Fort Townsend State Park, where we stopped for refreshments late morning on our way forward. We liked the ambience of the place so much that all of us decided to stop there again to eat our lunch as well.

The US Army built this fort in 1856 but abandoned it from 1859 to 1876 as "unfit." The revived fort lasted until 1895, when fire destroyed the barracks. It became active again during World War II. Since 1956, the State Parks has run the facility for the enjoyment of tourists like us.

After lunch, we continued driving south along the eastern shore of Discovery Bay. At the southern end of the bay, we merged into the scenic Olympic Highway (US 101), which flanks the eastern boundary of the Olympic National Park. We stopped fifteen miles further south at the Quilcene (pop 591) Ranger Station to savor the magnificent beauty of the Douglas-fir, spring blooming Pacific rhododendrons, Oregon grape, and salal in the Olympic National Forest land.

Our next stop was Shelton (pop 8,442), the administrative seat of Mason County, fifty-four miles to the south of Quilcene. Incorporated in 1890, the city was named after David Shelton, a delegate to the territorial legislature. Yoke-Sim, our team expert in food, splurged $14 to purchase a salmon from a vendor somewhere in the vicinity. We also took a photo of "Tollie," a ten-ton Shay locomotive adorning the city.

It was dinnertime when we reached Centralia (via Olympia), forty-three miles south of Shelton. We decided to compensate my mother for all the *dukkha* (suffering) we caused her through my *tanha* (desire) for endless travel by treating her with a grand dinner at the Cousins Family Restaurant in the city that a black man founded.

We returned home to Longview on Interstate 5 at about 8:00 p.m. after driving 256 miles during the day.

The very next day (Monday August 21, 1989), my mother left us to return to Australia.

CHAPTER 97

Washington: Camping in Olympic National Park on Our Return Journey Home

ALL GOOD THINGS must come to an end, the proverb asserts; so did my stint with the (Longview) *Daily News*.

I had to be back in Minnesota in time for the beginning of fall term at my university in Moorhead. So we—daughter Carmel (five); son Junius (nine); wife Yoke-Sim, and I—left Longview Saturday (August 26, 1989) in our Toyota Camry station wagon via the Olympic Peninsula and the Trans-Canada Highway.

Because three of us had thoroughly enjoyed our forays into Sequoia and Yosemite national parks in 1983 before Carmel's birth (see chapters 57 and 59); and all of us had fond memories of our experiences in Voyageurs National Park in 1988 (chapter 86); and my solo adventure in Volcano National Park in 1984 (chapter 81), we wanted to start our return journey with a taste of the Olympic National Park (ONP) in Washington.

The 922,561-acre ONP intrigued us because of its divisibility into three basic geographical regions: the Pacific coastline, the Olympic Mountains, and the temperate rain forest. In recognition of this unique three-dimensional combination, ONP became an International Biosphere Reserve in 1976. Five years later, UNESCO designated it a World Heritage Site.

President Theodore Roosevelt, an unabashed conservationist, created the Mount Olympus National Monument in 1909. In 1938, Congress authorized the park's re-designation as a national park, and President Franklin Roosevelt signed the legislation approving the status change. In 1988, Congress designated 95 percent of ONP as the Olympic Wilderness.

Saturday morning, we got up early to empty the apartment of all our belongings and pack them into the boot of our car. After leaving the apartment, we went to the Longview Safeway for coffee. Then, we left Longview for good at 8:00 a.m. or so on our way to ONP.

Our first stop was the familiar city of Centralia, forty-five miles to the north on I-5.

After filling up our car in Centralia, we headed thirty-five miles northwest on US 12 to Elma (pop 3,049) in Grays Harbor County.

Driving twenty-one miles west of Elmer, we stopped at Aberdeen (pop 16,461), known as the "Gateway to the Olympic Peninsula." We visited the Aberdeen Museum of History. In the early 1900s, Aberdeen had the reputation of being "one of the grittiest towns on the West Coast with many saloons, whorehouses, and gambling establishments populating the area" (Wikipedia). We also tarried in the adjoining city of Hoquiam (pop 9, 097) to rush through the Polson Park and museum and Hoquiam's Castle.

Day 1

In the vicinity of Hoquiam-Aberdeen-Cosmopolis, where US 12 merged with US101, we drove north to reach the southern boundary of the Olympic National Forest right into Quinault (pop 191), forty-four miles to the north.

Access to the temperate rain forest division of ONP is possible through the Quinault, Queets, and Hoh/Bogachiel valleys on the western flank of the park. We entered the ONP through the Quinault Valley, also known as the "Valley of the Rain Forest Giants."

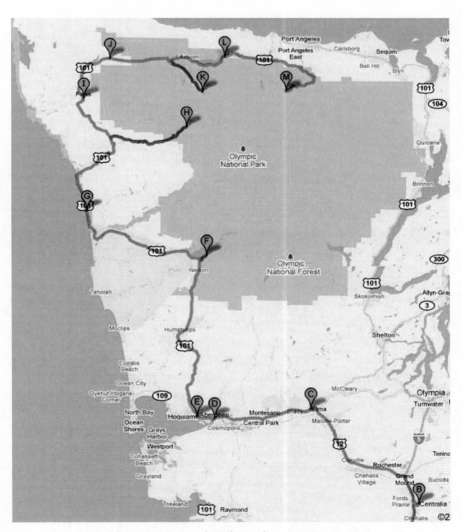

Map 97.1 Olympic National Park Exploration Route *A*, Longview (not in map); *B*, Centralia; *C*, Elma; *D*, Aberdeen; *E*, Hoquiam/ Grays Harbor; *F*, Quinault/Graves Creek; *G*, Kalaloch Lodge/ Queets; *H*, Hoh Rain Forest Campgrounds and Visitor Center; *I*, Forks; *J*, Sappho; *K*, Sol Duc Hot Springs Resort: *L*, Lake Crescent; *M*, Heart o' the Hills Campgrounds/Hurricane Ridge.

Quinault Rain Forest

The temperate Quinault Rain forest dominates the entire valley. This glacially carved valley, comprising the 7.6 square-mile Lake Quinault and the sixty-nine mile Quinault River, provides access to the second major division of ONP, the Olympic Mountains.

The Quinault Indian Nation owns Lake Quinault. The Quinault River marks the boundary of ONP for several miles before emptying into Lake Quinault. After the lake, the river flows southwest, reaching the ocean at Taholah—the approximate starting point of the third geographical division of ONP, the Pacific coastline.

(The Quinault Indian Reservation (pop 1,370), encompassing a land area of 316.331 sq. miles, lies to the west of the lake. About 60 percent of the reservation's population lives in the community of Taholah.)

A thirty-mile scenic loop around Quinault lake and the river enables visitors to go on scenic drives to spot the flora and fauna peculiar to a temperate rain forest, particularly the Roosevelt elk, the largest land mammal in the park, which serves as a preserve for some four thousand to five thousand of these elk. Other protected fauna thriving in the park's rain forest include the Pacific tree frog, Northern spotted owl, bobcat, cougar, raccoon, Olympic black bear, and black-tailed deer.

The facilities flanking the Quinault River include the Quinault Rain Forest Ranger Station on the North Shore and the Olympic National Forest/Park Information Station on the South Shore. The historic Lake Quinault Lodge and the Rain Forest Resort Village also stand on the South Shore.

The valley derives its nickname from the largest specimens of Western red cedar, Sitka spruce, western hemlock, Alaskan cedar, and mountain hemlock, as well as five of the top ten largest Douglas-firs, found in the forest. Other native flora that make the ONP Rain Forest their home include the big leaf maple, vine maple, red alder, and black cottonwood.

From Quinault, we cruised seventeen miles northeast on the South Shore of the lake and the river all the way to idyllic Graves Creek, where the facilities include two campgrounds. The cliffs of Mount Hoquiam, Mount

Olson, and Mount Lawson surrounded us as we ate our lunch enjoying the superlative charm of nature. We couldn't resist the temptation to hike about a half-mile on the Six Ridge Trail. However, we had to bear the inconvenience of continual drizzling endemic to rain forests.

We drove back on the same gravel road but shifted to the North Shore of the loop at North Fork. We rejoined US 101 at the southwestern edge of Lake Quinault and headed west to the coastal resort of Kalaloch, an unincorporated community, almost fifty miles from Graves Creek. We got off at the Kalaloch Lodge to walk along the Pacific Beach although it was chilly and foggy. The scenery varied from beaches (that might be sandy, rocky or boulder-strewn!) to cliffs plunging into the sea. Three national wildlife refuges and the Olympic Coast National Marine Sanctuary protect the marine environment and offshore islands.

About five miles to the south of Kalaloch is the tiny Native American community of Queets, which provides access to ONP's Pacific Beach hiking trails.

From Kalaloch, we followed US 101, which runs north and then turn northeast at the mouth of Hoh River bordering the 477-acre Hoh Indian Reservation (pop 102). At the junction where US 101 crosses the Hoh River to go northwest again, we turned east on Upper Hoh Road to reach the Hoh Rain Forest Campground, just to the west of the visitor center, about 6:30 p.m. We drove forty-one miles from Kalaloch to reach our destination of the day, translating to a driving stretch of 265 miles all the way from Longview.

Hoh Rain Forest

Howsoever tiring our relentless tour was, we were delighted to have explored two of the three geographical dimensions of ONP—the temperate rain forest and the uneven terrain of the Pacific coastline. We weren't fully prepared to explore the remaining dimension of ONP—the snow-capped peaks of the Mountains. Locations where snowy peaks sit side by side with rain forests are unusual.

Originating in the Ho Glacier on Mount Olympus (elev. 7,980 ft.), the Hoh River flows fifty-six miles west and empties itself into the Pacific

Ocean at the Hoh Indian Reservation. The final segment of the Hoh River marks the boundary between the ONP and the Indian reservation while also providing another point of road access to the rain forest in the Hoh Valley.

The Hoh River Campground is the trailhead of the Hoh River Trail, which follows the river through the Hoh Rain Forest from the campground to Mount Olympus. The Hoh Rain Forest accommodates the National Park Service Ranger Station from where backcountry trails extend deeper into the national park.

A popular 0.8-mile loop trail near the visitor center is the Hall of Mosses, which gives visitors a feel for the local ecosystem. It's a display of big leaf maple, Sitka spruce, and other temperate conifers covered in green and brown mosses. Along the trail, a side path of 200 feet leads to a grove of maple trees covered with moss.

Picture 97.1 Maples in the Hall of Mosses Trail at Hoh Rain Forest (August 2006). (Photo by Kevin Muckenthaler. *Source:* Wikimedia Commons)

Junius and I set up our tent in campground A for our overnight stay. Later, after eating our dinner, all of us attended the rangers' campfire program on "Lifestyle of the salmon on the Hoh, Queets, and Quinault Rivers."

Day 2

We kicked off Sunday (August 27) morning with a walk on the Hall of Mosses Trail. Then, we backtracked the Upper Hoh Road to head northwest on US 101 to Forks (pop 3,120) in Clallam County. The Forks Timber Museum did not exist at the time of our visit. However, we stopped in the town to buy groceries and get maps at the visitor center.

We spent the rest of the day with visits to the following places:

- Sappho, where we toured the Sol Duc Hatchery. The hatchery exhibited big salmon in the adult pond, which was fascinating.
- Sol Duc Hot Springs Resort "best known for its soaking pools, hot tubs, and a swimming pool that are heated with the nearby hot springs."
- Storm King Ranger Station at Crescent Lake. We ate our lunch here and then we walked a one-mile trail to see the ninety-foot Marymere Falls.
- Elwha River Valley to see Lake Mills formed by the Glines Canyon Dam (also known as Upper Elwha Dam), a 210-feet structure built in 1927. (Because the dam has drastically reduced the annual salmon run in the Elwha River watershed from more than 400,000 to less than 4,000 adult returns, the federal government has undertaken to decommission and demolish the dam starting 2011.)
- Pioneer Memorial Museum and Visitor Center in Port Angeles.

From Port Angeles, we drove to our final destination of the day—the Heart o' the Hills Campground to set up our tent for our overnight stay. But we hardly expected the highlight of the day to come last: our drive to the Hurricane Ridge on a 9 percent grade highway, 5,200 feet above sea level. As we headed toward the ridge, magnificent views of the snow-capped Mount Olympus, Mount Constance, and other Olympic mountains, whose sides and ridgelines are topped with massive glaciers, appeared on the horizon. We walked on nature trails to get clear views of the Strait of Juan de Fuca and the Vancouver Island in Canada, which we strained to see from Port Townsend the previous week. We also saw wild bear and elk roaming around the lodge.

(The Hanukkah Eve Windstorm of 2006 extensively damaged the Heart o' the Hills Campground. It was reopened in June 2007.)

Although we had explored almost the entirety of the scenic US 101 surrounding the ONP, our forays failed to encounter the mountain region of the park adequately.

Finally, back at the campgrounds, I took Carmel and Junius to the campfire program "The Geological Changes in the Olympic Peninsula." After another day of driving some 170 miles, we deserved a good night's sleep.

Picture 97.2 A view of Hurricane Ridge Trail at ONP (August 25, 2007). (Photo by Vranak. *Source:* Wikimedia Commons)

SHELTON A. GUNARATNE

CHAPTER 98

British Columbia: Victoria and Vancouver Bring Us Memories of Australia

MONDAY (AUGUST 28, 1989) morning, we—Carmel (five), Junius (nine), Yoke-Sim, and I—left the Olympic Peninsula of Washington from Port Angeles (pop 18,397), the biggest city in the peninsula, by ferry and landed in Victoria (pop 78,000) in British Columbia (pop 4.4 million), Canada. The current population of Canada is 34 million,

On arrival at Port Angeles ferry terminal, we lined up our car for the 12:45 p.m. ferry ride to Victoria on MV *Coho*. (In 1989, our ferry ride cost us $32, including $23 for the car. Today, the same package would cost $86, including $39.50 for the car.) Then, until the ferry's departure time, we visited the Port Angeles courthouse, library, and several downtown shops.

The 40 km (25 mile) ferry ride to Victoria, across the Strait of Juan de Fuca, took ninety minutes. The ride turned out to be great fun for Carmel and Junius, who observed the waters of the strait from all angles of the ferry. Because none us used Sri Lankan passports, the Canada immigration had no reason to deny us entry to the country. But we recalled the fuss that the Canada consul general in Seattle created when we sought a travel visa for my sister Rani barely a fortnight ago.

British Columbia (BC) was so named by Queen Victoria in 1858. It became the sixth province of Canada in 1871. Victoria, at the southern tip of Vancouver Island (map 98.1), is the capital of the province. However, the metropolitan area of Greater Victoria has a population of 330,000—translating to about 45 percent of the people who live on the 32,694 sq. km Vancouver Island. Vancouver (pop 578,041) on the mainland is the province's largest city. The metropolitan area of Vancouver, however, has a population of more than 2.1 million.

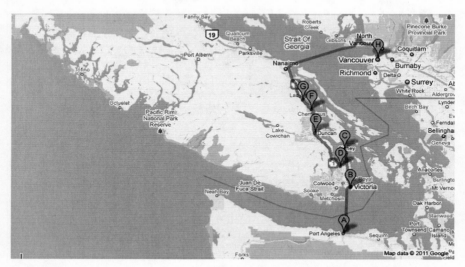

Map 98.1 Our route from Port Angeles, WA, through Vancouver Island to Vancouver, BC. *A*, Port Angeles, WA, Victoria, BC, Ferry; *B*, Victoria, capital of BC; *C*, McDonald Provincial Park (northern tip of Saanich Peninsula); *D*, Butchart Gardens; *E*, Duncan; *F*, Chemainus; *G*, Ladysmith; *H*, Nanaimo-Vancouver City Ferry.

So, whom shall we call by the demonym Vancouverite—a resident of Vancouver city or of Vancouver Island? Apparently, the people of British Columbia are so proud of their British colonial heritage that they have retained the name that Queen Victoria gave their province, as well as the name of their capital city named for her. Moreover, despite the confusion, they have retained the name of their island and their largest city named after Captain George Vancouver (1757-1798), the famous British explorer of the Pacific Coast.

Victoria's Attractions

It was sunny when we landed in Victoria's Inner Harbor, where the Trans-Canada Highway 1 begins on the western edge of Beacon Hill Park. We lost no time and drove 500 m from the Ferry Ramp to the Parliamentary Buildings to join the 3:00 p.m. tour.

After learning about the Parliamentary system of governance in British Columbia, we moved on to see a few more attractions in and around the Heritage Court.

- Thunderbird Park, a part of the Royal British Columbia Museum Cultural Precinct. The park is home to many totem poles (mostly Gitxsan, Haida, and Kwakwaka'wakw) and other First Nations monuments.
- The sixty-two bell Netherlands Centennial Carillon in front of the Royal British Columbia Museum. A gift of the Dutch community of British Columbia, the carillon was placed in 1967 to commemorate Canada's Centennial Year.
- The renovated turn-of-the century Empress Hotel, where visitors can enjoy their afternoon tea in the hotel's historic Tea Lobby. Served with scones, afternoon tea is a British ritual familiar in Australia and New Zealand as well. It reminded us of our decade in Australia. In our eyes, we could have easily imagined ourselves to be in Adelaide, Brisbane, Melbourne, Perth, or Sydney. We were having a whale of a time in Victoria, the city in British Columbia (although we could have confused it with the state of the same name in Australia).

We spent the late afternoon in the fourteen-hectare Butchart Gardens (800 Benvenuto Ave.) in Brentwood Bay, 23 km north of downtown Victoria. (Current summer admission is $29 per adult plus 12 percent harmonized sales tax.) The gardens, founded by Robert P. Butchart (1856-1943) and his wife Jennie at the turn of the century, attract more than a million visitors annually. It is a visual delight of flowers and shrubs. We were delighted to feast our eyes on its different floral gardens—Japanese, Rose, Sunken, Italian, and so forth; the Star Pond; the Concert Lawn; and the Show Greenhouse. We saw the Ross Fountain at its best with its lights on at night. We ate a picnic dinner and waited to see the "Just for Fun" stage show at 8:30 p.m. It was well worth our money. In addition, the gardens offer a collection of statuary and of birds to enhance its ambience.

We drove 18 km northeast from Butchart Gardens to camp overnight at the twenty-hectare McDonald Provincial Park (in Sidney, a variation of Sydney, Australia)—a very attractive, wooded campground facility located a short distance from the Swartz Bay ferry terminal, just off Highway 17 on the Saanich Peninsula.

Because the attractions we visited were not far from one another, our driving distance during the day was a mere 59 km (37 miles).

Picture 98.1 We feasted our eyes on the several floral gardens at the Butchart Gardens. The Sunken Gardens was one of our favorites (May 27, 2008). (Photo by W. Bardwin. *Source:* Wikimedia Commons)

Tuesday (August 29), we widened our area of exploration from the top to the bottom of Saanich Peninsula, which encompasses two of the fifteen most populous municipalities in British Columbia: Saanich and Victoria. In the morning, after we checked out of MacDonald campgrounds, we visited the ferry terminal at Swartz Bay, cruised the top of the peninsula along Lands End Road, then drove all the way south on West Saanich Road (Route 17A), turned east on Keating Cross Road to join Patricia Bay Highway 17, and stopped at Cordova Bay to see the Fable Cottage Estate, a fairytale home with an animated "fantasy forest." This owner-built private estate was open to tourists during the summer months. Knotted beams, barrel doors, crafted hand-adzed furniture, and family heirlooms were some of the intriguing features of the Fable Cottage.

(Since our visit in 1989, Fable Cottage has disappeared from its location in Cordova Bay. Its new location is Denman Island, north of Nanaimo and south of Comox, on the Strait of Georgia.)

Driving further south, we stopped at Mount Tolmie Park for a good view of Victoria. From its 120-meter summit, we had a sweeping, 360-degree view of Saanich, Victoria, the Olympic Mountains and Mount Baker. On the way up, we saw a number of man-made structures and natural pathways through rocky outcrops to explore. A Garry oak mountain meadow along the trail provides an ideal place for picnicking.

Then, via Richmond Avenue, we drove further south to the two-hectare Gonzales Hill Regional Park with hopes of visiting the Gonzales Observatory (built in 1914). Unfortunately, it was closed.

From the Observatory, we went to see the modern Tudor-style Government House and Gardens (1401 Rockland Ave.), the official residence of the lieutenant governor of British Columbia (currently Steven Point). Fire destroyed the first mansion in May 1899. Wikipedia elaborates that the walls of the present T-shaped structure "are of rusticated blue, grey and pink British Columbia granite with Haddington Island stone trim, and the roof, which is two stories high in itself, has steeply pitched, chalet-style gables and numerous dormer windows." The 14.6-hectare property associated with Government House is divided into a multitude of zones by plant life or garden style. Thus, the British Columbia native plant garden contains species unique to the province.

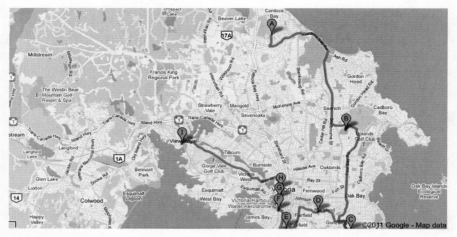

Map 98.2 Selected Attractions in City of Victoria, BC (August 29, 1989). *A*, Cordova Bay (Fable Cottage relocated on Denman Island, BC); *B*, Mount Tolmie; C=Gonzales Hill; *D*, Government House Gardens; *E*, Beacon Hill Park; *F*, Parliament Buildings/Inner Harbor Ferry Terminal; *G*, Bastion Square; *H*, Chinatown; *I*, Trans-Canada Highway 1 to Nanaimo-Vancouver Ferry Terminal.

We ate our lunch at Beacon Hill Park, about 2 km away from the Inner Harbor Ferry Ramp where we landed the day before. The sixty-two-hectare park is elegantly landscaped and manicured with bridges, lakes, and ponds, and an alpine and rock garden. Carmel and Junius enjoyed the park's Children's Farm attraction. We admired the forty-meter totem pole carved out of cedar by Chief Mungo Martin (1879-1962), alias *Nakapenkem*, a major contributor to Kwakwaka'wakw art, particularly wood sculpture and painting. The totem pole stood as another park attraction from 1956 to 2000.

In the early afternoon, we explored the Bastion Square overlooking the Victoria Harbor, where British colonial governor and fur trader James Douglas (1803-1877) first established Fort Victoria in 1843. Thanks to City Planner Roderick Clack, Bastion Square became an important heritage precinct in Victoria from the 1960s. It was the northern edge of Fort Victoria, and it became the center of civic life during the gold-rush era and afterward. Some of its buildings are among the oldest in Old Town and many are landmark structures in the city.

In a walking tour starting at the City Hall from Centennial Square, we went through Chinatown, the oldest one of its kind in Canada. The focal point of Chinatown is the five hundred to six hundred blocks of Fisgard Street, including famously narrow Fan Tan Alley, the old Chinese School, and a small selection of historic buildings and Chinese businesses. The visit to E. A. Morris tobacconist shop since 1892 was of special interest to me because it brought memories of my father's addiction to Jaffna-made *suruttus* (cigars).

Trans-Canada Highway

We realized that the law of diminishing returns was affecting our ability to enjoy all our hectic explorations. We had to start our journey on the Victoria-Winnipeg section of the Trans-Canada Highway (Highway 1) now because our schedule required us to leave Vancouver Island by evening and camp the night in the North Shore Mountains of Vancouver in the mainland.

The Trans-Canada Highway, uniformly designated as Highway 1 in the four western provinces, begins in Victoria, British Columbia, at the intersection of Douglas Street and Dallas Road (where the "Mile 0" plaque stands), and passes northward along the east coast of Vancouver Island for 99 km (62 miles) to Nanaimo (pop 78,692).

So we left downtown Victoria, got on Highway 1, and drove to Nanaimo, stopping at three places on the way—Duncan (pop 5,000), Chemainus (pop 4,100), and Ladysmith (pop 7,538). In Duncan, we saw the Glass Castle from outside. In Chemainus, we saw the wall murals of downtown buildings. In Ladysmith, we bought ice cream from a Malaysian vendor. In Nanaimo, we saw the Petroglyph (rock inscription) Park before we reached the ferry terminal. (Some call Nanaimo the Hub, Tub, and Pub City because of its association with the bathtub racing and the numerous "watering holes" in Old Nanaimo.)

From Nanaimo, we took the 7:00 p.m. ferry to cross the Strait of Georgia to Horseshoe Bay in West Vancouver—a distance of 48 km (30 miles). Our total fare was $29.

From West Vancouver, we drove 31 km east-northeast on Highway 1, past North Vancouver, to reach the 3,508-hectare Mount Seymour Provincial Park (established 1936), via Mount Seymour Parkway. We camped in the ski area at the top, with a beautiful view of Vancouver at night. For the record, we drove 220 km during the day.

Picture 98.2 View of the eastern flank, looking north—Mount Seymour Provincial Park, Vancouver, BC (September 2006). (Flank photo by Keith Freeman. *Source:* Wikimedia Commons)

SHELTON A. GUNARATNE

CHAPTER 99

British Columbia: Though Crazy for British Names, Canadians Omit Dickens

"**D**ICKENS" IS A small (eighty-four-block) neighborhood in east Vancouver, British Columbia. The neighborhood extends from East Twelfth Avenue (north boundary) to King Edward/ East Twenty-Fifth Avenue (south boundary) and from Fraser Street (west) to Knight Street (east). Kingsway runs diagonally through the neighborhood, which lies within the city-defined community of Kensington-Cedar Cottage. The area is dubbed "Dickens" because both of its two schools bear Charles Dickens's name.

As an avid fan of Charles Dickens, the famous nineteenth-century British novelist, I found it hard to swallow that the British Columbians have failed to name a single park, town, city, or province to memorialize Dickens even though they have overused the name of British explorer Captain George Vancouver (1757-1798) just as Americans have overused the name of President George Washington (1732-1799).

By ethnic origin, about one-half the population of British Columbia identify themselves as of English or Scottish origin. Another 18 percent identify themselves as Canadian. These three powerful ethnic groups explain the reason for the retention of British names and traditions (e.g., Victoria, Vancouver, High Tea at the Empress Hotel) more than a century and half after Queen Victoria declared the Colony of British Columbia a crown colony in 1858. Despite such abject loyalty to Britain, the British Columbia's majority, unlike Mr. Barkis (in David Copperfield), has *not been willing* to recognize Dickens! On his 1842 visit, Dickens found

Canada delightful after the disappointment of the United States. On the whole, Dickens found Canada a pleasant surprise.

These thoughts crossed my mind as we—Carmel (five), Junius (nine), Yoke-Sim, and I—passed through the so-called "Dickens" neighborhood in Vancouver Wednesday (August 30, 1989).

Because we camped overnight in one of the most scenic provincial parks in BC in a mountain wilderness setting encompassing several peaks, including Mount Bishop (1,509 meters), Mount Elsay, Runner Peak, and Mount Seymour (1,499 meters), we thought we would be able to capture the scenic splendor and do some hiking in the morning. The setting included several lakes and ponds too, including Elsay Lake (the largest), De Pencier Lake, Gopher Lake, and Goldie Lake. These lakes drained eastward into the Indian Arm. Other smaller lakes and ponds drained westward into the Seymour River.

Unfortunately, a thick fog had set in covering the mountains overnight dashing our hopes of enjoying scenic glory in the morning. We stopped at the café of the ski resort to pay our $10 camping fee and drove slowly downhill through thick fog for 13 km along the exit parkway to Highway 1. Thus, what should have been a scenic descent turned out to be a harrowing experience.

On the positive side, downtown Vancouver was only 30 km southwest of Mount Seymour PP campgrounds. Memories of my first visit to Vancouver some twenty-two years ago occupied my mind as we began our day's explorations.

Recalling the 1967 Visit

(See map 100.1, next chapter to trace this trip)

After completing my internship at the Eugene (Ore.) *Register-Guard*, I took off to Barrow, Alaska, to interview the Eskimos for my Assignment USA Project for the World Press Institute. I traveled by Greyhound bus from Eugene, Oregon, to Vancouver, British Columbia, via Seattle. An immigration official at the border crossing pointed out that my visa to reenter the US was no longer valid. Thus, my top priority on arrival at

Vancouver on a Monday (April 17, 1967) was to visit the US consul office to update my visa.

I toured downtown Vancouver by foot but could not see much of the city because I was scheduled to leave at 5:30 p.m. on the bus to Prince George (pop 70,981), 788 km to the north. The bus drove on Highway 1 (Trans-Canada Highway) for 344 km to Cache Creek (pop 1,037), and then followed Highway 97 (the "Caribou Trail"). I was lucky to sit by a lady who got on the bus at Abbotsford (pop 123,864) and she kept me in good cheer until she got off at Williams Lake (pop 10,744).

The bus stopped at Quesnel (pop 9,326) for morning tea and reached Prince George, "the British Columbia's Northern Capital," at 7:50 a.m. Tuesday.

The city originated as a trading post that fur trader Simon Fraser established in 1807 as Fort George, named for King George III. The city's dust repelled me, and the only thingamajig that caught my attention was a turbaned Sikh riding a motorcycle that I never expected to see in the caribou country.

I was delighted to leave Prince George two hours later on a Coachways bus, which headed northwest all the way to Prince Rupert (pop 12,815), a distance of 717 km on Highway 16. The bus stopped at Burns Lake (pop 2,107) Panhandle for lunch and at Cedarvale/*Minskinish* (unincorporated) in the Skeena River Valley for supper. Farms and the wilderness dominated the route.

Railway magnate Charles M. Hays founded Prince Rupert in 1910. He named the settlement after Prince Rupert of the Rhine, hoping for favors from the prince. This port city (nicknamed "the Rainbow City") is the land, air, and water transportation hub of British Columbia's North Coast.

Our bus reached the Prince Rupert terminal at about 10:30 p.m. Immediately, I started looking for overnight accommodation, when I ran into Paul Young, a Native American returning from service, who was also looking for a place to sleep. We joined forces and approached the Friendship House (744 Fraser St.), which allowed us to sleep on the floor of its dining room.

Wednesday morning, Paul and I had to arrange the tables of the Friendship House dining room as a return favor. A very good deal! Then, both of us got on board the ferry "Taku," which left Prince Rupert at 9:30 a.m. carrying people and their vehicles to all ports along the Alaska Panhandle. But that's another story (see chapter 4)

Back to 1989

Thus, I was no stranger to British Columbia whereas Carmel, Junius, and Yoke-Sim were. They already had a lesson on the vagaries of weather conditions in British Columbia as we descended the Mount Seymour Parkway zigzagging through Hidden Lake, Mystery Lake, Dog Mountain Dinky Peak, Flower Lake, and Mountain Forest. After a short distance to the west of Maplewood Park, we merged into Trans-Canada Highway 1, where we turned north on Lynn Valley Road to enter the 250-hectare Lynn Canyon Park—a forested park that features awesome creek and waterfall views and hiking trails through the temperate rain forest. Located 23 km south west of the Mount Seymour Provincial Park, the park comes under the authority of the District of North Vancouver municipality.

We spent more than one hour in the park hiking on the fifty-meter high Lynn Canyon Suspension Bridge (built in 1912) section of the Baden-Powell Trail, which runs 50 km from Horseshoe Bay to Deep Cove. (Wikipedia points out that this trail is host to the annual Knee Knackering North Shore Trail Run (or Knee Knacker), a half-day-long run along the entire length of the trail. The district is also home to the Grouse Grind hiking trail, a steep vertical climb sometimes referred to as "God's Stairmaster.")

On the far side of the bridge, a trail leads to a natural canyon-formed swimming pool (called the "Thirty Foot Pool"). The creek provides an ideal spot for cliff jumping. The park is a second growth forest, with most of the oldest trees aged eighty to hundred years. The park's five exhibits—its ecology center, plant gallery, animal gallery, human gallery, and Exploratorium—constitute another attraction. After leaving the park, we drove to Lynn Village shopping area in North Vancouver to nourish ourselves with whatever edibles we craved. From there, we went to the Park Royal mall in West Vancouver to collect maps and tour guides from the Royal Canadian Automobile Club.

　　SHELTON A. GUNARATNE

Map 99.1 Our tour route of Vancouver, BC (August 1989). *A,* Mount Seymour Provincial Park; *B,* Maplewood Farm; *C,* Lynn Canyon Park; *D,* North Vancouver; *E,* West Vancouver; *F,* Stanley Park; *G,* Holy Rosary Cathedral; *H,* Chinatown; *I,* Hotel Patricia; *J,* St. Roch National Historic Site; *K,* Jericho Beach Park; *L,* VanDusen Botanical Gardens; *M,* Quean Elizabeth Park; *N,* "Dickens" neighborhood (east Vancouver); *O,* Dear Lake Park/Burnaby.

Now, let me clear up possible nomenclature confusion. British Columbians have nonplused the world by naming too many places to memorialize Captain George Vancouver. What they call North Shore applies to the city of North Vancouver (pop 43,165); the District of North Vancouver (pop 82,562), which surrounds the city of North Vancouver; and West Vancouver (pop 42,131). These three are separate municipalities, each with its own mayor. The city of Vancouver (pop 642, 843) stands across the Salish Sea on its south shore. Located on the Burrard Peninsula, Vancouver lies between Burrard Inlet to the north and the Fraser River to the south. Greater Vancouver (pop 2.2 million) consists of twenty-one municipalities, including the four neighboring Vancouvers. The most populated municipalities in this group in rank order of population size are Vancouver, Surrey, Burnaby, Richmond, Coquitlam, Delta and Langley. In this light, the identification of "Dickens" as a neighborhood of east (lower cased) Vancouver is likely to increase confusion.

Picture 99.1 The Lynn Canyon Suspension Bridge (September 2006). (Photo by Tim Hollosy. *Source:* Wikimedia Commons)

We crossed the Burrard Inlet on the First Narrows Bridge (or Lions Gate Bridge) and landed on the 405-hectare Stanley Park (founded in 1888), which has an 8.8 km seawall surrounding it. Forested with trees—some more than hundred years old, the park offers more than 200 km of trails and roads. It attracts more than 8 million visitors a year. We ate lunch at the Prospect Point picnic area; then, we stopped to see the Third Beach, the Second Beach, and the totem poles. Our next visit was to downtown Vancouver, where we stopped at:

- Holy Rosary Cathedral (646 Richards St.) to see its stained-glass windows.

SHELTON A. GUNARATNE

- Harbor Center Complex, where we walked along the gaslight shopping area.
- Chinatown (centered on Pender Street), where we ate at a restaurant, and also visited the Dr. Sun Yat Sen Classical Chinese Garden, where Yoke-Sim felt quite at home.

We checked in at Hotel Patricia (203 East Hastings St.) to spend the night in relative comfort after four nights of camping outdoors. Later in the evening, I walked a few blocks east of the hotel to Oppenheimer Park, where I saw several courtesans parading themselves in an alley between Hastings and Cordova streets.

Thursday (August 31) morning, we continued our explorations in Vancouver.

First, we crossed the Burrard Bridge to visit the Saint Roch National Historic Site of the Vancouver Maritime Museum. Launched in May 1928, Saint Roch was the first ship to completely circumnavigate North America.

Then, we drove along the shore of the English Bay to Jericho Beach and the associated Jericho Park, from where we entered the scenic campus of the University of British Columbia. We passed the M.Y. Williams Geological Museum, which exhibits an 80-million-year-old Lambeosaurus found in Alberta in 1913, spectacular rocks, minerals, and fossils. The scenic beauty of the campus fascinated us.

For us, the main attraction of the day was the twenty-two-hectare VanDusen Botanical Gardens (est in 1975) in the Shaughnessy neighborhood. We spent about an hour in the gardens enjoying its outstanding plant collection gathered from all over the world. Its special attractions include carved totem poles, large stone sculptures, and a Korean Pavilion. Then, heading east, we stopped for lunch at Queen Elizabeth Park (4600 Cambie St.) on Little Mountain in King Edward Station neighborhood. A surprise attraction in this park was its sunken garden.

Finally, we drove past "Dickens" neighborhood in east Vancouver and stopped at Deer Lake Park in Burnaby, where we visited the art gallery and walked in the scenic rose and rhododendron gardens.

We concluded our tour of Vancouver at about 3:00 p.m. and drove 479 km northeast to Sicamous (pop 3,192), British Columbia, to camp overnight at the Yard Creek Provincial Park, where we arrived about 10:30 p.m. The day's travel distance totaled 554 km.

Picture 99.2 A montage of Vancouver images: (clockwise from top) Downtown Vancouver as seen from the southern shore of False Creek; University of British Columbia campus; Lions Gate Bridge; boats on the harbor; Granville Island; Chinatown gate; and totem poles in Stanley Park (2008). (Photo by Dolphin Jedi. *Source:* Wikimedia Commons)

(In the next chapter, I shall dwell on the drama of man versus nature that we encountered on that tedious drive.)

SHELTON A. GUNARATNE

CHAPTER 100

British Columbia: Drama on Canadian Rockies

RITISH COLUMBIA COVERS a land area of 925,186 sq. km with a population density of 4.8 people per square kilometer. One-half the British Columbia population lived in the Greater Vancouver metropolitan area. For me, the vast patches of uninhabited land I saw in my foray into Caribou Country in 1967 were utterly depressing.

The population density of the adjoining provinces of Alberta (5.8), Saskatchewan (1.7), and Manitoba (2.2) along Trans-Canada (Highway 1) was even thinner than that of British Columbia except for the slightly higher figure for Alberta. Thus, driving across Canada from Victoria, British Columbia, to Winnipeg, Manitoba, a distance of 2,457 km, with vast patches of sparsely inhabited barren land, straddling metropolitan conurbations would be as "interesting" as crossing the Nullarbor or the "Big Sky" country unless one were an authentic misanthrope.

After leaving Burnaby Thursday (August 31, 1989), we—Carmel (five), Junius (nine), Yoke-Sim, and I—drove 64 km southeast on Trans-Canada 1 to Abbotsford, where the highway turns northeast to reach Hope (pop 6,185), located on the confluence of Fraser and Coquihalla Rivers, about 84 km away.

About 7 km east of Hope, at an uninhabited location known as "Othello," we left Trans-Canada 1 to get on what was then British Columbia's only toll road, Highway 5 (also known as the Coquihalla Highway or "the Coke"). We thought it was worth the $10 toll to drive on the 186 km toll road (a freeway since 2008) rather than sticking on to Trans-Canada 1 all the way to Cache Creek and turn east to Kamloops, Besides, I had already been to Cache Creek and beyond on my 1967 journey on the Caribou Trail. The toll was well worth the extra distance of roughly 75 km we saved by taking "the Coke."

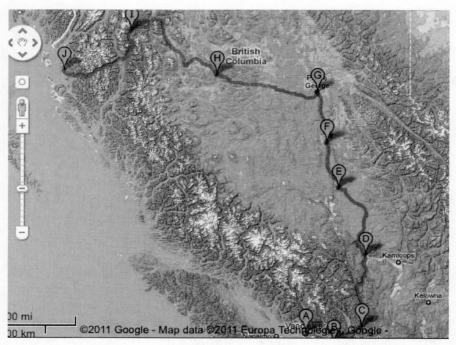

Map 100.1 From Vancouver to Prince Rupert via Prince George—my solo tour of British Columbia in 1967 (distance covered is 1,519 km). *A*, Vancouver; *B*, Abbotsford; *C*, Hope/Exit to Coquihalla toll road; *D*, Cache Creek/ Junction of Highway 97 and Trans-Canada (Highway 1); *E*, Williams Lake; *F*, Quesnel; *G*, Prince George; *H*, Burns Lake; *I*, Cedarvale/Minskinish; *J*, Prince Rupert.

Torrential Rain

Highway 5 generally follows the Coquihalla River for about 60 km near Hope. Some 35 km north of Othello, after passing through five interchanges, Highway 5 reaches the Great Bear snowshed, a landmark on the route. About 13 km north of the snowshed, after passing through another interchange and the 1,244-meter Coquihalla Pass, Highway 5 reaches (the former) tollbooth. It goes through three more interchanges and one mountain pass, the 1,444-meter Clapperton Creek Summit,

SHELTON A. GUNARATNE

in its remaining 72 km between Merritt (pop 6,998) and its end is at a junction of Highways 1 and 97 within the Afton area of Kamloops (pop 92,882), the largest community in the Thompson-Nicola Regional District and the location of the regional district's offices.

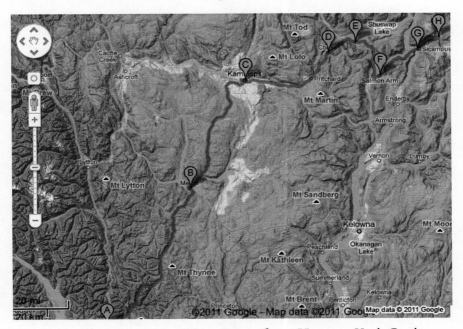

Map 100.2 Our 1989 Tour Route from Hope to Yard Creek Provincial Park (365 km). *A*, Hope/Othello; *B*, Merritt; *C*, Kamloops; *D*, Chase; *E*, Sorrento, *F*, Salmon's Arm; *G*, Sicamous; *H*, Yard Creek Provincial Park.

The mountainous terrain we passed through was prone to outbursts of torrential rain. Yoke-Sim drove our car on "the Coke" from Merritt to Kamloops when thunder and lightning warned us of an impending rainstorm. In Kamloops, we stopped at the Aberdeen shopping mall to buy some knickknacks; and at Safeway to purchase the food we needed for dinner. Currently, Aberdeen Mall is home to more than hundred stores and services including restaurants like East Side Mario's and New York Fries (Wikipedia).

Despite the threat of torrential rain, we decided to drive as far as possible to come close to the British Columbia-Alberta borderline—361 km further to the east.

Picture 100.1 A landmark feature of the southern leg of BC Highway 5 is the Great Bear Snowshed (September 2007). (Photo by Dimbeko. *Source*: Wikimedia Commons).

The threat materialized as I drove my faithful Toyota Camry wagon toward the village of Chase (pop 2,409), located on the south shore of Little Shuswap Lake. Trans-Canada 1 snakes around Mount Chase and Squilax Mountain to reach the unincorporated community of Sorrento on the southeastern edge of Shuswap Lake. Then, the road takes a sharp southward turn to reach the current city of Salmon Arm (pop 16,205) on the shores of Shuswap Lake where the Salmon River empties into the Salmon Arm reach of the lake. The 1998 wildfire destroyed five thousand hectares of forestland south of Salmon Arm, including twenty homes and fifteen barns.

Although my description of the mountainous terrain we crossed might conjure up images of scenic splendor, the conditions of driving through the Canadian Rockies imposed on us much fear and tension. The windshield wipers of our vehicle could not at times cope with the velocity of rainwater lashing on our vehicle. Road visibility diminished to near zero at times so much so that we realized the folly of taking up this unwinnable fight with nature by ignoring the ample warning signs of the impending rainstorm. Now, nature was punishing us with its combined forces of rain, wind, thunder, and lightning. Gripped by tension, Carmel and Junius hugged their pillows in the backseat of the car to distract themselves from the wrath of nature. We remembered the similar but less aggravating plight we faced when we drove through a thick fog Wednesday morning on the Mount Seymour Parkway.

Picture 100.2 Bastion Mountain as seen from Salmon Arm of Shuswap Lake (December 2010). (Photo by Metallurgist. *Source*: Wikimedia Commons).

The anger of the cosmic forces that control the skies appeared to have subsided by the time Trans-Canada Highway 1 took us 31 km northeast along the southern shore of Salmon Arm all the way to Sicamous (pop 3,132), located opposite the Bastion Bay. This area was the habitat of the Secwepemc or Shuswaps tribe of Native Americans before the influx of white settlers, particularly after the Big Bend Gold Rush of 1864.

It was 10:30 p.m. when we reached our campground in the Yard Creek Provincial Park in Malakwa, 16 km east of Sicamous. The British Columbia-Alberta boundary line was another 208 km to the northeast.

Yard Creek provided the rest we needed after driving a distance of 554 km during the day.

CHAPTER 101

British Columbia and Alberta: A B.C. Cop Fines Us $75 at the Border

E—CARMEL (FIVE), JUNIUS (nine), Yoke-Sim, and I—got up on Friday (September 1, 1989) morning watching the American dippers and a variety of little bird species dive into the icy waters of Yard Creek and "fly" along under the water, looking for their "yummy" water insects. We watched them on the rocks along the creek in the interior wet belt of cedar and hemlock forest and lush undergrowth.

We unabashedly relished the breath of cool fresh air scented by the overnight heavy rains that helped the creek to quench its perennial thirst for supplementary "fuel." We were privileged to occupy one of the 175-hectare park's sixty-five shaded campsites. We ate our breakfast at the park's log picnic shelter, and tried out some of the park's hiking trails.

Upon leaving Yard Creek, we continued driving east on Trans-Canada 1 and stopped at the Revelstoke Dam Visitor Center, 64 km to the east. We learnt that the hydroelectric Revelstoke Dam spanned the Columbia River—the very same river that determined the border between Washington and Oregon from the Tri-Cities (Richland-Kennewick-Pasco), Washington, to Astoria, Oregon. (see chapters 89 and 91). BC Hydro completed the powerhouse in 1984 with four units capable of generating 1,980 megawatts. (A fifth generating unit with the capacity to produce an additional 500 MW was scheduled to operate in 2010.)

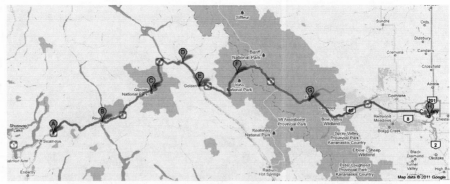

Map 101.1 Crossing the Canadian Rockies. *A*, Yard Creek PP; *B*, Revelstoke Dam/Visitor Center/Mount Revelstoke NP; *C*, Glacier NP; *D*, Donald (at) Columbia River northbound; *E*, Golden (at) Columbia River northbound; *F*, Field/Yoho NP/BC-Alberta boundary; *G*, Banff/Banff NP (Alberta); *H*, Calgary (Alberta).

Now we were witnessing the Canadian side of the vast Columbia River with Columbia Lake as its primary source. The mighty river flows 320 km northwest from Columbia Lake, then takes a steep southward turn at Kinbasket Lake to Mica Creek (pop 700) and flows into the 130 km long Lake Revelstoke, an artificial reservoir formed by the Revelstoke Dam, six km north of Revelstoke (pop 7,000). Revelstoke Dam is one of the fourteen hydroelectric projects on the mainstream of the Columbia River.

(The original highway from Revelstoke to Donald-Golden area followed the Columbia River around the Big Bend to avoid crossing Rogers Pass. We followed the new shortened Trans-Canada Highway 1 built over the pass between 1956 and 1962. This also allowed the construction of Mica Dam, which flooded part of the Big Bend as Kinbasket Lake.)

On the new Trans-Canada 1, we drove through the twenty-six-thousand-hectare Mount Revelstoke National Park, which was established in 1914. The park's two boardwalks have been the magnets of tourist attraction: the (five-hundred-meter) Giant Cedars Boardwalk interpretive trail that twists through a stand of old-growth western red cedar and hemlock trees, some more than eight hundred years old; and the (1.2-km) Skunk Cabbage Boardwalk interpretive trail that leads through valley bottom rain forest and fragile wetlands inhabited by muskrats, beavers, bears, and the strange skunk cabbage plant (Wikipedia).

Picture 101.1 Eastbound Canadian Pacific Railway freight train crossing the 600 feet-long Stoney Creek Bridge, 325 feet above the creek at Rogers Pass (1988). (Photo by David R. Spencer. *Source:* Wikimedia Commons)

Next, we headed further northeast to enter the 134,900-hectare Glacier National Park (established 1886), where we stopped at the Rogers Pass National Historic Site—the location of the park's visitor center. The site depicts the human history of the region through accounts of first climbs, last spikes, lives lost, and railway lines laid. Excited by the story of how the ferocious avalanches roaring down the Selkirk Mountains at speeds exceeding 300 km an hour caused the Canadian Pacific Railway to abandon its attempt to construct a railway line though the dense wilderness, we decided to walk along the track abandoned in 1910 ready to lay our lives at the mercy of the cosmic forces that decide the timing of avalanches. In 1910, while clearing one slide, another slide came down Avalanche Mountain, killing sixty-two men. Thereupon, the CPR "decided that the only way to keep the transportation corridor open was to tunnel under Mount Macdonald thereby eliminating 16 kilometers of the most hazardous railway line" (Wikipedia).

Ten glaciated peaks ranging from 2,600 m to 3,390 m in height dominate the Glacier National Park, which we left through its East Gate.

Continuing further east on Trans-Canada 1, we crossed the 2,000 km long Columbia River again at Donald (a small sawmilling community) from where we traveled 28 km south along the river to the town of Golden (pop 3,811), very close to the BC-Alberta boundary.

Golden, nestled in the Rocky Mountain Trench, is located at the confluence of Columbia and Kicking Horse Rivers. Three mountain ranges and five national parks surround the town. Columbia Lake, the source of Columbia River, lay 168 km further to the southern end of the trench. Because we had already explored British Columbia for five days, we did not want to spare more time to see the primary source of the river. Besides, we already had a close-up look at the Donald-Golden segment of the northbound first 320 km of the river, which makes an about turn at Kinbasket Lake.

We ate our lunch in Golden, where we also stopped at a bank to get Canadian currency for greenbacks. It dawned on us that we were now on a World Heritage Site recognized as such by UNESCO in 1984—the contiguous national parks of Yoho, Banff, Jasper, and Kootenay, as well as the Mount Robson, Mount Assiniboine, and Hamber provincial parks. However, because time was running out, we agreed to visit only the spots that weren't too far off from Trans-Canada 1.

Our next stop was Field, the headquarters of the 340,065-hectare Yoho National Park (established 1886), 58 km south northeast of Golden. Field is the last outpost of British Columbia with Banff occupying the Alberta side of the border and Yoho the British Columbia side. At Yoho, we went to see the Natural Bridge, a creation of the fast flowing Kicking Horse River and the Spiral Tunnels—two tunnels that make a gigantic loop inside the mountain. A train headed uphill would enter the lower tunnel and exit on the upper tunnel and then cross over the lower track on a trestle. The spiral tunnels were necessary to decrease the slope of the track, as it made its way up to Kicking Horse Pass.

An Unexpected Turn

We were about to leave British Columbia when we fell into a traffic trap set up by Her Majesty's British Columbia Provincial Police to make a fast buck. We drove downhill on Trans-Canada 1 from Watson Peak to Lake Louise with several vehicles trailing us. Traffic law did not permit overtaking on the highway marked with double solid lines. An elderly couple driving ahead of us at slow speed held up the smooth flow of traffic spreading impatience among the drivers who began to honk their horns. Yoke-Sim egged me on to overtake the vehicle of the elderly couple. Little did I know that the royal constabulary was waiting for me at the foothills to pull me up and express the displeasure of Her Majesty for violating British Columbia traffic laws. Officer S. Crowe, God bless him (I still remember his name!), issued me a warrant to appear in the traffic court or pay a fine of $75.

Touring Alberta

That sour experience made me happy to leave British Columbia behind and enter the province of Alberta (pop 3.7 million), the most populous of the three prairie provinces that we had to travel through on this journey—the other two being Saskatchewan and Manitoba. Alberta is named after Princess Louise Caroline Alberta (1848-1939), the fourth daughter of Queen Victoria and Prince Albert. People who identify themselves as British (47.5 percent) or Canadian (20.5 percent) make up more than two-thirds of the population. Calgary (pop 1.1 million) is Alberta's largest city. Edmonton (pop 730,372) is the province's capital.

After entering Alberta, we hopped over to the 1.7-million-hectare Banff National Park, the oldest national park of Canada established in 1885, two years after the discovery of the thermal mineral springs exhibited at the Cave and Basin National Historic Site. It constitutes the lowest component of nine sulfurous hot springs clustered in three groups on the northeast flank of Sulphur Mountain. We also visited the beautiful

Cascade Rock Gardens encircling the Park Administration Building. A trail winding through the terraced garden passes through arches, gazebos with seats, and blooming patches of flowers, and manicured lawns. At various turns are views of the surrounding mountains.

Picture 101.2 Banff, Alberta (2007). (Photo by Jiri Eischmann. *Source:* Wikimedia Commons).

From Banff (pop 8,721) town, we drove 129 km east to Calgary, where we arrived about 8:00 p.m., Mountain Time. Our driving distance for the whole day was 520 km. We checked into Windward Hotel (119 Twelfth Ave. SW) for the night.

CHAPTER 102

Alberta and Saskatchewan: On the Canadian Prairie from Calgary to Regina

THE FOUR OF us—daughter Carmel (five), son Junius (nine), wife Yoke-Sim, and I—spent Saturday (September 2, 1989) morning to get a sense of Calgary that is located in the Grassland region of southern Alberta. Two major rivers run through the city. The Bow River is the largest and flows from the west to the south. The Elbow River flows northward from the south until it converges with the Bow River near downtown.

In 1883, the Canadian Pacific Railway reached the area and built a rail station in Calgary, which soon turned into an important commercial and agricultural center. The CPR headquarters are located in Calgary today. After the arrival of the railway, the dominion government adopted the policy of leasing grazing land at minimal cost (up to 40,470 hectares for 2.5 cents per hectare per year). This policy enabled the establishment of large ranching operations in the outlying country near Calgary.

Already a transportation and distribution hub, Calgary quickly became the center of Canada's cattle marketing and meatpacking industries. The world famous Calgary Stampede, still held annually in July, grew from a small agricultural show and rodeo started in 1912 by four wealthy ranchers to "the greatest outdoor show on earth" (Wikipedia).

With the discovery of oil in Alberta, Calgary's economic ups and downs began to reflect the highs and lows of the oil industry. Today, while the oil and gas industry comprise an important part of the economy, Calgary city has invested a great deal into other areas such as tourism and high-tech manufacturing.

Our plan for the day was to continue east on Trans-Canada 1, cross the prairies into adjoining Saskatchewan, and stay overnight in Regina, the provincial capital of Saskatchewan. The distance between Calgary and Regina is 758 km. (But, at the end of the day, our deviations from Highway 1 caused us to drive more than 63 km extra.)

Morning in Calgary

We spent the morning getting to know downtown Calgary. Just three blocks to the north of Windward Inn where we spent the night, we gawked at the 191-meter Husky Tower (101 Ninth Ave SW) built at a cost of $3.5 million in 1967. Renamed Calgary Tower in 1971, it became notable for its revolving restaurant and its carillon. The 215-meter Petro-Canada Centre's west tower overtook the Calgary Tower as the tallest structure in Calgary in 1983.

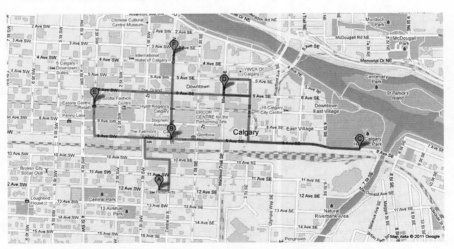

Map 102.1 Sites we visited in Calgary, Alberta (September 2, 1989). *A*, Windward Inn; *B*, Calgary/Husky Tower; *C*, Fort Calgary Historical Park@ confluence of Elbow River with Bow River; *D*, "The Family of Man" sculpture exhibit; *E*, Devonian Gardens@ The Core Shopping Center; *F*, Chinatown.

Next, we found our way to the Fort Calgary Interpretive Centre on Ninth Avenue Southeast at the confluence of Elbow River with the bigger Bow River. The North-West Mounted Police established the fort in 1875 to comply with a federal order to force out whiskey traders from the area. Originally called "The Elbow" or "Bow Fort," the fort made of pine and spruce logs was eventually named after a castle at Calgary Bay on Scotland's Isle of Mull. The fort was in operation until 1914.

Backtracking to downtown, we stopped at the Calgary Education Centre (515 Macleod Trail SE) to see the set of statues called "The Family of Man" that sculptor Mario Armengol (1909-1995) built for Britain's Pavilion at Expo '67. Maxwell Cummings & Sons purchased the 6.4-meter-tall metal statues and donated them to the Canadian Board of Education for public exhibition.

Then, we visited the one-hectare Devonian Gardens, a large indoor park and botanical garden located on the Stephen Avenue pedestrian mall. The park is enclosed with glass and covers one full city block on the top floor of The Core Shopping Centre, which was known as the Toronto Dominion Shopping Complex at the time of our visit. Opened in 1977, the construction of the project cost $9 million. (This attraction was scheduled to reopen in 2011 after its closure in 2008 for a major reconstruction.)

Picture 102.1 "The Family of Man" sculpture exhibit in downtown Calgary, Alberta (October 6, 2006). (Photo by Thivierr. *Source:* Wikimedia Commons).

SHELTON A. GUNARATNE

Finally, running short of time, we drove through Calgary's Chinatown district (pop 1,361), the fourth largest in Canada, on our way to rejoin Trans-Canada 1 for the day's long journey east. We found Chinatown along Centre Street in the northeast area of Downtown Calgary immediately north of the Downtown East Village. We ate lunch at a restaurant in Chinatown. Wikipedia attests that Calgary's Chinese Cultural Centre with its traditional architecture and decor (styled after the Temple of Heaven in Beijing) is the largest facility of its kind in North America.

Back on Trans-Canada 1

After leaving Calgary, our first stop on Trans-Canada 1 was Brooks (pop 12,498), about 186 km to the southeast. Located in the steppe region known as the Palliser's Triangle, Brooks has a semi-arid climate, which produces long, dry, and cold winters with little snowfall in comparison to the rest of Canada. We visited the Alberta Special Crops and Horticultural Research Centre, where we toured the rose garden and the perennial flower trials. However, to the dismay of Carmel and Junius, the wildlife center's pheasant-raising facility was closed for the day.

Map 102.2 From Calgary to Regina (758 km) *A*, Calgary, AB; *B*, Brooks, AB; *C*, Medicine Hat, AB; *D*, Walsh, AB; *E*, Maple Creek, SK; *F*, Swift Current, SK; *G*, Herbert, SK; *H*, Chaplin, SK; *I*, Moose Jaw, SK; *J*, Regina, SK.

Thereafter, we "explored" the prairies with brief stops in the following communities:

- Medicine Hat (pop 61,097), 107 km southeast of Brooks. Well, known for its natural gas fields, it is also called "The Gas City." We stopped at a downtown park for refreshments. The Badlands

Guardian Geological Feature, a landscape formation taking the form of a head wearing a feathered headdress, lies 40 km to the east of the city.

- Walsh (pop 55), about 53 km east of Medicine Hat. This hamlet lies immediately to the west of the Saskatchewan border.
- Maple Creek (pop 2,198), about 53 km east of Walsh. It is the town in Saskatchewan closest to the Alberta border. We stopped at the Tourist Information Centre, where a friendly guide helped us with the tourist literature we needed.
- Swift Current (pop 15,048), 138 km northeast of Maple Creek. It was 8:30 p.m. when we reached Swift Current where we bought gasoline and our food. We ate dinner at a quiet spot along a downtown street. Yoke-Sim took over driving from here to Regina.
- Herbert (pop 742), about 47 km northeast of Swift Current. The Herbert Train Station Museum is "the best place to stop for information on the town of Herbert" (Wikipedia).
- Chaplin (pop 292), about 44 km east of Herbert. In 1997, Chaplin Lake was designated a Western Hemispheric Shorebird Reserve Network site—the highest designation that a reserve can receive.
- Moose Jaw (pop 35,629), 85 km east of Chaplin. Its intriguing name was the reason we stopped in this city. Some say that the city derived its name from the shape of the Moose Jaw River. Others say that the name is a corruption of the Plains Cree word *moscâstani-sîpiy* (meaning "a warm place by the river"). The replica of "Mac the Moose" standing on the edge of the city reminded me of "Max the Moose," the emblem of Dryden, Ontario, that we saw as we traversed Trans-Canada 17 in 1988 (see chapter 87).

We arrived in Regina, 75 km east of Moose Jaw, close to midnight after crossing a long stretch of the prairies. Carmel and Junius helped me set up our tent on a site at the King's Acres Campground, 1 km east of Regina on East Gate Drive.

Our tired bodies were only too willing to yield to the call for sleep. Yet I could hear the sound of raindrops falling on our tent as we curled up in our sleeping bags intent on disregarding such minor distractions of nature.

SHELTON A. GUNARATNE

Picture 102.2 "Mac the Moose" stands on the edge of Moose Jaw, Saskatchewan (June 10, 2008). (Photo by Magnus Manske. *Source:* Wikimedia Commons).

CHAPTER 103

Saskatchewan and Manitoba: From Regina to Winnipeg

OUR RETURN JOURNEY from Longview, Washington, to Moorhead, Minnesota, via Trans-Canada 1 enabled us—Carmel (five), Junius (nine), Yoke-Sim, and I—to get a good grasp of the geographic and demographic features of Canada. Sunday (September 3, 1989) was our ninth day out on the road since we started the tour. Our plan was to quit Trans-Canada 1 at Winnipeg, 571 km further to the east, and drive another 357 km south on Manitoba 75 and Interstate 29 to reach Moorhead.

Saskatchewan, with its population of 1.1 million, is a sparsely inhabited province. Almost 45 percent of the province's inhabitants live in the capital city Regina (pop 210,000) and the province's largest city Saskatoon (pop 257,300), 257 km to the northwest of Regina. In terms of ethnic origin, 61 percent of Saskatchewanians identify themselves as British (26.5 percent English, 19.2 percent Scottish, and 15.3 percent Irish). German (30 percent) was the largest single ethnic group. (See chapter 99 for comparison with British Columbia). Originally a part of Northwest Territories, in 1905 Saskatchewan became the eighth province to join Canada.

Regina ("The Queen City") was the name that Princess Louise, the fourth daughter of Queen Victoria or *Le Victoria Regina*, gave the city in 1882 to honor the queen. Louise was then the wife of John Campbell, the Duke of Argyll (better known as Marquess of Lorne) who became the fourth governor-general of Canada (1878-1883). That the Reginans have kept the imperial name to this day attests to their willingness to be loyal to the British royalty. Just like the Victorians in British Columbia!

Wikipedia asserts that Regina was a *tabula rasa*, without topographical features other than the small spring run-off Wascana Creek. Early planners took advantage of such opportunity by damming the creek to create an artificial lake to the south of the central business district and constructing the elaborate 260-meter-long Albert Street Bridge across the new lake.

In 1906, Regina's importance was further assured when the new province of Saskatchewan made the city its capital. Wascana Centre, created around the focal point of Wascana Lake, remains Regina's signal attraction and contains the Provincial Legislative Building, both campuses of the University of Regina, the provincial museum of natural history, the Regina Conservatory (in the original Regina College buildings), the Saskatchewan Science Centre, the Norman MacKenzie Art Gallery and the Saskatchewan Centre of the Arts. Because of the pressure of time, we could not see all of them.

Exploring Regina

After leaving Kings Acres Campground in the morning, we began to explore several of the tourist attractions in Regina although the Sunday closures restricted our choice of what to see. From the Kings Acres Campground, where we camped overnight, we started the day with a visit to the Victoria Square Shopping Center, where we stopped at the Safeway supermarket to purchase the food we needed for the rest of the day. Located in the heart of Regina's East End, "the Vic Square Mall" was first opened in 1983. It currently accommodates more than forty-five stores and professional services.

Then, we headed west to explore downtown Regina, including the Market Square, where the hustle and bustle of a normal weekday eluded us. However, we thought that we succeeded in capturing the essence of Regina by patiently visiting a few key attractions, which kept us in the city until 3:00 p.m.

The star attraction we visited was the Royal Saskatchewan Museum (RSM), which was established in 1906 as a museum of natural history to "secure and preserve natural history specimens and objects of historical and ethnological interest" (Wikipedia). Between 1906 and

1945, the museum occupied several premises including those of the Provincial Legislative Building and the Normal School. After World War II, the provincial government built the current premises on the corner of Albert Street and College Avenue, the site of the abandoned Chateau Qu'Appelle Hotel, as a Saskatchewan Golden Jubilee project. Governor General Vincent Massey opened the new premises on May 16, 1955. To reflect the areas of devotion, the museum renamed itself the "Saskatchewan Museum of Natural History." This title stuck until 1993 when it received royal designation from Queen Elizabeth II and became the Royal Saskatchewan Museum (Wikipedia). "The museum had a very good display of geological development," I wrote in my diary.

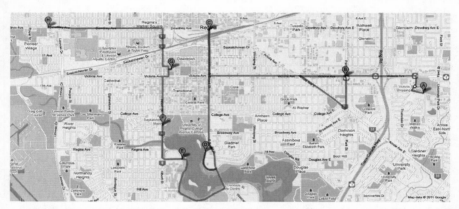

Map 103.1 Places we visited in Regina, Saskatchewan (September 3, 1989). *A*, Victoria Square Shopping Center/ the "Vic Square Mall"; *B*, Kings Acres Campground; *C*, Downtown Regina/ Market Square; *D*, Diefenbaker Homestead (Wascana Centre); *E*, Legislative Building (2405 Legislative Drive); *F*, Royal Saskatchewan Museum (2445 Albert Place); *G*, Royal Canadian Mounted Police Centennial Museum; *H*, Government House (4607 Dewdney Ave.).

The other attractions in Regina we visited in 1989 included the following:

- The Diefenbaker Homestead (located 1967-2004 on south side of Wascana Lake. Current location: Sukanen Ship Pioneer Village Museum, south of Moose Jaw). Driving south on Wascana Drive, we stopped at Wascana Place for coffee. Crossing over to Lakeshore Drive, we reached the then site of the Diefenbaker Homestead. John Diefenbaker was prime minister of Canada from 1957 through 1963. His "homestead" was moved from Borden to Regina in 1967. He died in 1979 at the age of eighty-four.

- The Provincial Legislative Building (2405 Legislative Drive overlooking Wascana Lake). Built between 1908 and 1912 in the Beaux Arts style at a cost of $ 1.75 million, the building was designed by the Maxwell brothers, Edward and William Sutherland, of Montreal. We joined a conducted tour of the building.

Picture 103.1 Saskatchewan Legislative Building in Regina (March 4, 2007). (Photo by Victor D. *Source:* Wikimedia Commons).

- Government House (4607 Dewdney Ave.), constructed in 1889 as the official residence of the lieutenant governor for the North-West Territories. The vice-regal offices and residence were moved out of Government House in the 1940s because of the anticolonial political climate of the time. In 1958, the original building was renamed Saskatchewan House. In 1984, the offices of the lieutenant governor (but not the residence) returned to the original building, which resumed the name Government

House. It is now "a museum of the 1900 period under Lt. Gov. Amédée Forget, and a hospitality facility for government and non-profit organizations" (Wikipedia). A female guide gave us an excellent tour of the quarters. We ate lunch at the premises of Government House, which some believe is a haunted mansion.

- The Royal Canadian Mounted Police Centennial Museum (RCMP; closed in 2006). Established in 1933, the museum operated in a number of facilities for its first sixty years. In 1973, Queen Elizabeth II officially opened the museum (on the site we visited) in honor of the RCMP's centennial. The museum exhibited many artifacts relating to the colorful history and traditions of the RCMP. The museum closed permanently in October 2006, and the collection moved to the RCMP Heritage Center, a $40-million project. Its phase 1 (located near the RCMP headquarters at 5907 Dewdney Ave.) opened in 2007.

Back on Highway 1

We left Regina midafternoon heading further east on Trans-Canada 1 intending to get as close as possible to Winnipeg, Manitoba.

Map 103.2 From Regina to Winnipeg—places of interest. Saskatchewan: *A*, Regina (capital); *B*, Indian Head; *C*, Grenfell; *D*, Crooked Lake Provincial Park; *E*, Whitewood; *F*, Fleming (border town) Manitoba: *G*, Kirkella (border hamlet); *H*, Virden; *I*, Brandon; *J*, Portage la Prairie; *K*, Winnipeg (capital).

Indian Head (pop, 1,758), 78 km east of Regina, was our first stop. This town is the location of the federally operated Prairie Farm Rehabilitation

Administration (PFRA) experimental farm and tree nursery that produces seedlings for shelterbelts. We visited the site and picnicked in the scenic premises.

At Grenfell (pop 947), 57 km southeast of Indian Head, we decided to skip the 51 km stretch of Trans-Canada 1 up to Whitewood (pop 869) because we wanted to enjoy the scenic splendor of spur Highway 247 running along the northern shores of Crooked Lake and Round Lake. We stopped at the Crooked Lake Provincial Park, where Yoke-Sim cooked a splendid dinner out of the groceries we purchased in the morning at the Safeway in Regina. The lakeshore scenery provided the ideal background to relish our meal. Carmel and Junius were ecstatic that they had a chance to play around for a while. Highway 47 north took us to the spur road, and Highway 9 brought us back to Trans-Canada 1 at Whitewood. Heavy rains slowed down our journey considerably as we reached the Whitewood junction. Thus, our unplanned detour added an extra 51 km to our journey and cost us almost two hours of extra travel time.

Picture 103.2 Crooked Lake Provincial Park in Saskatchewan

Some 70 km southeast of Whitewood, we crossed the Saskatchewan-Manitoba border lying between Fleming (pop 75) in Saskatchewan and Kirkella (an unincorporated hamlet) in Manitoba. Winnipeg (pop 633,451), the provincial capital of Manitoba, lay 330 km east of the Manitoba-Saskatchewan border.

Yoke-Sim took charge of driving at Virden (pop 3,020), stopped briefly at the McDonald's in Brandon (pop 46,000) for refreshments, and guided us all the way to Portage la Prairie (pop 12,728), which we reached at 1:00 a.m. Monday. Because we were thoroughly pooped out after traveling 607 km during the day, we agreed to call it quits even though Winnipeg was 84 km further away.

We camped overnight at the (now defunct) Norquay Beach Provincial Recreation Park, 16 km east of Portage la Prairie. We went to sleep confident that we could terminate our Canadian adventure Monday after a peek into Winnipeg.

CHAPTER 104

Manitoba: After Winnipeg, We Learn—Penny Wise, Pound Foolish

WHEN WE LEFT our home in Moorhead, Minnesota, July 17, 1989, on my summer internship and family holiday trip to the Pacific Northwest, we hoped to return to our own cozy "castle" to unwind and relax after our tedious ten-day camping trip through the Trans-Canada Highway 1 on September 4, 1989.

When we left home on this two and one-half month excursion, we kept our Moorhead home under lock and key. During my ten-year teaching stint in Rockhampton, Australia, we were wont to shut off power and other utilities when we left our Queensland-style home on stilts during long breaks. We expected to accrue substantial savings by applying the Oz practice to our new habitat in the Village Green area of Moorhead.

On our return home about 9:00 p.m. on Monday (September 4), we learnt the hard way that the application of the Oz practice to our Minnesota home was one of the "dumbest" things we had ever done. Our savings on utilities turned out to be peanuts compared to the losses we incurred by so doing.

To our surprise and dismay, we found our basement flooded with approximately five centimeters of water. Because we had shut off electricity, the sump pump hardwired to our home's electrical system had ceased to operate. (Homes with basements use this device to pump out water accumulated in a water-collecting sump pit.) The intrusion of water rendered the basement carpeting unusable and spoilt the collection of books and journals stacked in the bottom shelf of a couple of bookcases. Thus, we learned the wisdom expressed in the idiom "penny wise, pound foolish."

Background

Considering that we didn't arrive at our campsite, east of Portage la Prairie, until after 1:00 a.m. on Monday, we slept until late morning because we decided to take it easy on the final day of our travels. It was about 11:00 a.m. when we left our overnight campsite.

Back on Trans-Canada 1, as we crossed the meandering Assiniboine River a couple of times on our way to Winnipeg, we realized that we have been driving on the drainage basin of the 1,070 km Assiniboine from eastern Saskatchewan onwards.

The Assiniboine forks with the 885 km Red River of the North at "The Forks" park in downtown Winnipeg, the capital and the most populous city of the province of Manitoba. The Red, which originates at the confluence of the Bois de Sioux and Otter Tail Rivers in the United States, flows awkwardly from south to north through the flood-prone Red River Valley—encompassing the metropolitan areas of Fargo-Moorhead and Grand Forks—and empties itself into Lake Winnipeg in Manitoba that spews out into Hudson Bay.

Manitoba has a population of 1.2 million with almost 60 percent concentrated in the metropolitan Winnipeg area. The majority in the province, almost 55 percent, claims to be of British origin—English, 22.9 percent; Scottish, 18.5 percent; and Irish, 13.4 percent. Remarkably, 19.1 percent of Manitobans claim German ethnicity while 14.7 percent claim Ukrainian ethnicity. Almost 20 percent of these groups identify themselves to be Canadian as well.

Doings in Winnipeg

As we drove into the western outskirts of Winnipeg on Trans-Canada 1, the first tourist attraction we passed was *Grant's Old Mill* (2777 Portage Ave.). Cuthbert Grant, leader of the Métis at the Battle of Seven Oaks, established the first watermill of the Red River settlement on this site in

1829. The museum offers tours of the site to demonstrate how the early settlers used millstones to grind grain into flour.

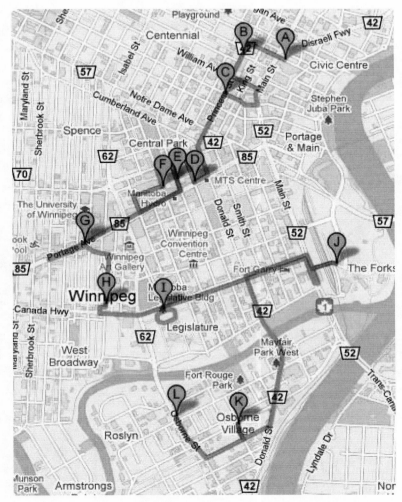

Map 104.1 Sites I visited in downtown Winnipeg 1989-1990. *A*, Manitoba Museum of Man (190 Rupert Ave.); *B*, Chinatown; *C*, Spaghetti Factory (291 Bannatyne Ave.); *D*, Times Bar (301 Hargrave St.); *E*, Winnipeg Free Press (300 Carlton St.); *F*, Promenade-on-the-Arc Motor Hotel (defunct); *G*, Canadian Broadcasting Corporation (541 Portage Ave.) *H*, Downtown Winnipeg; *I*, Legislative Building/Government House complex; *J*, The Forks Park/Market at intersection of Assiniboine and Red Rivers; *K*, McCoy Communications Ltd.; *L*, Yuk Yuk's comedy club (moved out).

Going further east, we stopped at the 445-hectare Assiniboine Park (established 1904), which includes the 283-hectare Assiniboine Forest to the south, Assiniboine Zoo, Assiniboine Conservatory, Assiniboine Park Pavilion, formal and informal gardens, a sculpture garden, a miniature railway, an outdoor band shell theatre for performing arts, and several other attractions. The Canadian predilection for British fads are again evident in this mammoth park, where English landscape style is applied to 36 percent of its total area. Carmel (five) and Junius (nine) found this vast parkland an ideal place to test their levels of energy. All of us thoroughly enjoyed the English Garden "for its luxuriant display of thousands of annual and perennial flowers" (Wikipedia).

Picture 104.1 Chinese Cultural Centre in Chinatown, Winnipeg (July 20, 2006). (Photo by Cayla. *Source:* Wikimedia Commons).

Assiniboine Park brought to my mind memories of Stanley Park in Vancouver, British Columbia (see chapter 99). Again, we had no illusions of visiting all the attractions that Winnipeg offered. We had to pick and choose a few that interested us within the limited time we spent in the city. We opted to visit the following:

1. *Winnipeg Chinatown* (pop 20,000). Because of her Chinese ethnicity, my wife Yoke-Sim insisted on visiting Chinatown located on King Street between James and Higgins Avenues. The pioneer Chinese established the site in 1908, but they failed to get official recognition until 1968. Pacific Avenue is the old heart of Chinatown with the most historic buildings. The Kingstown strip mall stands at the intersection of King Street and Henry Avenue. We ate a lavish lunch at the Kum Koon Garden (257 King St.) restaurant. Yoke-Sim splurged all the Canadian currency she had on purchasing Chinese groceries to take home.

2. *Manitoba Legislative Building* (450 Broadway). We joined the 3:30 p.m. guided tour of the seven-meter-tall building, which was originally named the Manitoba Parliament Building. Architects Frank W. Simon and Henry Boddington III designed the neoclassical-style building, the construction of which began in 1913. The lieutenant governor's reception room, located in the east corridor of the building, is an anachronism that violates the principles of human dignity by reserving it for the exclusive entertainment of royalty and similar dignitaries. Although maintained with the money collected from all taxpayers, its exclusivity implicitly degrades the ordinary people as scum. The fifty-seven-member Legislative Assembly and the lieutenant governor form the legislative branch of the government of Manitoba.

3. *Government House* (10 Kennedy St.), the official residence of the lieutenant governor of Manitoba. First opened in 1883, the Government House is located on the southeast side of the Legislative Building complex.

4. *The Forks* (in downtown Winnipeg), the confluence of the Assiniboine River with the Red River of the North, is currently a park, a playground, a market, a marina, and many other things. The Forks will be the site of the Canadian Museum for Human Rights (the first national museum outside of Ottawa). If all goes according to plan, it will open in 2012.

We left Winnipeg at about 4:00 p.m. Monday for the homeward journey to Fargo-Moorhead. We drove south on the highway that runs parallel to the Red River—on Manitoba 75 up to the Canadian border town of Emerson and then on Interstate 29 from the United States town of Pembina—until we reached our "castle," which was silently waiting to teach us a lesson.

Picture 104.2 The Assiniboine River forks with the Red River at The Forks in downtown Winnipeg (September 3, 2005). (Photo by Diderot. *Source:* Wikimedia Commons)

Six Months Later

Six months later, I visited Winnipeg again on a Thursday-Saturday study break (March 22-24, 1990). I was one of seven faculty members who accompanied twenty-eight mass communications majors on a field trip to study the operational mechanics of the mass media in Winnipeg.

Friday 8:00 a.m., we visited the premises of McKim Communications, Ltd. in Osborne Village. The company welcomed us with coffee and donuts. Their brief visual presentations on advertising and public relations were superb. John DaCastro was our contact with the company.

SHELTON A. GUNARATNE

On Friday at 10:00 a.m., we went to the premises of the Winnipeg Free Press (300 Carlton St.), where ombudsman Barry Mullin gave an impressive talk on the newspaper and gave us a tour of the facilities. Mullin said that the starting salary of a college graduate at a Canadian newspaper was about $35,000.

Then on Friday afternoon, we visited the premises of the Canadian Broadcasting Corporation (541 Portage Ave.). Our contact Alex Wash Shyn welcomed us and gave us a guided tour.

I became more familiar with the downtown layout of Winnipeg on this visit because I had the chance to gallivant the streets on my own.

We lodged the two nights of our stay in Manitoba at the (now defunct) Promenade-on-the-Ark Motor Hotel in downtown. On Thursday night, I joined three of my colleagues—Martin Grindeland, Mark Strand, and Bob Larson—to go to Times (301 Hargrave St.) for a beer. There, a laser-light show was scheduled to begin at 11:30 p.m. However, we were unwilling to hang around for the show.

On Friday night, the four of us decided to try out Mark Breslin's Yuk Yuk's (108 Osborne St.), a national comedy club chain in Canada, owned by stand-up comedian Mark Breslin and established in 1977 by Breslin and Joel Axler. This dinner-comedy combo adventure cost each of us a hefty $24. As the only non-white in the audience, I inevitably became the subject of the comedian's humor at one point of his delivery, punctuated with an abundance of expletives.

On Saturday morning, I ate breakfast at Portage Place with the same three colleagues. Then, in the shivering cold, we walked to the Manitoba Legislative Building, which I had already explored on my first visit. Strand was hung up on eating lunch at the Old Spaghetti Factory (291 Bannatyne Ave.), which we reached on our coach.

Our coach was scheduled to depart Winnipeg at 4:00 p.m. on Saturday to return home. In the meantime, I joined the group to visit The Manitoba Museum of Man-Nature (190 Rupert Ave.), the largest museum in Manitoba. (The current adult admission to all three of its features—the museum, the planetarium, and the science gallery—is $19.) At the planetarium, I saw a feature on satellites. The interpretive galleries of the museum focus on Earth History, Arctic/Sub-Arctic, Boreal Forest, Nonsuch, Hudson's Bay Company, Parklands/Mixed Woods, Grasslands and Urban. Nonsuch is a replica of a ship that sailed from England to the Hudson Bay in 1668.

SHELTON A. GUNARATNE

CHAPTER 105

Texas: San Antonio—Our Gateway to Big Bend National Park

HAVING CAMPED IN almost every national park in the West and the Midwest, I turned next to the South. My attention focused on the Big Bend National Park located in south Brewster County, Texas. The Big Bend National Park encompasses approximately 324,220 hectares. The mammoth size of the park becomes clear when you realize that almost one-quarter of the 1,000 miles of Rio Grande/River Bravo, which makes up the boundary between the United States and Mexico, flows through the Big Bend territory. Within the 118 twisting miles that also marks the southern boundary of the park, the river's southeasterly flow turns abruptly to the northeast thereby forming the "big bend" of the Rio Grande.

This geographical layout of Big Bend intrigued my family—daughter Carmel (seven); son Junius (eleven); spouse Yoke-Sim; and me—so much that we decided to skip the rigors of early wintry weather in our neck of the woods in Fargo-Moorhead in late November 1991 to enjoy the warmer sunshine of southwestern Texas for at least nine days.

We left Fargo at 8:00 a.m. on a Saturday (November 23, 1991). Ariyaratna Wijetunga, a faculty colleague of mine, gave us a ride to the Fargo Airport, where we boarded the Northwest flight to Minneapolis. There, we took another Northwest flight to Memphis, Tennessee. Then, we boarded yet another Northwest flight to San Antonio (pop 1.33 million), the second largest city in Texas after Houston.

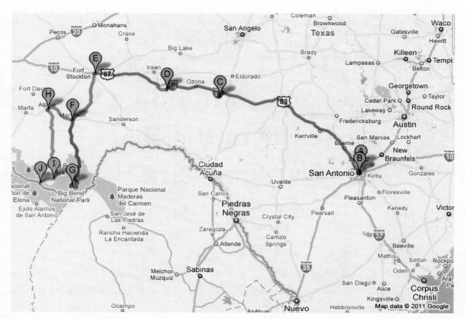

Map 105.1 Our tour route from San Antonio to Big Bend National Park (November 1991). *A*, San Antonio International Airport; *B*, Downtown San Antonio; *C*, Caverns of Sonora; *D*, Fort Lancaster on scenic highway 290; *E*, Fort Stockton; *F*, Marathon; *G*, Big Bend National Park Service Headquarters; *H*, Alpine; *I*, Study Butte-Terlingua; *J*, Lajitas.

On arrival in San Antonio at 5:00 p.m., we rented a Ford Taurus automatic from National® Car Rental. We used this vehicle as our storage and "home-away-from-home" for the duration of our entire trip. Next, we drove two miles southeast from the airport to Best Western Town House Motel (942 NE Loop 410) to check-in for our overnight stay in room 66. After settling down, we drove a dozen or so miles south and west on New Braunfels Avenue to downtown to buy our food and other camping needs at a Handy Andy supermarket on West Commerce Street.

On Sunday morning, we drove some 182 miles northwest on Interstate 10 to Sonora (pop 3,008), the administrative seat of Sutton County. Our plan was to tour San Antonio after we finished the more exciting exploration of the Big Bend National Park.

SHELTON A. GUNARATNE

Picture 105.1 Yoke-Sim stands by the side of a huge stalactite and a stalagmite during the tour of the Caverns of Sonora (November 24, 1991).

Because all four of us were cave buffs, we stopped to visit the Caverns of Sonora National Natural Landmark (1711 Private Road 4468), a star tourist attraction on this route, located eight miles west of Sonora. Wikipedia extols the landmark as "a world-class cave because of its stunning array of calcite (a carbonate mineral) crystal formations, especially helictites." Having paid a total of $24 for admission, we were happy to join the 11:30 a.m. tour of the caves, an exciting 1.5-hour experience that introduced us to an enormous variety of stalactites, the icicle-like elongated mineral formations that hang from the ceilings and sides of limestone caverns; stalagmites, the corresponding formations on the floor of the cavern; and helictites, which usually come out from cave walls horizontally and look like tangles of spaghetti. Jack Burch, a caver from Oklahoma, saw the cavern for the first time in 1956. It has been open to the public since July 1960.

Back on our way on Interstate 10, about seventy miles west of Sonora, we decided to take a scenic detour on SR 290 to see the thirty-three-hectare Fort Lancaster State Historic Site in the Pecos River Valley of Crockett County. Established by Captain Stephen Decatur Carpenter on August 20, 1855, Fort Lancaster was one of four forts built along the western Texas frontier "to guard the military supplies, commercial shipments, and immigrants" (Wikipedia) along the military route between San Antonio and El Paso.

Then, we got back to I-10 and drove another eighty miles northwest to Fort Stockton (pop 7,846), where we arrived at 5:00 p.m. We stayed overnight at Sands Motor Inn (1801 N. Dickinson Blvd.), where Carmel and Junius had a whale of a time in the facility's heated swimming pool and the Jacuzzi. We ate dinner at Kentucky Fried Chicken. We also shopped at Walmart to buy various knickknacks we needed.

On Monday (November 25,) morning, we toured the Fort Stockton historical district starting from the welcoming figure of Paisano Pete, the then world's largest (10 ft. tall and 22 ft. long) roadrunner (now demoted to second place by a challenger in Las Cruces, N.M.). Going south on Main Street, we had a quick look at the Annie Riggs Memorial Museum, Saint Joseph Catholic Church, Zero Stone Park, the Oldest House, etc. We also stopped to see the historic fort and other historic sites on the way. Built in 1859, the fort was named for US Naval Commodore Robert Field Stockton. Until abandoned in 1886, the fort provided employment for freighters and laborers and a market for farmers, stockmen, and merchants.

Picture 105.2 Paisano Pete, the world's largest roadrunner at the time of our visit, greeted us in Fort Stockton on November 25, 1991. (Photo by Talshiar. *Source:* Wikimedia Commons)

We left Fort Stockton about 10:00 a.m. on US 385 and headed southwest to Marathon (pop 470) in Brewster County (pop 13,000), one of the most sparsely populated areas of the country showing a density of one person per square mile. Most of the county's population resided in two towns: Marathon and Alpine (pop 6,460), which lie 86 and 117 miles respectively to the north and northwest of the park headquarters (1 Panther Drive). We stopped in Marathon to visit the historic Gage Hotel (205 N First St.), a restored hotel of the 1920s with original pine floors and woodwork. Another attraction in the town is La Loma del Chives, a unique eco village or hostel that demonstrates the applicability of sustainable technologies in enterprises such as organic gardens, papercrete construction, and in solar and wind projects. We skipped Alpine and the western gateway communities of Study Butte-Terlingua (pop 267), and Lajitas (pop 48), about fifteen miles apart, which have experienced growth in recent years but still lag behind Marathon and Alpine in terms of population.

Instead, Yoke-Sim took over driving at Marathon and continued southward on US 385 and entered the Big Bend NP from its northern entry point at Persimmon Gap, where we arrived at 12:50 p.m. But we found the ranger station there closed presumably for lunch. Therefore, we drove twenty-eight miles further south on Persimmon Gap Drive and stopped at the Panther Junction Visitor Center and park headquarters to pay the $5 park entrance fee and buy a couple of road guides to explore its attractions.

CHAPTER 106

Texas: Mule Riding in Mexican Border, Dipping Feet in Hot Springs, and Making Camping a Super Adventure

S I MENTIONED in chapter 105, we entered the Big Bend National Park through the three-mile long Persimmon Gap, the park's northern entrance or exit. Named for the Texas persimmon trees that grow in abundance in the nearby *arroyos* (desert washes), the gap has been a pass through the Santiago Mountains on the Comanche Trail, the Marathon-Boquillas stagecoach route, the Old Ore Road, and also a route used by the US Army.

A few miles south of the gap is the Dog Canyon Trail, forking east and leading to the Nine Point primitive campground. The waters from the Nine Point Draw and the Bore Spring Draw have cut the gorge that created the Dog Canyon, now considered the dividing line between Santiago Mountains and Dead Horse Mountains to the south. The story goes that the Dog Canyon was so named by an early traveler who found a dog guarding an abandoned ox-drawn wagon in the canyon.

One lesson we learnt on the first day of our visit to the Big Bend was this: Heavy rains transformed the desert washes into muddy raging torrents. When the flood subsided, the water sank into the gravel and continued to flow underground. We saw it happening before our very eyes!

Picture 106.1: Daughter Carmel (seven) and wife Yoke-Sim at the entrance to the Big Bend National Park (November 25, 1991).

Driving further south on Persimmon Gap Drive, we passed the Dagger Mountain, so named because of the Giant Daggers that grow along its slopes. We learned that the mountain took the shape of a dome or anticline when geological forces pushed up the molten rock under the limestone beds. We skipped the seven-mile improved auto trail that forks eastward to Dagger Flat and Sierra del Caballo Muerte. About two miles into the same trail lies the northern end of the Old Ore Road, which zigzags its way twenty-five miles to Rio Grande Village.

Then, we drove past Tornillo Flat, the expanse of flatlands on both sides of Tornillo Creek, the largest drainage in the park. Once covered with a solid growth of native grasses, this expanse has turned into one of the most barren areas of the park because of soil erosion caused by overgrazing. We learned that from our entry point at Persimmon Gap, we had ascended a long, gentle gravel road up to Tornillo Flat.

We, then, stopped at the Fossil Bones exhibit in the vicinity of Tornillo Creek Bridge. This was a display of bones imbedded in sandstone of early Eocene Age dating back to 50 million years. Among the bones were those of Coryphodon, an extinct mammal.

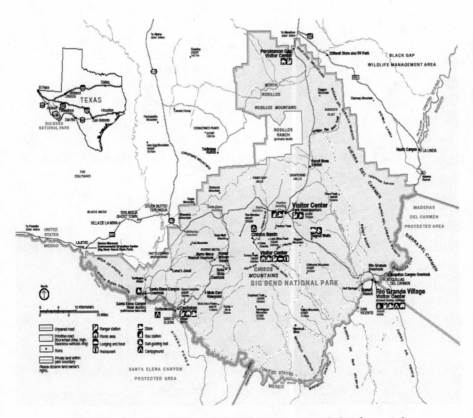

Map 106.1 Big Bend National Park. We camped the first night at Rio Grande Village Campground, the second night at Cottonwood Campground, and the third night at Chisos Basin Campground. (*Source:* US National Park Service)

Yet further to the south was the Hannold Draw, named after Nina Hannold, who homesteaded a ranch in the vicinity but died of blood poisoning in 1911 at the age of twenty-nine.

Finally, we arrived at the Big Bend National Park headquarters in Panther Junction (elevation 3,750 ft.) to pay for official admission to the park (currently $20 per car for one week) and to get advice from the visitors' center. We walked the adjoining Panther Path, a self-guided nature trail that orients the visitor to desert plants.

Rio Grande Village

We had to travel another twenty miles southeast on the scenic drive to the Rio Grande Village to get to the riparian site on the National Park Service campground we had reserved for our stay overnight. (The fee for camping was $5 compared to the current $14.) This drive offered us the chance to enjoy a variety of desert scenery, which became increasingly spectacular, as we got closer to Mexico's Sierra del Carmen, which took on a rosy glow at sunset.

On this drive, about 1.5 miles east of Panther Junction, is the so-called K-Bar ranch site—the location of the Chihuahuan Desert Research Station. Less than a mile from the ranch house, built in 1927, is the K-Bar primitive campground.

About five miles southeast of Panther Junction, we passed the primitive gravel road that heads southwest to Nugent Mountain; then, turns south to Glen Spring, on the western side of Chilicotal Mountain (4,108 ft.). Less than a mile ahead on the scenic drive, we stopped at Dugout Wells (so named because the first home built there was dug into the ground to form a dugout shelter), where we walked along a short self-guiding loop named the Chihuahuan Desert Nature Trail.

Closer to the Rio Grande Village, just after passing the turnoff to Old Ore Road, we drove through a short tunnel and stopped at the Rio Grande Overlook to view Sierra del Carmen in its magnificent splendor.

Immediately thereafter, we reached the Rio Grande Village campground, where we set up our tent, cooked and ate our dinner, and curled into our sleeping bags, hoping for a good night's slumber. But severe cold caused us misery in the dead of night, forcing us to wrap ourselves in our jackets.

Day 2 at Big Bend

Tuesday (November 26, 1991) morning, we woke up to the calls of coyotes. (I almost felt that the rangers had orchestrated these calls of their wild chums to clear the campgrounds early.) After eating breakfast at the camp in a riparian setting, we began to explore the Rio Grande Village and its surroundings until midafternoon.

Our exploration began with a walk through the one-quarter-mile Rio Grande Village Nature Trail in the southeastern corner of the campground. The trail provided a delightful introduction to the flora and fauna in the area.

Then, we explored the banks of Rio Grande just across the Mexican community of Ojo Caliente in Coahuila State. We learned that Rio Grande Village was about twenty-five miles northeast of Mariscal Canyon, the location of Rio Grande's "big bend." (We were short of time to drive fifteen miles southwest on River Road East to Solis and then hike through Cross Canyon Trail and Mariscal Canyon Rim Trail to Talley to view the splendor of the massive gorge at the "big bend" itself.)

Known as Rio Bravo del Norte in Mexico, the Rio Grande flows from its headwaters near Alamosa, Colorado, through New Mexico and down the Texas-Mexico border through Big Bend to Brownsville and the Gulf of Mexico. It offers spectacular views of high mountains, the desert floor, wild animals, beautiful sunrises and sunsets, breathtaking flora and fauna, and just about everything.

We ambled to the visitors' center to get advice on our travel plans and to watch a short documentary on the area. Thereafter, we took off five miles east on the Rio Grande Village Drive to the Boquillas Canyon Overlook so that we could get a view of the canyon before visiting it. The limestone cliffs we passed through were rampant with hechtia, a plant of the pineapple family.

We reached the entrance to the 1.4-mile (round-trip) Boquillas Canyon Trail along the riverbank. The trail climbs over a low limestone hill and drops to the banks of the Rio Grande near some Indian mortar holes. We had great views of the river and mouth of Boquillas Canyon. We noted the 150-feet cliffs on each side of the canyon.

The adventure of the day commenced after we reached the international crossing to the "primitive" village of Boquillas del Carmen (next to Ojo Caliente) in the Mexican state of Coahuila.

Operated entirely by the Mexican villagers, it is an informal crossing at the end of a dirt road over a hill that descends to the river. You can cross over to Mexico by alerting the operators of the rowboats on the opposite riverbank. Soon, we received a boat ride to Boquillas del Carmen for a fare of $2 per adult—the cheapest fare we paid for landing in a foreign country! No passports or visas were involved just like when I stepped into Canada from the United States during our visit to the Voyageurs National Park in Minnesota in 1988 (see chapter 86).

We could not refuse the locals' offer of renting us two mules (donkey-horse hybrids) at $3 each for the duration of our visit. Thus, we turned into "Yankee doodles who went to town riding on their ponies" to the utter delight of Carmel and Junius. In town, we ate a delicious authentic Mexican lunch comprising burritos, tacos, and tamales downed with beer and Coke—all for $5. We rode the mules back to the river for our 2:00 p.m. return boat ride to Rio Grande Village in Big Bend National Park.

Picture 106.2 Son Junius (eleven) and daughter Carmel (seven) along the Boquillas Canyon Trail (November 26, 1991).

Picture 106.3 The author and wife Yoke-Sim riding their rented mules from the Mexican town of Boquillas del Carmen to the international crossing along Rio Bravo del Norte for the 2:00 p.m. rowboat ride to the United States (November 26, 1991).

(*Note*: Wikipedia explains that until the 7/11 terrorist attack on the US, Boquillas del Carmen functioned as a small (300 resident) town that was primarily dependent on the Big Bend tourist trade, with visitors crossing the Rio Grande to visit the village's bar, restaurant, and taco stands. Tourism options included pony and donkey rentals, parties at Park Bar, and overnight stays at a local bed and breakfast, The Buzzard's Roost. All that ended in 2001. In 2011, however, the federal government announced its intention to reopen the Texas-Mexico border crossings.)

Before we left Rio Grande Village on our return journey to Panther Junction, we wanted to visit another landmark in the vicinity. So back on the scenic drive, about a mile west of the Tornillo Creek Bridge, we turned south into a two-mile gravel road that follows a rather rough wash through the limestone hills to a point overlooking the confluence of Tornillo Creek and the Rio Grande. J. O. Langford, who homesteaded here in 1908, built a house on the bluff above the spring to create a health resort using the spring's natural hot water for baths. Langford sold the property to the state of Texas in 1942. We were in the famous Hot Springs. We gave into our natural instincts and dipped our hands and feet into the hot springs to enjoy the sensation. We crossed the Big Bend National Park from the southeast to the southwest via the park headquarters at Panther Junction and spent the rest of the afternoon exploring Ross Maxwell Scenic Drive. We camped overnight at the National Park Service's Cottonwood Campground adjacent to Castolon.

CHAPTER 107

Texas: Leaving Big Bend with Fond Memories and Circling Around to Absorb Its Ambience

ON OUR WAY to Cottonwood Campground in the Rio Grande floodplain Tuesday (November 26) late afternoon, we focused on exploring the area along the Ross Maxwell Scenic Drive. Because we did not have adequate time Tuesday to explore all the tourist spots on this scenic drive, we spent much of Wednesday as well to cover the spots we missed. However, so as not to confuse the reader, I shall comment on the attractions we encountered in spatial order from north to south as if we covered everything on the forward journey to Cottonwood.

The thirty mile Ross Maxwell Scenic Drive, which follows a fault line along the eastern edge of Burro Mesa, starts at Castolon/Santa Elena Junction, about thirteen miles west of Panther Junction. Burro Mesa, so named for the herd of wild burros (donkeys) that used it as their grazing ground, is a gently westward-sloping mesa standing high above the surrounding desert floor to the northwest of the Chisos Mountains. At its highest point the mesa reaches an elevation of 4,431 feet. The much slower erosion of the hard, igneous rocks crowning Burro Mesa in comparison to the softer rocks on the opposing side of the fault has over time down-dropped one side of the valley accommodating the fault line.

The Chisos Mountains, which form a great wall across the valley to the east, provided us with vistas of incredible rock formations as we drove south. At one point, we looked through the igneous wall to see Casa Grande (5,401 ft.) framed by the Window (4,600 ft.). Evidence shows that Oak Creek, which flowed down the drainage below the Window, was a clear stream that created the best grassland in West Texas in the 1880s. Greedy ranchers brought thousands of cattle, sheep, and goats to this area and the overgrazing caused severe erosion to the extent that the creek stopped flowing. Oak Creek today is a far cry from what it used to be.

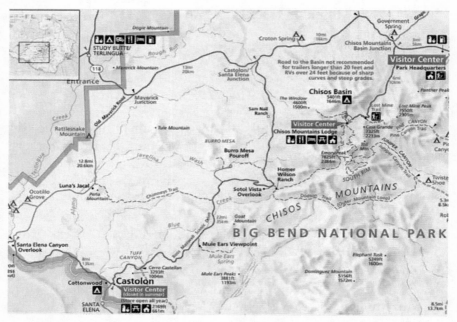

Map 107.1 Western section of Big Bend National Park showing the route and landmarks between Cottonwood/Castolon and Chisos-Basin campgrounds. (*Source*: US National Park Service)

Not too far away, a short path forking to the west takes the visitor to the abandoned Old Sam Nail Ranch house along Cottonwood Creek that Sam Nail and his younger brother Jim built in 1916. The house had a concrete floor, a viga and cane ceiling, and a corrugated metal roof. Close to the Nail ranch are several rock outcroppings that resemble rock walls or dikes. We crossed one of these dikes that ran up the hillside more than a mile to the east.

Next, at the parking lot on the highest point of the drive, the Homer Wilson (Blue Creek) Canyon Overlook provides a good view of the "red rock" upper Blue Creek Canyon and the restored bunkhouse of the defunct Homer Wilson Ranch, one of the largest in the region prior to the establishment of the park 1933-1944. Blue Creek is the main drainage area west from the high Chisos Mountains. A short trail leads down to the ranch buildings and connects with the Blue Creek Canyon and Dodson trails. Emory Peak (7,832 ft.), the highest point of the Big Bend National Park, lying majestically to the northeast of the ranch, seemed to exhort hikers to visit its peak.

Picture 107.1 The author with Casa Grande in the background (November 28, 1991).

A short distance away is the Sotol Vista Overlook. The park pundits advice the hoi polloi not to bypass it because the "view from the end of this short road is one of the best in the park and the first point along the Castolon Road from which you can see Santa Elena Canyon"—still fourteen straight miles to the southwest. Sotol Vista is so named because of the heavy growth of sotols—large bright green plants with sharp teeth along the margins of the leaves—that cover the Sotol Vista ridge.

Those who want to see the Burro Mesa Pouroff can turn west on the 1.5-mile side road that runs north to the base of the colorful cliffs of Burro Mesa. There, they can hike the one-half mile trail into a hidden box canyon to a high pouroff or dry (water) fall. A variety of desert wash plants and magnificent geology are the other attractions.

Closer to the southern end of the scenic drive, we stopped in the parking area at Mule Ears Viewpoint to see the landmark Mule Ears Peaks formed by dikes that erosion has sculptured into the shape of the ears of a mule. About a mile to the northwest of the peaks is the Mule Ears Spring. As you proceed further south, another landmark, Tuff Canyon, appears on the west side of the scenic drive. (Park pundits opine that these two landmarks are worthy of in-depth exploration.) Tuff Canyon was carved out of soft volcanic tuff (compressed ash). Travelers can easily observe the deep and narrow canyon from two viewing platforms. They can also enter and hike through the gorge.

We reached the floodplain of Rio Grande at the southern end of the scenic drive and turned west to Cottonwood Campground, adjacent to Old Castolon, the location of the park's oldest building used from 1900-1924. We were in the Castolon Historic District. Castolon, originally established as a cavalry camp, later served as the headquarters of the La Harmonia Company. At the campground, we ate a delightful dinner at Campsite 18, where we spent another riparian night.

Day 3 in Big Bend

Wednesday (November 27), soon after breakfast, we left the campground and drove eight miles west along the Rio Grande floodplain to the Santa Elena Canyon Overlook, the starting point of 1.7-mile Santa Elena Canyon Nature Trail, "one of the grandest spectacles in the park." After viewing the mammoth (1,500 ft.) cliffs of the spectacular canyon from the overlook, we waded across the Terlingua Creek to reach the nature trail, which climbs several short switchbacks and then gradually descends along the banks of the Rio Grande/Rio Bravo del Norte. Lush riparian vegetation and towering vertical cliffs of solid limestone surround the hikers. The thrill of the day for me was when I cooed Aussie-style in the middle of the trail, and I heard the canyon returning my echo loud and clear!

Picture 107.2 Carmel (seven) and Junius (eleven) at Campsite 18 of Cottonwood Campground, where we set up our tent to stay overnight on Tuesday (November 26, 1991).

Picture 107.3 The author, his wife Yoke-Sim, and their daughter Carmel in the "echo chamber" of the Santa Elena Canyon (November 26, 1991).

When we backtracked our way on the floodplain to Cottonwood, we found hardly any evidence that this expanse of flatland was a center of cotton farming from 1921 until the record flood of 1974 that destroyed the farmland and deposited the heavy ginning machinery at the bottom of the river. The foundation of the gin is visible adjacent to the Cottonwood Campground.

From Cottonwood, we drove a mile southeast to Rio Grande to see the crossover point to the Mexican village of Ejido del Santa Elena. Before 7/11, Mexicans from this village in Chihuahua State had crossed the border freely to shop at Castolon. For the sake of history, we too stopped at La Harmonia Company store to buy some groceries for camping. Then, we resumed our return journey north on Ross Maxwell Scenic Drive after a pause to look at Cerro Castellan (3,293 ft.). I have already mentioned the landmarks along this drive that we explored both on this trip and on the day before. We ate lunch at Mule Ears Overlook.

SHELTON A. GUNARATNE

At the Castolon/Santa Elena Junction, we turned northeast on Maverick Drive and then turned southwest into the seven-mile Basin Drive at Chisos Mountains Basin Junction to get to Chisos Basin Campground. The Basin Drive descends around a series of sharp curves to some 5,400 feet in the Chisos Basin, where we set up our tent on Campsite 34, which became our "home" for our final night at Big Ben National Park. The Chisos Mountains surrounded us. I felt that Casa Grande (7,325 ft.) and Emory Peak (7,825 ft.), just to the south of the campground, were staring at us.

Later, all of us went to the Upper Basin to hike on two trails—the 0.3-mile Window View Trail and the 1.6-mile Chisos Basin Loop Trail. After dark, we used a torch to guide us along a trail to the Chisos Mountains Lodge to enjoy its facilities for a short while. But the kids complained about the walk in the dark.

Gracias, Big Bend

We said good-bye to Big Bend on Thanksgiving Thursday (November 28). But we wanted to do another hike before we left. We decided to skip the five-hour hike to the summit of Emory Peak on the Pinnacle Trail in favor of hiking the 4.6-mile (round-trip) Lost Mine Trail, "one of the best trails in the park." The trail begins at the parking area on the south side of the road just west of the Panther Pass (5,679 ft.). It offers a self-guided tour of the park's flora, fauna, and scenery that increased our knowledge of desert plants, animals, and geology exponentially over the two hours and forty minutes we took to complete the hike. Carmel and Junius enjoyed this experience of self-learning. However, we did not make it to the Lost Mine Peak (7,550 ft.), the second highest peak in the park that looks like a jagged ridge in the skyline.

We left Panther Pass at 11:30 a.m., and said good-bye to our newfound *amigo* Big Bend National Park at Maverick Junction, the park's western exit or entry point. We realized that three days was not adequate to see all the numerous features of the park. For example, we had to skip the many attractions along Maverick Drive (Government Hills, Tule Mountain, etc.) and Old Maverick Drive (Old Canyon Outlook, Terlingua Abaja, etc.).

Our exit route to Sanderson, Texas—our destination for the day—circled the Big Bend National Park. This deliberately chosen longer route, which more than doubled the distance to our destination than through the shorter route via SR 118 (see map 107.2), reminded me of the Sinhala allusion "Parangia Kotte giya wagai" (like the route the natives used to lead the Portuguese to the kingdom of Kotte to create the illusion of a longer distance)

We stopped in Lajitas for lunch. Then, we proceeded northwest along the Rio Grande to Presidio (pop, 4,167), where we crossed the river for a brief visit to the Mexican town of Manuel Ojinaga (pop 20,744), the administrative seat of the municipality of Ojinaga. We had to pay a toll of $2 to recross the Presidio-Ojinaga International Bridge. Then, we drove northeast to Marfa and east to Alpine and Marathon, where we arrived at 6:00 p.m. The historic Gauge Hotel in Marathon enticed us to celebrate Thanksgiving with a grand dinner, which cost us $40.

Finally, off we drove to Sanderson, fifty-four miles further east, where we spent the night at the Desert Air Motel.

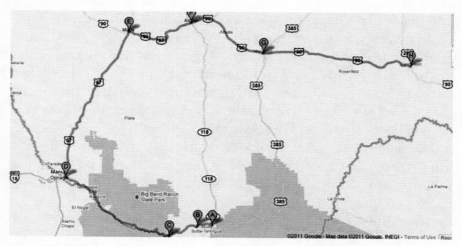

Map 107.2 Our exit route from Big Bend National Park to Sanderson, Texas (239 miles) on Thanksgiving Day 1991. *A*, Study Butte (west of Maverick Junction, Big Bend NP); *B*, Terlingua; *C*, Lajitas; *D*, Presidio (opposite Mexican city of Manuel Ojinaga in Chihuahua); *E*, Marfa; *F*, Alpine; *G*, Marathon; *H*, Sanderson.

SHELTON A. GUNARATNE

CHAPTER 108

Texas: On Rio Grande Route Back to San Antonio

AFTER THE ARDUOUS exploration of the Big Bend National Park and a cozy overnight in Sanderson (pop 861) in Terrell County, we—daughter Carmel, son Junius, wife Yoke-Sim, and I—left our motel at 7:30 a.m. Friday (November 29, 1991) to continue our return journey east to San Antonio (pop 1.3 million), Texas's second largest city. Whereas we traveled on Interstate 10 on our forward journey to Big Bend, we were now traveling on US 90 on our return journey so that we could drive parallel to the eastern section of Rio Grande as it meandered its way through Brownsville to its confluence with Gulf of Mexico.

Our first stop was Langtry (pop 145), sixty-one miles from Sanderson, in Val Verde County. Originally established in 1892 as Eagle Nest, a grading camp for railroad workers, it was later named after George Langtry, a railroad engineer and foreman who supervised immigrant Chinese workers. But today, this small community has gained a touch of notoriety as the place where "Judge" Phantly Roy Bean Jr. (1825-1903), the "Law West of the Pecos," had his saloon and practiced a kind of law. Curiosity forced us to stop at the Judge Roy Bean Visitor Center, where we also thoroughly enjoyed the botanical garden with native desert plants. Legend has it that Bean, who came from Kentucky, held court in his saloon along the Rio Grande in a desolate stretch of the Chihuahuan Desert of Southwest Texas.

From Langtry, US 90 runs southeast parallel to Rio Grande for sixty miles all the way to Del Rio (pop 44,286), the administrative seat of Val Verde County. On this stretch of the road, we stopped at Pecos River Picnic Area for refreshments. Then, we crossed the 26,300-hectare

Amistad Reservoir and the surrounding recreation area on Rio Grande at its confluence with Devils River and stopped to view the impressive Amistad Dam (completed in 1969) on the US-Mexico border. Here, we were thrilled to cross over to the Mexican state of Coahuila and drive the fourteen miles to Ciudad Acuña (pop 134,233), where we ate lunch at San Andres Fried Chicken Cafeteria on Avenue Lopez Mateos for just $5.50!

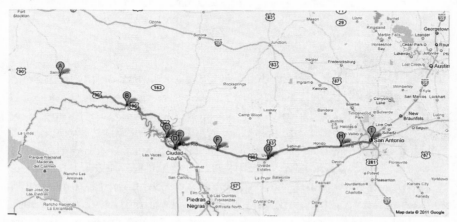

Map 108.1 The Rio Grande route from Sanderson to San Antonio (286 miles). *A*, Sanderson; *B*, Langtry; *C*, Amistad Dam/Amistad Reservoir; *D*, Ciudad Acuña in Coahuila, Mexico; *E*, Del Rio, Brackettville; *F*, Uvalde; *G*, Castroville; *H*, San Antonio.

I learnt that this was the border city wherefrom radio pioneer John R. Brinkley, a US citizen, began the era of Mexican border "blaster radio"—radio stations broadcasting from various Mexican cities near the border to attract US advertising. In the 1930s, these border stations had to operate under the laws of Mexico. In 1933, the Mexican government shut down a Brinkley-controlled station named XER-AM (in what was then called Villa Acuña). However, in 1935, the government gave the OK to a border blaster with the call letters XERA, also controlled by Brinkley but ostensibly owned by Ramón D. Bósquez Vitela. Wikipedia elaborates:

> Brinkley used the old buildings of XER but installed a new 500 kilowatt transmitter. The new directional antenna of XERA allowed Brinkley to claim that his station had an effective radiated propagation of one megawatt. One of his Texas engineers called XERA "the world's most powerful broadcasting station."

SHELTON A. GUNARATNE

Picture 108.1 The author with Junius (left) and Carmel at the US-Mexico border at Amistad Dam before they crossed over to Coahuila State for a fourteen-mile drive to Ciudad Acuña (November 29, 1991).

But XERA also came to a halt in 1939 when Mexico revoked the station's license. XERF commenced operations in 1947 as a new station (now branded as La Poderosa or "the Powerful") using the old facilities of Brinkley's XERA but with no other connection to Brinkley.

After mulling over the birthplace of border blasters, we paid a toll of $1.95 to cross the Del Río-Ciudad Acuña International Bridge to return to the United States. Del Rio lay six miles to the northeast of Acuña. At the bridge, Rio Grande and we also had to end our parallel company. We continued to drive east on US 90 to San Antonio while the river turned southeast eager to dislodge everything it carried in its belly into the mighty gulf. The Whitehead Memorial Museum downtown preserves the history of Del Rio. Just to the east of Del Rio is Laughlin Air Force Base, the busiest pilot training base in the US Air Force.

Next, we stopped at Brackettville (pop 1,876), the seat of Kinney County. Founded in 1852 as Las Moras (the name of a nearby spring and the creek it feeds), the town was later renamed Brackett after Oscar B. Brackett, the owner of the first dry goods store in the area. Tied strongly to nearby Fort Clark's fortunes, Brackettville—suffix "ville" was added in 1873—had a larger proportion of Black Seminoles (people of mixed African American and Seminole ancestry) than the rest of West Texas. Their language, Afro-Seminole Creole, is still spoken by some in Brackettville. North of town is a tourist attraction called Alamo Village, which was built in the 1950s as the set of John Wayne's movie *The Alamo* (Wikipedia).

We passed through Uvalde (pop 14,929), the seat of Uvalde County. When Reading Wood Black founded the town in 1853, it was named Encina. Three years later, a reorganization of the county made this town the county seat and renamed it for Juan de Ugalde (1729-1816), the Spanish governor of Coahuila from 1777 to 1783. Wikipedia says that Uvalde is usually considered the southern limit of the Texas Hill Country or the most northerly part of South Texas. The town has the only known bottler of cactus juice. Another attraction is John Nance Garner Museum memorializing the vice president of the United States from 1933 to 1941.

When we reached the western outskirts of San Antonio, we stopped at Castroville (pop 2,664) in Medina County to visit the Landmark Inn State Historic Site, featuring a series of cut limestone structures laid up with adobe-type mortar and covered with whitewashed lime plaster. The solid stonewalls of the buildings (of an inn established in 1824) vary between eighteen and twenty-four inches thick. What attracted our attention most was the two-story stone bathhouse that has an exterior stair and balcony. According to tradition, the upper room, which served as a tank, was lined with lead. During the Civil War, the Confederates melted this lead to furnish bullets for use.

Exploring San Antonio

Following our foray into Big Bend National Park, we returned to downtown San Antonio (see chapter 105) about 4:30 p.m. Friday (November 29) just in time to visit the Institute of Texan Cultures (801 E. Durango Blvd.) in HemisFair Plaza, a short walk from the Alamo and the River Walk, two of the outstanding tourist attractions in San Antonio. Inaugurated in 1965, the institute is part of the University of Texas at San Antonio. It serves as the state's primary center for multicultural education with exhibits, programs, and events like the Texas Folklife Festival, an annual celebration of the more than twenty-six ethnicities that make up the population of Texas.

Next, we drove through a traffic snarl to visit the Alamo (300 Alamo Plaza), an edifice built in 1718 to house Mission San Antonio de Valero, a Roman Catholic mission and fortress compound. It was the site of the Battle of the Alamo in 1836 in which the Texan army defeated the Mexican army. The chapel of the Alamo Mission is known as the "Shrine of Texas Liberty." We toured the chapel, as well as the Long Barracks, which contains a small museum with paintings, weapons, and other artifacts from the era of the Texas Revolution. We saw additional artifacts displayed in another complex building, alongside a large diorama that recreates the compound as it existed in 1836. A large mural, known as the Wall of History, portrays the history of the Alamo complex from its mission days to modern times. About 5 million people visit the Alamo every year. (Admission is free.)

From the Alamo, we turned into the River Walk (also known as Paseo del Río), a network of walkways along the banks of the San Antonio River, one story beneath downtown. Bars, shops, and restaurants lined the River Walk as an important part of the city's urban scene.

> The River Walk winds and loops under bridges as two parallel sidewalks lined with restaurants and shops, connecting the major tourist draws from the Alamo to Rivercenter mall, to the Arneson River Theatre close to La Villita, to HemisFair Park, to the Tower Life Building, to the San Antonio Museum of Art, and the Pearl Brewery. During the annual springtime Fiesta San Antonio, the River Parade features flowery floats that literally float (Wikipedia).

We learned that the idea to create the River Walk came up as a solution to the 1921 devastating floods that engulfed San Antonio, killing fifty people. Work on the project began in 1926 under the able guidance of architect Robert Hugman.

We found walking along the River Walk difficult because of the vast crowds that had gathered to see the River Walk Lighting Ceremony and Holiday River Parade. However, we enjoyed joining the crowds and viewing the parade. We also visited La Villita while waiting for the parade. After eating dinner at the downtown McDonald's, we drove all the way to the Best Western Townhouse—the same motel we stayed on Saturday (November 23) on our first arrival in the city—to spend the night.

Picture 108.2 A view of the San Antonio River Walk (1997). (Photo by Billy Halthorn. *Source:* Wikimedia Commons)

(I did a much more thorough exploration of the River Walk when I returned to San Antonio fourteen years later to attend the Association for Education in Journalism and Mass Communication Convention in 2005 (August 11-13).

Northwest informed us Saturday (November 30) that we had to spend another day in San Antonio because weather conditions prevented the airline from landing in Minneapolis. National Car Rental rented us another Ford Taurus automatic for a day when we returned the car we had rented for a week. Thus, we spent another day exploring San Antonio. Among the spots we decided to visit were the following:

- The Marion Koogler McNay Art Museum (600 N New Braunfels Ave.), where we spent about one hour in the delightful surroundings of a 9.3-hectare garden. The museum, opened in 1950, was named after American painter McNay and has been expanded to include galleries of medieval and Renaissance artwork and a larger collection of twentieth-century European and American modernist work. (Admission is free.)

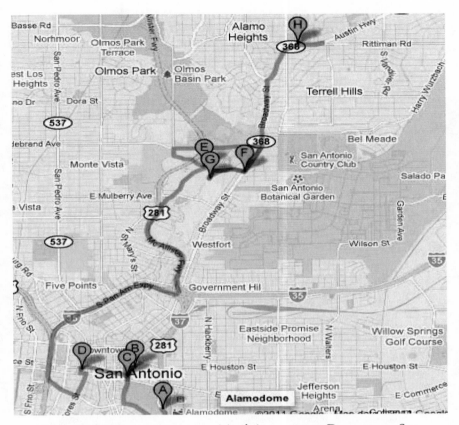

Map 108.2 Attractions we visited in or near Downtown San Antonio. *A*, Institute of Texan Cultures; *B*, the Alamo/Shrine of Texas Liberty; *C*, River Walk along San Antonio River; *D*, Spanish Governor's Palace; *E*, San Antonio Zoo and Aquarium; *F*, Witte Museum; *G*, Brackenridge Park; *H*, McNay Art Museum.

- The fourteen-hectare San Antonio Zoo and Aquarium in Brackenridge Park (3903 St. Mary's St.), where we spent a couple of hours looking at a collection of some 3,500 animals representing 750 species. The zoo's annual attendance exceeds 1 million. (Current general admission is $10.75.) We ate lunch at the adjoining sunken oriental garden.

- The Witte Museum (3801 Broadway), which focuses on the natural sciences with emphasis on South Texas and the history of Texas and the Southwest. It is dedicated to the history, science, and culture of the region. The permanent collection represents ethnography (study of social and cultural changes), decorative arts and textiles, and science. (Current general admission is $8.)

- The Spanish Governor's Palace (at Camaron and West Commerce) on Military Plaza. The keystone above the front entrance contains the coat-of-arms of Spanish King Ferdinand VI along with the date 1749. Wikipedia says the building was actually the residence and working offices of the local presidio captain and not the palace for the region's Spanish governor. (Current general admission is $2.)

Because Carmel and Junius started to show signs of boredom, we returned to our motel late afternoon to rest and get ready for our return journey to Minnesota. On Sunday (December 1), we returned our rented car to National Car Rental agent at San Antonio Airport, where we boarded the 6:10 a.m. Northwest flight to Memphis.

(The Sunday edition of the *Forum* (February 9, 1992), the daily newspaper of Fargo, North Dakota, published a condensed and different version of our Texas adventure.)

CHAPTER 109

Nevada: Las Vegas—Fountains of Bellagio Draw Many to Paradise

DURING A FOUR-DAY visit to Las Vegas, Nevada, mid-November 2011, we—my spouse and I—literally visited Paradise in its magnificent splendor to enjoy the sight and sound of the Fountains of Bellagio dancing to the tunes of the soothing songs of Frank Sinatra's "Luck be a lady," Johnny Mathis's "We need a little Christmas," Madonna's "Santa Baby," Gene Kelly's "Singing in the rain," Luciano Pavarotti's "Rondine al Nido," and many others.

The Fountains of Bellagio—a vast, choreographed water feature with performances set to light and music—enchanted us. We agreed that it was one of the highlights of our visit.

The dancing waters lulled the romantically inclined among the spectators gathered around the 1,000-feet-long lake along the Las Vegas Strip, into spontaneous dancing. The awesome sight of serpentine streams of water blast 245 feet in the air vertically and diagonally mixed with an assortment of horizontal waves thrilled us all.

We were truly in Paradise (pop 223,127), an unincorporated town, which includes most of the four-mile long Strip, where some the world's renowned hotels are located. Paradise is a part of Las Vegas metropolitan area (pop 1.9 million) but not of Las Vegas city (pop 583,756).

The Bellagio opened in 1998 replacing the legendary Dunes hotel and casino. (On my first visit to Las Vegas forty-four years ago, January 3-4, 1967, I spent quite some time at the Dunes casino.) Famed for its elegance, the 3,933-room Bellagio resort is most notable for its nine-acre

(3.6-ha.) manmade lake between the building and the Strip. The fountain is formed as a pair of large concentric rings and a long, curved arc, with two smaller circles attached to the arc near each end. Hyper-shooters and extreme shooters fire jets rising to almost the height of Bellagio's main tower. Robotic water jets called Oarsman nozzles create a nearly infinite variety of patterns to synchronize with the sound of music. A fog generating device rises from beneath the water to blanket the entire lake with fog, while some four thousand individually controllable underwater lights follow the water patterns' precise movements, sparkling on the water or glowing through the fog.

Picture 109.1 The Fountains of Bellagio at night. (Picture taken by user izx in January 2006. *Source:* Wikimedia Commons)

The Fountains of Bellagio, designed by Water Entertainment Technologies (WET), run every day on the half hour and every quarter hour during the evening. It's free to all. Inside Bellagio, Dale Chihuly's Fiori di Como, composed of more than two thousand hand-blown glass flowers, covers two thousand square feet of the lobby ceiling. Bellagio is also home to Cirque du Soleil's aquatic production *O*.

The Bellagio offers three other signature attractions—the Bellagio Gallery of Fine Art, the Conservatory, and the Bank Nightclub. We enjoyed the feel of the two giant pumpkins in the conservatory and botanical gardens.

SHELTON A. GUNARATNE

After

Picture 109.2 The author in the promenade of the Bellagio overlooking the lake that turns into the Fountains of Bellagio. In the background is Paris Las Vegas (November 15, 2011).

Along the Strip, north of the Bellagio, we found another magnificent exhibit called the Volcano at the entrance to The Mirage, a 3,044-room hotel and casino opened in 1989 to replace the Castaways, which had operated from 1963 in the premises once occupied by the famous Red Rooster Nite Club.

The Mirage's artificial volcano "erupts" nightly from seven to midnight on the hour, yet another free spectacle for walkers and gawkers on the Strip. A man-made mountain rising some fifty feet from a palm-fringed lagoon, the exhibit looks and sounds quite like a real volcano; thanks to its technological upgrade in 2008.

After the opening of its sister property Bellagio, WET Design that created the Fountains of Bellagio also improved the technology behind the volcano effect to make it more spectacular. The effects include massive fireballs, choreographed to a hypnotic music score by composer Zakir Hussain and former Grateful Dead drummer Mickey Hart. A new soundtrack complete with the sounds of actual volcanoes erupting gives the spectators an even more enhanced experience.

The Mirage, designed to fit its French Polynesia theme, has two other signature attractions—the Dolphin Habitat and the Siegfried and Hoyt's Secret Garden. The hotel's atrium has a hundred-foot-tall glass dome that shelters a living rain forest of palms, banana plants, and other tropical flora.

We found another free exhibit at the very end of the Forum Shops at Caesars Palace—the Roman-themed resort opened in 1966—between the Bellagio and the Mirage. It is a free show with large, moving statues acting out a short play, running every hour on the hour. However, its faulty sound system associated with the intense reverb and the thunderous sound effects makes the conversation unintelligible to the spectators—a drama about two offspring vying to be the successor to their father's throne.

Caesars has 3,349 rooms in five towers: Augustus, Centurion, Roman, Palace, and Forum. Its signature attractions are the Forum Shops, a high-end shopping mall comprising some 160 shops and haute couture boutiques, as well as 11 gourmet restaurants. This is a top celebrity-sighting spot in Las Vegas.

Caesars also offers various other shows. We spent an evening at the Spiegelworld located in front of Caesars Palace to see the ninety-minute show titled *Absinthe*, an over-the-top, circus-style comedy for adults interspersed with stunts. We had no clue about the nature of the show until we went to the venue because we got complimentary tickets from a vendor who tried to entice us into a business scam. We were too fascinated by the incredible stunts when *Absinthe*'s ringmaster, The Gazillionaire, warned the audience,

"If you're offended by words like f—or s—, you just might be at the wrong f—in' show."

Just to the north of The Mirage is the 2,884-room Treasure Island Hotel and Casino, opened in 1983. These two hotels, which share a common tropical ambience, are connected by tram. Treasure Island presents a free

SHELTON A. GUNARATNE

entertainment spectacular called the Sirens of TI every day using the hotel's Sirens' Cove as the backdrop.

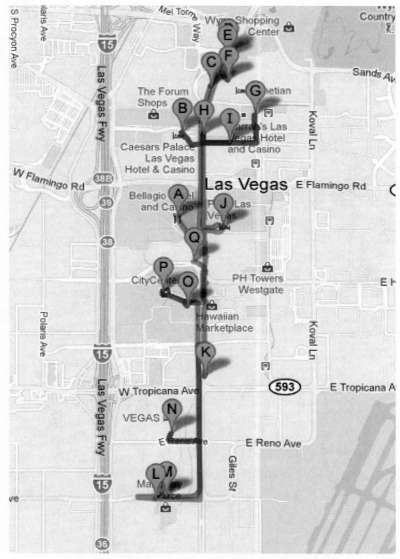

Map 109. 1 Major Hotels and Casinos on the Las Vegas Strip.
East of the Strip: *A*, Bellagio; *B*, Caesars Palace; *C*, The Mirage; *D*, Treasure Island. West of the Strip: *E*, The Palazzo; *F*, The Venetian; *G*, Harrah's; *H*, Imperial Palace; *I*, The Flamingo; *J*, Paris Las Vegas;ʼ *K*, MGM Grand. East of the Strip: *L*, Mandalay Bay; *M*, Luxor; *N*, Excalibur; *O*, Mandarin Oriental; *P*, Aria; *Q*, Cosmopolitan.

We spent another evening at the Phantom Theater of the Venetian, a luxury resort with 4,059 suites and rooms opened in 1999 to replace the old Sands Hotel. Located just to the north of Harrah's, where we stayed on this trip, the Venetian presents a remarkable facsimile of Venice's architectural glory. The ultra-plush Palazzo, in effect to the northern extension of the Venetian, was opened in 2007 with 3,068 suites. (In 1967, I stayed at the Riviera, the Strip's first high-rise opened in 1960, located further north.) This group of hotels constitutes the western flank of the Strip facing The Mirage.

We were curious about the $40-million theater designed to look like a nineteenth-century Parisian opera house. Overall, we enjoyed the ninety-five-minute musical *Phantom: The Las Vegas Spectacular,* featuring every song from the original Andrew Lloyd Webber *The Phantom of the Opera*. The special effects and the costumes were just fantastic. The tickets cost us $25 each from a discount dealer. We concur with the reviewer who observed:

"Sets change seamlessly before your eyes. There are no blackouts, no costume changes, and almost no down time. It feels as if you are watching a movie, except it's being performed live, right before your eyes."

Walking further south of Harrah's, we passed the 2,640-room Imperial Palace (opened in 1979), whose signature attraction is The Auto Collection. A tram interconnects the Imperial Palace with MGM Grand in the south with stopovers at the Flamingo and Paris Las Vegas.

Opened in 1946, the 3,626-room Flamingo is one of the oldest hotels in Las Vegas. We spent some time at its garden courtyard enjoying the Wildlife Habitat, its signature attraction, which included flamingoes and other birds.

Paris Las Vegas is a 2,915-room hotel opened in 1999 with Paris as its theme. The hotel includes a half scale, 541-foot (165 m) tall replica of the Eiffel Tower, a sign in the shape of the Montgolfier balloon, a two-thirds size Arc de Triomphe, a replica of La Fontaine des Mers, and a 1,200-seat theater called Le Théâtre des Arts. The front of the hotel suggests the Paris Opera House and the Louvre.

Flanking Paris is Baily's to the north and Planet Hollywood to the south. MGM Grand was the largest in the world when it opened in 1993. With 6,582 rooms, it has used Hollywood as its theme. Its signature attractions are its Lion Habitat, CBS Television City, Tabu, and Studio 54. Its neighbor to the south is Tropicana.

One morning, we took a bus ride from Harrah's to Mandalay Bay in the south to explore the resorts and casinos on the eastern flank of the Strip up to the City Center.

The 3,309-room Mandalay Bay Resort and Casino was opened in 1999. It has three signature attractions: the Shark Reef Aquarium, which displays numerous different species of sharks, rays, fish, reptiles, and marine invertebrates; the House of Blues, a chain of thirteen live music concert halls and restaurants in major markets throughout the United States; and Mandalay Beach.

A free tram interconnects MGM-owned Mandalay Bay with Luxor and Excalibur to the north, also MGM-owned.

Named and themed after Luxor (ancient Thebes in Egypt), the 4,407-room Luxor opened in 1993. Its signature attractions include the two-level LAX Nightclub for celebrities, the ultra-elite Noir Bar, and several additional nightlife destinations—CatHouse, Aurora, Liquidity, Flight, High Bar, and Play Bar.

Themed after Camelot (the legendary King Arthur's court), the 3,981-room Excalibur opened in 1990. Excalibur is home to two permanent shows—the all-male revue *Thunder from Down Under* and the medieval themed dinner show *Tournament of Kings.*

Finally, in the City Center, we did a quick tour of the plush hotels built after 2008—the 1,495-room Vdara, the 392-room Mandarin Oriental, the 4,004-room Aria, and the 2,995-room Cosmopolitan.

All these hotels were in Paradise. Being human, we could not cover all the hotels along the Strip.

We conclude that Las Vegas represents the epitome of opulence, conspicuous consumption, and degenerate living. It's the playground of the super-upper-and-aspiring classes. We watched the drama of man versus man, man versus self, and man versus nature each time we passed through a casino—greedy habitual gamblers losing money to machines programmed not to lose. Evil-minded Mara failed to tempt us to the charming slot machines. However, we confess that we sinned because we gave way to our gastronomic instincts.

If you have the urge to splurge, do visit the Sin City. Be aware that hotels have excess capacity. Look for inexpensive airfare-hotel deals. If you go, do as we did: avoid the one-armed bandits.

AFTERWORD

IN GENERAL, KEEPING diaries is a part of Western culture that focuses on the individual or self *(atta)*. Diaries help the folks with a sense of achievement to write their autobiographies with authenticity and accuracy.

In general, keeping diaries is not a part of Eastern culture that focuses on the extended family, group or community. Buddhism asserts that the three marks of existence are impermanence *(anicca),* sorrow *(dukkha),* and no-self *(anatta).* If existence means a stream of consciousness (rather than a soul/self) in a continuous state of becoming, then there cannot be a first person singular "I" or "me." Therefore, in the absence of a self, an "autobiography" is an oxymoron.

Yet, "I" call this book a compendium of "my autobiographical" notes based on "my diary" entries over "my lifespan." Thus, a Buddhist may consider this book to be an exercise in self-delusion. The fact, however, is that this book is the product of dependent co-origination because everything "I" wrote in "my diaries" and gathered from elsewhere came from others, for example, my mother.

Reverting to the Western first person singular, I started writing "The Travels of a Journalist" series in December 2009 in succession to "The Journey of a Journalist" series, which began in mid-2009. In effect, I completed writing the bulk of this book during the period 2009-2010. In the Buddhist sense, this book is the shared product of a constantly changing stream of consciousness, not the work of an "individual" with an eternal soul.

Readers can hobnob with the leading characters of the author's birth village in a companion book titled *Village Life in the '40s: Memories of a Lankan Expatriate* (Bloomington, Ind.: iUniverse, 2012).

INDEX

V

W

Y

Z

Edwards Brothers Malloy
Thorofare, NJ USA
November 8, 2012